The FOOTBALL ASSOCIATION YEARBOOK 1994-1995

THE FOOTBALL ASSOCIATION

The FOOTBALL ASSOCIATION YEARBOOK 1994–1995

PELHAM BOOKS

LONDON

PELHAM BOOKS

Published by the Penguin Group
27 Wrights Lane, London W8 5TZ, England
Viking Penguin, Inc. 375 Hudson Street, New York, NY 10014, USA
Penguin Books Australia Ltd, Ringwood, Victoria, Australia
Penguin Books Canada Ltd, 10 Alcorn Avenue, Toronto, Ontario, Canada M4V 3B2
Penguin Books (NZ) Ltd, 182–190 Wairau Road, Auckland 10, New Zealand

Penguin Books Ltd, Registered Offices: Harmondsworth, Middlesex, England
First published 1994

Made and printed in Great Britain by
Butler & Tanner Ltd, Frome, Somerset

ISBN 0 7207 2048 6

A CIP catalogue record for this book is available from the British Library.

The moral right of the author has been asserted

Photo credits
The Publishers are grateful to the following for permission to reproduce
copyright photographs in the book: Action Images pages 8, 12, 19, 30, 41, 44,
45, 49, 50, 85, 90, 92, 108, 116, 152.

Production in association with Book Production Consultants,
25 High Street, Chesterton, Cambridge CB4 1ND

Contents

THE FOOTBALL ASSOCIATION
PUBLICATIONS FOR SEASON 1994–1995

	Price (£)	Post/Pack
FA Diary 1994–95	3.25	–
FA Yearbook 1994–95	8.99	85p
FA Handbook 1994–95	6.00	–
FA News Annual 1993–94	1.80	58p
Soccer Tactics and Skills	10.99	2.40
The Winning Formula	9.99	1.90
Football Training Can Be Fun	6.99	85p
Financing and Taxation of Clubs	2.95	58p
Soccer Star	2.95	51p
Laws of Association Football*	4.50	38p
Arrangement of Fixtures	40p	24p
Know The Game Soccer	1.99	38p
Flying Start Soccer (hard cover)	6.50	51p
(soft cover)	2.95	35p
Official History of The FA	16.95	4.20
FA Complete Guide to England Players 1945–93	14.99	1.90
FA Quiz Book	4.99	85p

* *formerly the 'Referees' Chart'*

All these publications are available from:

FA Publications,
9 Wyllyotts Place,
Potters Bar,
Hertfordshire EN6 2JD.

Payment may be made by credit card (Visa/Access only)
by telephoning 'FA Publications' on 0707 651840.

FA Chief Executive's Report

Season 1994–95 will see some momentous changes in the way we develop our best young players. If all goes to plan, the English footballer of the future will be better able to compete on technical terms with his German, Italian and Dutch counterparts.

Already the signs are encouraging. In 1993 England won the European Under-18 Championship; in 1993–94 the England Under-16 team headed a qualifying group including Italy and Holland to reach the finals in Ireland last April, before going out to the Ukraine on penalties in the quarter-final. The work undertaken in the Centres of Excellence since their formation in 1984 is bearing fruit.

Now the radical changes The Football Association announced in the Blueprint for the Future of Football in 1991 and negotiated with The F.A. Premier League, The Football League and The English Schools' Football Association are coming on stream.

The purpose of the programme for excellence is to identify young players of exceptional promise between the ages of 9 and 16 and place them in an environment conducive to successful development.

Centres of Excellence can now coach boys on an unlimited number of occasions each week and offer Centres Football on Sundays. Centres Football means matches between Centres of Excellence, or similar.

Licences to operate Centres are granted subject to strict criteria.

Clubs are allowed to register up to 30, 45 or 60 boys in the various age categories. These restrictions on 'over-signing' will hopefully prevent boys stagnating with little chance of progress at the biggest clubs.

Football for young players is now divided into three categories.

Category	TYPE OF FOOTBALL
A	International Football Professional Football Clubs' junior and youth teams Football Association Centres Football and Coaching
B	All Schools Football
C	Local Youth Leagues Community Football Activities

Boys registered at Centres of Excellence are only allowed to play in category A or B football, unless there is little football available in those categories. In this case, they are allowed to play in category C. Control will be the responsibility of the directors of the Centres of Excellence.

To avoid overplay, the following priority list has been established.

1. International Matches
2. Preparation for International Matches
3. Trials for selection of Squads for International Matches
4. Trials for The Football Association National School
5. ESFA Summer Selection Course/Courses

The total number of games which outstanding young players play has been reduced to a maximum of 60 games, including international games and preparation and trials for those games. The 60 games are divided as follows:

35 games for schools, including International games
25 games for Centres Football.

It is emphasised that the maximum number of games will be 60. If, however, local arrangements facilitate a deviation from the 35 games for Schools or the 25 games for Centres football, this will be permissible provided the grand total does not exceed 60 games for any one boy in any one season. Included in this total are those games to which a player is released under these regulations in Category C.

The prime objective is to give more time for coaching talented young players and for them to play in coached games. However, in the early and later parts of the season priority will be given to Schools Football in the event of any clash.

Players from 9 to 14 can only be registered at a Centre of Excellence within one hour's travelling distance of home. Centres Football will be primarily small side games for boys under 12.

In another move towards excellence, The Football Association wants our young children to develop their skills through small sided games. In the past we have restricted the Under 9's for competitive football; now we are encouraging them to be involved in activities such as the F.A. Coca-Cola Mini-Soccer, which will provide more involvement, more enjoyment, and the development of technique.

We have the total support of the other football bodies involved, and now we look forward to reaping the rewards of what is, we believe, a massive step forward in the development of our young players.

Graham Kelly
Chief Executive
The Football Association

WORLD CUP FINALS 1930–1990

Year/venue	Winner		Runner-up	Result
1930 Montevideo	Uruguay	v	Argentina	4–2
1934 Rome	Italy	v	Czechoslovakia	2–1*
1938 Paris	Italy	v	Hungary	4–2
1950 Rio de Janeiro	Uruguay	v	Brazil	2–1
1954 Berne	West Germany	v	Hungary	3–2
1958 Stockholm	Brazil	v	Sweden	5–2
1962 Santiago	Brazil	v	Czechoslovakia	3–1
1966 Wembley	England	v	West Germany	4–2*
1970 Mexico City	Brazil	v	Italy	4–1
1974 Munich	West Germany	v	Holland	2–1
1978 Buenos Aires	Argentina	v	Holland	3–1*
1982 Madrid	Italy	v	West Germany	3–1
1986 Mexico City	Argentina	v	West Germany	3–2
1990 Rome	West Germany	v	Argentina	1–0

* *after extra time*

EUROPEAN CHAMPIONSHIP FINALS 1960–1992

Year/venue	Winner		Runner-up	Result
1960 Paris	USSR	v	Yugoslavia	2–1
1964 Madrid	Spain	v	USSR	2–1
1968 Rome	Italy	v	Yugoslavia	2–0†
1972 Brussels	West Germany	v	USSR	3–0
1976 Belgrade	Czechoslovakia	v	West Germany	2–2††
1980 Rome	West Germany	v	Belgium	2–1
1984 Paris	France	v	Spain	2–0
1988 Munich	Holland	v	USSR	2–0
1992 Gothenburg	Denmark	v	Germany	2–0

† *after 1-1 draw*
†† *won on penalty-kicks*

EUROPEAN CHAMPION CLUBS' CUP WINNERS 1956–1994

Year/venue		Winner		Runners–up	Result
1956	Paris	Real Madrid	v	Stade de Rheims	4–3
1957	Madrid	Real Madrid	v	Fiorentina	2–0
1958	Brussels	Real Madrid	v	AC Milan	3–2*
1959	Stuttgart	Real Madrid	v	Stade de Rheims	2–0
1960	Glasgow	Real Madrid	v	Eintracht Frankfurt	7–3
1961	Berne	Benfica	v	Barcelona	3–2
1962	Amsterdam	Benfica	v	Real Madrid	5–3
1963	Wembley	AC Milan	v	Benfica	2–1
1964	Vienna	Inter-Milan	v	Real Madrid	3–1
1965	Madrid	Inter-Milan	v	Benfica	1–0
1966	Brussels	Real Madrid	v	Partizan Belgrade	2–1
1967	Lisbon	Celtic	v	Inter-Milan	2–1
1968	Wembley	Manchester United	v	Benfica	4–1*
1969	Madrid	AC Milan	v	Ajax Amsterdam	4–1
1970	Milan	Feyenoord	v	Celtic	2–1*
1971	Wembley	Ajax Amsterdam	v	Panathinaikos	2–0
1972	Rotterdam	Ajax Amsterdam	v	Inter-Milan	2–0
1973	Belgrade	Ajax Amsterdam	v	Juventus	1–0
1974	Brussels	Bayern Munich	v	Atletico Madrid	1–1
	Brussels	Bayern Munich	v	Atletico Madrid	4–0
1975	Paris	Bayern Munich	v	Leeds United	2–0
1976	Glasgow	Bayern Munich	v	St Etienne	1–0
1977	Rome	Liverpool	v	Borussia Mönchengladbach	3–1
1978	Wembley	Liverpool	v	FC Bruges	1–0
1979	Munich	Nottingham Forest	v	Malmö	1–0
1980	Madrid	Nottingham Forest	v	Hamburg	1–0
1981	Paris	Liverpool	v	Real Madrid	1–0
1982	Rotterdam	Aston Villa	v	Bayern Munich	1–0
1983	Athens	Hamburg	v	Juventus	1–0
1984	Rome	Liverpool	v	Roma	1–1**
1985	Brussels	Juventus	v	Liverpool	1–0
1986	Seville	Steaua Bucharest	v	Barcelona	0–0**
1987	Vienna	Porto	v	Bayern Munich	2–1
1988	Stuttgart	PSV Eindhoven	v	Benfica	0–0**
1989	Barcelona	AC Milan	v	Steaua Bucharest	4–0
1990	Vienna	AC Milan	v	Benfica	1–0
1991	Bari	Red Star Belgrade	v	Marseille	0–0**
1992	Wembley	Barcelona	v	Sampdoria	1–0*
1993	Munich	Marseille	v	AC Milan	1–0
1994	Athens	AC Milan	v	Barcelona	4–0

* after extra time
** won on penalty-kicks

EUROPEAN CUP WINNERS' CUP WINNERS 1961–1994

Year/venue		Winner		Runners–up	Result
1961		A.C. Fiorentina	v	Glasgow Rangers	4–1†
1962	Glasgow	Atletico Madrid	v	Fiorentina	1–1
	Stuttgart	Atletico Madrid	v	Fiorentina	3–0
1963	Rotterdam	Tottenham Hotspur	v	Atletico Madrid	5–1
1964	Brussels	Sporting Lisbon	v	MTK Budapest	3–3*
	Antwerp	Sporting Lisbon	v	MTK Budapest	1–0

Year/venue		Winner		Runners–up	Result
1965	Wembley	West Ham United	v	Munich 1860	2–0
1966	Glasgow	Borussia Dortmund	v	Liverpool	2–1*
1967	Nuremberg	Bayern Munich	v	Rangers	1–0*
1968	Rotterdam	AC Milan	v	Hamburg	2–0
1969	Basle	Slovan Bratislava	v	Barcelona	3–2
1970	Vienna	Manchester City	v	Gornik Zabrze	2–1
1971	Athens	Chelsea	v	Real Madrid	1–1*
	Athens	Chelsea	v	Real Madrid	2–1
1972	Barcelona	Glasgow Rangers	v	Moscow Dynamo	3–2
1973	Salonika	AC Milan	v	Leeds United	1–0
1974	Rotterdam	Magdeburg	v	AC Milan	2–0
1975	Basle	Dynamo Kiev	v	Ferencvaros	3–0
1976	Brussels	Anderlecht	v	West Ham United	4–2
1977	Amsterdam	Hamburg	v	Anderlecht	2–0
1978	Paris	Anderlecht	v	Austria Vienna	4–0
1979	Basle	Barcelona	v	Fortuna Düsseldorf	4–3*
1980	Brussels	Valencia	v	Arsenal	0–0**
1981	Düsseldorf	Dynamo Tbilisi	v	Carl Zeiss Jena	2–1
1982	Barcelona	Barcelona	v	Standard Liège	2–1
1983	Gothenburg	Aberdeen	v	Real Madrid	2–1*
1984	Basle	Juventus	v	Porto	2–1
1985	Rotterdam	Everton	v	Rapid Vienna	3–1
1986	Lyon	Dynamo Kiev	v	Atletico Madrid	3–0
1987	Athens	Ajax Amsterdam	v	Lokomotiv Leipzig	1–0
1988	Strasbourg	Mechelen	v	Ajax Amsterdam	1–0
1989	Berne	Barcelona	v	Sampdoria	2–0
1990	Gothenburg	Sampdoria	v	Anderlecht	2–0*
1991	Rotterdam	Manchester United	v	Barcelona	2–1
1992	Lisbon	Werder Bremen	v	Monaco	2–0
1993	Wembley	Parma	v	Royal Antwerp	3–1
1994	Copenhagen	Arsenal	v	Parma	1–0

† *aggregate over two legs*
* *after extra time*
** *won on penalty-kicks*

UEFA CUP WINNERS 1958–1994

(Known also as the Inter Cities Fairs' Cup until 1971. Two-leg finals except in 1964 and 1965. Aggregate scores)

Year	Winner		Runners–up	Result
1958	Barcelona	v	London	8–2
1960	Barcelona	v	Birmingham	4–1
1961	Roma	v	Birmingham	4–2
1962	Valencia	v	Barcelona	7–3
1963	Valencia	v	Dynamo Zagreb	4–1
1964	Zaragoza	v	Valencia	2–1
1965	Ferencvaros	v	Juventus	1–0
1966	Barcelona	v	Zaragoza	4–3
1967	Dynamo Zagreb	v	Leeds United	2–0
1968	Leeds United	v	Ferencvaros	1–0
1969	Newcastle United	v	Ujpest Dozsa	6–2
1970	Arsenal	v	Anderlecht	4–3
1971	Leeds United	v	Juventus	3–3*

Year	Winner		Runners–up	Result
1972	Tottenham Hotspur	v	Wolverhampton Wanderers	3–2
1973	Liverpool	v	Borussia Mönchengladbach	3–2
1974	Feyenoord	v	Tottenham Hotspur	4–2
1975	Borussia Mönchengladbach	v	Twente Enschede	5–1
1976	Liverpool	v	FC Bruges	4–3
1977	Juventus	v	Bilbao	2–2
1978	PSV Eindhoven	v	Bastia	3–0
1979	Borussia Mönchengladbach	v	Red Star Belgrade	2–1
1980	Eintracht Frankfurt	v	Borussia Mönchengladbach	3–3*
1981	Ipswich Town	v	AZ 67 Alkmaar	5–4
1982	IFK Gothenburg	v	Hamburg	4–0
1983	Anderlecht	v	Benfica	2–1
1984	Tottenham Hotspur	v	Anderlecht	2–2†
1985	Real Madrid	v	Videoton	3–1
1986	Real Madrid	v	Cologne	5–3
1987	IFK Gothenburg	v	Dundee United	2–1
1988	Bayer Leverkusen	v	Español	3–3†
1989	Napoli	v	Stuttgart	5–4
1990	Juventus	v	Fiorentina	3–1
1991	Inter-Milan	v	Roma	2–1
1992	Ajax Amsterdam	v	Torino	2–2*
1993	Juventus	v	Borussia Dortmund	6–1
1994	Inter-Milan	v	Casino Salzburg	2–0

*   *won on away goals rule*
†   *won on penalty-kicks*

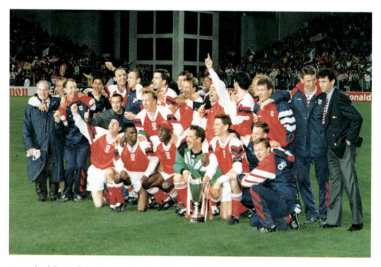

Arsenal celebrate their victory in the Cup Winners' Cup Final in Copenhagen.

Review of the European Season

For a long time another Italian clean sweep of the three UEFA club competitions looked very much on the cards. In 1990 AC Milan had won the Champions' Cup, Sampdoria the Cup Winners' Cup and Juventus (beating Fiorentina in the final) the UEFA Cup. A repeat four years later loomed as AC Milan won through to their seventh Champions' final, Inter faced unfancied Casino Salzburg over two legs in the UEFA Cup final and Parma found themselves within ninety minutes of retaining the Cup Winners' Cup.

It was George Graham's Arsenal, proven Cup specialists after becoming the first club to win the FA Cup and League Cup in the same season, who rewrote the script. They accounted for Torino in the Cup Winners' Cup quarter-final, winning 1-0 (Kevin Campbell) on aggregate, and beat Parma in the Copenhagen final to lift their first European trophy for 24 years. A left-foot volley from Alan Smith on the edge of the box punished a sloppy piece of Italian defending midway through the first half, and the goal proved sufficient to release Parma's grip on the trophy they had won so stylishly at Wembley twelve months earlier.

Arsenal had to be defensively strong and as generally pragmatic as ever to survive. They had been forced to take the field at the Parken Stadium without leading scorer Ian Wright (in tears during the home leg of the semi-final after collecting the booking that meant he was suspended for the final) and leading markers Keown and Jensen (the latter the victim of a horrific tackle during an international which put him out for the season). Tony Adams, the captain, gave a performance of towering authority in the heart of the defence and the relatively inexperienced Morrow tracked Parma's talented play-maker, Zola, throughout the match and managed to reduce his effectiveness. Parma had their chances – Brolin struck the inside of a post when it was 0–0 and Seaman touched a stinging shot from Zola over the top – but Arsenal stood firm.

Exactly a week later (11 May) Inter-Milan set up a possible 'double' for the Italian city when they won the UEFA Cup in front of 80,000 at the San Siro by beating Salzburg 1-0. Wim Jonk, the Dutchman who joined the club with compatriot Bergkamp in the previous summer, scored on 63 minutes and it came just in time for Inter, who were struggling to hold on to a 1–0 lead from the first leg of the final in Vienna. Italian clubs have now won the UEFA Cup five times in six years.

And so to the Olympic Stadium in Athens on 18 May for the 39th European Cup Final and a match between two great champions, AC Milan and Barcelona, both of whom had again won their respective leagues in 1993–94.

Without ace sweeper Franco Baresi (suspended) to marshal the defence, the pressure was on Milan striker Daniel Massaro to make the most of the type of chances he had missed in the previous year's final, when his side crashed unexpectedly to Marseille. He did not disappoint, scoring a brace in the first half (22 and 45 minutes). Barcelona's celebrated twin strike-force of the Brazilian Romario and Bulgarian Stoichkov had one shot between them in this period, and the Spanish team were faced with the proverbial mountain to climb. Even without Baresi and Costacurta, Milan still had a pretty mean defence.

Two minutes after the interval Savicevic lobbed the ball from a distance over a back-pedalling Zubizarreta after breaking clear down the right touchline and the match was effectively over as a contest. Midfielder Desailly, a French International, ventured upfield to find himself ideally placed to score a fourth on 58 minutes, skilfully curling the ball round the goalkeeper. Milan had equalled their winning scoreline in the 1989 final, and the most prestigious prize in European club football was theirs for the fifth time.

Philip Don from England, a late replacement as referee, showed eight yellow cards. England's representative in the Champions' Cup, Manchester United, lost to Galatasaray (Turkey) in the Second Round on the away goals rule.

EURO 96: Schedule of Matches

A	**WEMBLEY – VILLA PARK**
B	**ELLAND ROAD – ST JAMES' PARK**
C	**OLD TRAFFORD – ANFIELD**
D	**HILLSBOROUGH – CITY GROUND**

1.	Saturday 8th June	A1 – A2	Wembley
2.	Sunday 9th June	B1 – B2	Elland Road
3.		C1 – C2	Old Trafford
4.		D1 – D2	Hillsborough
5.	Monday 10th June	A3 – A4	Villa Park
6.		B3 – B4	St James' Park
7.	Tuesday 11th June	C3 – C4	Anfield
8.		D3 – D4	City Ground
9.	Thursday 13th June	A2 – A3	Villa Park
10.		B2 – B3	St James' Park
11.	Friday 14th June	C2 – C3	Anfield
12.		D2 – D3	City Ground
13.	Saturday 15th June	A4 – A1	Wembley
14.		B4 – B1	Elland Road
15.	Sunday 16th June	C4 – C1	Old Trafford
16.		D4 – D1	Hillsborough
17.	Tuesday 18th June	A4 – A2	Villa Park
18.		B4 – B2	St James' Park
19.		A3 – A1	Wembley
20.		B3 – B1	Elland Road
21.	Wednesday 19th June	C4 – C2	Anfield
22.		D4 – D2	City Ground
23.		C3 – C1	Old Trafford
24.		D3 – D1	Hillsborough
25.	Saturday 22nd June	1B – 2A	Anfield
26.		2B – 1A	Wembley
27.	Sunday 23rd June	1C – 2D	Old Trafford
28.		2C – 1D	Villa Park
29.	Wednesday 26th June	1 v 4	Old Trafford
30.		2 v 3	Wembley
31.	Sunday 30th June	Final	Wembley

European Championship 1996

Qualifying Competition

Group 1

(France, Romania, Poland, Israel,
Slovakia, Azerbaijan)

7. 9.94	Slovakia – France
7. 9.94	Romania – Azerbaijan
8.10.94	France – Romania
12.10.94	Israel – Slovakia
12.10.94	Poland – Azerbaijan
12.11.94	Romania – Slovakia
16.11.94	Poland – France
16.11.94	Azerbaijan – Israel
14.12.94	Azerbaijan – France
14.12.94	Israel – Romania
2.95*	Israel – Poland
29. 3.95	Romania – Poland
29. 3.95	Israel – France
29. 3.95	Slovakia – Azerbaijan
26. 4.95	France – Slovakia
26. 4.95	Poland – Israel
26. 4.95	Azerbaijan – Romania
7. 6.95	Poland – Slovakia
7. 6.95	Romania – Israel
16. 8.95	France – Poland
16. 8.95	Azerbaijan – Slovakia
6. 9.95	France – Azerbaijan
6. 9.95	Slovakia – Israel
6. 9.95	Poland – Romania
11.10.95	Romania – France
11.10.95	Israel – Azerbaijan
11.10.95	Slovakia – Poland
15.11.95	Slovakia – Romania
15.11.95	Azerbaijan – Poland
15.11.95	France – Israel

Group 2

(Denmark, Spain, Belgium, F.Y.R.
Macedonia, Cyprus, Armenia)

7. 9.94	Cyprus – Spain
7. 9.94	FYR Macedonia – Denmark
7. 9.94	Belgium – Armenia
8.10.94	Armenia – Cyprus
12.10.94	Denmark – Belgium
12.10.94	FYR Macedonia – Spain
16.11.94	Belgium – FYR Macedonia
16.11.94	Spain – Denmark
16.11.94	Cyprus – Armenia
17.12.94	Belgium – Spain
17.12.94	FYR Macedonia – Cyprus

must be confirmed by the Committee

25. 3.95**	Armenia – FYR Macedonia
29. 3.95	Spain – Belgium
29. 3.95	Cyprus – Denmark
26. 4.95	Armenia – Spain
26. 4.95	Belgium – Cyprus
26. 4.95	Denmark – FYR Macedonia
7. 6.95	Denmark – Cyprus
7. 6.95	FYR Macedonia – Belgium
7. 6.95	Spain – Armenia
16. 8.95	Armenia – Denmark
6. 9.95	Belgium – Denmark
6. 9.95	Spain – Cyprus
6. 9.95	FYR Macedonia – Armenia
7.10.95	Armenia – Belgium
11.10.95	Denmark – Spain
11.10.95	Cyprus – FYR Macedonia
15.11.95	Spain – FYR Macedonia
15.11.95	Cyprus – Belgium
15.11.95	Denmark – Armenia

Group 3

(Sweden, Switzerland, Hungary, Iceland,
Turkey)

7. 9.94	Iceland – Sweden
7. 9.94	Hungary – Turkey
12.10.94	Turkey – Iceland
12.10.94	Switzerland – Sweden
16.11.94	Switzerland – Iceland
16.11.94	Sweden – Hungary
14.12.94	Turkey – Switzerland
29. 3.95	Turkey – Sweden
29. 3.95	Hungary – Switzerland
26. 4.95	Hungary – Sweden
26. 4.95	Switzerland – Turkey
1. 6.95	Sweden – Iceland
11. 6.95*	Iceland – Hungary
16. 8.95	Iceland – Switzerland
6. 9.95	Sweden – Switzerland
6. 9.95	Turkey – Hungary
11.10.95	Switzerland – Hungary
11.10.95	Iceland – Turkey
11.11.95	Hungary – Iceland
15.11.95	Sweden – Turkey

Group 4

(Italy, Ukraine, Croatia, Lithuania,
Estonia, Slovenia)

4. 9.94	Estonia – Croatia
7. 9.94	Slovenia – Italy

** *Ev. 10.5.95*

15

7. 9.94	Ukraine – Lithuania
9.10.94	Croatia – Lithuania
12.10.94	Estonia – Italy
12.10.94	Ukraine – Slovenia
13.11.94	Ukraine – Estonia
16.11.94	Slovenia – Lithuania
16.11.94	Italy – Croatia
25. 3.95	Italy – Estonia
25. 3.95	Croatia – Ukraine
29. 3.95	Slovenia – Estonia
29. 3.95	Ukraine – Italy
29. 3.95	Lithuania – Croatia
26. 4.95	Lithuania – Italy
26. 4.95	Croatia – Slovenia
26. 4.95	Estonia – Ukraine
7. 6.95	Lithuania – Slovenia
11. 6.95	Estonia – Slovenia
11. 6.95	Ukraine – Croatia
16. 8.95	Estonia – Lithuania
3. 9.95	Croatia – Estonia
6. 9.95	Italy – Slovenia
6. 9.95	Lithuania – Ukraine
8.10.95	Croatia – Italy
11.10.95	Slovenia – Ukraine
11.10.95	Lithuania – Estonia
11.11.95	Italy – Ukraine
15.11.95	Slovenia – Croatia
15.11.95	Italy – Lithuania

Group 5

(Netherlands, Norway, Czech Republic, Belarus, Malta, Luxembourg)

6. 9.94	Czech Republic – Malta
7. 9.94	Luxembourg – Netherlands
7. 9.94	Norway – Belarus
12.10.94	Malta – Czech Republic
12.10.94	Belarus – Luxembourg
12.10.94	Norway – Netherlands
16.11.94	Belarus – Norway
16.11.94	Netherlands – Czech Republic
14.12.94	Malta – Norway
14.12.94	Netherlands – Luxembourg
22. 2.95*	Malta – Luxembourg
29. 3.95	Czech Republic – Belarus
29. 3.95	Luxembourg – Norway
29. 3.95	Netherlands – Malta
26. 4.95	Belarus – Malta
26. 4.95	Czech Republic – Netherlands
26. 4.95	Norway – Luxembourg
7. 6.95	Belarus – Netherlands
7. 6.95	Luxembourg – Czech Republic
7. 6.95	Norway – Malta
16. 8.95	Norway – Czech Republic
6. 9.95	Czech Republic – Norway
6. 9.95	Luxembourg – Malta

6. 9.95	Netherlands – Belarus
7.10.95	Belarus – Czech Republic
8.10.95	Malta – Netherlands
11.10.95	Luxembourg – Belarus
12.11.95	Malta – Belarus
15.11.95	Czech Republic – Luxembourg
15.11.95	Netherlands – Norway

Group 6

(Rep. of Ireland, Portugal, Northern Ireland, Austria, Latvia, Liechtenstein)

20. 4.94*	N. Ireland – Liechtenstein
7. 9.94	Liechtenstein – Austria
7. 9.94	N. Ireland – Portugal
7. 9.94	Latvia – Rep. of Ireland
9.10.94	Latvia – Portugal
12.10.94	Austria – N. Ireland
12.10.94	Rep. of Ireland – Liechtenstein
13.11.94	Portugal – Austria
15.11.94	Liechtenstein – Latvia
16.11.94	N. Ireland – Rep. of Ireland
18.12.94	Portugal – Liechtenstein
29. 3.95	Rep. of Ireland – N. Ireland
29. 3.95	Austria – Latvia
26. 4.95	Rep. of Ireland – Portugal
26. 4.95	Latvia – N. Ireland
26. 4.95	Austria – Liechtenstein
3. 6.95*	Portugal – Latvia
4. 6.95*	Liechtenstein – Rep. of Ireland
7. 6.95	N. Ireland – Latvia
11. 6.95	Rep. of Ireland – Austria
15. 8.95	Liechtenstein – Portugal
16. 8.95	Latvia – Austria
3. 9.95	Portugal – N. Ireland
6. 9.95	Austria – Rep. of Ireland
6. 9.95	Latvia – Liechtenstein
11.10.95	Rep. of Ireland – Latvia
11.10.95	Austria – Portugal
11.10.95	Liechtenstein – N. Ireland
15.11.95	Portugal – Rep. of Ireland
15.11.95	N. Ireland – Austria

Group 7

(Germany, Wales, Bulgaria, Georgia, Albania, Moldova)

7. 9.94	Wales – Albania
7. 9.94	Germany – Moldova
12.10.94	Moldova – Wales
12.10.94	Bulgaria – Georgia
16.11.94	Albania – Germany
16.11.94	Georgia – Wales
16.11.94	Bulgaria – Moldova
14.12.94	Wales – Bulgaria

14.12.94	Moldova – Germany		7. 9.94	Faroe Islands – Greece
14.12.94	Albania – Georgia		12.10.94	Scotland – Faroe Islands
18.12.94	Germany – Albania		12.10.94	Greece – Finland
29. 3.95	Georgia – Germany		12.10.94	Russia – San Marino
29. 3.95	Bulgaria – Wales		16.11.94	Scotland – Russia
29. 3.95	Albania – Moldova		16.11.94	Greece – San Marino
26. 4.95	Germany – Wales		16.11.94	Finland – Faroe Islands
26. 4.95	Moldova – Bulgaria		14.12.94	Finland – San Marino
26. 4.95	Georgia – Albania		18.12.94	Greece – Scotland
7. 6.95	Bulgaria – Germany		29. 3.95	Russia – Scotland
7. 6.95	Wales – Georgia		29. 3.95	San Marino – Finland
7. 6.95	Moldova – Albania		26. 4.95	San Marino – Scotland
6. 9.95	Germany – Georgia		26. 4.95	Greece – Russia
6. 9.95	Wales – Moldova		26. 4.95	Faroe Islands – Finland
6. 9.95	Albania – Bulgaria		6. 5.95*	Russia – Faroe Islands
7.10.95	Bulgaria – Albania		7. 6.95	Faroe Islands – Scotland
8.10.95	Germany – Moldova		7. 6.95	San Marino – Russia
11.10.95	Wales – Germany		11. 6.95	Finland – Greece
11.10.95	Georgia – Bulgaria		16. 8.95	Scotland – Greece
15.11.95	Germany – Bulgaria		16. 8.95	Finland – Russia
15.11.95	Albania – Wales		16. 8.95*	Faroe Islands – San Marino
15.11.95	Moldova – Georgia		6. 9.95	Scotland – Finland
			6. 9.95	Faroe Islands – Russia

Group 8

(Russia, Greece, Scotland, Finland, Faroe
Islands, San Marino)

7. 9.94	Finland – Scotland		6. 9.95	San Marino – Greece
			11.10.95	Russia – Greece
			11.10.95	Scotland – Faroe Islands
			15.11.95	Scotland – San Marino
			15.11.95	Russia – Finland
			15.11.95	Greece – Faroe Islands

must be confirmed by the Committee

England's Full International Record 1872–1994

(Up to and including 22nd May 1994)

| | HOME | | | | | | AWAY | | | | | |
	P	W	D	L	For	Agst	P	W	D	L	For	Agst
Albania	1	1	0	0	5	0	1	1	0	0	2	0
Argentina	5	3	2	0	10	6	5	1	2	2	5	5
Australia	–	–	–	–	–	–	5	3	2	0	5	2
Austria	5	3	1	1	18	9	10	5	2	3	36	16
Belgium	4	3	1	0	17	3	14	10	3	1	50	21
Bohemia	–	–	–	–	–	–	1	1	0	0	4	0
Brazil	7	2	4	1	9	7	10	1	3	6	6	15
Bulgaria	2	1	1	0	3	1	3	2	1	0	4	0
Cameroon	1	1	0	0	2	0	1	1	0	0	3	2
Canada	–	–	–	–	–	–	1	1	0	0	1	0
Chile	1	0	1	0	0	0	3	2	1	0	4	1
Colombia	1	0	1	0	1	1	1	1	0	0	4	0
Cyprus	1	1	0	0	5	0	1	1	0	0	1	0
Czechoslovakia	5	4	1	0	13	6	7	3	2	2	12	9
Denmark	6	5	0	1	9	3	8	4	4	0	18	8
Ecuador	–	–	–	–	–	–	1	1	0	0	2	0
Egypt	–	–	–	–	–	–	2	2	0	0	5	0
FIFA	1	0	1	0	4	4	–	–	–	–	–	–
Finland	2	2	0	0	7	1	7	6	1	0	27	5
France	8	6	2	0	23	4	14	9	1	4	39	23
Germany, East	2	2	0	0	4	1	2	1	1	0	3	2
Germany (and West)	8	5	0	3	15	9	13	4	4	5	22	19
Greece	3	2	1	0	8	0	3	3	0	0	7	1
Holland	6	2	3	1	14	8	6	2	2	2	4	6
Hungary	7	6	0	1	18	9	11	6	1	4	29	18
Iceland	–	–	–	–	–	–	1	0	1	0	1	1
Ireland, Northern	49	40	6	3	169	36	47	34	10	3	150	44
Ireland, Republic of	6	3	2	1	11	6	7	2	4	1	8	6
Israel	–	–	–	–	–	–	2	1	1	0	2	1
Italy	6	3	2	1	9	5	11	3	3	5	16	17
Kuwait	–	–	–	–	–	–	1	1	0	0	1	0
Luxembourg	3	3	0	0	18	1	4	4	0	0	20	2
Malaysia	–	–	–	–	–	–	1	1	0	0	4	2
Malta	1	1	0	0	5	0	1	1	0	0	1	0
Mexico	2	2	0	0	10	0	4	1	1	2	4	3
Morocco	–	–	–	–	–	–	1	0	1	0	0	0
New Zealand	–	–	–	–	–	–	2	2	0	0	3	0
Norway	4	2	2	0	9	1	5	3	0	2	17	6
Paraguay	–	–	–	–	–	–	1	1	0	0	3	0
Peru	–	–	–	–	–	–	2	1	0	1	5	4
Poland	5	3	2	0	10	2	6	2	3	1	6	4
Portugal	6	5	1	0	12	4	9	3	4	2	23	13
Rest of Europe.	1	1	0	0	3	0	–	–	–	–	–	–
Rest of the World	1	1	0	0	2	1	–	–	–	–	–	–
San Marino	1	1	0	0	6	0	1	1	0	0	7	1
Romania	3	0	3	0	2	2	5	2	2	1	4	2
Saudi Arabia	–	–	–	–	–	–	1	0	1	0	1	1
Scotland	53	25	11	17	115	87	54	18	13	23	73	81
Spain	6	5	0	1	19	6	11	5	2	4	16	14
Sweden	4	2	1	1	9	6	10	4	3	3	15	10
Switzerland	5	3	2	0	12	3	10	7	0	3	25	9

	HOME				Goals		AWAY				Goals	
	P	W	D	L	For	Agst	P	W	D	L	For	Agst
Tunisia	–	–	–	–	–	–	1	0	1	0	1	1
Turkey	2	2	0	0	13	0	3	2	1	0	9	0
USA	–	–	–	–	–	–	6	4	0	2	29	7
USSR (and CIS)	4	2	1	1	10	5	8	3	3	2	11	10
Uruguay	3	1	1	1	3	3	5	1	1	3	5	9
Wales	49	32	9	8	126	46	48	30	12	6	113	44
Yugoslavia	7	4	3	0	15	7	7	1	2	4	8	13
TOTAL	299	192	65	42	778	293	406	210	99	97	876	458

GRAND TOTAL

Played	Won	Drawn	Lost	Goals	
				For	Against
705	402	164	139	1654	751

The England Squad in 1994.

England's Goalscorers 1946–1994

(Up to and including 22nd May 1994)

Charlton, R	49	Edwards	5	Moore	2
Lineker	48	Hitchens	5	Perry	2
Greaves	44	Latchford	5	Pointer	2
Finney	30	Neal	5	Royle	2
Lofthouse	30	Pearson, S C (Stan)	5	Smith, A	2
Robson, B	26	Pearson, J S (Stuart)	5	Taylor, P	2
Hurst	24	Pickering, F	5	Tueart	2
Mortensen	23	Wright, I	5	Wignall	2
Platt	23	Adams	4	Worthington	2
Channon	21	Barnes, P	4	A'Court	1
Keegan	21	Bull	4	Anderton	1
Peters	20	Dixon, K	4	Astall	1
Haynes	18	Hassall	4	Beattie	1
Hunt, R	18	Pearce	4	Bowles	1
Lawton	16	Revie	4	Bradford	1
Taylor, T	16	Robson, R	4	Bridges	1
Woodcock	16	Steven	4	Chamberlain	1
Chivers	13	Watson, D	4	Crawford	1
Mariner	13	Webb	4	Dixon, L	1
Smith, R	13	Baker	3	Goddard	1
Francis, T	12	Blissett	3	Hirst	1
Douglas	11	Butcher	3	Hughes, E	1
Mannion	11	Currie	3	Kay	1
Barnes, J	11	Elliott	3	Keown	1
Clarke, A	10	Francis, G	3	Kidd	1
Flowers, R	10	Grainger	3	Langton	1
Lee, F	10	Kennedy, R	3	Lawler	1
Milburn	10	McDermott	3	Lee, J	1
Wilshaw	10	Matthews, S	3	Mabbutt	1
Beardsley	9	Morris	3	Marsh	1
Bell	9	O'Grady	3	Medley	1
Bentley	9	Peacock	3	Melia	1
Hateley	9	Ramsey	3	Merson	1
Ball	8	Sewell	3	Mullery	1
Broadis	8	Shearer	3	Nicholls	1
Byrne, J	8	Wilkins	3	Nicholson	1
Hoddle	8	Wright, W	3	Palmer	1
Kevan	8	Allen, R	2	Parry	1
Connelly	7	Anderson	2	Sansom	1
Coppell	7	Bradley	2	Shackleton	1
Paine	7	Broadbent	2	Stiles	1
Charlton, J	6	Brooks	2	Summerbee	1
Gascoigne	6	Cowans	2	Tambling	1
Johnson	6	Eastham	2	Thompson, P B (Phil)	1
Macdonald	6	Ferdinand	2	Viollet	1
Mullen	6	Froggatt, J	2	Wallace	1
Rowley	6	Froggatt, R	2	Walsh	1
Waddle	6	Haines	2	Weller	1
Atyeo	5	Hancocks	2	Wise	1
Baily	5	Hunter	2	Withe	1
Brooking	5	Ince	2	Wright, M	1
Carter	5	Lee, S	2		

England Caps 1872–1994

(Up to and including 22nd May 1994)

Abbott W (Everton)	1	Balmer W (Everton)	1
A'Court A (Liverpool)	5	Bamber J (Liverpool)	1
Adams T (Arsenal)	31	Bambridge A (Swifts)	3
Adcock H (Leicester City)	5	Bambridge E C (Swifts)	18
Alcock C (Wanderers)	1	Bambridge E H (Swifts)	1
Alderson J (C Palace)	1	Banks G (Leicester, Stoke)	73
Aldridge A (WBA, Walsall Town Swifts)	2	Banks H (Millwall)	1
Allen A (Stoke)	3	Banks T (Bolton)	6
Allen A (Aston Villa)	1	Bannister W (Burnley, Bolton)	2
Allen C (QPR, Spurs)	5	Barclay R (Sheff Wed)	3
Allen H (Wolves)	5	Bardsley D (QPR)	2
Allen J (Portsmouth)	2	Barham M (Norwich City)	2
Allen R (WBA)	5	Barkas S (Man City)	5
Alsford W (Spurs)	1	Barker J (Derby County)	11
Amos A (Old Carthusians)	2	Barker R (Herts Rangers)	1
Anderson R (Old Etonians)	1	Barker R R (Casuals)	1
Anderson S (Sunderland)	2	Barlow R (WBA)	1
Anderson V (Nottm Forest,		Barnes J (Watford, Liverpool)	73
Arsenal, Man Utd)	30	Barnes P (Man City, WBA, Leeds Utd)	22
Anderton D (Spurs)	3	Barnet H (Royal Engeneers)	1
Angus J (Burnley)	1	Barrass M (Bolton)	3
Armfield J (Blackpool)	43	Barrett A (Fulham)	1
Armitage G (Charlton)	1	Barrett E (Oldham, Aston Villa)	3
Armstrong D (Middlesbrough,		Barrett J (West Ham Utd)	1
Southampton)	3	Barry L (Leicester City)	5
Armstrong K (Chelsea)	1	Barson F (Aston Villa)	1
Arnold J (Fulham)	1	Barton J (Blackburn)	1
Arthur J (Blackburn)	7	Barton P (Birmingham)	7
Ashcroft J (Woolwich Arsenal)	3	Bassett W (WBA)	16
Ashmore G (WBA)	1	Bastard S (Upton Park)	1
Ashton C (Corinthians)	1	Bastin C (Arsenal)	21
Ashurst W (Notts County)	5	Batty D (Leeds Utd, Blackburn)	15
Astall G (Birmingham)	2	Baugh R (Stafford Road, Wolves)	2
Astle J (WBA)	5	Bayliss A (WBA)	1
Aston J (Man Utd)	17	Baynham R (Luton)	3
Athersmith W (Aston Villa)	12	Beardsley P (Newcastle, Liverpool)	52
Atyeo J (Bristol City)	6	Beasant D (Chelsea)	2
Austin S (Man City)	1	Beasley A (Huddersfield)	1
		Beats W (Wolves)	2
Bach P (Sunderland)	1	Beattie K (Ipswich)	9
Bache J (Aston Villa)	7	Becton F (Preston, Liverpool)	2
Baddeley T (Wolves)	5	Bedford H (Blackpool)	2
Bagshaw J (Derby County)	1	Bell C (Man City)	48
Bailey G (Man Utd)	2	Bennett W (Sheff Utd)	2
Bailey H (Leicester Fosse)	5	Benson R (Sheff Utd)	1
Bailey M (Charlton)	2	Bentley R (Chelsea)	12
Bailey N (Clapham Rovers)	19	Beresford J (Aston Villa)	1
Baily E (Spurs)	9	Berry A (Oxford Univ)	1
Bain J (Oxford Univ)	1	Berry J (Man Utd)	4
Baker A (Arsenal)	1	Bestall J (Grimsby)	1
Baker B (Everton, Chelsea)	2	Betmead H (Grimsby)	1
Baker J (Hibernian, Arsenal)	8	Betts M (Old Harrovians)	1
Ball A (Blackpool Everton,		Betts W (Sheff Wed)	1
Arsenal)	72	Beverley J (Blackburn)	3
Ball J (Bury)	1	Birkett R H (Clapham Rovers)	1

Birkett R (Middlesbrough)	1
Birley F (Oxford Univ, Wanderers)	2
Birtles G (Nottm Forest)	3
Bishop S (Leicester City)	4
Blackburn F (Blackburn)	3
Blackburn G (Aston Villa)	1
Blenkinsop E (Sheff Wed)	26
Bliss H (Spurs)	1
Blissett L (Watford)	14
Blockley J (Arsenal)	1
Bloomer S (Derby County, Middlesbrough)	23
Blunstone F (Chelsea)	5
Bond R (Preston, Bradford City)	8
Bonetti P (Chelsea)	7
Bonsor A (Wanderers)	2
Booth F (Man City)	1
Booth T (Blackburn, Everton)	2
Bould S (Arsenal)	2
Bowden E (Arsenal)	6
Bower A (Corinthians)	5
Bowers J (Derby County)	3
Bowles S (QPR)	5
Bowser S (WBA)	1
Boyer P (Norwich)	1
Boyes W (WBA, Everton)	3
Boyle T (Burnley)	1
Brabrook P (Chelsea)	3
Bracewell P (Everton)	3
Bradford G (Bristol Rovers)	1
Bradford J (Birmingham)	12
Bradley W (Man Utd)	3
Bradshaw F (Sheff Wed)	1
Bradshaw T (Liverpool)	1
Bradshaw W (Blackburn)	4
Brann G (Swifts)	3
Brawn W (Aston Villa)	2
Bray J (Man City)	6
Brayshaw E (Sheff Wed)	1
Bridges B (Chelsea)	4
Bridgett A (Sunderland)	11
Brindle T (Darwen)	2
Brittleton J (Sheff Wed)	5
Britton C (Everton)	9
Broadbent P (Wolves)	7
Broadis I (Man City, Newcastle)	14
Brockbank J (Cambridge Univ)	1
Brodie J B (Wolves)	3
Bromilow T G (Liverpool)	5
Bromley-Davenport W E (Oxford Univ)	2
Brook E (Man City)	18
Brooking T (West Ham)	47
Brooks J (Spurs)	3
Broome F H (Aston Villa)	7
Brown A (Aston Villa)	3
Brown A S (Sheff Utd)	2
Brown G (Huddersfield, Aston Villa)	9

Brown J (Blackburn)	5
Brown J H (Sheff Wed)	6
Brown K (West Ham)	1
Brown T (WBA)	1
Brown W (West Ham)	1
Bruton J (Burnley)	3
Bryant W (Clapton)	1
Buchan C (Sunderland)	6
Buchanan W (Clapham Rovers)	1
Buckley F C (Derby County)	1
Bull S (Wolves)	13
Bullock F E (Huddersfield)	1
Bullock N (Bury)	3
Burgess H (Man City)	4
Burgess H (Sheff Wed)	4
Burnup C (Cambridge Univ)	1
Burrows H (Sheff Wed)	3
Burton F E (Nottm Forest)	1
Bury L (Cambridge Univ, Old Etonians)	2
Butcher T (Ipswich, Rangers)	77
Butler J (Arsenal)	1
Butler W (Bolton)	1
Byrne G (Liverpool)	2
Byrne J J (C Palace, West Ham)	11
Byrne R (Man Utd)	33
Callaghan I (Liverpool)	4
Calvey J (Nottm Forest)	1
Campbell A (Blackburn, Huddersfield)	8
Camsell, G (Middlesbrough)	9
Capes A (Stoke)	1
Carr J (Middlesbrough)	2
Carr J (Newcastle)	2
Carr W H (Owlerton)	1
Carter H S (Sunderland, Derby County)	13
Carter J H (WBA)	3
Catlin A E (Sheff Wed)	5
Chadwick A (Southampton)	2
Chadwick E (Everton)	7
Chamberlain M (Stoke)	8
Chambers H (Liverpool)	8
Channon M (Southampton, Man City)	46
Charles G (Nottm Forest)	2
Charlton J (Leeds Utd)	35
Charlton R (Man Utd)	106
Charnley R (Blackpool)	1
Charnsley C (Small Heath)	1
Chedgzoy S (Everton)	8
Chenery C (C Palace)	3
Cherry T (Leeds Utd)	27
Chilton A (Man Utd)	2
Chippendale H (Blackburn)	1
Chivers M (Spurs)	24
Christian E (Old Etonians)	1
Clamp E (Wolves)	4
Clapton D (Arsenal)	1
Clare T (Stoke)	4
Clarke A (Leeds Utd)	19
Clarke H (Spurs)	1

Clay T (Spurs)	4
Clayton R (Blackburn)	35
Clegg J (Sheff Wed)	1
Clegg W (Sheff Wed, Sheff Albion)	2
Clemence R (Liverpool, Spurs)	61
Clement D (QPR)	5
Clough B (Middlesbrough)	2
Clough N (Nottm Forest)	14
Coates R (Burnley, Spurs)	4
Cobbold W (Cambridge Univ, Old Carthusians)	9
Cock J (Huddersfield, Chelsea)	2
Cockburn H (Man Utd)	13
Cohen G (Fulham)	37
Colclough H (C Palace)	1
Coleman E (Dulwich Hamlet)	1
Coleman J (Woolwich Arsenal)	1
Common A (Sheff Utd, Middlesbrough)	3
Compton L H (Arsenal)	2
Conlin J (Bradford City)	1
Connelly J (Burnley, Man Utd)	20
Cook T E (Brighton)	1
Cooper N C (Cambridge Univ)	1
Cooper T (Derby County)	15
Cooper T (Leeds Utd)	20
Coppell S (Man Utd)	42
Copping W (Leeds Utd, Arsenal)	20
Corbett B (Corinthians)	1
Corbett R (Old Malvernians)	1
Corbett W (Birmingham)	3
Corrigan J (Manchester C.)	9
Cottee A (West Ham, Everton)	7
Cotterill G (Cambridge Univ, Old Brightonians)	4
Cottle J (Bristol City)	1
Cowan S (Man City)	3
Cowans G (Aston Villa, Bari)	10
Cowell A (Blackburn)	1
Cox J (Liverpool)	3
Cox J D (Derby County)	1
Crabtree J (Burnley, Aston Villa)	14
Crawford J F (Chelsea)	1
Crawford R (Ipswich)	2
Crawshaw T (Sheff Wed)	10
Crayston W (Arsenal)	8
Creek N (Corinthians)	1
Cresswell W (South Shields, Sunderland, Everton)	7
Crompton R (Blackburn)	41
Crooks S (Derby County)	26
Crowe C (Wolves)	1
Cuggy F (Sunderland)	2
Cullis S (Wolves)	12
Cunliffe A (Blackburn)	2
Cunliffe D (Portsmouth)	1
Cunliffe J (Everton)	1
Cunningham L (WBA, Real Madrid)	6
Curle K (Man City)	3
Currey E (Oxford Univ)	2

Currie A (Sheff Utd, Leeds Utd)	17
Cursham A (Notts County)	6
Cursham H (Notts County)	8
Daft H (Notts County)	5
Daley A (Aston Villa)	7
Danks T (Nottm Forest)	1
Davenport J (Bolton)	2
Davenport P (Nottm Forest)	1
Davis G (Derby County)	2
Davis H (Sheff Wed)	3
Davison J (Sheff Wed)	1
Dawson J (Burnley)	2
Day S (Old Malvernians)	3
Dean W (Everton)	16
Deane B (Sheffield U.)	3
Deeley N (Wolves)	2
Devey J (Aston Villa)	2
Devonshire A (West Ham)	8
Dewhurst F (Preston)	9
Dewhurst G (Liverpool Ramblers)	1
Dickinson J (Portsmouth)	48
Dimmock J (Spurs)	3
Ditchburn E (Spurs)	6
Dix R (Derby County)	1
Dixon J (Notts County)	1
Dixon K (Chelsea)	8
Dixon L (Arsenal)	21
Dobson A (Notts County)	4
Dobson C (Notts County)	1
Dobson M (Burnley, Everton)	5
Doggart A (Corinthians)	1
Dorigo T (Chelsea, Leeds Utd)	15
Dorrell A (Aston Villa)	4
Douglas B (Blackburn)	36
Downs R (Everton)	1
Doyle M (Manchester C.)	5
Drake E (Arsenal)	5
Ducat A (Woolwich Arsenal, Aston Villa)	6
Dunn A T (Cambridge Univ, Old Etonians)	4
Duxbury M (Man Utd)	10
Earle S (Clapton, West Ham)	2
Eastham G (Arsenal)	19
Eastham G R (Bolton)	1
Eckersley W (Blackburn)	17
Edwards D (Man Utd)	18
Edwards J (Shropshire Wanderers)	1
Edwards W (Leeds Utd)	16
Ellerington W (Southampton)	2
Elliott G (Middlesbrough)	3
Elliott W (Burnley)	5
Evans R (Sheff Utd)	4
Ewer F (Casuals)	2
Fairclough P (Old Foresters)	1
Fairhurst D (Newcastle)	1
Fantham J (Sheff Wed)	1

Fashanu J (Wimbledon)	2
Felton W (Sheff Wed)	1
Fenton M (Middlesbrough)	1
Fenwick T (QPR, Spurs)	20
Ferdinand L (QPR)	6
Field E (Clapham Rovers)	2
Finney T (Preston)	76
Fleming H (Swindon)	11
Fletcher A (Wolves)	2
Flowers R (Wolves)	49
Flowers T (Southampton, Blackburn)	2
Forman F (Nottm Forest)	9
Forman F R (Nottm Forest)	3
Forrest J (Blackburn)	11
Fort J (Millwall)	1
Foster R (Oxford Univ, Corinthians)	5
Foster S (Brighton & Hove Albion)	3
Foulke W (Sheff Utd)	1
Foulkes W (Man Utd)	1
Fox F (Gillingham)	1
Francis G (QPR)	12
Francis T (Birmingham, Nottm Forest, Man City, Sampdoria)	52
Franklin C (Stoke)	27
Freeman B (Everton, Burnley)	5
Froggatt J (Portsmouth)	13
Froggatt R (Sheff Wed)	4
Fry C (Corinthians)	1
Furness W (Leeds Utd)	1
Galley T (Wolves)	2
Gardner T (Aston Villa)	2
Garfield B (WBA)	1
Garratty W (Aston Villa)	1
Garrett T (Blackpool)	3
Gascoigne P (Spurs, Lazio)	29
Gates E (Ipswich)	2
Gay L (Cambridge Univ, Old Brightonians)	3
Geary F (Everton)	2
Geaves R (Clapham Rovers)	1
Gee C (Everton)	3
Geldard A (Everton)	4
George C (Derby County)	1
George W (Aston Villa)	3
Gibbins W (Clapton)	2
Gidman J (Aston Villa)	1
Gillard I (QPR)	3
Gilliat W (Old Carthusians)	1
Goddard P (West Ham)	1
Goodall F (Huddersfield)	25
Goodall J (Preston, Derby County)	14
Goodhart H (Old Etonians)	3
Goodwyn A (Royal Engineers)	1
Goodyer A (Nottm Forest)	1
Gosling R (Old Etonians)	5
Gosnell A (Newcastle)	1
Gough H (Sheff Utd)	1
Goulden L (West Ham)	14

Graham L (Millwall)	2
Graham T (Nottm Forest)	2
Grainger C (Sheff Utd, Sunderland)	7
Gray A (Crystal Palace)	1
Greaves J (Chelsea, Spurs)	57
Green G (Sheff Utd)	8
Green T (Wanderers)	1
Greenhalgh E (Notts County)	2
Greenhoff B (Man Utd, Leeds Utd)	18
Greenwood D (Blackburn)	2
Gregory J (QPR)	6
Grimsdell A (Spurs)	6
Grosvenor A (Birmingham)	3
Gunn W (Notts County)	2
Gurney R (Sunderland)	1
Hacking J (Oldham)	3
Hadley N (WBA)	1
Hagan J (Sheffield U.)	1
Haines J (WBA)	1
Hall A (Aston Villa)	1
Hall G (Spurs)	10
Hall J (Birmingham)	17
Halse H (Man Utd)	1
Hammond H (Oxford Univ)	1
Hampson J (Blackpool)	3
Hampton H (Aston Villa)	4
Hancocks J (Wolves)	3
Hapgood E (Arsenal)	30
Hardinge H (Sheff Utd)	1
Hardman H (Everton)	4
Hardwick G (Middlesbrough)	13
Hardy H (Stockport County)	1
Hardy S (Liverpool, Aston Villa)	21
Harford M (Luton Town)	2
Hargreaves F (Blackburn)	3
Hargreaves J (Blackburn)	2
Harper E (Blackburn)	1
Harris G (Burnley)	1
Harris P (Portsmouth)	2
Harris S (Cambridge Univ, Old Westminsters)	6
Harrison A (Old Westminsters)	2
Harrison G (Everton)	2
Harrow J (Chelsea)	2
Hart E (Leeds Utd)	8
Hartley F (Oxford City)	1
Harvey A (Wednesbury Strollers)	1
Harvey J (Everton)	1
Hassall H (Huddersfield, Bolton)	5
Hateley M (Portsmouth AC Milan, Monaco, Rangers)	32
Hawkes R (Luton)	5
Haworth G (Accrington)	5
Hawtrey J (Old Etonians)	2
Haygarth E (Swifts)	1
Haynes J (Fulham)	56
Healless H (Blackburn)	2
Hector K (Derby County)	2

Hedley G (Sheff Utd)	1
Hegan K (Corinthians)	4
Hellawell M (Birmingham)	2
Henfrey A (Cambridge Univ, Corinthians)	5
Henry R (Spurs)	1
Heron F (Wanderers)	1
Heron G (Uxbridge, Wanderers)	5
Hibbert W (Bury)	1
Hibbs H (Birmingham)	25
Hill F (Bolton)	2
Hill G (Man Utd)	6
Hill J (Burnley)	11
Hill R (Luton)	3
Hill R H (Millwall)	1
Hillman J (Burnley)	1
Hills A (Old Harrovians)	1
Hilsdon G (Chelsea)	8
Hine E (Leicester City)	6
Hinton A (Wolves, Nottm Forest)	3
Hirst D (Sheff Wed)	3
Hitchens G (Aston Villa, Inter-Milan)	7
Hobbis H (Charlton)	2
Hoddle G (Spurs, Monaco)	53
Hodge S (Aston Villa, Spurs, Nottm Forest)	24
Hodgetts D (Aston Villa)	6
Hodgkinson A (Sheffield U)	5
Hodgson G (Liverpool)	3
Hodkinson J (Blackburn)	3
Hogg W (Sunderland)	3
Holdcroft G (Preston)	2
Holden A (Bolton)	5
Holden G (Wednesbury OA)	4
Holden-White C (Corinthians)	2
Holford T (Stoke)	1
Holley G (Sunderland)	10
Holliday E (Middlesbrough)	3
Hollins J (Chelsea)	1
Holmes R (Preston)	7
Holt J (Everton, Reading)	10
Hopkinson E (Bolton)	14
Hossack A (Corinthians)	2
Houghton W (Aston Villa)	7
Houlker A (Blackburn, Portsmouth, Southampton)	5
Howarth R (Preston, Everton)	5
Howe D (WBA)	23
Howe J (Derby)	3
Howell L (Wanderers)	1
Howell R (Sheff Utd, Liverpool)	2
Hudson A (Stoke)	2
Hudson J (Sheffield)	1
Hudspeth F (Newcastle)	1
Hufton A (West Ham)	6
Hughes E (Liverpool, Wolves)	62
Hughes L (Liverpool)	3
Hulme J (Arsenal)	9
Humphreys P (Notts County)	1

Hunt G (Spurs)	3
Hunt Rev. K (Leyton)	2
Hunt R (Liverpool)	34
Hunt S (WBA)	2
Hunter J (Sheff Heeley)	7
Hunter N (Leeds Utd)	28
Hurst G (West Ham)	49
Ince P (Man Utd)	14
Iremonger J (Nottm Forest)	2
Jack D (Bolton, Arsenal)	9
Jackson E (Oxford Univ)	1
Jarrett B (Cambridge Univ)	3
Jefferis F (Everton)	2
Jezzard B (Fulham)	2
Johnson D (Ipswich, Liverpool)	8
Johnson E (Saltley Coll, Stoke)	2
Johnson J (Stoke)	5
Johnson T (Man City, Everton)	5
Johnson W (Sheff Utd)	6
Johnston H (Blackpool)	10
Jones A (Walsall Swifts, Great Lever)	3
Jones H (Blackburn)	6
Jones H (Nottm Forrest)	1
Jones M (Sheffield U, Leeds Utd)	3
Jones R (Liverpool)	4
Jones W (Bristol City)	1
Jones W (Liverpool)	2
Joy B (Casuals)	1
Kail E (Dulwich Hamlet)	3
Kay T (Everton)	1
Kean F (Sheff Wed, Bolton)	9
Keegan K (Liverpool, SV Hamburg, Southampton)	63
Keen E (Derby County)	4
Kelly R (Burnley, Sunderland, Huddersfield)	14
Kennedy A (Liverpool)	2
Kennedy R (Liverpool)	17
Kenyon-Slaney (Wanderers)	1
Keown M (Everton, Arsenal)	11
Kevan D (WBA)	14
Kidd B (Man Utd)	2
King R (Oxford Univ)	1
Kingsford R (Wanderers)	1
Kingsley M (Newcastle)	1
Kinsey G (Wolves, Derby County)	4
Kirchen A (Arsenal)	3
Kirton W (Aston Villa)	1
Knight A (Portsmouth)	1
Knowles C (Spurs)	4
Labone B (Everton)	26
Lampard F (West Ham)	2
Langley J (Fulham)	3
Langton R (Blackburn Preston, Bolton)	11
Latchford R (Everton)	12

Latheron E (Blackburn)	2
Lawler C (Liverpool)	4
Lawton T (Everton, Chelsea, Notts County)	23
Leach T (Sheff Wed)	2
Leake A (Aston Villa)	5
Lee E (Southampton)	1
Lee F (Manchester C.)	27
Lee J (Derby)	1
Lee S (Liverpool)	14
Leighton J (Nottm Forest)	1
Le Saux G (Blackburn)	3
Le Tissier M (Southampton)	3
Lilley H (Sheff Utd)	1
Linacre H (Nottm Forest)	2
Lindley T (Cambridge Univ, Nottm Forest)	13
Lindsay A (Liverpool)	4
Lindsay W (Wanderers)	1
Lineker G (Leicester Everton, Barcelona, Spurs)	80
Lintott E (QPR, Bradford City)	7
Lipsham H (Sheff Utd)	1
Little B (Aston Villa)	1
Lloyd L (Liverpool, Nottm Forest)	4
Lockett A (Stoke)	1
Lodge L (Cambridge Univ, Corinthians)	5
Lofthouse J (Blackburn, Accrington)	7
Lofthouse N (Bolton)	33
Longworth E (Liverpool)	5
Lowder A (Wolves)	1
Lowe E (Aston Villa)	3
Lucas T (Liverpool)	3
Luntley E (Nottm Forest)	2
Lyttelton Hon A (Cambridge Univ)	1
Lyttelton Hon E (Cambridge Univ)	1
Mabbutt G (Spurs)	16
Macauley R (Cambridge Unive)	1
Macdonald M (Newcastle)	14
Macrae S (Notts County)	6
McCall J (Preston)	5
McDermott T (Liverpool)	25
McDonald C (Burnley)	8
McFarland R (Derby County)	28
McGarry W (Huddersfield)	4
McGuinness W (Man Utd)	2
McInroy A (Sunderland)	1
McMahon S (Liverpool)	17
McNab R (Arsenal)	4
McNeal R (WBA)	2
McNeil M (Middlesbrough)	9
Maddison F (Oxford Univ)	1
Madeley P (Leeds Utd)	24
Magee T (WBA)	5
Makepeace H (Everton)	4
Male C (Arsenal)	19
Mannion W (Middlesbrough)	26
Mariner P (Ipswich, Arsenal)	35

Marsden J (Darwen)	1
Marsden W (Sheff Wed)	3
Marsh R (QPR, Manchester C)	9
Marshall T (Darwen)	2
Martin A (West Ham)	17
Martin H (Sunderland)	1
Martyn N (Crystal Palace)	3
Marwood B (Arsenal)	1
Maskrey H (Derby County)	1
Mason C (Wolves)	3
Matthews R (Coventry)	5
Matthews S (Stoke, Blackpool)	54
Matthews V (Sheff Utd)	2
Maynard W (1st Surrey Rifles)	2
Meadows J (Man City)	1
Medley L (Spurs)	6
Meehan T (Chelsea)	1
Melia J (Liverpool)	2
Mercer D (Sheff Utd)	2
Mercer J (Everton)	5
Merrick G (Birmingham)	23
Merson P (Arsenal)	14
Metcalfe V (Huddersfield)	2
Mew J (Man Utd)	1
Middleditch B (Corinthians)	1
Milburn J (Newcastle)	13
Miller B (Burnley)	1
Miller H (Charlton)	1
Mills G (Chelsea)	3
Mills M (Ipswich)	42
Milne G (Liverpool)	14
Milton A (Arsenal)	1
Milward A (Everton)	4
Mitchell C (Upton Park)	5
Mitchell J (Man City)	1
Moffat H (Oldham)	1
Molyneux G (Southampton)	4
Moon W (Old Westminsters)	7
Moore H (Notts County)	2
Moore J (Derby County)	1
Moore R (West Ham)	108
Moore W (West Ham)	1
Mordue J (Sunderland)	2
Morice C (Barnes)	1
Morley A (Aston Villa)	6
Morley H (Notts County)	1
Morren T (Sheff Utd)	1
Morris F (WBA)	2
Morris J (Derby)	3
Morris W (Wolves)	3
Morse H (Notts County)	1
Mort T (Aston Villa)	3
Morten A (C Palace)	1
Mortensen S (Blackpool)	25
Morton J (West Ham)	1
Mosforth W (Sheff Wed, Sheff Albion)	9
Moss F (Arsenal)	4
Moss F (Aston Villa)	5
Mosscrop E (Burnley)	2

Mozley B (Derby)	3	Perryman S (Spurs)	1
Mullen J (Wolves)	12	Peters M (West Ham, Spurs)	67
Mullery A (Spurs)	35	Phelan M (Man Utd)	1
		Phillips L (Portsmouth)	3
Neal P (Liverpool)	50	Pickering F (Everton)	3
Needham E (Sheff Utd)	16	Pickering J (Sheff Utd)	1
Newton K (Blackburn, Everton)	27	Pickering N (Sunderland)	1
Nicholls J (WBA)	2	Pike T (Cambridge Univ)	1
Nicholson W (Spurs)	1	Pilkington B (Burnley)	1
Nish D (Derby)	5	Plant J (Bury)	1
Norman M (Spurs)	23	Platt D (Aston Villa, Bari, Juventus,	
Nuttall H (Bolton)	3	Sampdoria)	48
		Plum S (Charlton)	1
Oakley W (Oxford Univ, Corinthians)	16	Pointer R (Burnley)	3
O'Dowd J (Chelsea)	3	Porteous T (Sunderland)	1
O'Grady M (Huddersfield, Leeds Utd)	2	Priest A (Sheff Utd)	1
Ogilvie R (Clapham Rovers)	1	Prinsep J (Clapham Rovers)	1
Oliver L (Fulham)	1	Puddefoot S (Blackburn)	2
Olney B (Aston Villa)	2	Pye J (Wolves)	1
Osborne F (Fulham, Spurs)	4	Pym R (Bolton)	3
Osborne R (Leicester City)	1		
Osgood P (Chelsea)	4	Quantrill A (Derby County)	4
Osman R (Ipswich)	11	Quixall A (Sheffield W.)	5
Ottaway C (Oxford Univ)	2		
Owen J (Sheffield)	1	Radford J (Arsenal)	2
Owen S (Luton)	3	Raikes G (Oxford Univ)	4
		Ramsey A (Southampton, Spurs)	32
Page L (Burnley)	7	Rawlings A (Preston)	1
Paine T (Southampton)	19	Rawlings W (Southampton)	2
Pallister G (Middlesbrough, Man Utd)	13	Rawlinson J (Cambridge Univ)	1
Palmer C (Sheff Wed)	18	Rawson H (Royal Engineers)	1
Pantling H (Sheff Utd)	1	Rawson W (Oxford Univ)	2
Paravacini P J de (Cambridge Univ)	3	Read A (Tufnell Park)	1
Parker P (QPR, Man Utd)	19	Reader J (WBA)	1
Parker T (Southampton)	1	Reaney P (Leeds Utd)	3
Parkes P (QPR)	1	Reeves K (Norwich, Man City)	2
Parkinson J (Liverpool)	2	Regis C (WBA, Coventry)	5
Parr P (Oxford Univ)	1	Reid P (Everton)	13
Parry E (Old Carthusians)	3	Revie D (Manchester C.)	6
Parry R (Bolton)	2	Reynolds J (WBA, Aston Villa)	8
Patchitt B (Corinthians)	2	Richards C (Nottm Forest)	1
Pawson F (Cambridge Univ, Swifts)	2	Richards G (Derby County)	1
Payne J (Luton)	1	Richards J (Wolves)	1
Peacock A (Middlesbrough, Leeds Utd)	6	Richardson J (Newcastle)	2
Peacock J (Middlesbrough)	3	Richardson K (Aston Villa)	1
Pearce S (Nottm Forest)	56	Richardson W (WBA)	1
Pearson H (WBA)	1	Rickaby S (WBA)	1
Pearson J H (Crewe)	1	Rigby A (Blackburn)	5
Pearson J S (Stuart) (Man Utd)	15	Rimmer E (Sheff Wed)	4
Pearson S C (Stan) (Man Utd)	8	Rimmer J (Arsenal)	1
Pease W (Middlesbrough)	1	Ripley S (Blackburn)	1
Pegg D (Man Utd)	1	Rix G (Arsenal)	17
Pejic M (Stoke)	4	Robb G (Spurs)	1
Pelly F (Old Foresters)	3	Roberts C (Man Utd)	3
Pennington J (WBA)	25	Roberts F (Man City)	4
Pentland F (Middlesbrough)	5	Roberts G (Spurs)	6
Perry C (WBA)	3	Roberts H (Arsenal)	1
Perry T (WBA)	1	Roberts H (Millwall)	1
Perry W (Blackpool)	3	Roberts R (WBA)	3

Roberts W (Preston) 2
Robinson J (Sheff Wed) 4
Robinson J W (Derby County, New
  Brighton Tower, Southampton) 11
Robson B (WBA, Man Utd) 90
Robson R (WBA) 20
Rocastle D (Arsenal) 14
Rose W (Wolves, Preston) 5
Rostron T (Darwen) 2
Rowe A (Spurs) 1
Rowley J (Man Utd) 6
Rowley W (Stoke) 2
Royle J (Everton, Manchester C) 6
Ruddlesdin H (Sheff Wed) 3
Ruffell J (West Ham) 6
Russell B (Royal Engineers) 1
Rutherford J (Newcastle) 11

Sadler D (Man Utd) 4
Sagar C (Bury) 2
Sagar E (Everton) 4
Salako J (Crystal Palace) 5
Sandford E (WBA) 1
Sandilands R (Old Westminsters) 5
Sands J (Nottm Forest) 1
Sansom K (C Palace, Arsenal) 86
Saunders F (Swifts) 1
Savage A (C Palace) 1
Sayer J (Stoke) 1
Scattergood E (Derby County) 1
Schofield J (Stoke) 3
Scott L (Arsenal) 17
Scott W (Brentford) 1
Seaman D (QPR, Arsenal) 14
Seddon J (Bolton) 6
Seed J (Spurs) 5
Settle J (Bury, Everton) 6
Sewell J (Sheffield W.) 6
Sewell W (Blackburn) 1
Shackleton L (Sunderland) 5
Sharp J (Everton) 2
Sharpe L (Man Utd) 8
Shaw G E (WBA) 1
Shaw G L (Sheff Utd) 5
Shea D (Blackburn) 2
Shearer A (Southampton, Blackburn) 10
Shellito K (Chelsea) 1
Shelton A (Notts County) 6
Shelton C (Notts Rangers) 1
Shepherd A (Bolton, Newcastle) 2
Sheringham T (Spurs) 2
Shilton P (Leicester, Stoke, Nottm
  Forest, Southampton, Derby County) 125
Shimwell E (Blackpool) 1
Shutt G (Stoke) 1
Silcock J (Man Utd) 3
Sillett P (Chelsea) 3
Simms E (Luton) 1
Simpson J (Blackburn) 8

Sinton A (QPR) 12
Slater W (Wolves) 12
Smalley T (Wolves) 1
Smart T (Aston Villa) 5
Smith A (Nottm Forest) 3
Smith A K (Oxford Univ) 1
Smith A M (Arsenal) 13
Smith B (Spurs) 2
Smith C E (C Palace) 1
Smith G O (Oxford Univ, Old
  Carthusians, Corinthians) 20
Smith H (Reading) 4
Smith J (WBA) 2
Smith Joe (Bolton) 5
Smith J C R (Millwall) 2
Smith J W (Portsmouth) 3
Smith Leslie (Brentford) 1
Smith Lionel (Arsenal) 6
Smith R A (Spurs) 15
Smith S (Aston Villa) 1
Smith S C (Leicester City) 1
Smith T (Birmingham) 2
Smith T (Liverpool) 1
Smith W H (Huddersfield) 3
Sorby T (Thursday Wanderers) 1
Southworth J (Blackburn) 3
Sparks F (Herts Rangers, Clapham Rovers)3
Spence J (Man Utd) 2
Spence R (Chelsea) 2
Spencer C (Newcastle) 2
Spencer H (Aston Villa) 6
Spiksley F (Sheff Wed) 7
Spilsbury B (Cambridge Univ) 3
Spink N (Aston Villa) 1
Spouncer W (Nottm Forest) 1
Springett R (Sheffield W.) 33
Sproston B (Leeds Utd, Spurs,
  Man City) 11
Squire R (Cambridge Univ) 3
Stanbrough M (Olc Carthusians) 1
Staniforth R (Huddersfield) 8
Starling R (Sheff Wed, Aston Villa) 2
Statham D (WBA) 3
Steele F (Stoke) 6
Stein B (Luton) 1
Stephenson C (Huddersfield) 1
Stephenson G (Derby County,
  Sheff Wed) 3
Stephenson J (Leeds Utd) 2
Stepney A (Man Utd) 1
Sterland M (Sheffield Wed) 1
Steven T (Everton, Rangers, Marseille) 36
Stevens G A (Spurs) 7
Stevens G (Everton, Rangers) 46
Stewart J (Sheff Wed, Newcastle) 3
Stewart P (Spurs) 3
Stiles N (Man Utd) 28
Stoker J (Birmingham) 3
Storer H (Derby County) 2

Storey P (Arsenal)	19	
Storey-Moore I (Nottm Forest)	1	
Strange A (Sheff Wed)	20	
Stratford A (Wanderers)	1	
Streten B (Luton)	1	
Sturgess A (Sheff Utd)	2	
Summerbee M (Man City)	8	
Sunderland A (Arsenal)	1	
Sutcliffe J (Bolton, Millwall)	5	
Swan P (Sheffield Wed)	19	
Swepstone H (Pilgrims)	6	
Swift F (Manchester C)	19	
Tait G (Birmingham Excelsior)	1	
Talbot B (Ipswich, Arsenal)	6	
Tambling R (Chelsea)	3	
Tate J (Aston Villa)	3	
Taylor E (Blackpool)	1	
Taylor E H (Huddersfield)	8	
Taylor J (Fulham)	2	
Taylor P H (Liverpool)	3	
Taylor P J (C Palace)	4	
Taylor T (Man Utd)	19	
Temple D (Everton)	1	
Thickett H (Sheff Utd)	2	
Thomas D (Coventry)	2	
Thomas D (QPR)	8	
Thomas G (Crystal Palace)	9	
Thomas M (Arsenal)	2	
Thompson P (Peter) (Liverpool)	16	
Thompson P (Phil) (Liverpool)	42	
Thompson T (Aston Villa, Preston)	2	
Thomson R (Wolves)	8	
Thornewell G (Derby County)	4	
Thornley I (Man City)	1	
Tilson S (Man City)	4	
Titmuss F (Southampton)	2	
Todd C (Derby)	27	
Toone G (Notts County)	2	
Topham A (Casuals)	1	
Topham R (Wolves, Casuals)	2	
Towers A (Sunderland)	3	
Townley W (Blackburn)	2	
Townrow J (Clapton Orient)	2	
Tremelling D (Birmingham)	1	
Tresadern J (West Ham)	2	
Tueart D (Man City)	6	
Tunstall F (Sheff Utd)	7	
Turnbull R (Bradford City)	1	
Turner A (Southampton)	2	
Turner H (Huddersfield)	2	
Turner J (Bolton, Stoke, Derby County)	3	
Tweedy G (Grimsby)	1	
Ufton D (Charlton)	1	
Underwood A (Stoke)	2	
Urwin T (Middlesbrough, Newcastle)	4	
Utley G (Barnsley)	1	

Vaughton O (Aston Villa)	5	
Veitch C (Newcastle)	6	
Veitch J (Old Westminsters)	1	
Venables T (Chelsea)	2	
Vidal R (Oxford Univ)	1	
Viljoen C (Ipswich)	2	
Viollet D (Man Utd)	2	
Von Donop (Royal Engineers)	2	
Wace H (Wanderers)	3	
Waddle C (Newcastle, Spurs, Marseille)	62	
Wadsworth S (Huddersfield)	9	
Wainscoat W (Leeds Utd)	1	
Waiters A (Blackpool)	5	
Walden F (Spurs)	2	
Walker D (Nottm Forest, Sampdoria, Sheff Wed)	59	
Walker W (Aston Villa)	18	
Wall G (Man Utd)	7	
Wallace C (Aston Villa)	3	
Wallace D (Southampton)	1	
Walsh P (Luton)	5	
Walters A (Cambridge Univ, Old Carthusians)	9	
Walters M (Rangers)	1	
Walters P (Oxford Univ, Old Carthusians	13	
Walton N (Blackburn)	1	
Ward J (Blackburn Olympic)	1	
Ward P (Brighton and Hove Albion)	1	
Ward T (Derby County)	2	
Waring T (Aston Villa)	5	
Warner C (Upton Park)	1	
Warren B (Derby County, Chelsea)	22	
Waterfield G (Burnley)	1	
Watson D (Norwich, Everton)	12	
Watson D (Sunderland, Man City, Werder Bremen, Southampton, Stoke)	65	
Watson V (West Ham)	5	
Watson W (Burnley)	3	
Watson W (Sunderland)	4	
Weaver S (Newcastle)	3	
Webb G (West Ham)	2	
Webb N (Nottm Forest, Man Utd)	26	
Webster M (Middlesbrough)	3	
Wedlock W (Bristol City)	26	
Weir D (Bolton)	2	
Welch R de C (Wanderers, Harrow Chequers)	2	
Weller K (Leicester)	4	
Welsh D (Charlton)	3	
West G (Everton)	3	
Westwood R (Bolton)	6	
Whateley O (Aston Villa)	2	
Wheeler J (Bolton)	1	
Wheldon G (Aston Villa)	4	
White D (Man City)	1	
White T (Everton)	1	
Whitehead J (Accrington, Blackburn)	2	

Whitfield H (Old Etonians)	1	Withe P (Aston Villa)	11
Whitham M (Sheff Utd)	1	Wollaston C (Wanderers)	4
Whitworth S (Leicester)	7	Wolstenholme S (Everton, Blackburn)	3
Whymark T (Ipswich)	1	Wood H (Wolves)	3
Widdowson S (Nottm Forest)	1	Wood R (Man Utd)	3
Wignall F (Nottm Forest)	2	Woodcock T (Nottm Forest,	
Wilkes A (Aston Villa)	5	Cologne, Arsenal)	42
Wilkins R (Chelsea, Man Utd,		Woodger G (Oldham)	1
AC Milan)	84	Woodhall G (WBA)	2
Wilkinson B (Sheff Utd)	1	Woodley Y (Chelsea)	19
Wilkinson L (Oxford Univ)	1	Woods C (Norwich, Rangers,	
Williams B (Wolves)	24	Sheff Wed)	43
Williams O (Clapton Orient)	2	Woodward V (Spurs, Chelsea)	23
Williams S (Southampton)	6	Woosnam M (Man City)	1
Williams W (WBA)	6	Worrall F (Portsmouth)	2
Williamson E (Arsenal)	2	Worthington F (Leicester City)	8
Williamson R (Middlesbrough)	7	Wreford-Brown C (Oxford Univ,	
Willingham C (Huddersfield)	12	Old Carthusians)	4
Willis A (Spurs)	1	Wright E (Cambridge Univ)	1
Wilshaw D (Wolves)	12	Wright I (C Palace, Arsenal)	18
Wilson C P (Hendon)	2	Wright J (Newcastle)	1
Wilson C W (Oxford Univ)	2	Wright J (Southampton, Derby	
Wilson G (Sheff Wed)	12	County, Liverpool)	43
Wilson G P (Corinthians)	2	Wright T (Everton)	11
Wilson R (Huddersfield, Everton)	63	Wright W (Wolves)	105
Wilson T (Huddersfield)	1	Wylie J (Wanderers)	1
Winckworth W (Old Westminsters)	2		
Windridge J (Chelsea)	8	Yates J (Burnley)	1
Wingfield-Straford C (Royal Engineers)	1	York R (Aston Villa)	2
Winterburn N (Arsenal)	2	Young A (Huddersfield)	9
Wise D (Chelsea)	6	Young G (Sheffield Wed)	1

David Platt, Daren Anderton and Peter Beardsley celebrate win v Denmark.

England Senior Caps 1993–1994

	Poland	Holland	San Marino	Denmark	Greece	Norway
D. Seaman (Arsenal)	1	1	1	1		1
R. Jones (Liverpool)	2				2	2
S. Pearce (Nottingham Forest)	3		3		2*	
P. Ince (Manchester United)	4	4	4	4		4
G. Pallister (Manchester United)	5	5	5	6		
T. Adams (Arsenal)	6	6		5	6	6
D. Platt (Sampdoria)	7	7	7	7	7	7
P. Gascoigne (Lazio)	8			8		
L. Ferdinand (Queens Park Rangers)	9		9			
I. Wright (Arsenal)	10	10*	10		10*	11*
L. Sharpe (Manchester United)	11	11				
P. Parker (Manchester United)		2		2		
T. Dorigo (Leeds United)		3				
C. Palmer (Sheffield Wednesday)		8				
A. Shearer (Blackburn Rovers)		9		9	9	9
P. Merson (Arsenal)		10			8	
A. Sinton (Sheffield Wednesday)		8*	11			
L. Dixon (Arsenal)			2			
D. Walker (Sheffield Wednesday)			6			
S. Ripley (Blackburn Rovers)			8			
G. Le Saux (Blackburn Rovers)				3	3	3
P. Beardsley (Newcastle United)				10	10	10
D. Anderton (Tottenham Hotspur)				11	11	11
D. Batty (Blackburn Rovers)				4*		
M. Le Tissier (Southampton)				8*	11*	4*
T. Flowers (Blackburn Rovers)					1	
K. Richardson (Aston Villa)					4	
S. Bould (Arsenal)					5	5
D. Wise (Chelsea)						8

substitute

Under-21 International Matches 1976–1994

UQ = UEFA Competition Qualifier
UF = UEFA Competition Finals

v Albania

| 1989 | 7/3 | Shkoder | W2–1 (UQ) |
| 1989 | 25/4 | Ipswich | W2–0 (UQ) |

v Belgium

| 1994 | 5/6 | Berre | W2–1 |

v Brazil

| 1993 | 11/6 | Draguignan | D0–0 |

v Bulgaria

1979	5/6	Pernik	W3–1 (UQ)
1979	20/11	Leicester	W5–0 (UQ)
1989	5/6	Toulon	L2–3

v Czech Republic

| 1993 | 9/6 | Saint Cyr | D1–1 |

v Czechoslovakia

| 1990 | 27/4 | Toulon | W2–1 |
| 1992 | 26/5 | Toulon | L1–2 |

v Denmark

1978	19/9	Hvidovre	W2–1 (UQ)
1979	11/9	Watford	W1–0 (UQ)
1982	21/9	Hvidovre	W4–1 (UQ)
1983	20/9	Norwich	W4–1 (UQ)
1986	12/3	Copenhagen	W1–0 (UF)
1986	26/3	Manchester City	D1–1 (UF)
1988	13/9	Watford	D0–0
1994	8/3	Brentford	W1–0

v Finland

1977	26/5	Helsinki	W1–0 (UQ)
1977	12/10	Hull	W8–1 (UQ)
1984	16/10	Southampton	W2–0 (UQ)
1985	21/5	Mikkeli	L1–3 (UQ)

v France

1984	28/2	Sheffield Wed	W6–1 (UF)
1984	28/3	Rouen	W1–0 (UF)
1987	11/6	Toulon	L0–2
1988	13/4	Besançon	L2–4 (UF)
1988	27/4	Arsenal	D2–2 (UF)
1988	12/6	Toulon	L2–4
1990	23/5	Aix en Provence	W7–3
1991	3/6	Toulon	W1–0

1992	28/5	Aubagne	D0–0
1993	15/6	Toulon	W1–0
1994	31/5	Aubagne	L0–3

v East Germany

| 1980 | 16/4 | Sheffield United | L1–2 (UF) |
| 1980 | 23/4 | Jena | L0–1 (UF) |

v West Germany

1982	21/9	Sheffield United	W3–1 (UF)
1982	12/10	Bremen	L2–3 (UF)
1987	8/9	Lüdenscheid	L0–2

v Germany

| 1991 | 10/9 | Scunthorpe | W2–1 |

v Greece

1982	16/11	Piraeus	L1–0 (UQ)
1983	29/3	Portsmouth	W2–1 (UQ)
1989	7/2	Patras	L0–1

v Holland

| 1993 | 27/4 | Portsmouth | W3–0 (UQ) |
| 1993 | 12/10 | Utrecht | D1–1 (UQ) |

v Hungary

1981	5/6	Keszthely	W2–1 (UQ)
1981	17/11	Nottingham	W2–0 (UQ)
1983	26/4	Newcastle	W1–0 (UQ)
1983	11/10	Nyiregyhaza	W2–0 (UQ)
1990	11/9	Southampton	W3–1
1992	12/5	Vac	D2–2

v Israel

| 1985 | 27/2 | Tel Aviv | W2–1 |

v Italy

1978	8/3	Manchester City	W2–1 (UF)
1978	5/4	Rome	D0–0 (UF)
1984	18/4	Manchester City	W3–1 (UF)
1984	2/5	Florence	L0–1 (UF)
1986	9/4	Pisa	L0–2 (UF)
1986	23/4	Swindon	D1–1 (UF)

v Mexico

1988	5/6	Toulon	W2–1
1991	29/5	Vitrolles	W6–0
1992	24/5	Six-Fours	D1–1

v Morocco

| 1987 | 7/6 | Toulon | W2–0 |
| 1988 | 9/6 | Toulon | W1–0 |

v Norway

1977	1/6	Bergen	W2–1 (UQ)
1977	6/9	Brighton	W6–0 (UQ)
1980	9/9	Southampton	W3–0
1981	8/9	Drammen	D0–0
1992	13/10	Peterborough	L0–2 (UQ)
1993	1/6	Stavanger	D1–1 (UQ)

v Poland

1982	17/3	Warsaw	W2-1 (UF)
1982	7/4	West Ham	D2-2 (UF)
1989	2/6	Plymouth	W2-1 (UQ)
1989	10/10	Jastrzebie Zdroj	W3-1 (UQ)
1990	16/10	Tottenham	L0-1 (UQ)
1991	12/11	Pila	L1-2 (UQ)
1993	28/5	Jastrzebie Zdroj	W4–1 (UQ)
1993	7/9	Millwall	L1-2 (UQ)

v Portugal

1987	13/6	Sollies-Pont	D0–0
1990	21/5	Six-Fours	L0-1
1993	7/6	Miramas	W2-0
1994	7/6	Toulon	W2-0

v Republic of Ireland

1981	25/2	Liverpool	W1-0
1985	25/3	Portsmouth	W3-2
1989	9/6	Six-Fours	D0-0
1990	13/11	Cork	W3-0 (UQ)
1991	26/3	Brentford	W3-0 (UQ)

v Romania

1980	14/10	Ploesti	L0-4 (UQ)
1981	28/4	Swindon	W3-0 (UQ)
1985	30/4	Brasov	D0–0 (UQ)
1985	9/9	Ipswich	W3-0 (UQ)

v Russia

1994	29/5	Bandol	W2-0

v San Marino

1993	16/2	Luton	W6–0 (UQ)
1993	17/11	San Marino	W4-0 (UQ)

v Scotland

1977	27/4	Sheffield United	W1-0
1980	12/2	Coventry	W2–1 (UF)
1980	4/3	Aberdeen	D0-0 (UF)
1982	19/4	Glasgow	W1–0 (UF)
1982	28/4	Manchester City	D1-1 (UF)
1988	16/2	Aberdeen	W1–0 (UF)
1989	22/3	Nottingham	W1–0 (UF)
1993	13/6	La Ciotat	W1-0

v Senegal

1989	7/6	Sainte-Maxime	W6-1
1991	27/5	Arles	W2-1

v Spain

1984	17/5	Seville	W1-0 (UF)
1984	24/5	Sheffield United	W2-0 (UF)
1987	18/2	Burgos	W2-1
1992	8/9	Burgos	W1-0

v Sweden

1979	9/6	Vasteras	W2-1
1986	9/9	Oestersund	D1–1
1988	18/10	Coventry	D1-1 (UQ)
1989	5/9	Uppsala	L0-1 (UQ)

v Switzerland

1980	18/11	Ipswich	W5-0 (UQ)
1981	31/5	Neuenburg	D0-0 (UQ)
1988	28/5	Lausanne	D1–1

v Turkey

1984	13/11	Bursa	D0–0 (UQ)
1985	15/10	Bristol	W3–0 (UQ)
1987	28/4	Izmir	D0–0 (UQ)
1987	13/10	Sheffield	D1-1 (UQ)
1991	30/4	Izmir	D2-2 (UQ)
1991	15/10	Reading	W2–0 (UQ)
1992	17/11	Leyton	L1–0 (UQ)
1993	30/3	Izmir	D0–0 (UQ)

v USA

1989	11/6	Toulon	L0–2
1994	2/6	Arles	W3–0

v USSR

1987	9/6	La Ciotat	D0-0
1988	7/6	Six-Fours	W1–0
1990	25/5	Toulon	W2-1
1991	31/5	Aix-en-Provence	W2–1

v Wales

1976	15/12	Wolverhampton	D0–0
1979	6/2	Swansea	W1–0
1990	5/12	Tranmere	D0-0

v Yugoslavia

1978	19/4	Novi Sad	L1-2 (UF)
1978	2/5	Manchester City	D1-1 (UF)
1986	11/11	Peterborough	D1-1 (UQ)
1987	10/11	Zemun	W5-1 (UQ)

England Under-21 Caps 1976–1994

(Up to and including 7th June 1994)

Ablett G (Liverpool)	1	Chapman L (Stoke City)	1
Adams N (Everton)	1	Charles G (Nottm Forest)	4
Adams T (Arsenal)	5	Chettle S (Nottm Forest)	12
Allen B (QPR)	8	Clark L (Newcastle)	11
Allen C (QPR, C Palace)	3	Clough N (Nottm Forest)	15
Allen M (QPR)	2	Cole A (Arsenal, Newcastle)	8
Allen P (West Ham, Spurs)	3	Coney D (Fulham)	4
Anderson V (Nottm Forest)	1	Connor T (Brighton & Hove Albion)	1
Anderton D (Spurs)	12	Cooke R (Spurs)	1
Andrews I (Leicester City)	1	Cooper C (Middlesbrough)	8
Ardley N (Wimbledon)	10	Corrigan J (Man City)	3
Atkinson B (Sunderland)	6	Cottee T (West Ham)	8
Atherton P (Coventry)	1	Cowans G (Aston Villa)	5
Awford A (Portsmouth)	9	Cox N (Aston Villa)	6
Bailey G (Man Utd)	14	Cranson I (Ipswich Town)	5
Baker G (Southampton)	2	Crooks G (Stoke City)	4
Bannister G (Sheff Wed)	1	Crossley M (Nottm Forest)	3
Barker S (Blackburn)	4	Cundy J (Chelsea)	3
Barmby N (Spurs)	1	Cunningham L (WBA)	6
Barnes J (Watford)	2	Curbishley A (Birmingham)	1
Barnes P (Man City)	9	Daniel P (Hull City)	7
Barrett E (Oldham)	4	Davis P (Arsenal)	11
Bart-Williams C (Sheff Wed)	8	D'Avray M (Ipswich)	2
Batty D (Leeds Utd)	7	Deehan J (Aston Villa)	7
Bazeley D (Watford)	1	Dennis M (Birmingham)	3
Beagrie P (Sheff Utd)	2	Dickens A (West Ham)	1
Beardsmore R (Man Utd)	5	Dicks J (West Ham)	4
Beeston C (Stoke)	1	Digby F (Swindon)	5
Bertschin K (Birmingham)	3	Dillon K (Birmingham)	1
Birtles G (Nottm Forest)	2	Dixon K (Chelsea)	1
Blackwell D (Wimbledon)	6	Dobson T (Coventry City)	4
Blake M (Aston Villa)	8	Dodd J (Southampton)	8
Blissett L (Watford)	4	Donowa L (Norwich City)	3
Bracewell P (Stoke, Sunderland, Everton)	13	Dorigo T (Aston Villa)	11
		Dozzell J (Ipswich)	9
Bradshaw P (Wolves)	4	Draper M (Notts County)	3
Breacker T (Luton Town)	2	Duxbury M (Man Utd)	7
Brennan M (Ipswich)	5	Dyer B (C Palace)	5
Brightwell I (Man City)	4	Dyson P (Coventry City)	4
Brock K (Oxford Utd)	4	Eadie D (Norwich)	2
Bull S (Wolves)	5	Ebbrell J (Everton)	14
Burrows D (WBA, Liverpool)	7	Edghill R (Man City)	2
Butcher T (Ipswich)	7	Ehiogu U (Aston Villa)	15
Butters G (Spurs)	3	Elliott P (Luton, Aston Villa)	3
Butterworth I (Coventry City, Nottm Forest)	8	Fairclough C (Nottm Forest, Spurs)	7
		Fairclough D (Liverpool)	1
Caesar G (Arsenal)	3	Fashanu Justin (Norwich, Nottm Forest)	11
Callaghan N (Watford)	9		
Campbell K (Arsenal)	4	Fear P (Wimbledon)	3
Campbell S (Spurs)	6	Fenwick T (QPR)	11
Carr C (Fulham)	1	Fereday W (QPR)	5
Carr F (Nottm Forest)	9	Flitcroft G (Man City)	10
Caton T (Man City, Arsenal)	14	Flowers T (Southampton)	3
Chamberlain M (Stoke)	4	Forsyth M (Derby County)	1

Foster S (Brighton & Hove Albion)	1
Fowler R (Liverpool)	4
Froggatt S (Aston Villa)	2
Futcher P (Luton, Man City)	11
Gabbiadini M (Sunderland)	2
Gale T (Fulham)	1
Gascoigne P (Newcastle)	13
Gayle H (Birmingham)	3
Gerrard P (Oldham)	11
Gernon I (Ipswich)	1
Gibbs N (Watford)	5
Gibson C (Aston Villa)	1
Gilbert W (C Palace)	11
Goddard P (West Ham)	8
Gordon D (C Palace)	5
Gordon D (Norwich)	4
Gray A (Aston Villa)	2
Haigh P (Hull)	1
Hall R (Southampton)	11
Hardyman P (Portsmouth)	2
Hateley M (Coventry City, Portsmouth)	10
Hayes M (Arsenal)	3
Hazell R (Wolves)	1
Heaney N (Arsenal)	6
Heath A (Stoke, Everton)	8
Hendon I (Spurs)	7
Hesford I (Blackpool)	7
Hilaire V (C Palace)	9
Hillier D (Arsenal)	1
Hinchcliffe A (Man City)	1
Hinshelwood P (C Palace)	2
Hirst D (Sheff Wed)	7
Hoddle G (Spurs)	12
Hodge S (Nottm Forest, Aston Villa)	8
Hodgson D (Middlesbrough, Liverpool)	7
Holdsworth D (Watford)	1
Horne B (Millwall)	5
Hucker P (QPR)	2
Impey A (QPR)	1
Ince P (West Ham United)	2
Jackson M (Everton)	10
James D (Watford)	10
James J (Luton)	2
Jemson N (Nottm Forest)	1
Joachim J (Leicester)	1
Johnson T (Notts County, Derby)	7
Johnston C (Middlesbrough)	2
Jones C (Spurs)	1
Jones D (Everton)	1
Jones R (Liverpool)	2
Keegan G (Oldham)	1
Kenny W (Everton)	1
Keown M (Aston Villa)	8
Kerslake D (QPR)	1
Kilcline B (Notts County)	2
King A (Everton)	2
Kitson P (Leicester, Derby)	7
Knight A (Portsmouth)	2
Knight I (Sheff Wed)	2
Lake P (Man City)	5
Langley T (Chelsea)	1
Lee D (Chelsea)	10
Lee R (Charlton)	2
Lee S (Liverpool)	6
Le Saux G (Chelsea)	4
Lowe D (Ipswich)	2
Lukic J (Leeds Utd)	7
Lund G (Grimsby)	3
Mabbutt G (Bristol Rovers, Spurs)	7
McCall S (Ipswich)	6
McDonald N (Newcastle)	5
McGrath L (Coventry City)	1
Mackenzie S (WBA)	3
McLeary A (Millwall)	1
McMahon S (Everton, Aston Villa)	6
McManaman S (Liverpool)	7
Makin C (Oldham)	5
Marriott A (Nottm Forest)	1
Martin L (Man Utd)	2
Martyn N (Bristol Rovers)	11
Matteo D (Liverpool)	3
Matthew D (Chelsea)	9
May A (Man City)	1
Merson P (Arsenal)	4
Middleton J (Nottm Forest, Derby County)	3
Miller A (Arsenal)	4
Mills G (Nottm Forest)	2
Mimms R (Rotherham, Everton)	3
Minto S (Charlton)	6
Moran S (Southampton)	2
Morgan S (Leicester)	2
Mortimer P (Charlton)	2
Moses R (WBA, Man Utd)	8
Mountfield D (Everton)	1
Muggleton C (Leicester City)	1
Mutch A (Wolves)	1
Nethercott S (Spurs)	6
Newell M (Luton Town)	4
Newton E (Chelsea)	2
Nicholls A (Plymouth)	1
Oakes M (Aston Villa)	5
Oldfield D (Luton)	1
Olney I (Aston Villa)	10
Ord R (Sunderland)	3
Osman R (Ipswich)	7
Owen G (Man City, WBA)	22
Painter I (Stoke)	1
Palmer C (Sheff Wed)	4
Parker G (Hull, Nottm Forest)	6
Parker P (Fulham)	8
Parkes P (QPR)	1
Parkin S (Stoke City)	5
Parlour R (Arsenal)	11
Peach D (Southampton)	6
Peake A (Leicester City)	1

Pearce S (Nottm Forest) 1
Pickering N (Sunderland, Coventry City) 15
Platt D (Aston Villa) 3
Porter G (Watford) 12
Pressman K (Sheff Wed) 1
Proctor M (Middlesbrough,
    Nottm Forest) 4
Ramage C (Derby County) 3
Ranson R (Man City) 10
Redknapp J (Liverpool) 16
Redmond S (Man City) 14
Reeves K (Norwich, Man City) 10
Regis C (WBA) 6
Reid N (Man City) 6
Reid P (Bolton) 6
Richards J (Wolves) 2
Rideout P (Aston Villa, Bari) 5
Ripley S (Middlesbrough) 8
Ritchie A (Brighton & Hove Albion) 1
Rix G (Arsenal) 7
Robins M (Man Utd) 6
Robson B (WBA) 7
Robson S (Arsenal, West Ham) 6
Rocastle D (Arsenal) 14
Rodger G (Coventry City) 4
Rosario R (Norwich) 4
Rowell G (Sunderland) 1
Ruddock N (Southampton) 4
Ryan J (Oldham Athletic) 1
Samways V (Spurs) 5
Sansom K (Crystal Palace) 8
Seaman D (Birmingham) 10
Sedgley S (Coventry City, Spurs) 11
Sellars S (Blackburn) 3
Selley I (Arsenal) 3
Sharpe L (Man Utd) 8
Shaw G (Aston Villa) 7
Shearer A (Southampton) 11
Shelton G (Sheff Wed) 1
Sheringham T (Millwall) 1
Sheron M (Man City) 16
Sherwood T (Norwich City) 4
Shipperley N (Chelsea) 1
Simpson P (Man City) 5
Sims S (Leicester City) 10
Sinclair T (QPR) 8
Sinnott L (Watford) 1
Slater S (West Ham) 3
Small B (Aston Villa) 12
Smith D (Coventry City) 10
Smith M (Sheff Wed) 5
Snodin I (Doncaster) 4
Statham B (Spurs) 3
Statham D (WBA) 6
Stein B (Luton) 3
Sterland M (Sheff Wed) 7
Steven T (Everton) 2

Stevens G (Everton) 1
Stevens G (Brighton & Hove Albion,
    Spurs) 7
Stewart P (Man City) 1
Stuart G (Chelsea) 5
Suckling P (Coventry City,
    Man City, C Palace) 10
Summerbee N (Swindon) 3
Sunderland A (Wolves) 1
Sutch D (Norwich) 4
Sutton C (Norwich) 13
Swindlehurst D (C Palace) 1
Talbot B (Ipswich) 1
Thomas D (Coventry City, Spurs) 7
Thomas M (Arsenal) 12
Thomas M (Luton) 3
Thomas R (Watford) 1
Thompson G (Coventry City) 6
Thorn A (Wimbledon) 5
Tiler C (Barnsley, Nottm Forest) 13
Venison B (Sunderland) 10
Vinnicombe C (Rangers) 12
Waddle C (Newcastle) 1
Walker D (Nottm Forest) 7
Walker I (Spurs) 9
Wallace D (Southampton) 14
Wallace Ray (Southampton) 4
Wallace Rod (Southampton) 11
Walsh G (Man Utd) 2
Walsh P (Luton Town) 4
Walters M (Aston Villa) 9
Ward P (Brighton & Hove Albion) 2
Warhurst P (Oldham, Sheff Wed) 8
Watson D (Barnsley) 4
Watson D (Norwich) 7
Watson G (Sheff Wed) 2
Watson S (Newcastle) 5
Webb N (Portsmouth,
    Nottm Forest) 3
Whelan P (Ipswich) 3
White D (Man City) 6
Whyte C (Arsenal) 4
Wicks S (QPR) 1
Wilkins R (Chelsea) 1
Wilkinson P (Grimsby, Everton) 4
Williams P (Charlton) 4
Williams P (Derby County) 6
Williams S (Southampton) 14
Winterburn N (Wimbledon) 1
Wise D (Wimbledon) 1
Woodcock A (Nottm Forest) 2
Woods C (Nottm Forest, QPR,
    Norwich) 6
Wright A (Blackburn) 2
Wright M (Southampton) 4
Wright W (Everton) 6
Yates D (Notts County) 5

England Under-21 Caps 1993–1994

	Poland	Holland	San Marino	Denmark	Russia	France	United States	Belgium	Portugal
I. Walker (Tottenham Hotspur)	1								
M. Jackson (Everton)	2								
B. Small (Aston Villa)	3		3						
N. Cox (Aston Villa)	4		6						
U. Ehiogu (Aston Villa)	5	5	5						
G. Flitcroft (Manchester City)	6	7							
D. Anderton (Tottenham Hotspur)	7		7						
C. Sutton (Norwich City)	8	4	9	9					
A. Cole (Newcastle United)	9	9							
J. Redknapp (Liverpool)	10	10*		7	7	7	7	7	7
S. McManaman (Liverpool)	11								
M. Sheron (Manchester City)	7*	8	8						
N. Ardley (Wimbledon)	10*	2	2						
D. Watson (Barnsley)		1	1						
S. Minto (Charlton Athletic)		3							
A. Awford (Portsmouth)		6							
L. Clark (Newcastle United)		10							
T. Sinclair (Queens Park Rangers)		11	11	11	11	11	11	11	11
E. Newton (Chelsea)		4							
R. Fowler (Liverpool)			10		9*	10	10		
N. Shipperley (Chelsea)			10*						
S. Watson (Newcastle United)			11*	2					
P. Gerrard (Oldham Athletic)				1	1				
R. Edghill (Manchester City)				3	2				
S. Campbell (Tottenham Hotspur)				4	4	4	4	4	4
S. Nethercott (Tottenham Hotspur)				5	5	5	5	5	5
R. Parlour (Arsenal)				6	6			6	6
N. Barmby (Tottenham Hotspur)				8					
C. Bart-Williams (Sheffield Wednesday)				10	10	6		10	10
M. Oakes (Aston Villa)				1*		1*	1	1	1
J. Joachim (Leicester City)				8*					
D. Gordon (Crystal Palace)					3	3	3	3	3
P. Fear (Wimbledon)					8	8	10*		
B. Dyer (Crystal Palace)					9	9	9	9	9
C. Makin (Oldham Athletic)					2*	2	2	2	2
I. Selley (Arsenal)					6*	6*	6		
A. Nicholls (Plymouth Argyle)					1				
D. Matteo (Liverpool)					3*			8	8
D. Eadie (Norwich City)					8*	8			

substitute

England B International Matches 1949–1994

v *Algeria*

1990 11/12	Algiers	D0-0

v *Australia*

1980 17/11	Birmingham	W1-0

v *CIS*

1992 28/4	Moscow	D1-1

v *Czechoslovakia*

1978 28/11	Prague	W1-0
1990 24/4	Sunderland	W2-0
1992 24/3	Ceske Budejovice	W1-0

v *Finland*

1949 15/5	Helsinki	W4-0

v *France*

1952 22/5	Le Havre	L1-7
1992 18/2	QPR	W3-0

v *West Germany*

1954 24/3	Gelsenkirchen	W4-0
1955 23/3	Sheffield	D1-1
1978 21/2	Augsburg	W2-1

v *Holland*

1949 18/5	Amsterdam	W4-0
1950 22/2	Newcastle	W1-0
1950 17/5	Amsterdam	L0-3
1952 26/3	Amsterdam	W1-0

v *Iceland*

1989 19/5	Reykjavik	W2-0
1991 27/4	Watford	W1-0

v *Italy*

1950 11/5	Milan	L0-5
1989 14/11	Brighton	D1-1

v *Luxembourg*

1950 21/5	Luxembourg	W2-1

v *Malaysia*

1978 30/5	Kuala Lumpur	D1-1

v *Malta*

1987 14/10	Ta'Qali	W2-0

v *New Zealand*

1978 7/6	Christchurch	W4-0
1978 11/6	Wellington	W3-1
1978 14/6	Auckland	W4-0
1979 15/10	Leyton Orient	W4-1
1984 13/11	Nottingham Forest	W2-0

v *Northern Ireland*

1994 10/5	Sheffield	W4-2

v *Norway*

1989 22/5	Stavanger	W1-0

v *Republic of Ireland*

1990 27/3	Cork	L1-4

v *Scotland*

1953 11/3	Edinburgh	D2-2
1954 3/3	Sunderland	D1-1
1956 29/2	Dundee	D2-2
1957 6/2	Birmingham	W4-1

v *Singapore*

1978 18/6	Singapore	W8-0

v *Spain*

1980 26/3	Sunderland	W1-0
1981 25/3	Granada	L2-3
1991 18/12	Castellon	W1-0

v *Switzerland*

1950 18/1	Sheffield	W5-0
1954 22/5	Basle	L0-2
1956 21/3	Southampton	W4-1
1989 16/5	Winterthur	W2-0
1991 20/5	Walsall	W2-1

v *USA*

1980 14/10	Manchester	W1-0

v *Wales*

1991 5/2	Swansea	W1-0

v *Yugoslavia*

1954 16/5	Ljubljana	L1-2
1955 19/10	Manchester	W5-1
1989 12/12	Millwall	W2-1

England B Caps 1978–1994

(Up to and including 10th May 1994)

Ablett G (Liverpool)	1	Fairclough C (Spurs)	1
Adams T (Arsenal)	4	Fairclough D (Liverpool)	1
Anderson V (Nottingham Forest)	7	Fashanu J (Nottingham Forest)	1
Armstrong C (Crystal Palace)	1	Flanagan M (Charlton and Crystal Palace)	3
Armstrong D (Middlesbrough)	2	Ford T (WBA)	3
Atkinson D (Sheffield Wednesday)	1	Forsyth M (Derby County)	1
Bailey G (Manchester United)	2	Fox R (Newcastle)	1
Bailey J (Everton)	1	Gabbiadini M (Sunderland)	1
Barnes P (WBA)	1	Gallagher J (Birmingham)	1
Barrett E (Oldham Athletic)	4	Gascoigne P (Tottenham)	4
Barton W (Wimbledon)	2	Geddis D (Ipswich Town)	1
Bart-Williams C (Sheffield Wednesday)	1	Gibson C (Aston Villa)	1
Batson B (WBA)	3	Gidman J (Aston Villa)	2
Batty D (Leeds United)	5	Goddard P (West Ham United)	1
Beagrie P (Everton)	2	Gordon D (Norwich City)	2
Beardsley P (Liverpool)	2	Greenhoff B (Manchester United)	1
Beasant D (Wimbledon)	7	Harford M (Luton Town)	1
Beresford J (Newcastle)	1	Hazell R (Wolves)	1
Birtles G (Nottingham Forest)	1	Heath A (Everton)	1
Bishop I (West Ham United)	1	Hilaire V (Crystal Palace)	1
Blissett L (Watford)	1	Hill G (Man Utd and Derby County)	6
Bond K (Norwich and Manchester City)	2	Hirst D (Sheffield Wednesday)	3
Borrows B (Coventry City)	1	Hoddle G (Tottenham)	2
Bould S (Arsenal)	1	Hodge S (Nottingham Forest)	2
Brock K (QPR)	1	Holdsworth D (Wimbledon)	1
Bruce S (Norwich City)	1	Hollins J (QPR.)	5
Bull S (Wolves)	5	Hurlock T (Millwall)	3
Burrows D (Liverpool)	3	Ince P (Man Utd)	1
Butcher T (Ipswich Town)	1	Jobson R (Oldham)	2
Callaghan N (Watford)	1	Johnston C (Liverpool)	1
Campbell K (Arsenal)	1	Joseph R (Wimbledon)	2
Chapman L (Leeds United)	1	Kennedy A (Liverpool)	7
Clough N (Nottingham Forest)	3	Keown M (Everton)	1
Corrigan J (Manchester City)	10	King P (Sheffield Wednesday)	1
Coton T (Manchester City)	1	Lake P (Manchester City)	1
Cowans G (Aston Villa)	2	Langley T (Chelsea)	3
Crook I (Norwich City)	1	Laws B (Nottingham Forest)	1
Cunningham L (WBA)	1	Lee R (Newcastle)	1
Curle K (Wimbledon and Man City)	4	Le Saux G (Chelsea)	2
Daley S (Wolves)	6	Le Tissier M (Southampton)	5
Daley T (Aston Villa)	1	Lineker G (Leicester City)	1
Davenport P (Nottingham Forest)	1	Linighan A (Norwich City)	4
Davis P (Arsenal)	1	Lukic J (Leeds United)	1
Deane B (Sheffield United)	3	Lyons M (Everton)	1
Devonshire A (West Ham United)	1	McCall S (Ipswich Town)	1
Dicks J (West Ham)	2	McDermott T (Liverpool)	1
Dixon L (Arsenal)	4	McLeary A (Millwall)	3
Dorigo T (Chelsea, Leeds Utd)	7	McMahon S (A Villa and Liverpool)	2
Ebbrell J (Everton)	1	Mabbutt G (Tottenham)	9
Edghill R (Manchester City)	1	Mackenzie S (Man City and Charlton)	3
Elliott P (Celtic)	1	Mariner P (Ipswich Town)	7
Elliott S (Sunderland)	3	Martin A (West Ham United)	2
Eves M (Wolves)	3	Martyn N (Bristol Rovers and C Palace)	6

Merson P (Arsenal)	3
Money R (Liverpool)	1
Morley T (Aston Villa)	2
Mortimer D (Aston Villa)	3
Mountfield D (Everton)	1
Mowbray T (Middlesbrough)	3
Mutch A (Wolves)	3
Naylor S (WBA)	3
Needham D (Nottingham Forest)	6
Newell M (Everton)	2
Osman R (Ipswich Town)	2
Owen G (Manchester City)	7
Pallister G (Middlesbrough, Man Utd)	9
Palmer C (Sheffield Wednesday)	5
Parker G (Nottingham Forest)	1
Parker P (QPR)	3
Parkes P (West Ham United)	2
Peach D (Southampton)	1
Platt D (Aston Villa)	3
Power P (Manchester City)	1
Preece D (Luton Town)	3
Pressman K (Sheffield Wednesday)	1
Reeves K (Manchester City)	3
Regis C (WBA)	3
Richards J (Wolves)	3
Rix G (Arsenal)	3
Roberts G (Tottenham)	1
Robson B (WBA, Man Utd)	3
Rocastle D (Arsenal)	2
Roeder G (Orient and QPR)	5
Sansom K (Crystal Palace)	2
Scales J (Wimbledon)	1
Seaman D (QPR)	6
Sharpe L (Man Utd)	1
Shearer A (Southampton)	1

Sims S (Leicester City)	1
Sinton A (QPR)	3
Slater S (West Ham United)	2
Smith A (Arsenal)	4
Snodin I (Everton)	2
Speight M (Sheffield United)	4
Spink N (Aston Villa)	2
Statham D (WBA)	2
Sterland M (Sheffield Wed, Leeds)	3
Stevens G (Everton)	1
Stewart P (Tottenham)	5
Stubbs A (Bolton)	1
Summerbee N (Swindon)	1
Sunderland A (Arsenal)	7
Sutton C (Norwich)	1
Talbot B (Ipswich and Arsenal)	8
Thomas G (Crystal Palace)	3
Thomas M (Liverpool)	5
Thomas M (Tottenham Hotspur)	1
Thompson P (Liverpool)	1
Waldron M (Southampton)	1
Wallace D (Manchester United)	1
Wallace R (Southampton)	1
Walters M (Rangers)	1
Ward P (Nottingham Forest)	2
Webb N (Manchester United)	4
White D (Manchester City)	1
Williams P (Charlton Athletic)	3
Williams S (Southampton)	4
Winterburn N (Arsenal)	3
Wise D (Wimbledon)	3
Woodcock T (Cologne)	1
Woods C (Norwich, Rangers)	2
Wright B (Everton)	2
Wright I (Crystal Palace)	3

England's International Matches 1993–1994

7th September 1993, Millwall
England 1   Poland 2
(Under-21)

England's hopes of qualifying for the quarter-finals of the European Under-21 Championship were all but dashed at Millwall's brand new 'Den'. A skilful, but at times cynical Polish team – they had six players cautioned on the night – survived a catalogue of scoring chances to end England's ten-match unbeaten run. There were echoes from 1973 as Polish goalkeeper Majdan, dubbed 'Tomaszewski the Second' by England Under-21 boss Lawrie McMenemy, continually denied the home side.

England might have scored inside two minutes through Sutton, but it was Poland who grabbed an early lead. Villa's Cox was ruled to have fouled Kucharski on seven minutes and, though Walker got a hand to Baluszynski's penalty, he could not quite keep it out. Cole immediately had a header cleared off the line and after that there were near misses galore – as McManaman curled a shot wide, a Flitcroft effort clipped the bar and Sutton had a header turned away for a corner.

The pattern continued after half-time as Majdan performed heroics to beat away Sheron's fierce shot and launch himself to save a 35-yard drive from Ehiogu. England remained frustrated and were then mortified to concede another fortuitous Polish goal with just eleven minutes left. The lively Kubica's strike in off the post came completely against the run of play and England stormed back for Ehiogu to reduce the arrears. Cole almost equalised at the end, but was foiled by a world-class stop from Majdan. It was an ominous sign for the seniors.

A great start for England: Les Ferdinand scores after five minutes.

England: Walker, Jackson, Small, Cox, Ehiogu, Flitcroft, Anderton (Sheron), Sutton, Cole, Redknapp (Ardley), McManaman.
Poland: Majdan, Hajton, Mosor, Stolarczyk, Wojtala, Ruta (Bocusz), Baluszynski (Dabrowski), Ledwon, Kubica, Wojciechowski, Kucharski.
Referee: O.B. Christensen (Denmark).
Attendance: 5,930.

8th September 1993, Wembley
England 3   Poland 0

A rousing performance by England put them back on course for qualification for the 1994 World Cup Finals, as Graham Taylor's determined team were given a standing ovation by the Wembley crowd at the end of a memorable 3–0 victory. After a disappointing summer England had gone into the match knowing that anything less than two points would almost certainly have ended their hopes of making it to the States.

An adventurous team, full of attacking power, had the crowd on their feet after just 40 seconds, as Sharpe's centre from the left reached Gascoigne and his shot hit giant Polish goalkeeper Bako. An early goal to settle the nerves was essential and it was not long in coming. Platt split the Polish defence with a magnificent 50-yard pass and Ferdinand, in one action, controlled the ball and beat Bako from eight yards. It was the QPR striker's second goal in five internationals, but hugely more significant than the one he had scored on his debut against San Marino.

England had stamped their authority on the match to such a great extent that Seaman had not been required to make a save in the first half-hour. Even then, Kosecki's 20-yard effort hardly caused him palpitations. Then there was acute disappointment as Gascoigne was cautioned for a challenge on Brzeczek: it meant he would be suspended for the return match with Holland.

England increased their lead three minutes after half-time. A free-kick by Jones was headed on by Ferdinand to Gascoigne and the Lazio midfielder beat Brzeczek before scoring with an unstoppable right-foot volley. Pearce, back as England's captain, made it 3-0 on 53 minutes with a typically ferocious shot from 25 yards after Gascoigne had cleverly teed the ball up from Sharpe's short free-kick. There were no more goals to cheer after that, but England supporters who had been in a mood to get behind the team from the start were delighted with England's courageous display.

England: Seaman, Jones, Pearce, Ince, Pallister, Adams, Platt, Gascoigne, Ferdinand, Wright, Sharpe.
Poland: Bako, Czachowski, Brzeczek, Kozminski, Lesiak, Warzycha R., Swierczewski, Adamczuk (Bak), Furtok (Ziober), Kosecki, Lesniak.
Referee: F. van den Wijngaert (Belgium).
Attendance: 71,220.

12th October 1993, Utrecht
Holland 1   England 1
(Under-21)

England Under-21s stuck to their task well after being given the run-around by their Dutch counterparts in Utrecht. Opting for a cautious approach by employing a five-man defence, England were consequently outnumbered in midfield and were chasing shadows for much of the first half. England's first attempt on goal, a 25-yarder from Cole which sailed high over the bar, did not arrive until the 30th minute, while Barnsley goalkeeper Watson had been kept busy by contrast.

Watson missed his punch on a deep cross from Verhagen and was grateful to see full-back Ardley hack the ball clear from the line. But, when a Dutch goal finally came on 52 minutes – Mutsaers scored from close range after a one-two with fellow midfielder Klomp – it had the effect of sparking England into life.

Ten minutes later the visitors were on level terms. Dutch goalkeeper Moens parried away Ardley's corner, but the ball landed conveniently for Sutton to nod it goalwards and Flitcroft to turn it home. After that it was England who looked more likely to score the winner, with Cole and Redknapp going close. Unfortunately England's faint hopes of making the quarter-finals had now been extinguished.

Holland: Moens, Verhagen, van Hoogdalem, van Gastel, van de Looi, Buskermolen, Klomp (Gesthuizen), Loeffen (Rorije), Pahlplatz, Mutsaers, Hoekstra.
England: Watson, Ardley, Minto, Sutton, Ehiogu, Awford, Flitcroft, Sheron, Cole, Clark (Redknapp), Sinclair.
Referee: L. Gadosi (Slovakia).
Attendance: 3,300.

13th October 1993, Rotterdam
Holland 2   England 0

Graham Taylor's team were desperately unlucky not to get anything out of this match. Pointless England's slim hopes of going to America now rested on their scoring the proverbial hatful of goals against San Marino and Poland's beating Holland on the same day. A controversial incident in the 60th minute had virtually decided the outcome of the match in Rotterdam, as the German referee elected to be lenient with Koeman when the Dutch captain should clearly have been sent off.

Koeman pulled down Platt as the England forward was about to enter the Dutch penalty area with only goalkeeper de Goey to beat. It was an obvious case of serious foul play – the 'professional foul' – but the crack Barcelona defender was only shown a yellow card. Needless to say England's free-kick – at the time of the offence many watchers had seen it as a penalty – came to nothing.

A minute later, ironically, Holland were awarded a free-kick in a similar position on the edge of the England penalty area after Ince had fouled Wouters. Koeman's first effort, a typically powerful shot, was blocked by Ince who was then cautioned for encroaching. The retaken kick was chipped over the England wall and past Seaman's desperate lunge towards his right-hand post. There had been something almost inevitable about the goal.

Seaman made a superb double save from Bergkamp and Rijkaard before Holland wrapped things up with a second strike on 70 minutes. There was even a debatable element to this goal, as the Inter-Milan forward Bergkamp appeared to control the ball with a hand before running on to slot the ball into the corner. Overall England had performed well, and there was sympathy for the team at home. It had just not been their night.

Holland: de Goey, de Wolf, Koeman R., de Boer F., Rijkaard, Wouters, Koeman E., Bergkamp, Overmars (Winter), de Boer R. (Van Gobbel), Roy.
England: Seaman, Parker, Dorigo, Ince, Pallister, Adams, Platt, Palmer (Sinton), Shearer, Merson (Wright), Sharpe.
Referee: K.J. Assenmacher (Germany).
Attendance: 48,000.

17th November 1993, San Marino
San Marino 0   England 4
(Under-21)

England were expected to win easily and they did rattle in four goals without reply. The opposition was poor and the visitors would surely have scored more on a better playing surface. In the cold of a November evening in the Serraville Stadium in San Marino, before a meagre crowd of about 200, Liverpool's Robbie Fowler improved his credentials with an encouraging debut at Under-21 level.

Fowler had scored freely for the England Youth team, helping them to win the UEFA Championship four months earlier, and he had made such an impact in Liverpool's first team that he was already inviting favourable comparisons with the great Ian Rush. Part of a very attacking line-up in San Marino, Fowler had scored within three minutes of the start as an avalanche of England goals on the night looked probable.

Les Ferdinand is on target in Bologna.

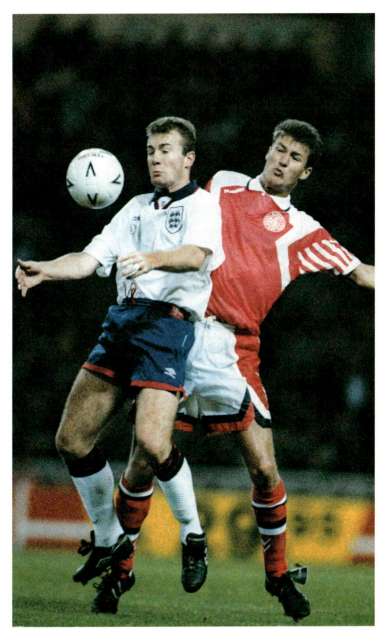

Alan Shearer is shadowed by Danish defender Reiper.

Anderton (10 minutes) and Sutton (43 minutes) gave England a 3–0 lead at the break. But motivation was difficult in the conditions and there was only one more goal in the second half – from Sheron. Chelsea's young striker Shipperley came off the bench to replace Fowler with eight minutes to go.

San Marino: Ceccoli, Casadei, Bacciocchi, Moroni, Valentini, Corbelli, Zanotti, Francini, Gatti, Gasperoni, Ugolini.
England: Watson D., Ardley, Small, Newton, Ehiogu, Cox, Anderton, Sheron, Sutton, Fowler (Shipperley), Sinclair (Watson S.).
Referee: Lubos (Slovakia).
Attendance: 200.

17th November 1993, Bologna
San Marino 1   England 7

England bowed out of the 1994 World Cup, thereby failing to make the finals for the first time in sixteen years, before a sparse crowd in Bologna's Renato Dall'Ara Stadium. They also suffered the embarrassment of conceding a goal to the minnows of European international football inside the first few seconds. The low point of England's tortuous qualifying campaign arrived when Pearce underhit a back-pass to Seaman which presented Gualtieri with an offer he could hardly refuse.

Defeat against the part-timers was, of course, unthinkable and England pulled themselves together for Ince to pick up a loose ball on 22 minutes and rifle in his first international goal with a right-footer from just outside the box. Wright notched the first of his four goals on 33 minutes, following an error by San Marino goalkeeper and team-bus driver Benedettini, and Ferdinand took advantage of another goalkeeping indiscretion to tap England 3–1 ahead four minutes later.

With the chances of a result for San Marino receding into oblivion, England were sufficiently relaxed to register another four goals in the second half. Wright headed in Ferdinand's centre thirty seconds after the restart, Ince netted his second on 73 minutes and Wright completed his hat-trick four minutes later from Pallister's long punt. Wright added his fourth in injury time, thereby equalling Platt's tally at Wembley, but San Marino had almost caused further embarrassment when Bacciocchi struck an upright.

England's 400th international victory proved to be a hollow one. The news from Poland was bad: Holland had won 3–1 to clinch their spot in America. Within a week Graham Taylor had resigned as England Team Manager.

San Marino: Benedettini, Valentini (Gobbi), Gennari, Zanotti, Canti, Guerra, Manzaroli, Della Valle, Bacciocchi (Mazza), Bonini, Gualtieri.
England: Seaman, Dixon, Pearce, Ince, Pallister, Walker, Platt, Ripley, Ferdinand, Wright, Sinton.
Referee: Mohammed Nazri (Malaysia).
Attendance: 2,378.

8th March 1994, Brentford
England 1   Denmark 0
(Under-21)

The first international fixture after England's new management team had been put in place – an Under-21 match against the Danes at Brentford – was watched by a record home crowd (11,553) for a friendly at that level. Terry Venables had been sworn in as the new 'England Coach' at Wembley on 28th January and he had appointed the greatly respected Dave Sexton, who had guided England to two UEFA Championships (in 1982 and 1984), as the new boss of the Under-21s after Lawrie McMenemy.

So the expected renaissance began at Griffin Park and, just to prove the point, Sexton brought in five new caps – Edghill, Sinclair and Tottenham trio Campbell, Nethercott and Barmby – and a refined playing style which involved a lot of low passes, played to feet. Denmark were outplayed in the first half as Redknapp and Sinclair moved around sharply and Sutton showed excellent vision and timing up front. England should have been three or four goals to the good by the end of the half, but they finished it goalless – and also Barmby-less, the diminutive Spurs midfielder having been stretchered away after hurting his left knee in a collision with Stensgaard.

England had clearly been unsettled by the popular Barmby's departure and there was a feeling that the enthusiastic crowd would be denied the sight of a goal by the home side, although England continued to move forward purposefully, with Parlour and the speedy Joachim prominent down the right. Then, almost out of the blue, Sinclair scored with a snap shot from just outside the box on 71 minutes and that was enough to win it.

England: Gerrard (Oakes), Watson, Edghill, Campbell, Nethercott, Parlour, Redknapp, Barmby (Joachim), Sutton, Bart-Williams, Sinclair.
Denmark: Stensgaard, Rytter, Nielsen M., Nielsen P., Bisgaard, Sorenson P., Sorenson J. (Nonbo), Petersen C., Rasmussen, Bech (Poulsen), Petersen U.
Referee: R. Jol (Holland).
Attendance: 11,553.

9th March 1994
England 1   Denmark 0

England seemed to have genuine hope for the future as Terry Venables' new-look team beat the reigning European champions before an appreciative Wembley crowd. Venables' first match as England coach could hardly have gone better: he introduced a fluid system of play, with players rotating and swapping positions, which both the team and the crowd clearly liked. The Danes had little or no answer to it.

The first step on the road to the 1996 European Championship – England, as hosts, do not have to qualify and will therefore play friendlies as preparation – was overcome with few problems. Seaman was called into serious action just once, when he produced a brilliant stop to deny Brian Laudrup on 59 minutes. Platt and Beardsley, the latter back for his 50th cap after a three-year gap, were England's most influential players, while Anderton and Le Saux had impressive debuts.

England's most consistent goalscorer since Lineker's retirement after Euro 92, David Platt, once again found the back of the net to win the match for the home side. Le Saux won possession deep in his own half, making ground down the left before finding his Blackburn team-mate Shearer with a 40-yard pass. Shearer lost his marker to thread the ball cleverly through for Platt to sweep it left-footed past Schmeichel from 12 yards in the 17th minute. It was the Sampdoria player's 21st goal in 46 internationals, a total which left him ninth in the post-war list of England marksmen.

Denmark tightened up their defence in the second half, but the barrage continued as England retained possession whenever they could and waited for an opening. Tottenham's Anderton, who sparkled throughout in a roving role, must have thought he had crowned his debut with a classic goal on 57 minutes. He lifted the ball over Schmeichel, only for Danish captain Olsen to make a last-ditch clearance on the line. At the end of a great night the Wembley thousands roared their approval to signal the start of a new era for the England team.

England: Seaman, Parker, Le Saux, Ince (Batty), Adams, Pallister, Platt, Gascoigne (Le Tissier), Shearer, Beardsley, Anderton.
Denmark: Schmeichel, Vilfort (Frederiksen), Kjeldbjerg, Olsen, Rieper, Laudrup B., Jensen, Larsen, Laudrup M., Dethlefsen, Christensen.
Referee: J. Uilenberg (Holland).
Attendance: 71,970.

10th May 1994
England 'B' 4   Northern Ireland 'B' 2

Less than 24 hours before Terry Venables named his England senior squad for the Wembley matches with Greece and Norway, he took a 'B' team to Hillsborough which included a number of players with aspirations to feature in that squad. Arsenal's Paul Merson, already with 13 caps, was the game's outstanding player and Newcastle's Robert Lee also caught the eye.

An inexperienced Irish team were not expected to provide stiff opposition, but they took the lead on 14 minutes when an unmarked O'Boyle turned Dennison's cross past Pressman from close in and, though they failed to sustain their early promise, they were close to getting a result inasmuch as England's fourth goal did not arrive until the final minute.

A slightly dishevelled-looking England team quickly recovered their poise after going behind, and within ten minutes goals by Holdsworth (17 minutes) and Merson (24 minutes) gave the home side an advantage of their own. Then Quinn outpaced Bould to flick the ball past Pressman for an equaliser, before the England skipper scored with a diving header to make it 3–2 at the interval. A more disjointed second half saw a wave of substitutions and, ultimately, a clinching goal from Scales.

England: Pressman (Martyn), Barton (Edghill), Scales, Bould, Beresford, Fox (Summerbee), Lee, Bart-Williams (Stubbs), Merson, Holdsworth, Sutton (Armstrong).
Northern Ireland: Fettis, Lomas, McGibbon (Hunter), Patterson, Horlock, Dennison, Lennon (McMahon), O'Neill (Miller), Black, O'Boyle, Quinn (Robinson).
Referee: S. Lodge (Barnsley).
Attendance: 8,281.

Darren Anderton scores his first international goal as England take the lead against Greece.

17th May 1994, Wembley
England 5   Greece 0

England's opponents in the first of two Wembley friendlies inside six days were Greece, shortly to be taking part in their first World Cup Finals. Without any star names, the Greeks drew a meagre crowd to Wembley on a cold, damp evening, and they fared badly on the pitch after a bright start.

Greece had some good early possession, and from one Hantzidis cross a slipping Adams deflected the ball uncomfortably close to Flowers' left-hand post. But England, as fluent as they had been in Venables' first match, began to demonstrate that football is about more than making pretty passing patterns and showed a directness that soon had the World Cup qualifiers floundering.

England went ahead on 23 minutes. Le Saux speared in a low centre from the left and the sprawling Karkamanis spilled the ball to allow Anderton a tap in from eight yards. Platt, the captain, then assisted with one goal and scored another to make it 3–0 at the break. First he tricked his way with close control past a bemused Tsalouchidis inside the box before rolling the ball gently back from the byline for Beardsley to sweep home. Then Kalitzakis tripped Shearer and Platt beat Karkamanis comprehensively from the penalty mark.

The rout continued with another England goal ten minutes into the second half. The goalkeeper parried Anderton's lunging effort, Shearer lobbed the ball towards the far post and Platt launched himself higher than two Greek defenders to head it high into the net. It was his 23rd England goal and it left him just one behind Geoff Hurst. Ten minutes on and it became 5–0 as Shearer's blistering shot from the right bounced under Karkamanis' dive. It was a night when England could do no wrong.

England: Flowers, Jones (Pearce), Le Saux, Richardson, Bould, Adams, Platt, Merson, Shearer, Beardsley (Wright), Anderton (Le Tissier).
Greece: Karkamanis, Apostolakis, Karagiannis, Kolitsidakis (Karataidis), Kalitzakis, Tsalouchidis, Hantzidis (Mitropoulos), Nioplias, Machlas (Saravakos), Kofidis (Kostis), Tsiantakis.
Referee: J. McCluskey (Scotland).
Attendance: 23,659.

22nd May 1994, Wembley
England 0   Norway 0

England found Norway, another team bound for the USA, an altogether different proposition to Greece and had to settle in the end for a draw. But at least they maintained their record of not having conceded a goal during Terry Venables' period as coach. The Norwegians had taken three points off England in the World Cup qualifiers and, as if trying to prove there had been nothing freakish about their Oslo victory last year, they played unadventurously with a multi-layered defence in order to avoid defeat.

England played with just Shearer up front, but he did not enjoy much support and toiled away on his own, often attempting to hold the ball up with two or three Norwegian defenders snapping at his heels. The home side did get the ball in the net once – when Thorstvedt could only palm Shearer's free-kick against the inside of his near post and Platt followed up for a ridiculously easy tap-in. But the Danish referee ruled that he had not yet given permission for the kick to be taken. The Blackburn striker's second effort drifted inches wide of the other post.

Norway had now registered nine clean sheets in twelve games and lost just four of their last 29 matches. Their Wembley result was further proof of the fact they

David Platt tussles with Bohinen of Norway.

were in the World Cup finals on merit. They used the occasion to hone their 4-5-1 formation and system and the England players found it hard to lift themselves one more time at the end of a demanding nine-month season.

It was a slow-tempo match of few scoring chances. Seaman turned round Orjan Berg's fierce shot in the seventh minute and then needed two tries to stop an effort from Jakobsen. An instant Platt shot on 36 minutes caused Thorstvedt some discomfort, but overall it was a frustrating afternoon for Venables' team – and for the crowd.

England: Seaman, Jones, Le Saux, Ince (Le Tissier), Bould, Adams, Platt, Wise, Shearer, Beardsley, Anderton (Wright).
Norway: Thorstvedt (By Rise), Berg H., Johnsen, Bratseth, Nilsen (Haland), Flo, Berg O. (Ingebrigtsen), Bohinen, Fjortoft (Sorloth), Rekdal, Jakobsen.
Referee: K. Nielsen (Denmark).
Attendance: 64,327.

29th May 1994, Bandol
England 2   Russia 0
(Under-21)

England made an impressive start to their defence of the Toulon Under-21 Tournament with a comfortable victory in the opening match against Russia. England coach Terry Venables arrived in the south of France in time to see an England team with three new caps – Gordon and Dyer of Crystal Palace and Wimbledon's Fear – achieve a win through superior work-rate and greater determination.

After a slow start England went in front when Bart-Williams' free-kick from the right was headed firmly home by Sinclair for his second goal in successive Under-21 internationals. England were operating a similar formation to the one being developed at senior level, with Dyer playing in the Shearer role, and they increased their lead on 58 minutes from the penalty mark. Dyer was hauled down by Russian goalkeeper Mikhail Kharine (brother of Chelsea's Dmitri) and Bart-Williams slotted in the kick.

Gerrard in England's goal had little to do in the first half but produced an outstanding save to block Faizulin's effort after the break. Parlour had to leave the field after Pozemov's challenge and make way for his Arsenal team-mate Selley, one of the Cup Winners' Cup heroes who was winning his first Under-21 cap.

England: Gerrard, Edghill (Makin), Gordon, Campbell, Nethercott, Parlour (Selley), Redknapp, Fear, Dyer (Fowler), Bart-Williams, Sinclair.
Russia: Kharine, Karlachov, Lipko, Kuprianov, Bavykin (Savichenko), Berketov, Mamontiev (Pozemov), Klivev, Konovalov, Nekrassov, Dmitriev.
Referee: L. Schelings (Belgium).

31st May 1994, Aubagne
France 3   England 0
(Under-21)

A disappointing defeat against the hosts left the holders (England) needing to beat the United States in the last group match to have any hope of reaching the semi-finals. The England camp had received a blow early in the day: Paul Gerrard, the

Oldham Athletic goalkeeper with 11 caps at Under-21 level, injured his left knee and was forced to fly home. His replacement against France, Nicholls of Plymouth, had the misfortune to be involved in a penalty incident inside the first two minutes of the match. Argyle's first capped player ever at this level was put under pressure as Nethercott mistimed a pass back and he brought down Maurice inside the box. Micoud converted the kick.

England came close to equalising early in the second half, when Sinclair and Fear engineered a chance for Fowler, but the Liverpool striker failed from close range. On 55 minutes Baudry hit a long shot over Nicholls' head for a second French goal. Then another misunderstanding involving Nethercott and his goalkeeper resulted in a third, Abou finding the top right-hand corner after Pires had touched the ball to him from an indirect free-kick eight yards from the English goal.

France: Coupey, Candela, Terrier, Dorado, Laville, Bonnissel, Micoud, Baudry, Pires, Abou, Maurice (Vairelles).
England: Nicholls (Oakes), Makin, Gordon (Matteo), Campbell, Nethercott, Bart-Williams (Selley), Redknapp, Fear (Eadie), Dyer, Fowler, Sinclair.
Referee: V. Melo Pereira (Portugal).

2nd June 1994, Arles
England 3   United States 0
(Under-21)

England bounced back with a convincing win against the Americans and Dave Sexton's side thereby progressed to the last four as runners up in the group to France. The host nation had drawn 0-0 with Russia in Cannes to grab the top spot.

In a vastly improved performance from the defeat in Aubagne, England opened the scoring in a very one-sided match on 14 minutes. Dyer, Palace's new million-pound striker, bundled in his first Under-21 goal after Sinclair's header from Eadie's cross had been blocked. Oakes was rarely threatened in England's goal and the lead was extended on 61 minutes when Fowler converted Sinclair's cross moments before being substituted.

England's victory was completed six minutes from time from the penalty mark. Dyer was upended by American goalkeeper Grafer and skipper Redknapp, whose pass had put the Palace teenager through, hit home the kick.

England: Oakes, Makin, Gordon, Campbell, Nethercott, Selley, Redknapp, Eadie, Dyer, Fowler (Fear), Sinclair.
United States: Grafer, Hejduk, Wood, Berhalter, Pollard, McKeon, Vargas (Kelly), Baba, Jonas, Amani-Dove, Lanza.
Referee: A. Trentalange (Italy).

5th June 1994, Berre
England 2   Belgium 1
(Under-21)

England were in trouble before the match in Berre L'Etaing, near Marseille, had even started. The coach carrying the party from Toulon broke down 40 miles from its destination and there was a danger that the England team would miss the game.

But alternative transport was swiftly found and the team went on to reach the tournament final as goals from Campbell and Dyer sank the Belgians.

The main difficulty once the match had begun was the gale-force mistral gusts that made controlled football almost impossible. But, with the wind behind them in the first period, England quickly opened their account. Skipper Redknapp's corner-kick swung in to cause chaos in the Belgian defence and Campbell poked the ball in.

England increased their lead on 57 minutes when Liverpool midfielder Matteo put in a low cross and Dyer side-footed his second goal in successive games. Belgium hit back when their giant striker Peeters converted a cross from Genaux, but England held on to make the final. Coach Dave Sexton hailed the win as one of the best during his time in charge of the Under-21 side.

England: Oakes, Makin, Gordon, Campbell, Nethercott, Parlour, Redknapp, Matteo, Dyer, Bart-Williams, Sinclair.
Belgium: Beeken, Deflandre, Smeets, Verjans, Vreven, Genaux, Peiremans, Huysmans (Snoeckx), Remy, Peeters, Van Gompel.
Referee: M. Meier (Switzerland).

7th June 1994, Toulon
England 2   Portugal 0
(Under-21)

Palace striker Bruce Dyer, who had become the first seven-figure teenage signing three months earlier, grabbed a vital goal to help England to retain the Toulon trophy. He finished as the tournament's top scorer after Trevor Sinclair had given England the lead shortly after half-time.

It was England's fourth triumph in five years of the annual end-of-season tournament. They controlled the midfield, with man-of-the-match Parlour and 'most elegant player' Redknapp outstanding, and it was the latter whose corner-kick three minutes into the second half was headed down by Nethercott for Sinclair to volley in.

England extended their lead on 55 minutes when Parlour's astute through-ball sent Bart-Williams clear. The Sheffield Wednesday midfielder shrugged off Henriques' tackle before squaring the ball precisely for the irrepressible Dyer to shoot home. The rugged Portuguese had fully tested England's nerve with some cynical fouling, but solid goalkeeping from Oakes ensured success. Prior to the match the Belgian coach had said: 'They (the Portuguese) have no idea of fair play like the British teams have.'

England: Oakes, Makin, Gordon, Campbell, Nethercott, Parlour, Redknapp, Matteo, Dyer, Bart-Williams, Sinclair.
Portugal: Morais P. (Sampaio), Renato (Morais N.), Litos, Afonso, Henriques, Costa (Ribeiro), Adalberto, Calado, Marco Paulo (Veira), Simao, Bambo.
Referee: J van Vliet (Holland).

England's full international teams 1946–1994

(Up to and including 22nd May 1994)

*captain   †own goal   Small numerals goals scored   Numbers after sub player replaced

versus	venue	Result	1	2	3	4	5
1946–47							
Northern Ireland	A	7–2	Swift	Scott	Hardwick*	W Wright	Franklin
Republic of Ireland	A	1–0	Swift	Scott	Hardwick*	W Wright	Franklin
Wales	H	3–0	Swift	Scott	Hardwick*	W Wright	Franklin
Holland	H	8–2	Swift	Scott	Hardwick*	W Wright	Franklin
Scotland	H	1–1	Swift	Scott	Hardwick*	W Wright	Franklin
France	H	3–0	Swift	Scott	Hardwick*	W Wright	Franklin
Switzerland	A	0–1	Swift	Scott	Hardwick*	W Wright	Franklin
Portugal	A	10–0	Swift	Scott	Hardwick*	W Wright	Franklin
1947–48							
Belgium	A	5–2	Swift	Scott	Hardwick*	Ward	Franklin
Wales	A	3–0	Swift	Scott	Hardwick*	P Taylor	Franklin
Northern Ireland	H	2–2	Swift	Scott	Hardwick*	P Taylor	Franklin
Sweden	H	4–2	Swift	Scott	Hardwick*	P Taylor	Franklin
Scotland	A	2–0	Swift	Scott	Hardwick*	W Wright	Franklin
Italy	A	4–0	Swift*	Scott	J Howe	W Wright	Franklin
1948–49							
Denmark	A	0–0	Swift*	Scott	Aston	W Wright	Franklin
Ireland	A	6–2	Swift	Scott	J Howe	W Wright*	Franklin
Wales	H	1–0	Swift	Scott	Aston	Ward	Franklin
Switzerland	H	6–0	Ditchburn	Ramsey	Aston	W Wright*	Franklin
Scotland	H	1–3	Swift	Aston	J Howe	W Wright*	Franklin
Sweden	A	1–3	Ditchburn	Shimwell	Aston	W Wright*	Franklin
Norway	A	4–1	Swift	Ellerington	Aston	W Wright*	Franklin
France	A	3–1	Williams	Ellerington	Aston	W Wright*	Franklin
1949–50							
Republic of Ireland	H	0–2	Williams	Mozley	Aston	W Wright*	Franklin
Wales	A	4–1	Williams	Mozley	Aston	W Wright*	Franklin
Northern Ireland	H	9–2	Streten	Mozley	Aston	Watson	Franklin
Italy	H	2–0	Williams	Ramsey	Aston	Watson	Franklin
Scotland	A	1–0	Williams	Ramsey	Aston	W Wright*	Franklin
Portugal	A	5–3	Williams	Ramsey	Aston	W Wright*	WH Jones
Belgium	A	4–1	Williams	Ramsey	Aston	W Wright*	WH Jones
Chile	N	2–0	Williams	Ramsey	Aston	W Wright*	L Hughes
USA	N	0–1	Williams	Ramsey	Aston	W Wright*	L Hughes
Spain	N	0–1	Williams	Ramsey	Eckersley	W Wright*	L Hughes
1950–51							
Northern Ireland	A	4–1	Williams	Ramsey	Aston	W Wright*[1]	Chilton
Wales	H	4–2	Williams	Ramsey*	L Smith	Watson	L Compton
Yugoslavia	H	2–2	Williams	Ramsey[1]	Eckersley	Watson	L Compton
Scotland	H	2–3	Williams	Ramsey	Eckersley	Johnston	J Froggatt
Argentina	H	2–1	Williams	Ramsey	Eckersley	W Wright*	J Taylor
Portugal	H	5–2	Williams	Ramsey*	Eckersley	Nicholson[1]	J Taylor
1951–52							
France	H	2–2	Williams	Ramsey	Willis	W Wright*	Chilton
Wales	A	1–1	Williams	Ramsey	L Smith	W Wright*	Barrass
Northern Ireland	H	2–0	Merrick	Ramsey	L Smith	W Wright*	Barrass
Austria	H	2–2	Merrick	Ramsey[1]	Eckersley	W Wright*	J Froggatt

54

6	7	8	9	10	11	Substitutes
Cockburn	Finney[1]	Carter[1]	Lawton[1]	Mannion[3]	Langton[1]	
Cockburn	Finney[1]	Carter	Lawton	Mannion	Langton	
Cockburn	Finney	Carter	Lawton[1]	Mannion[2]	Langton	
Johnston	Finney[1]	Carter[2]	Lawton[4]	Mannion[1]	Langton	
Johnston	S Matthews	Carter[1]	Lawton	Mannion	Mullen	
Lowe	Finney[1]	Carter[1]	Lawton	Mannion[1]	Langton	
Lowe	S Matthews	Carter	Lawton	Mannion	Langton	
Lowe	S Matthews[1]	Mortensen[4]	Lawton[4]	Mannion	Finney[1]	
W Wright	S Matthews	Mortensen[1]	Lawton[2]	Mannion	Finney[2]	
W Wright	S Matthews	Mortensen[1]	Lawton[1]	Mannion	Finney[1]	
W Wright	S Matthews	Mortensen	Lawton[1]	Mannion[1]	Finney	
W Wright	Finney	Mortensen[3]	Lawton[1]	Mannion	Langton	
Cockburn	S Matthews	Mortensen[1]	Lawton	Pearson	Finney[1]	
Cockburn	S Matthews	Mortensen[1]	Lawton[1]	Mannion	Finney[2]	
Cockburn	S Matthews	Hagan	Lawton	Shackleton	Langton	
Cockburn	S Matthews[1]	Mortensen[3]	Milburn[1]	Pearson[1]	Finney	
W Wright*	S Matthews	Mortensen	Milburn	Shackleton	Finney[1]	
Cockburn	S Matthews	J Rowley[1]	Milburn[1]	Haines[2]	Hancocks[2]	
Cockburn	S Matthews	Mortensen	Milburn[1]	Pearson	Finney	
Cockburn	Finney[1]	Mortensen	Bentley	J Rowley	Langton	
Dickinson	Finney[1]	Morris[1]	Mortensen	Mannion	Mullen[1]	†
Dickinson	Finney	Morris[2]	J Rowley	Mannion	Mullen	
Dickinson	P Harris	Morris	Pye	Mannion	Finney	
Dickinson	Finney	Mortensen[1]	Milburn[3]	Shackleton	Hancocks	
W Wright*	Finney	Mortensen[2]	J Rowley[4]	Pearson[2]	J Froggatt[1]	
W Wright*[1]	Finney	Mortensen	J Rowley[1]	Pearson	J Froggatt	
Dickinson	Finney	Mannion	Mortensen	Bentley[1]	Langton	
Dickinson	Milburn	Mortensen[1]	Bentley	Mannion	Finney[4]	
Dickinson	Milburn	Mortensen[1]	Bentley[1]	Mannion[1]	Finney	Mullen(7)[1]
Dickinson	Finney	Mannion[1]	Bentley	Mortensen[1]	Mullen	
Dickinson	Finney	Mannion	Bentley	Mortensen	Mullen	
Dickinson	S Matthews	Mortensen	Milburn	E Baily	Finney	
Dickinson	S Matthews	Mannion	J Lee[1]	E Baily[2]	Langton	
Dickinson	Finney	Mannion[1]	Milburn[1]	E Baily[2]	Medley	
Dickinson	Hancocks	Mannion	Lofthouse[2]	E Baily	Medley	
W Wright*	S Matthews	Mannion	Mortensen	Hassall[1]	Finney[1]	
Cockburn	Finney	Mortensen[1]	Milburn[1]	Hassall	Metcalfe	
Cockburn	Finney[1]	Pearson	Milburn[2]	Hassall[1]	Metcalfe	
Cockburn	Finney	Mannion	Milburn	Hassall	Medley[1]	†
Dickinson	Finney	T Thompson	Lofthouse	E Baily[1]	Medley	
Dickinson	Finney	Sewell	Lofthouse[2]	Phillips	Medley	
Dickinson	Milton	Broadis	Lofthouse[1]	E Baily	Medley	

versus	venue	Result	1	2	3	4	5
Scotland	A	2–1	Merrick	Ramsey	Garrett	W Wright*	J Froggatt
Italy	A	1–1	Merrick	Ramsey	Garrett	W Wright*	J Froggatt
Austria	A	3–2	Merrick	Ramsey	Eckersley	W Wright*	J Froggatt
Switzerland	A	3–0	Merrick	Ramsey	Eckersley	W Wright*	J Froggatt
1952–53							
Northern Ireland	A	2–2	Merrick	Ramsey	Eckersley	W Wright*	J Froggatt
Wales	H	5–2	Merrick	Ramsey	L Smith	W Wright*	J Froggatt[1]
Belgium	H	5–0	Merrick	Ramsey	L Smith	W Wright*	J Froggatt
Scotland	H	2–2	Merrick	Ramsey	L Smith	W Wright*	Barrass
Argentina	A	0–0	Merrick	Ramsey	Eckersley	W Wright*	Johnston
Chile	A	2–1	Merrick	Ramsey	Eckersley	W Wright*	Johnston
Uruguay	A	1–2	Merrick	Ramsey	Eckersley	W Wright*	Johnston
USA	A	6–3	Ditchburn	Ramsey	Eckersley	W Wright*	Johnston
1953–54							
Wales	A	4–1	Merrick	Garrett	Eckersley	W Wright*	Johnston
FIFA	H	4–4	Merrick	Ramsey[1]	Eckersley	W Wright*	Ufton
Ireland	H	3–1	Merrick	Rickaby	Eckersley	W Wright*	Johnston
Hungary	H	3–6	Merrick	Ramsey[1]	Eckersley	W Wright*	Johnston
Scotland	A	4–2	Merrick	Staniforth	R Byrne	W Wright*	H Clarke
Yugoslavia	A	0–1	Merrick	Staniforth	R Byrne	W Wright*	Owen
Hungary	A	1–7	Merrick	Staniforth	R Byrne	W Wright*	Owen
Belgium	N	4–4	Merrick	Staniforth	R Byrne	W Wright*	Owen
Switzerland	N	2–0	Merrick	Staniforth	R Byrne	McGarry	W Wright*
Uruguay	N	2–4	Merrick	Staniforth	R Byrne	McGarry	W Wright*
1954–55							
Northern Ireland	A	2–0	Wood	Foulkes	R Byrne	Wheeler	W Wright*
Wales	H	3–2	Wood	Staniforth	R Byrne	Phillips	W Wright*
West Germany	H	3–1	Williams	Staniforth	R Byrne	Phillips	W Wright*
Scotland	H	7–2	Williams	Meadows	R Byrne	Armstrong	W Wright*
France	A	0–1	Williams	P Sillett	R Byrne	Flowers	W Wright*
Spain	A	1–1	Williams	P Sillett	R Byrne	Dickinson	W Wright*
Portugal	A	1–3	Williams	P Sillett	R Byrne	Dickinson	W Wright*
1955–56							
Denmark	A	5–1	Baynham	Hall	R Byrne	McGarry	W Wright*
Wales	A	1–2	Williams	Hall	R Byrne	McGarry	W Wright*
Northern Ireland	H	3–0	Baynham	Hall	R Byrne	Clayton	W Wright*
Spain	H	4–1	Baynham	Hall	R Byrne	Clayton	W Wright*
Scotland	A	1–1	R Matthews	Hall	R Byrne	Dickinson	W Wright*
Brazil	H	4–2	R Matthews	Hall	R Byrne	Clayton	W Wright*
Sweden	A	0–0	R Matthews	Hall	R Byrne	Clayton	W Wright*
Finland	A	5–1	Wood	Hall	R Byrne	Clayton	W Wright*
West Germany	A	3–1	R Matthews	Hall	R Byrne	Clayton	W Wright*
1956–57							
Northern Ireland	A	1–1	R Matthews	Hall	R Byrne	Clayton	W Wright*
Wales	H	3–1	Ditchburn	Hall	R Byrne	Clayton	W Wright*
Yugoslavia	H	3–0	Ditchburn	Hall	R Byrne	Clayton	W Wright*
Denmark	H	5–2	Ditchburn	Hall	R Byrne	Clayton	W Wright*
Scotland	H	2–1	Hodgkinson	Hall	R Byrne	Clayton	W Wright*
Republic of Ireland	H	5–1	Hodgkinson	Hall	R Byrne	Clayton	W Wright*
Denmark	A	4–1	Hodgkinson	Hall	R Byrne	Clayton	W Wright*
Republic of Ireland	A	1–1	Hodgkinson	Hall	R Byrne	Clayton	W Wright*
1957–58							
Wales	A	4–0	Hopkinson	D Howe	R Byrne	Clayton	W Wright*

6	7	8	9	10	11	*Substitutes*
Dickinson	Finney	Broadis	Lofthouse	Pearson[2]	J Rowley	
Dickinson	Finney	Broadis[1]	Lofthouse	Pearson	Elliott	
Dickinson	Finney	Sewell[1]	Lofthouse[2]	E Baily	Elliott	
Dickinson	R Allen	Sewell[1]	Lofthouse[2]	E Baily	Finney	
Dickinson	Finney	Sewell	Lofthouse[1]	E Baily	Elliott[1]	
Dickinson	Finney[1]	R Froggatt	Lofthouse[2]	Bentley[1]	Elliott	
Dickinson	Finney	Bentley	Lofthouse[2]	R Froggatt[1]	Elliott[2]	
Dickinson	Finney	Broadis[2]	Lofthouse	R Froggatt	J Froggatt	
Dickinson	Finney	Broadis	Lofthouse	T Taylor	Berry	
Dickinson	Finney	Broadis	Lofthouse[1]	T Taylor[1]	Berry	
Dickinson	Finney	Broadis	Lofthouse	T Taylor[1]	Berry	
Dickinson	Finney[2]	Broadis[1]	Lofthouse[2]	R Froggatt[1]	J Froggatt	
Dickinson	Finney	Quixall	Lofthouse[2]	Wilshaw[2]	Mullen	
Dickinson	S Matthews	Mortensen[1]	Lofthouse	Quixall	Mullen[2]	
Dickinson	S Matthews	Quixall	Lofthouse[1]	Hassall[2]	Mullen	
Dickinson	S Matthews	E Taylor	Mortensen[1]	Sewell[1]	Robb	
Dickinson	Finney	Broadis[1]	R Allen[1]	Nicholls[1]	Mullen[1]	
Dickinson	Finney	Broadis	R Allen	Nicholls	Mullen	
Dickinson	P Harris	Sewell	Jezzard	Broadis[1]	Finney	
Dickinson	S Matthews	Broadis[2]	Lofthouse[2]	T Taylor	Finney	
Dickinson	Finney	Broadis	T Taylor	Wilshaw[1]	Mullen[1]	
Dickinson	S Matthews	Broadis	Lofthouse[1]	Wilshaw	Finney[1]	
Barlow	S Matthews	Revie[1]	Lofthouse	Haynes[1]	Pilkington	
Slater	S Matthews	Bentley[3]	R Allen	Shackleton	Blunstone	
Slater	S Matthews	Bentley[1]	R Allen[1]	Shackleton[1]	Finney	
Edwards	S Matthews	Revie[1]	Lofthouse[2]	Wilshaw[4]	Blunstone	
Edwards	S Matthews	Revie	Lofthouse	Wilshaw	Blunstone	
Edwards	S Matthews	Bentley[1]	Lofthouse	Quixall	Wilshaw	
Edwards	S Matthews	Bentley[1]	Lofthouse	Wilshaw	Blunstone	Quixall(9)
Dickinson	Milburn	Revie[2]	Lofthouse[2]	Bradford[1]	Finney	
Dickinson	S Matthews	Revie	Lofthouse	Wilshaw	Finney	†
Dickinson	Finney[1]	Haynes	Jezzard	Wilshaw[2]	Perry	
Dickinson	Finney[1]	Atyeo[1]	Lofthouse	Haynes	Perry[2]	
Edwards	Finney	T Taylor	Lofthouse	Haynes[1]	Perry	
Edwards	S Matthews	Atyeo	T Taylor[2]	Haynes	Grainger[2]	
Edwards	Berry	Atyeo	T Taylor	Haynes	Grainger	
Edwards	Astall[1]	Haynes[1]	T Taylor	Wilshaw[1]	Grainger	Lofthouse(9)[2]
Edwards[1]	Astall	Haynes[1]	T Taylor	Wilshaw	Grainger[1]	
Edwards	S Matthews[1]	Revie	T Taylor	Wilshaw	Grainger	
Dickinson	S Matthews	Brooks[1]	Finney[1]	Haynes[1]	Grainger	
Dickinson	S Matthews	Brooks[1]	Finney	Haynes	Blunstone	T Taylor (10)[2]
Dickinson	S Matthews	Brooks	T Taylor[3]	Edwards[2]	Finney	
Edwards[1]	S Matthews	T Thompson	Finney	Kevan[1]	Grainger	
Edwards	S Matthews	Atyeo[2]	T Taylor[3]	Haynes	Finney	
Edwards	S Matthews	Atyeo[1]	T Taylor[2]	Haynes[1]	Finney	
Edwards	Finney	Atyeo[1]	T Taylor	Haynes	Pegg	
Edwards	Douglas	Kevan	T Taylor	Haynes[2]	Finney[1]	†

versus	venue	Result	1	2	3	4	5
Northern Ireland	H	2–3	Hopkinson	D Howe	R Byrne	Clayton	W Wright*
France	H	4–0	Hopkinson	D Howe	R Byrne	Clayton	W Wright*
Scotland	A	4–0	Hopkinson	D Howe	Langley	Clayton	W Wright*
Portugal	H	2–1	Hopkinson	D Howe	Langley	Clayton	W Wright*
Yugoslavia	A	0–5	Hopkinson	D Howe	Langley	Clayton	W Wright*
USSR	A	1–1	McDonald	D Howe	T Banks	Clamp	W Wright*
USSR	N	2–2	McDonald	D Howe	T Banks	Clamp	W Wright*
Brazil	N	0–0	McDonald	D Howe	T Banks	Clamp	W Wright*
Austria	N	2–2	McDonald	D Howe	T Banks	Clamp	W Wright*
USSR	N	0–1	McDonald	D Howe	T Banks	Clayton	W Wright*
1958–59							
Northern Ireland	A	3–3	McDonald	D Howe	T Banks	Clayton	W Wright*
USSR	H	5–0	McDonald	D Howe	G Shaw	Clayton	W Wright*
Wales	H	2–2	McDonald	D Howe	G Shaw	Clayton	W Wright*
Scotland	H	1–0	Hopkinson	D Howe	G Shaw	Clayton	W Wright*
Italy	H	2–2	Hopkinson	D Howe	G Shaw	Clayton	W Wright*
Brazil	A	0–2	Hopkinson	D Howe	Armfield	Clayton	W Wright*
Peru	A	1–4	Hopkinson	D Howe	Armfield	Clayton	W Wright*
Mexico	A	1–2	Hopkinson	D Howe	Armfield	Clayton	W Wright*
USA	A	8–1	Hopkinson	D Howe	Armfield	Clayton	W Wright*
1959–60							
Wales	A	1–1	Hopkinson	D Howe	A Allen	Clayton*	T Smith
Sweden	H	2–3	Hopkinson	D Howe	A Allen	Clayton*	T Smith
Northern Ireland	H	2–1	R Springett	D Howe	A Allen	Clayton*	Brown
Scotland	A	1–1	R Springett	Armfield	Wilson	Clayton*	Slater
Yugoslavia	H	3–3	R Springett	Armfield	Wilson	Clayton*	Swan
Spain	A	0–3	R Springett	Armfield	Wilson	R Robson	Swan
Hungary	A	0–2	R Springett	Armfield	Wilson	R Robson	Swan
1960–61							
Northern Ireland	A	5–2	R Springett	Armfield	McNeil	R Robson	Swan
Luxembourg	A	9–0	R Springett	Armfield	McNeil	R Robson	Swan
Spain	H	4–2	R Springett	Armfield	McNeil	R Robson	Swan
Wales	H	5–1	Hodgkinson	Armfield	McNeil	R Robson	Swan
Scotland	H	9–3	R Springett	Armfield	McNeil	R Robson¹	Swan
Mexico	H	8–0	R Springett	Armfield	McNeil	R Robson¹	Swan
Portugal	A	1–1	R Springett	Armfield	McNeil	R Robson	Swan
Italy	A	3–2	R Springett	Armfield	McNeil	R Robson	Swan
Austria	A	1–3	R Springett	Armfield	Angus	Miller	Swan
1961–62							
Luxembourg	H	4–1	R Springett	Armfield*	McNeil	R Robson	Swan
Wales	A	1–1	R Springett	Armfield	Wilson	R Robson	Swan
Portugal	H	2–0	R Springett	Armfield	Wilson	R Robson	Swan
Northern Ireland	H	1–1	R Springett	Armfield	Wilson	R Robson	Swan
Austria	H	3–1	R Springett	Armfield	Wilson	Anderson	Swan
Scotland	A	0–2	R Springett	Armfield	Wilson	Anderson	Swan
Switzerland	H	3–1	R Springett	Armfield	Wilson	R Robson	Swan
Peru	A	4–0	R Springett	Armfield	Wilson	Moore	Norman
Hungary	N	1–2	R Springett	Armfield	Wilson	Moore	Norman
Argentina	N	3–1	R Springett	Armfield	Wilson	Moore	Norman
Bulgaria	N	0–0	R Springett	Armfield	Wilson	Moore	Norman
Brazil	N	1–3	R Springett	Armfield	Wilson	Moore	Norman
1962–63							
France	H	1–1	R Springett	Armfield*	Wilson	Moore	Norman
Northern Ireland	A	3–1	R Springett	Armfield*	Wilson	Moore	Labone

6	7	8	9	10	11	Substitutes
Edwards[1]	Douglas	Kevan	T Taylor	Haynes	A'Court[1]	
Edwards	Douglas	R Robson[2]	T Taylor[2]	Haynes	Finney	
Slater	Douglas[1]	R Charlton[1]	Kevan[2]	Haynes	Finney	
Slater	Douglas	R Charlton[2]	Kevan	Haynes	Finney	
Slater	Douglas	R Charlton	Kevan	Haynes	Finney	
Slater .	Douglas	R Robson	Kevan[1]	Haynes	Finney	
Slater	Douglas	R Robson	Kevan[1]	Haynes	Finney[1]	
Slater	Douglas	R Robson	Kevan	Haynes	A'Court	
Slater	Douglas	R Robson	Kevan[1]	Haynes[1]	A'Court	
Slater	Brabrook	Broadbent	Kevan	Haynes	A'Court	
McGuinness	Brabrook	Broadbent	R Charlton[2]	Haynes	Finney[1]	
Slater	Douglas	R Charlton[1]	Lofthouse[1]	Haynes[3]	Finney	
Flowers	Clapton	Broadbent[2]	Lofthouse	Haynes	A'Court	
Flowers	Douglas	Broadbent	R Charlton[1]	Haynes	Holden	
Flowers	Bradley[1]	Broadbent	R Charlton[1]	Haynes	Holden	
Flowers	Deeley	Broadbent	R Charlton	Haynes	Holden	
Flowers	Deeley	Greaves[1]	R Charlton	Haynes	Holden	
McGuinness	Holden	Greaves	Kevan[1]	Haynes	R Charlton	Flowers(6) Bradley(7)
Flowers[2]	Bradley[1]	Greaves	Kevan[1]	Haynes[1]	R Charlton[3]	
Flowers	Connelly	Greaves[1]	Clough	R Charlton	Holliday	
Flowers	Connelly[1]	Greaves	Clough	R Charlton[1]	Holliday	
Flowers	Connelly	Haynes	Baker[1]	Parry[1]	Holliday	
Flowers	Connelly	Broadbent	Baker	Parry	R Charlton[1]	
Flowers	Douglas[1]	Haynes[1]	Baker	Greaves[1]	R Charlton	
Flowers	Brabrook	Haynes*	Baker	Greaves	R Charlton	
Flowers	Douglas	Haynes*	Baker	Viollet	R Charlton	
Flowers	Douglas[1]	Greaves[2]	R Smith[1]	Haynes*	R Charlton[1]	
Flowers	Douglas	Greaves[3]	R Smith[2]	Haynes*[1]	R Charlton[3]	
Flowers	Douglas[1]	Greaves[1]	R Smith[2]	Haynes*	R Charlton	
Flowers	Douglas	Greaves[2]	R Smith[1]	Haynes*[1]	R Charlton[1]	
Flowers	Douglas[1]	Greaves[3]	R Smith[2]	Haynes*[2]	R Charlton	
Flowers[1]	Douglas[2]	Kevan	Hitchens[1]	Haynes*	R Charlton[3]	
Flowers[1]	Douglas	Greaves	R Smith	Haynes*	R Charlton	
Flowers	Douglas	Greaves[1]	Hitchens[2]	Haynes*	R Charlton	
Flowers	Douglas	Greaves[1]	Hitchens	Haynes*	R Charlton	
Flowers	Douglas	Fantham	Pointer[1]	Viollet[1]	R Charlton[2]	
Flowers	Connelly	Douglas[1]	Pointer	Haynes*	R Charlton	
Flowers	Connelly[1]	Douglas	Pointer[1]	Haynes*	R Charlton	
Flowers	Douglas	J Byrne	Crawford	Haynes*	R Charlton[1]	
Flowers[1]	Connelly	Hunt[1]	Crawford[1]	Haynes*	R Charlton	
Flowers	Douglas	Greaves	R Smith	Haynes*	R Charlton	
Flowers[1]	Connelly[1]	Greaves	Hitchens[1]	Haynes*	R Charlton	
Flowers[1]	Douglas	Greaves[3]	Hitchens	Haynes*	R Charlton	
Flowers[1]	Douglas	Greaves	Hitchens	Haynes*	R Charlton	
Flowers[1]	Douglas	Greaves[1]	Peacock	Haynes*	R Charlton[1]	
Flowers	Douglas	Greaves	Peacock	Haynes*	R Charlton	
Flowers	Douglas	Greaves	Hitchens[1]	Haynes*	R Charlton	
Flowers[1]	Hellawell	Crowe	Charnley	Greaves	A Hinton	
Flowers	Hellawell	F Hill	Peacock	Greaves[1]	O'Grady[2]	

versus	venue	Result	1	2	3	4	5
Wales	H	4–0	R Springett	Armfield*	G Shaw	Moore	Labone
France	A	2–5	R Springett	Armfield*	Henry	Moore	Labone
Scotland	H	1–2	G Banks	Armfield*	G Byrne	Moore	Norman
Brazil	H	1–1	G Banks	Armfield*	Wilson	Milne	Norman
Czechoslovakia	A	4–2	G Banks	Shellito	Wilson	Milne	Norman
East Germany	A	2–1	G Banks	Armfield*	Wilson	Milne	Norman
Switzerland	A	8–1	R Springett	Armfield*	Wilson	Kay[1]	Moore
1963–64							
Wales	A	4–0	G Banks	Armfield*	Wilson	Milne	Norman
Rest of the World	H	2–1	G Banks	Armfield*	Wilson	Milne	Norman
Northern Ireland	H	8–3	G Banks	Armfield*	R Thomson	Milne	Norman
Scotland	A	0–1	G Banks	Armfield*	Wilson	Milne	Norman
Uruguay	H	2–1	G Banks	Cohen	Wilson	Milne	Norman
Portugal	A	4–3	G Banks	Cohen	Wilson	Milne	Norman
Republic of Ireland	A	3–1	Waiters	Cohen	Wilson	Milne	Flowers
USA	A	10–0	G Banks	Cohen	R Thomson	M Bailey	Norman
Brazil	A	1–5	Waiters	Cohen	Wilson	Milne	Norman
Portugal	N	1–1	G Banks	R Thomson	Wilson	Flowers	Norman
Argentina	N	0–1	G Banks	R Thomson	Wilson	Milne	Norman
1964–65							
Northern Ireland	A	4–3	G Banks	Cohen	R Thomson	Milne	Norman
Belgium	H	2–2	Waiters	Cohen	R Thomson	Milne	Norman
Wales	H	2–1	Waiters	Cohen	R Thomson	M Bailey	Flowers*
Holland	A	1–1	Waiters	Cohen	R Thomson	Mullery	Norman
Scotland	H	2–2	G Banks	Cohen	Wilson	Stiles	J Charlton
Hungary	H	1–0	G Banks	Cohen	Wilson	Stiles	J Charlton
Yugoslavia	A	1–1	G Banks	Cohen	Wilson	Stiles	J Charlton
West Germany	A	1–0	G Banks	Cohen	Wilson	Flowers	J Charlton
Sweden	A	2–1	G Banks	Cohen	Wilson	Stiles	J Charlton
1965–66							
Wales	A	0–0	R Springett	Cohen	Wilson	Stiles	J Charlton
Austria	H	2–3	R Springett	Cohen	Wilson	Stiles	J Charlton
Northern Ireland	H	2–1	G Banks	Cohen	Wilson	Stiles	J Charlton
Spain	A	2–0	G Banks	Cohen	Wilson	Stiles	J Charlton
Poland	H	1–1	G Banks	Cohen	Wilson	Stiles	J Charlton
West Germany	H	1–0	G Banks	Cohen	K Newton	Moore*	J Charlton
Scotland	A	4–3	G Banks	Cohen	K Newton	Stiles	J Charlton
Yugoslavia	H	2–0	G Banks	Armfield*	Wilson	Peters	J Charlton
Finland	A	3–0	G Banks	Armfield*	Wilson	Peters[1]	J Charlton[1]
Norway	A	6–1	R Springett	Cohen	G Byrne	Stiles	Flowers
Denmark	A	2–0	Bonetti	Cohen	Wilson	Stiles	J Charlton[1]
Poland	A	1–0	G Banks	Cohen	Wilson	Stiles	J Charlton
Uruguay	H	0–0	G Banks	Cohen	Wilson	Stiles	J Charlton
Mexico	H	2–0	G Banks	Cohen	Wilson	Stiles	J Charlton
France	H	2–0	G Banks	Cohen	Wilson	Stiles	J Charlton
Argentina	H	1–0	G Banks	Cohen	Wilson	Stiles	J Charlton
Portugal	H	2–1	G Banks	Cohen	Wilson	Stiles	J Charlton
West Germany	H	4–2	G Banks	Cohen	Wilson	Stiles	J Charlton
1966–67							
Northern Ireland	A	2–0	G Banks	Cohen	Wilson	Stiles	J Charlton
Czechoslovakia	H	0–0	G Banks	Cohen	Wilson	Stiles	J Charlton
Wales	H	5–1	G Banks	Cohen	Wilson	Stiles	J Charlton[1]
Scotland	H	2–3	G Banks	Cohen	Wilson	Stiles	J Charlton[1]
Spain	H	2–0	Bonetti	Cohen	K Newton	Mullery	Labone

6	7	8	9	10	11	*Substitutes*
Flowers	Connelly[1]	F Hill	Peacock[2]	Greaves[1]	Tambling	
Flowers	Connelly	Tambling[1]	R Smith[1]	Greaves	R Charlton	
Flowers	Douglas[1]	Greaves	R Smith	Melia	R Charlton	
Moore	Douglas[1]	Greaves	R Smith	Eastham	R Charlton	
Moore*	Paine	Greaves[2]	R Smith[1]	Eastham	R Charlton[1]	
Moore	Paine	Hunt[1]	R Smith	Eastham	R Charlton[1]	
Flowers	Douglas[1]	Greaves	J Byrne[2]	Melia[1]	R Charlton[3]	
Moore	Paine	Greaves[1]	R Smith[2]	Eastham	R Charlton[1]	
Moore	Paine[1]	Greaves[1]	R Smith	Eastham	R Charlton	
Moore	Paine[3]	Greaves[4]	R Smith[1]	Eastham	R Charlton	
Moore	Paine	Hunt	J Byrne	Eastham	R Charlton	
Moore*	Paine	Greaves	J Byrne[2]	Eastham	R Charlton	
Moore*	P Thompson	Greaves	J Byrne[3]	Eastham	R Charlton[1]	
Moore*	P Thompson	Greaves[1]	J Byrne[1]	Eastham[1]	R Charlton	
Flowers*	Paine[2]	Hunt[4]	Pickering[3]	Eastham	P Thompson	R Charlton(10)[1]
Moore*	P Thompson	Greaves[1]	J Byrne	Eastham	R Charlton	
Moore*	Paine	Greaves	J Byrne	Hunt[1]	P Thompson	
Moore*	P Thompson	Greaves*	J Byrne	Eastham	R Charlton	
Moore*	Paine	Greaves[3]	Pickering[1]	R Charlton	P Thompson	
Moore*	P Thompson	Greaves	Pickering[1]	Venables	A Hinton	†
Young	P Thompson	Hunt	Wignall[2]	J Byrne	A Hinton	
Flowers*	P Thompson	Greaves[1]	Wignall	Venables	R Charlton	
Moore*	P Thompson	Greaves[1]	Bridges	J Byrne	R Charlton[1]	
Moore*	Paine	Greaves[1]	Bridges	Eastham	Connelly	
Moore*	Paine	Greaves	Bridges[1]	Ball	Connelly	
Moore*	Paine[1]	Ball	M Jones	Eastham	Temple	
Moore*	Paine	Ball[1]	M Jones	Eastham	Connelly[1]	
Moore*	Paine	Greaves	Peacock	R Charlton	Connelly	
Moore*	Paine	Greaves	Bridges	R Charlton[1]	Connelly[1]	
Moore*	P Thompson	Baker[1]	Peacock[1]	R Charlton	Connelly	
Moore*	Ball	Hunt[1]	Baker[1]	Eastham	R Charlton	Hunter(9)
Moore*[1]	Ball	Hunt	Baker	Eastham	G Harris	
Hunter	Ball	Hunt	Stiles1	G Hurst	R Charlton	Wilson(3)
Moore*	Ball	Hunt[2]	R Charlton[1]	G Hurst[1]	Connelly	
Hunter	Paine	Greaves[1]	R Charlton[1]	G Hurst	Tambling	
Hunter	Callaghan	Hunt[1]	R Charlton	G Hurst	Ball	
Moore*[1]	Paine	Greaves[4]	R Charlton	Hunt	Connelly[1]	
Moore*	Ball	Greaves	G Hurst	Eastham[1]	Connelly	
Moore*	Ball	Greaves	R Charlton	Hunt[1]	Peters	
Moore*	Ball	Greaves	R Charlton	Hunt	Connelly	
Moore*	Paine	Greaves	R Charlton[1]	Hunt[1]	Peters	
Moore*	Callaghan	Greaves	R Charlton	Hunt[2]	Peters	
Moore*	Ball	G Hurst[1]	R Charlton	Hunt	Peters	
Moore*	Ball	G Hurst	R Charlton[2]	Hunt	Peters	
Moore*	Ball	G Hurst[3]	R Charlton	Hunt	Peters[1]	
Moore*	Ball	G Hurst	R Charlton	Hunt[1]	Peters[1]	
Moore*	Ball	G Hurst	R Charlton	Hunt	Peters	
Moore*	Ball	G Hurst[2]	R Charlton[1]	Hunt	Peters	†
Moore*	Ball	Greaves	R Charlton[1]	G Hurst[1]	Peters	
Moore*	Ball	Greaves[1]	G Hurst	Hunt[1]	Hollins	

versus	venue	Result	1	2	3	4	5
Austria	A	1–0	Bonetti	K Newton	Wilson	Mullery	Labone
1967–68							
Wales	A	3–0	G Banks	Cohen	K Newton	Mullery	J Charlton
Northern Ireland	H	2–0	G Banks	Cohen	Wilson	Mullery	Sadler
USSR	H	2–2	G Banks	C Knowles	Wilson	Mullery	Sadler
Scotland	A	1–1	G Banks	K Newton	Wilson	Mullery	Labone
Spain	H	1–0	G Banks	C Knowles	Wilson	Mullery	J Charlton
Spain	A	2–1	Bonetti	K Newton	Wilson	Mullery	Labone
Sweden	H	3–1	Stepney	K Newton	C Knowles	Mullery	Labone
West Germany	A	0–1	G Banks	K Newton	C Knowles	Hunter	Labone
Yugoslavia	N	0–1	G Banks	K Newton	Wilson	Mullery	Labone
USSR	N	2–0	G Banks	T Wright	Wilson	Stiles	Labone
1968–69							
Romania	A	0–0	G Banks	T Wright	K Newton	Mullery	Labone
Bulgaria	H	1–1	West	K Newton	McNab	Mullery	Labone
Romania	H	1–1	G Banks	T Wright	McNab	Stiles	J Charlton[1]
France	H	5–0	G Banks	K Newton	Cooper	Mullery	J Charlton
Northern Ireland	A	3–1	G Banks	K Newton	McNab	Mullery	Labone
Wales	H	2–1	West	K Newton	Cooper	Moore*	J Charlton
Scotland	H	4–1	G Banks	K Newton	Cooper	Mullery	Labone
Mexico	A	0–0	West	K Newton	Cooper	Mullery	Labone
Uruguay	A	2–1	G Banks	T Wright	K Newton	Mullery	Labone
Brazil	A	1–2	G Banks	T Wright	K Newton	Mullery	Labone
1969–70							
Holland	A	1–0	Bonetti	T Wright	E Hughes	Mullery	J Charlton
Portugal	H	1–0	Bonetti	Reaney	E Hughes	Mullery	J Charlton[1]
Holland	H	0–0	G Banks	K Newton	Cooper	Peters	J Charlton
Belgium	A	3–1	G Banks	T Wright	Cooper	Moore*	Labone
Wales	A	1–1	G Banks	T Wright	E Hughes	Mullery	Labone
Northern Ireland	H	3–1	G Banks	K Newton	E Hughes	Mullery	Moore*
Scotland	A	0–0	G Banks	K Newton	E Hughes	Stiles	Labone
Colombia	A	4–0	G Banks	K Newton	Cooper	Mullery	Labone
Ecuador	A	2–0	G Banks	K Newton	Cooper	Mullery	Labone
Romania	N	1–0	G Banks	K Newton	Cooper	Mullery	Labone
Brazil	N	0–1	G Banks	T Wright	Cooper	Mullery	Labone
Czechoslovakia	N	1–0	G Banks	K Newton	Cooper	Mullery	J Charlton
West Germany	N	2–3	Bonetti	K Newton	Cooper	Mullery[1]	Labone
1970–71							
East Germany	H	3–1	Shilton	E Hughes	Cooper	Mullery	Sadler
Malta	A	1–0	G Banks	Reaney	E Hughes	Mullery*	McFarland
Greece	H	3–0	G Banks	Storey	E Hughes	Mullery	McFarland
Malta	H	5–0	G Banks	Lawler[1]	Cooper	Moore*	McFarland
Northern Ireland	A	1–0	G Banks	Madeley	Cooper	Storey	McFarland
Wales	H	0–0	Shilton	Lawler	Cooper	T Smith	Lloyd
Scotland	H	3–1	G Banks	Lawler	Cooper	Storey	McFarland
1971–72							
Switzerland	A	3–2	G Banks	Lawler	Cooper	Mullery	McFarland
Switzerland	H	1–1	Shilton	Madeley	Cooper	Storey	Lloyd
Greece	A	2–0	G Banks	Madeley	E Hughes	Bell	McFarland
West Germany	H	1–3	G Banks	Madeley	E Hughes	Bell	Moore*
West Germany	A	0–0	G Banks	Madeley	E Hughes	Storey	McFarland
Wales	A	3–0	G Banks	Madeley	E Hughes[1]	Storey	McFarland
Northern Ireland	H	0–1	Shilton	Todd	E Hughes	Storey	Lloyd
Scotland	A	1–0	G Banks	Madeley	E Hughes	Storey	McFarland

6	7	8	9	10	11	Substitutes
Moore*	Ball[1]	Greaves	Hurst, G	Hunt	Hunter	
Moore*	Ball[1]	Hunt	R Charlton[1]	G Hurst	Peters[1]	
Moore*	P Thompson	Hunt	R Charlton[1]	G Hurst[1]	Peters	
Moore*	Ball[1]	Hunt	R Charlton	G Hurst	Peters[1]	
Moore*	Ball	G Hurst	Summerbee	R Charlton	Peters[1]	
Moore*	Ball	Hunt	Summerbee	R Charlton[1]	Peters	
Moore*	Ball	Peters[1]	R Charlton	Hunt	Hunter[1]	
Moore*	Bell	Peters[1]	R Charlton[1]	Hunt[1]	Hunter	G Hurst(9)
Moore*	Ball	Bell	Summerbee	G Hurst	P Thompson	
Moore*	Ball	Peters	R Charlton	Hunt	Hunter	
Moore*	Hunter	Hunt	R Charlton[1]	G Hurst[1]	Peters	
Moore*	Ball	Hunt	R Charlton	G Hurst	Peters	McNab(2)
Moore*	F Lee	Bell	R Charlton	G Hurst[1]	Peters	Reaney(2)
Hunter	Radford	Hunt	R Charlton*	G Hurst	Ball	
Moore*	F Lee[1]	Bell	G Hurst[3]	Peters	O'Grady[1]	
Moore*	Ball	F Lee[1]	R Charlton	G Hurst[1]	Peters[1]	
Hunter	F Lee[1]	Bell	Astle	R Charlton[1]	Ball	
Moore*	F Lee	Ball	R Charlton	G Hurst[2]	Peters[2]	
Moore*	F Lee	Ball	R Charlton	G Hurst	Peters	T Wright(2)
Moore*	F Lee[1]	Bell	G Hurst[1]	Ball	Peters	
Moore*	Ball	Bell[1]	R Charlton	G Hurst	Peters	
Moore*	F Lee	Bell[1]	R Charlton	G Hurst	Peters	P Thompson(7)
Moore*	F Lee	Bell	Astle	R Charlton	Ball	Peters(8)
Hunter	F Lee	Bell	M Jones	R Charlton*	Storey-Moore	Mullery(7) G Hurst(9)
E Hughes	F Lee	Ball[2]	Osgood	G Hurst[1]	Peters	
Moore*	F Lee[1]	Ball	R Charlton	G Hurst	Peters	
Stiles	Coates	Kidd	R Charlton[1]	G Hurst[1]	Peters[1]	Bell(2)
Moore*	P Thompson	Ball	Astle	G Hurst	Peters	Mullery(7)
Moore*	F Lee	Ball[1]	R Charlton[1]	G Hurst	Peters[2]	
Moore*	F Lee[1]	Ball	R Charlton	G Hurst	Peters	Kidd(7)[1] Sadler(9)
Moore*	F Lee	Ball	R Charlton	G Hurst[1]	Peters	T Wright(2) Osgood(7)
Moore*	F Lee	Ball	R Charlton	G Hurst	Peters	Astle(7) Bell(9)
Moore*	Bell	R Charlton	Astle	A Clarke[1]	Peters	Ball(8) Osgood(10)
Moore*	F Lee	Ball	R Charlton	G Hurst	Peters[1]	Bell(9) Hunter(11)
Moore*	F Lee[1]	Ball	G Hurst	A Clarke[1]	Peters[1]	
Hunter	Ball	Chivers	Royle	Harvey	Peters[1]	
Moore*	F Lee[1]	Ball	Chivers[1]	G Hurst[1]	Peters	Coates(8)
E Hughes	F Lee[1]	Coates	Chivers[2]	A Clarke[1]	Peters	Ball(11)
Moore*	F Lee	Ball	Chivers	A Clarke[1]	Peters	
E Hughes	F Lee	Coates	G Hurst	Coates	Peters*	A Clarke(8)
Moore*	F Lee	Ball	Chivers[2]	G Hurst	Peters[1]	A Clarke(7)
Moore*	F Lee	Madeley	Chivers[1]	G Hurst[1]	Peters	†Radford(10)
Moore*	Summerbee[1]	Ball	G Hurst	F Lee	E Hughes	Chivers(7) Marsh(10)
Moore*	F Lee	Ball	Chivers[1]	G Hurst[1]	Peters	
Hunter	F Lee[1]	Ball	Chivers	G Hurst	Peters	Marsh(10)
Moore*	Ball	Bell	Chivers	Marsh	Hunter	Summerbee(10) Peters(11)
Moore*	Summerbee	Bell[1]	MacDonald	Marsh1	Hunter	
Hunter	Summerbee	Bell*	MacDonald	Marsh	Currie	Chivers(9) Peters(11)
Moore*	Ball[1]	Bell	Chivers	Marsh	Hunter	MacDonald(10)

versus	*venue*	*Result*	1	2	3	4	5
1972–73							
Yugoslavia	H	1–1	Shilton	M Mills	Lampard	Storey	Blockley
Wales	A	1–0	Clemence	Storey	E Hughes	Hunter	McFarland
Wales	H	1–1	Clemence	Storey	E Hughes	Hunter[1]	McFarland
Scotland	A	5–0	Shilton	Storey	E Hughes	Bell	Madeley
Northern Ireland	A	2–1	Shilton	Storey	Nish	Bell	McFarland
Wales	H	3–0	Shilton	Storey	E Hughes	Bell	McFarland
Scotland	H	1–0	Shilton	Storey	E Hughes	Bell	McFarland
Czechoslovakia	A	1–1	Shilton	Madeley	Storey	Bell	McFarland
Poland	A	0–2	Shilton	Madeley	E Hughes	Storcy	McFarland
USSR	A	2–1	Shilton	Madeley	E Hughes	Storey	McFarland
Italy	A	0–2	Shilton	Madeley	E Hughes	Storey	McFarland
1973–74							
Austria	H	7–0	Shilton	Madeley	E Hughes	Bell[1]	McFarland
Poland	H	1–1	Shilton	Madeley	E Hughes	Bell	McFarland
Italy	H	0–1	Shilton	Madeley	E Hughes	Bell	McFarland
Portugal	A	0–0	Parkes	Nish	Pejic	Dobson	Watson
Wales	A	2–0	Shilton	Nish	Pejic	E Hughes*	McFarland
Northern Ireland	H	1–0	Shilton	Nish	Pejic	E Hughes*	McFarland
Scotland	A	0–2	Shilton	Nish	Pejic	E Hughes*	Hunter
Argentina	H	2–2	Shilton	E Hughes*	Lindsay	Todd	Watson
East Germany	A	1–1	Clemence	E Hughes*	Lindsay	Todd	Watson
Bulgaria	A	1–0	Clemence	E Hughes*	Todd	Watson	Lindsay
Yugoslavia	A	2–2	Clemence	E Hughes*	Lindsay	Todd	Watson
1974–75							
Czechoslovakia	H	3–0	Clemence	Madeley	E Hughes*	Dobson	Watson
Portugal	H	0–0	Clemence	Madeley	Watson	E Hughes	Cooper
West Germany	H	2–0	Clemence	Whitworth	Gillard	Bell[1]	Watson
Cyprus	H	5–0	Shilton	Madeley	Watson	Todd	Beattie
Cyprus	A	1–0	Clemence	Whitworth	Beattie	Watson	Todd
Northern Ireland	A	0–0	Clemence	Whitworth	E Hughes	Bell	Watson
Wales	H	2–2	Clemence	Whitworth	Gillard	G Francis	Watson
Scotland	H	5–1	Clemence	Whitworth	Beattie[1]	Bell[1]	Watson
1975–76							
Switzerland	A	2–1	Clemence	Whitworth	Todd	Watson	Beattie
Czechoslovakia	A	1–2	Clemence	Madeley	Gillard	G Francis*	McFarland
Portugal	A	1–1	Clemence	Whitworth	Beattie	G Francis*	Watson
Wales	A	2–1	Clemence	Cherry	M Mills	Neal	P Thompson
Wales	A	1–0	Clemence	Clement	M Mills	Towers	B Greenhoff
Northern Ireland	H	4–0	Clemence	Todd	M Mills	P Thompson	B Greenhoff
Scotland	A	1–2	Clemence	Todd	M Mills	P Thompson	McFarland
Brazil	N	0–1	Clemence	Todd	Doyle	P Thompson	Doyle
Italy	N	3–2	Rimmer	Clement	Neal	P Thompson[1]	Doyle
Finland	A	4–1	Clemence	Todd	M Mills	P Thompson	Madeley
1976–77							
Republic of Ireland	H	1–1	Clemence	Todd	Madeley	Cherry	McFarland
Finland	H	2–1	Clemence	Todd	Beattie	P Thompson	Greenhoff
Italy	A	0–2	Clemence	Clement	M Mills	B Greenhoff	McFarland
Holland	H	0–2	Clemence	Clement	Beattie	Doyle	Watson
Luxembourg	H	5–0	Clemence	Gidman	Cherry	Kennedy[1]	Watson
Northern Ireland	A	2–1	Shilton	Cherry	M Mills	Greenhoff	Watson
Wales	H	0–1	Shilton	Neal	M Mills	Greenhoff	Watson
Scotland	H	1–2	Clemence	Neal	M Mills	Greenhoff	Watson

6	7	8	9	10	11	Substitutes
Moore*	Ball	Channon	Royle[1]	Bell	Marsh	
Moore*	Keegan	Chivers	Marsh	Bell[1]	Ball	
Moore*	Keegan	Bell	Chivers	Marsh	Ball	
Moore*	Ball	Channon[1]	Chivers[1]	A Clarke[2]	Peters	†
Moore*	Ball	Channon	Chivers[2]	Richards	Peters	
Moore*	Ball	Channon[1]	Chivers[1]	A Clarke	Peters[1]	
Moore*	Ball	Channon	Chivers	A Clarke	Peters[1]	
Moore*	Ball	Channon	Chivers	A Clarke[1]	Peters	
Moore*	Ball	Bell	Chivers	A Clarke	Peters	
Moore*	Currie	Channon	Chivers[1]	A Clarke	Peters	† MacDonald(10) Hunter(11) Summerbee(8)
Moore*	Currie	Channon	Chivers	A Clarke	Peters	
Hunter	Currie[1]	Channon[2]	Chivers[1]	A Clarke[2]	Peters*	
Hunter	Currie	Channon	Chivers	A Clarke[1]	Peters*	Hector(9)
Moore*	Currie	Channon	Osgood	A Clarke	Peters	Hector(10)
Todd	Bowles	Channon	MacDonald	Brooking	Peters*	Ball(9)
Todd	Keegan[1]	Bell	Channon	Weller	Bowles[1]	
Todd	Keegan	Weller[1]	Channon	Bell	Bowles	Hunter(5) Worthington(11)
Todd	Channon	Bell	Worthington	Weller	Peters	Watson(5) MacDonald(9)
Bell	Keegan	Channon[1]	Worthington[1]	Weller	Brooking	
Dobson	Keegan	Channon[1]	Worthington	Bell	Brooking	
Dobson	Brooking	Bell	Keegan	Channon	Worthington[1]	
Dobson	Keegan[1]	Channon[1]	Worthington	Bell	Brooking	MacDonald(9)
Hunter	Bell[2]	G Francis	Worthington	Channon[1]	Keegan	Brooking(4) Thomas(9)
Brooking	G Francis	Bell	Thomas	Channon	A Clarke	Todd(5) Worthington(11)
Todd	Ball*	MacDonald[1]	Channon	Hudson	Keegan	
Bell	Ball*	Hudson	Channon	MacDonald[5]	Keegan	Thomas(9)
Bell	Thomas	Ball*	Channon	MacDonald	Keegan[1]	E Hughes(3) Tueart(11)
Todd	Ball*	Viljoen	MacDonald	Keegan	Tueart	Channon(9)
Todd	Ball*	Channon	Johnson[2]	Viljoen	Thomas	Little(8)
Todd	Ball*	Channon	Johnson[1]	G Francis[2]	Keegan	Thomas(11)
Bell	Currie	G Francis	Channon[1]	Johnson	Keegan[1]	MacDonald(10)
Todd	Keegan	Channon[1]	MacDonald	A Clarke	Bell	Watson(5) Thomas(8)
Todd	Keegan	Channon[1]	MacDonald	Brooking	Madeley	A Clarke(11) Thomas(9)
Doyle	Keegan*	Channon	Boyer	Brooking	Kennedy[1]	Clement(2) P Taylor(8)[1]
P Thompson	Keegan	G Francis*	Pearson	Kennedy	P Taylor[1]	
R Kennedy	Keegan	G Francis*[1]	Pearson[1]	Channon[2]	P Taylor	Towers(11) Royle(7)
R Kennedy	Keegan	G Francis*	Pearson	Channon[1]	P Taylor	Cherry(9) Doyle(5)
G Francis	Cherry	Brooking	Keegan	Pearson	Channon	
Towers	Wilkins	Brooking	Royle	Channon*[2]	Hill	Corrigan(1) M Mills(3)
Cherry	Keegan[2]	Channon[1]	S Pearson[1]	Brooking	G Francis*	
Greenhoff	Keegan*	Wilkins	Pearson[1]	Brooking	George	Hill(11)
Wilkins	Keegan*	Channon	Royle[1]	Brooking	Tueart[1]	M Mills(10) Hill(11)
E Hughes	Keegan*	Channon	Bowles	Cherry	Brooking	Beattie(2)
Madeley	Keegan*	Greenhoff	T Francis	Bowles	Brooking	Todd(8) S Pearson(6)
E Hughes	Keegan*[1]	Channon[2]	Royle	T Francis[1]	Hill	Mariner(9)
Todd	Wilkins	Channon*[1]	Mariner	Brooking	Tueart[1]	Talbot(7)
E Hughes	Keegan*	Channon	Pearson	Brooking	R Kennedy	Tueart(10)
E Hughes*	T Francis	Channon[1]	Pearson	Talbot	R Kennedy	Cherry(4) Tueart(11)

versus	venue	Result	1	2	3	4	5
Brazil	A	0–0	Clemence	Neal	Cherry	B Greenhoff	Watson
Argentina	A	1–1	Clemence	Neal	Cherry	B Greenhoff	Watson
Uruguay	A	0–0	Clemence	Neal	Cherry	B Greenhoff	Watson
1977–78							
Switzerland	H	0–0	Clemence	Neal	Cherry	McDermott	Watson
Luxembourg	A	2–0	Clemence	Cherry	Watson	E Hughes*	R Kennedy[1]
Italy	H	2–0	Clemence	Neal	Cherry	Wilkins	Watson
West Germany	A	1–2	Clemence	Neal	M Mills	Wilkins	Watson
Brazil	H	1–1	Corrigan	M Mills	Cherry	B Greenhoff	Watson
Wales	A	3–1	Shilton	M Mills*	Cherry	B Greenhoff	Watson
Northern Ireland	H	1–0	Clemence	Neal[1]	M Mills	Wilkins	Watson
Scotland	A	1–0	Clemence	Neal	M Mills	Currie	Watson
Hungary	H	4–1	Shilton	Neal[1]	M Mills	Wilkins	Watson
1978–79							
Denmark	A	4–3	Clemence	Neal[1]	M Mills	Wilkins	Watson
Republic of Ireland	A	1–1	Clemence	Neal	M Mills	Wilkins	Watson
Czechoslovakia	H	1–0	Shilton	Anderson	Cherry	P Thompson	Watson
Northern Ireland	H	4–0	Clemence	Neal	M Mills	Currie	Watson[1]
Northern Ireland	A	2–0	Clemence	Neal	M Mills*	P Thompson	Watson[1]
Wales	H	0–0	Corrigan	Cherry	Sansom	Wilkins	Watson
Scotland	H	3–1	Clemence	Neal	M Mills	P Thompson	Watson
Bulgaria	A	3–0	Clemence	Neal	M Mills	P Thompson	Watson[1]
Sweden	A	0–0	Shilton	Anderson	Cherry	McDermott	Watson
Austria	A	3–4	Shilton	Neal	M Mills	P Thompson	Watson
1979–80							
Denmark	H	1–0	Clemence	Neal	M Mills	P Thompson	Watson
Northern Ireland	A	5–1	Shilton	Neal	M Mills	P Thompson	Watson
Bulgaria	H	2–0	Clemence	Anderson	Sansom	P Thompson*	Watson[1]
Republic of Ireland	H	2–0	Clemence	Cherry	Sansom	P Thompson	Watson
Spain	A	2–0	Shilton	Neal	M Mills	P Thompson	Watson
Argentina	H	3–1	Clemence	Neal	Sansom	P Thompson	Watson
Wales	A	1–4	Clemence	Neal	Cherry	P Thompson*	Lloyd
Northern Ireland	H	1–1	Corrigan	Cherry	Sansom	E Hughes	Watson
Scotland	A	2–0	Clemence	Cherry	Sansom	P Thompson*	Watson
Australia	A	2–1	Corrigan	Cherry*	Lampard	Talbot	Osman
Belgium	N	1–1	Clemence	Neal	Sansom	P Thompson	Watson
Italy	A	0–1	Shilton	Neal	Sansom	P Thompson	Watson
Spain	N	2–1	Clemence	Anderson	M Mills	P Thompson	Watson
1980–81							
Norway	H	4–0	Shilton	Anderson	Sansom	P Thompson*	Watson
Romania	A	1–2	Clemence	Neal	Sansom	P Thompson*	Watson
Switzerland	H	2–1	Shilton	Neal	Sansom	Robson	Watson
Spain	H	1–2	Clemence	Neal	Sansom	Robson	Butcher
Romania	H	0–0	Shilton	Anderson	Sansom	Robson	Watson*
Brazil	H	0–1	Clemence*	Neal	Sansom	Robson	Martin
Wales	H	0–0	Corrigan	Anderson	Sansom	Robson	Watson*
Scotland	H	0–1	Corrigan	Anderson	Sansom	Wilkins	Watson*
Switzerland	A	1–2	Clemence	M Mills	Sansom	Wilkins	Watson
Hungary	A	3–1	Clemence	Neal	M Mills	P Thompson	Watson
1981–82							
Norway	A	1–2	Clemence	Neal	M Mills	P Thompson	Osman
Hungary	H	1–0	Shilton	Neal	M Mills	P Thompson	Martin

6	7	8	9	10	11	Substitutes
E Hughes	Keegan*	T Francis	Pearson	Wilkins	Talbot	Channon(9) R Kennedy(10)
E Hughes	Keegan*	Channon	Pearson[1]	Wilkins	Talbot	R Kennedy(4)
E Hughes	Keegan*	Channon	Pearson	Wilkins	Talbot	
E Hughes*	Keegan	Channon	T Francis	R Kennedy	Callaghan	Hill(8) Wilkins(11)
Callaghan	McDermott	Wilkins	T Francis	Mariner[1]	G Hill	Whymark(7) Beattie(3)
E Hughes*	Keegan[1]	Coppell	R Latchford	Brooking[1]	P Barnes	Pearson(9) T Francis(7)
E Hughes*	Keegan	Coppell	S Pearson	Brooking	P Barnes	T Francis(7)
Currie	Keegan*[1]	Coppell	R Latchford	T Francis	P Barnes	
Wilkins	Coppell	T Francis	R Latchford[1]	Brooking	P Barnes[1]	Currie(3)[1] Mariner(9)
E Hughes*	Currie	Coppell	Pearson	Woodcock	B Greenhoff	
E Hughes*	Wilkins	Coppell[1]	Mariner	T Francis	P Barnes	B Greenhoff(6)Brooking(9)
E Hughes*	Keegan	Coppell	T Francis[1]	Brooking	P Barnes[1]	B Greenhoff(5) Currie(8)[1]
E Hughes*	Keegan[2]	Coppell	Latchford[1]	Brooking	P Barnes	
E Hughes*	Keegan	Coppell	Latchford[1]	Brooking	P Barnes	P Thompson(5)Woodcock(11)
Wilkins	Keegan*	Coppell[1]	Woodcock	Currie	P Barnes	Latchford(9)
E Hughes*	Keegan[1]	Coppell	Latchford[2]	Brooking	P Barnes	
Wilkins	Coppell[1]	Wilkins	Latchford	Currie	P Barnes	
E Hughes*	Keegan	Wilkins	Latchford	McDermott	Cunningham	Coppell(7) Brooking(4)
Wilkins	Keegan*[1]	Coppell[1]	Latchford	Brooking	P Barnes[1]	
Wilkins	Keegan*[1]	Coppell	Latchford	Brooking	P Barnes[1]	T Francis(9) Woodcock(11)
E Hughes*	Keegan	T Francis	T Francis	Woodcock	Cunningham	Wilkins(4) Brooking(8)
Wilkins1	Keegan*[1]	Coppell[1]	Latchford	Brooking	P Barnes	Clemence(1) T Francis(9) Cunningham(11)
Wilkins	Coppell	McDermott	Keegan*[1]	Brooking	P Barnes	
Wilkins	Keegan*	Coppell	T Francis[2]	Brooking	Woodcock[2]	† McDermott(10)
Wilkins	Reeves	Hoddle[1]	T Francis	Kennedy	Woodcock	
Robson	Keegan*[2]	McDermott	Johnson	Woodcock	Cunningham	Coppell(9)
Wilkins	Keegan*	Coppell	T Francis[1]	R Kennedy	Woodcock[1]	E Hughes(2) Cunningham(9)
Wilkins	Keegan*[1]	Coppell	Johnson[2]	Woodcock	R Kennedy	Cherry(2) Birtles(9) Brooking(11)
R Kennedy	Coppell	Hoddle	Mariner[1]	Brooking	Barnes	Sansom(2) Wilkins(5)
Wilkins	Reeves	Wilkins	Johnson[1]	Brooking	Devonshire	Mariner(7)
Wilkins	Coppell[1]	McDermott	Johnson	Mariner	Brooking[1]	E Hughes(10)
Butcher	Robson	Hoddle[1]	Mariner[1]	Hoddle[1]	Armstrong	B Greenhoff(7) Ward(10) Devonshire(11)
Wilkins[1]	Keegan*	Coppell	Johnson	Woodcock	Brooking	McDermott(8) R Kennedy(9)
Wilkins	Keegan*	Coppell	Birtles	R Kennedy	Woodcock	Mariner(9)
Wilkins	McDermott	Hoddle	Keegan*	Woodcock[1]	Brooking[1]	Cherry(3) Mariner(8)
Robson	Gates	McDermott[2]	Mariner[1]	Woodcock[1]	Rix	
Robson	Rix	McDermott	Birtles	Woodcock[1]	Gates	Cunningham(9) Coppell(11)
M Mills*	Coppell	McDermott	Mariner[1]	Brooking	Woodcock	† Rix(10)
Osman	Keegan*	T Francis	Mariner	Brooking	Hoddle[1]	P Barnes(8) Wilkins(10)
Osman	Wilkins	Brooking	Coppell	T Francis	Woodcock	McDermott(11)
Wilkins	Coppell	McDermott	Withe	Rix	P Barnes	
Wilkins	Coppell	Hoddle	Withe	Rix	P Barnes	Woodcock(9)
Robson	Coppell	Hoddle	Withe	Rix	Woodcock	Martin(5) T Francis(11)
Osman	Keegan*	Robson	Keegan	Mariner	T Francis	McDermott(11)[1] P Barnes(5)
Robson	Keegan*[1]	McDermott	Mariner	Brooking[2]	Keegan*[1]	Wilkins(10)
Robson[1]	Keegan*	T Francis	Mariner	Hoddle	McDermott	Withe(9) P Barnes(10)
Robson	Keegan*	Coppell	Mariner[1]	Brooking	McDermott	Morley(8)

67

versus	venue	Result	1	2	3	4	5
Northern Ireland	H	4–0	Clemence	Anderson	Sansom	Wilkins1	Watson
Wales	A	1–0	Corrigan	Neal	Sansom	P Thompson*	Butcher
Holland	H	2–0	Shilton*	Neal	Sansom	P Thompson	Foster
Scotland	A	1–0	Shilton	M Mills	Sansom	P Thompson	Butcher
Iceland	A	1–1	Corrigan	Anderson	Neal*	Watson	Osman
Finland	A	4–1	Clemence	M Mills	Sansom	P Thompson	Martin
France	N	3–1	Shilton	M Mills*	Sansom	P Thompson	Butcher
Czechoslovakia	N	2–0	Shilton	M Mills*	Sansom	P Thompson	Butcher
Kuwait	N	1–0	Shilton	Neal	M Mills*	P Thompson	Foster
West Germany	N	0–0	Shilton	M Mills*	Sansom	P Thompson	Butcher
Spain	A	0–0	Shilton	M Mills*	Sansom	P Thompson	Butcher
1982–83							
Denmark	A	2–2	Shilton	Neal	Sansom	Wilkins*	Osman
West Germany	H	1–2	Shilton	Mabbutt	Sansom	P Thompson	Butcher
Greece	A	3–0	Shilton	Neal	Sansom	P Thompson	Martin
Luxembourg	H	9–0	Clemence	Neal1	Sansom	Robson*	Martin
Wales	H	2–1	Shilton*	Neal1	Statham	S Lee	Martin
Greece	H	0–0	Shilton*	Neal	Sansom	S Lee	Martin
Hungary	H	2–0	Shilton*	Neal	Sansom	S Lee	Martin
Northern Ireland	A	0–0	Shilton*	Neal	Sansom	Hoddle	Roberts
Scotland	H	2–0	Shilton	Neal	Sansom	S Lee	Roberts
Australia	A	0–0	Shilton*	Thomas	Statham	Williams	Osman
Australia	A	1–0	Shilton*	Neal	Statham	Barham	Osman
Australia	A	1–1	Shilton*	Neal	Pickering	S Lee	Osman
1983–84							
Denmark	H	0–1	Shilton	Neal	Sansom	S Lee	Osman
Hungary	A	3–0	Shilton	Gregory	Sansom	S Lee1	Martin
Luxembourg	A	4–0	Clemence	Duxbury	Sansom	S Lee	Martin
France	A	0–2	Shilton	Duxbury	Sansom	S Lee	Roberts
Northern Ireland	H	1–0	Shilton	Anderson	A Kennedy	S Lee	Roberts
Wales	A	0–1	Shilton	Duxbury	A Kennedy	S Lee	Martin
Scotland	A	1–1	Shilton	Duxbury	Sansom	Wilkins	Roberts
USSR	H	0–2	Shilton	Duxbury	Sansom	Wilkins	Roberts
Brazil	A	2–0	Shilton	Duxbury	Sansom	Wilkins	Watson
Uruguay	A	0–2	Shilton	Duxbury	Sansom	Wilkins	Watson
Chile	A	0–0	Shilton	Duxbury	Sansom	Wilkins	Watson
1984–85							
East Germany	H	1–0	Shilton	Duxbury	Sansom	Williams	Wright
Finland	H	5–0	Shilton	Duxbury	Sansom1	Williams	Wright
Turkey	A	8–0	Shilton	Anderson1	Sansom	Williams	Wright
Northern Ireland	A	1–0	Shilton	Anderson	Sansom	Steven	Martin
Republic of Ireland	H	2–1	Bailey	Anderson	Sansom	Steven1	Wright
Romania	A	0–0	Shilton	Anderson	Sansom	Steven	Wright
Finland	A	1–1	Shilton	Anderson	Sansom	Steven	Fenwick
Scotland	A	0–1	Shilton	Anderson	Sansom	Hoddle	Fenwick
Italy	N	1–2	Shilton	Stevens	Sansom	Steven	Wright
Mexico	A	0–1	Bailey	Anderson	Sansom	Hoddle	Fenwick
West Germany	N	3–0	Shilton	Stevens	Sansom	Hoddle	Wright
USA	A	5–0	Woods	Anderson	Sansom	Hoddle	Fenwick

6	7	8	9	10	11	*Substitutes*
Foster	Keegan*[1]	Robson[1]	T Francis	Hoddle[1]	Morley	Regis(9) Woodcock(11)
Robson	Wilkins	T Francis[1]	Withe	Hoddle	Morley	McDermott(8) Regis(10)
Robson	Wilkins	Devonshire	Mariner[1]	McDermott	Woodcock[1]	Rix(8) Barnes(9)
Robson	Keegan*	Coppell	Mariner[1]	Brooking	Wilkins	McDermott(7) T Francis(9)
McDermott	Hoddle	Devonshire	Withe	Regis	Morley	Perryman(8) Goddard(10)[1]
Robson[2]	Keegan*	Coppell	Mariner[2]	Brooking	Wilkins	Rix(6) T Francis(8) Woodcock(10)
Robson[2]	Coppell	T Francis	Mariner[1]	Rix	Wilkins	Neal(3)
Robson	Coppell	T Francis[1]	Mariner	Rix	Wilkins	† Hoddle(6)
Hoddle	Coppell	T Francis[1]	Mariner	Rix	Wilkins	
Robson	Coppell	T Francis	Mariner	Rix	Wilkins	Woodcock(8)
Robson	Rix	T Francis	Mariner	Woodcock	Wilkins	Brooking(7) Keegan(10)
Butcher	Morley	Robson	Mariner	T Francis[2]	Rix	Hill(7)
Wilkins*	R Hill	Regis	Mariner	Armstrong	Devonshire	Woodcock(8)[1] Blissett(9) Rix(10)
Robson*	S Lee[1]	Mabbutt	Mariner	Woodcock[2]	Morley	† Chamberlain(7)[1] Hoddle(11)[1]
Butcher	Coppell[1]	S Lee	Woodcock[1]	Blissett[3]	Mabbutt	
Butcher[1]	Mabbutt	Blissett	Mariner	Cowans	Devonshire	
Butcher	Coppell	Mabbutt	T Francis	Woodcock	Devonshire	Blissett(10) Rix(11)
Butcher	Mabbutt	T Francis[1]	Withe[1]	Blissett	Cowans	
Butcher	Mabbutt	T Francis	Withe	Blissett	Cowans	J Barnes(10)
Butcher	Robson*[1]	T Francis	Withe	Hoddle	Cowans[1]	Mabbutt(7) Blissett(9)
Butcher	Barham	Gregory	Blissett	T Francis	Cowans	J Barnes(3) Walsh(9)
Butcher	Gregory	T Francis	Walsh[1]	Cowans	J Barnes	Williams(3)
Butcher	Gregory	T Francis[1]	Walsh	Cowans	J Barnes	Spink(1) Thomas(2) Blissett(9)
Butcher	Wilkins*	Gregory	Mariner	T Francis	J Barnes	Blissett(4) Chamberlain(11)
Butcher	Robson*	Hoddle[1]	Mariner[1]	Blissett	Mabbutt	Withe(10)
Butcher[1]	Robson*[2]	Hoddle	Mariner[1]	Woodcock	Devonshire	J Barnes(10)
Butcher	Robson*	Stein	Walsh	Hoddle	Williams	J Barnes(4) Woodcock(8)
Butcher	Robson*	Wilkins	Woodcock[1]	T Francis	Rix	
Wright	Wilkins*	Gregory	Walsh	Woodcock	Armstrong	Fenwick(5) Blissett(11)
Fenwick	Chamberlain	Robson*	Woodcock[1]	Blissett	J Barnes	Hunt(7) Lineker(9)
Fenwick	Chamberlain	Robson*	T Francis	Blissett	J Barnes	Hateley(9) Hunt(11)
Fenwick	Robson*	Chamberlain	Hateley[1]	Woodcock	J Barnes[1]	Allen(10)
Fenwick	Robson*	Chamberlain	Hateley	Allen	J Barnes	Woodcock(10)
Fenwick	Robson*	Chamberlain	Hateley	Allen	J Barnes	S Lee(8)
Butcher	Robson*[1]	Wilkins	Mariner	Woodcock	J Barnes	Hateley(9) T Francis(10)
Butcher	Robson*[1]	Wilkins	Hateley[2]	Woodcock[1]	J Barnes	GA Stevens(2) Chamberlain(7)
Butcher	Robson*[3]	Wilkins	Withe	Woodcock[2]	J Barnes[2]	GA Stevens(4) Francis(10)
Butcher	Steven	Wilkins*	Hateley[1]	Woodcock	J Barnes	T Francis(10)
Butcher	Robson*	Wilkins	Hateley	Lineker[1]	Waddle	Hoddle(7) Davenport(9)
Butcher	Robson*	Wilkins	Mariner	T Francis	J Barnes	Lineker(9) Waddle(11)
Butcher	Robson*	Wilkins	Hateley[1]	T Francis	J Barnes	Waddle(4)
Butcher	Robson*	Wilkins	Hateley	T Francis	J Barnes	Lineker(4) Waddle(11)
Butcher	Robson*	Wilkins	Hateley[1]	T Francis	Waddle	Hoddle(4) Lineker(10) J Barnes(11)
Watson	Robson*	Wilkins	Hateley	T Francis	J Barnes	K Dixon(4) Reid(8) Waddle(11)
Butcher	Robson*[1]	Reid	K Dixon[2]	Lineker	Waddle	Bracewell(7) J Barnes(10)
Butcher	Robson*	Bracewell	K Dixon[2]	Lineker[2]	Waddle	Watson(3) Steven(4)[1] Reid(7) J Barnes(11)

versus	venue	Result	1	2	3	4	5
1985–86							
Romania	H	1–1	Shilton	Stevens	Sansom	Reid	Wright
Turkey	H	5–0	Shilton	Stevens	Sansom	Hoddle	Wright
Northern Ireland	H	0–0	Shilton	GA Stevens	Sansom	Hoddle	Wright
Egypt	A	4–0	Shilton	Stevens	Sansom	Cowans[1]	Wright
Israel	A	2–1	Shilton	Stevens	Sansom	Hoddle	Martin
USSR	A	1–0	Shilton	Anderson	Sansom	Hoddle	Wright
Scotland	H	2–1	Shilton	Stevens	Sansom	Hoddle[1]	Watson
Mexico	N	3–0	Shilton	Anderson	Sansom	Hoddle	Fenwick
Canada	A	1–0	Shilton	Stevens	Sansom	Hoddle	Martin
Portugal	N	0–1	Shilton	Stevens	Sansom	Hoddle	Fenwick
Morocco	N	0–0	Shilton	Stevens	Sansom	Hoddle	Fenwick
Poland	N	3–0	Shilton*	Stevens	Sansom	Hoddle	Fenwick
Paraguay	N	3–0	Shilton*	Stevens	Sansom	Hoddle	Martin
Argentina	N	1–2	Shilton*	Stevens	Sansom	Hoddle	Fenwick
1986–87							
Sweden	A	0–1	Shilton*	Anderson	Sansom	Hoddle	Martin
Northern Ireland	H	3–0	Shilton	Anderson	Sansom	Hoddle	Watson
Yugoslavia	H	2–0	Woods	Anderson[1]	Sansom	Hoddle	Wright
Spain	A	4–2	Shilton	Anderson	Sansom	Hoddle	Adams
Northern Ireland	A	2–0	Shilton	Anderson	Sansom	Mabbutt	Wright
Turkey	A	0–0	Woods	Anderson	Sansom	Hoddle	Adams
Brazil	H	1–1	Shilton	Stevens	Pearce	Reid	Adams
Scotland	A	0–0	Woods	Stevens	Pearce	Hoddle	Wright
1987–88							
West Germany	A	1–3	Shilton*	Anderson	Sansom	Hoddle	Adams
Turkey	H	8–0	Shilton	Stevens	Sansom	Steven	Adams
Yugoslavia	A	4–1	Shilton	Stevens	Sansom	Steven	Adams[1]
Israel	A	0–0	Woods	Stevens	Pearce	Webb	Watson
Holland	H	2–2	Shilton	Stevens	Sansom	Steven	Adams[1]
Hungary	A	0–0	Woods	Anderson	Pearce	Steven	Adams
Scotland	H	1–0	Shilton	Stevens	Sansom	Webb	Watson
Colombia	H	1–1	Shilton	Anderson	Sansom	McMahon	Wright
Switzerland	A	1–0	Shilton	Stevens	Sansom	Webb	Wright
Republic of Ireland	N	0–1	Shilton	Stevens	Sansom	Webb	Wright
Holland	N	1–3	Shilton	Stevens	Sansom	Hoddle	Wright
USSR	N	1–3	Woods	Stevens	Sansom	Hoddle	Watson
1988–89							
Denmark	H	1–0	Shilton	Stevens	Pearce	Rocastle	Adams
Sweden	H	0–0	Shilton	Stevens	Pearce	Webb	Adams
Saudi Arabia	A	1–1	Seaman	Sterland	Pearce	M Thomas	Adams[1]
Greece	A	2–1	Shilton	Stevens	Pearce	Webb	Walker
Albania	A	2–0	Shilton	Stevens	Pearce	Webb	Walker
Albania	H	5–0	Shilton	Stevens	Pearce	Webb	Walker
Chile	H	0–0	Shilton	Parker	Pearce	Webb	Walker
Scotland	A	2–0	Shilton	Stevens	Pearce	Webb	Walker

6	7	8	9	10	11	Substitutes
Fenwick	Robson*	Hoddle[1]	Hateley	Lineker	Waddle	Woodcock(10) J Barnes(11)
Fenwick	Robson*[1]	Wilkins	Hateley	Lineker[3]	Waddle[1]	Steven(7) Woodcock(9)
Fenwick	Bracewell	Wilkins*	K Dixon	Lineker	Waddle	
Fenwick	Steven[1]	Wilkins*	Hateley	Lineker	Wallace[1]	† Woods(1) Hill(7) Beardsley(10)
Butcher	Robson*[2]	Wilkins	Dixon	Beardsley	Waddle	Woods(1) Woodcock(9) J Barnes(10)
Butcher	Cowans	Wilkins*	Beardsley	Lineker	Waddle[1]	Hodge(7) Steven(11)
Butcher[1]	Wilkins*	T Francis	Hateley	Hodge	Waddle	Reid(7) GA Stevens(10)
Butcher	Robson*	Wilkins	Hateley[2]	Beardsley[1]	Waddle	GA Stevens(7) Steven(8) K Dixon(9) J Barnes(11)
Butcher	Hodge	Wilkins*	Hateley[1]	Lineker	Waddle	Woods(1) Reid(8) Beardsley(10) J Barnes(11)
Butcher	Robson*	Wilkins	Hateley	Lineker	Waddle	Hodge(7) Beardsley(11)
Butcher	Robson*	Wilkins	Hateley	Lineker	Waddle	Hodge(7) GA Stevens(9)
Butcher	Hodge	Reid	Beardsley	Lineker[3]	Steven	Waddle(9) K Dixon(10)
Butcher	Hodge	Reid	Beardsley[1]	Lineker[2]	Steven	GA Stevens(8) Hateley(9)
Butcher	Hodge	Reid	Beardsley	Lineker[1]	Steven	Waddle(8) J Barnes(11)
Butcher	Steven	Wilkins	K Dixon	Hodge	J Barnes	Cottee(7) Waddle(11)
Butcher	Robson*	Hodge	Beardsley	Lineker[2]	Waddle[1]	Cottee(9)
Butcher*	Mabbutt[1]	Hodge	Beardsley	Lineker	Waddle	Wilkins(8) Steven(11)
Butcher	Robson*	Hodge	Beardsley	Lineker[4]	Waddle	Woods(1) Steven(11)
Butcher	Robson*[1]	Hodge	Beardsley	Lineker	Waddle[1]	Woods(1)
Mabbutt	Robson*	Hodge	Allen	Lineker	Waddle	J Barnes(8) Hateley(9)
Butcher	Robson*	J Barnes	Beardsley	Lineker[1]	Waddle	Hateley(10)
Butcher	Robson*	Hodge	Beardsley	Hateley	Waddle	
Mabbutt	Reid	J Barnes	Beardsley	Lineker[1]	Waddle	Pearce(3) Webb(4) Hateley(11)
Butcher	Robson*[1]	Webb[1]	Beardsley[1]	Lineker[3]	J Barnes[2]	Hoddle(4) Regis(9)
Butcher	Robson*[1]	Webb	Beardsley[1]	Lineker	J Barnes[1]	Reid(7) Hoddle(8)
Wright	Allen	McMahon	Beardsley*	J Barnes	Waddle	Fenwick(6) Harford(7)
Watson	Robson*	Webb	Beardsley	Lineker[1]	J Barnes	Wright(6) Hoddle(8) Hateley(9)
Pallister	Robson*	McMahon	Beardsley	Lineker	Waddle	Stevens(3) Hateley(9) Cottee(10) Hoddle(11)
Adams	Robson*	Steven	Beardsley[1]	Lineker	J Barnes	Waddle(8)
Adams	Robson*	Waddle	Beardsley	Lineker[1]	J Barnes	Hoddle(8) Hateley(9)
Adams	Robson*	Steven	Beardsley	Lineker[1]	J Barnes	Woods(1) Watson(6) Reid(7) Waddle(8)
Adams	Robson*	Waddle	Beardsley	Lineker	J Barnes	Hoddle(4) Hateley(9)
Adams	Robson*[1]	Steven	Beardsley	Lineker	J Barnes	Waddle(8) Hateley(9)
Adams[1]	Robson*	Steven	McMahon	Lineker	J Barnes	Webb(9) Hateley(10)
Butcher	Robson*	Webb[1]	Harford	Beardsley	Hodge	Woods(1) Walker(5) Cottee(9) Gascoigne(10)
Butcher	Robson*	Beardsley	Waddle	Lineker	J Barnes	Walker(5) Cottee(11)
Pallister	Robson*	Rocastle	Beardsley	Lineker	Waddle	Gascoigne(4) A Smith(9) Marwood(11)
Butcher	Robson*[1]	Rocastle	A Smith	Lineker	J Barnes[1]	Beardsley(9)
Butcher	Robson*[1]	Rocastle	Waddle	Lineker	J Barnes[1]	Beardsley(9) A Smith(10)
Butcher	Robson*	Rocastle	Beardsley[2]	Lineker[1]	Waddle[1]	Parker(2) Gascoigne(8)[1]
Butcher	Robson*	Gascoigne	Clough	Fashanu	Waddle	Cottee(10)
Butcher	Robson*	Steven	Fashanu	Cottee	Waddle[1]	Bull(9)[1] Gascoigne(10)

versus	venue	Result	1	2	3	4	5
Poland	H	3–0	Shilton	Stevens	Pearce	Webb[1]	Walker
Denmark	A	1–1	Shilton	Parker	Pearce	Webb	Walker
1989–90							
Sweden	A	0–0	Shilton	Stevens	Pearce	Webb	Walker
Poland	A	0–0	Shilton	Stevens	Pearce	McMahon	Walker
Italy	H	0–0	Shilton	Stevens	Pearce	McMahon	Walker
Yugoslavia	H	2–1	Shilton	Parker	Pearce	Thomas	Walker
Brazil	H	1–0	Shilton	Stevens	Pearce	McMahon	Walker
Czechoslovakia	H	4–2	Shilton	Dixon	Pearce[1]	Steven	Walker
Denmark	H	1–0	Shilton	Stevens	Pearce	McMahon	Walker
Uruguay	H	1–2	Shilton	Parker	Pearce	Hodge	Walker
Tunisia	A	1–1	Shilton	Stevens	Pearce	Hodge	Walker
Republic of Ireland	N	1–1	Shilton	Stevens	Pearce	Gascoigne	Walker
Holland	N	0–0	Shilton	Parker	Pearce	Wright	Walker
Egypt	N	1–0	Shilton*	Parker	Pearce	Gascoigne	Walker
Belgium	N	1–0	Shilton	Parker	Pearce	Wright	Walker
Cameroon	N	3–2	Shilton	Parker	Pearce	Wright	Walker
West Germany	N	1–1	Shilton	Parker	Pearce	Wright	Walker
Italy	A	1–2	Shilton*	Stevens	Dorigo	Parker	Walker
1990–91							
Hungary	H	1–0	Woods	Dixon	Pearce	Parker	Walker
Poland	H	2–0	Woods	Dixon	Pearce	Parker	Walker
Republic of Ireland	A	1–1	Woods	Dixon	Pearce	Adams	Walker
Cameroon	H	2–0	Seaman	Dixon	Pearce	Steven	Walker
Rep. of Ireland	H	1–1	Seaman	Dixon[1]	Pearce	Adams	Walker
Turkey	A	1–0	Seaman	Dixon	Pearce	Wise[1]	Walker
USSR	H	3–1	Woods	Stevens	Dorigo	Wise	Parker
Argentina	H	2–2	Seaman	Dixon	Pearce	Batty	Walker
Australia	A	1–0	Woods	Parker	Pearce	Batty	Walker
New Zealand	A	1–0	Woods	Parker	Pearce	Batty	Walker
New Zealand	A	2–0	Woods	Charles	Pearce*[1]	Wise	Walker
Malaysia	A	4–2	Woods	Charles	Pearce	Batty	Walker
1991–92							
Germany	H	0–1	Woods	Dixon	Dorigo	Batty	Pallister
Turkey	H	1–0	Woods	Dixon	Pearce	Batty	Walker
Poland	A	1–1	Woods	Dixon	Pearce	Gray	Walker
France	H	2–0	Woods	R Jones	Pearce*	Keown	Walker
Czechoslovakia	A	2–2	Seaman	Keown[1]	Pearce*	Rocastle	Walker
CIS	A	2–2	Woods	Stevens	Sinton	Palmer	Walker
Hungary	A	1–0	Martyn	Stevens	Dorigo	Curle	Walker
Brazil	H	1–1	Woods	Stevens	Dorigo	Palmer	Walker
Finland	A	2–1	Woods	Stevens	Pearce	Keown	Walker
Denmark	N	0–0	Woods	Curle	Pearce	Palmer	Walker
France	N	0–0	Woods	Batty	Pearce	Palmer	Walker
Sweden	A	1–2	Woods	Batty	Pearce	Keown	Walker

6	7	8	9	10	11	Substitutes
Butcher	Robson*	Waddle	Beardsley	Lineker[1]	J Barnes[1]	Rocastle(8) A Smith(9)
Butcher	Robson*	Rocastle	Beardsley	Lineker[1]	J Barnes	Seaman(1) McMahon(4) Bull(9) Waddle(11)
Butcher*	Beardsley	McMahon	Waddle	Lineker	J Barnes	Gascoigne(4) Rocastle(11)
Butcher	Robson*	Rocastle	Beardsley	Lineker	Waddle	
Butcher	Robson*	Waddle	Beardsley	Lineker	J Barnes	Beasant(1) Winterburn(3) Hodge(4) Phelan(7)Platt(9)
Butcher	Robson*[2]	Rocastle	Bull	Lineker	Waddle	Beasant(1) Dorigo(3)Platt(4) McMahon(7)Hodge(8)
Butcher*	Platt	Waddle	Beardsley	Lineker[1]	J Barnes	Woods(1) Gascoigne(9)
Butcher	Robson*	Gascoigne[1]	Bull[2]	Lineker	Hodge	Seaman(1) Dorigo(3) Wright(5) McMahon(7)
Butcher*	Hodge	Gascoigne	Waddle	Lineker[1]	J Barnes	Woods(1) Dorigo(3) Platt(4) Rocastle(9)Bull(10)
Butcher	Robson*	Gascoigne	Waddle	Lineker	J Barnes[1]	Beardsley(4) Bull(10)
Butcher	Robson*	Waddle	Gascoigne	Lineker	J Barnes	Beardsley(4) Wright(6) Platt(8) Bull(10)[1]
Butcher	Waddle	Robson*	Beardsley	Lineker[1]	J Barnes	McMahon(9) Bull(10)
Butcher	Robson*	Waddle	Gascoigne	Lineker	J Barnes	Platt(7) Bull(8)
Wright[1]	McMahon	Waddle	Bull	Lineker	J Barnes	Platt(8) Beardsley(9)
Butcher*	McMahon	Waddle	Gascoigne	Lineker	J Barnes	Platt(7)[1] Bull(11)
Butcher*	Platt[1]	Waddle	Gascoigne	Lineker[2]	J Barnes	Steven(6) Beardsley(11)
Butcher*	Platt	Waddle	Gascoigne	Lineker[1]	Beardsley	Steven(6)
Wright	Platt[1]	Steven	McMahon	Lineker	Beardsley	Waddle(6) Webb(9)
Wright	Platt	Gascoigne	Bull	Lineker*[1]	J Barnes	Dorigo(3) Waddle(9)
Wright	Platt	Gascoigne	Bull	Lineker*[1]	J Barnes	Beardsley(9)[1] Waddle(10)
Wright	Platt[1]	Cowans	Beardsley	Lineker*	McMahon	
Wright	Robson	Gascoigne	I Wright	Lineker*[2]	J Barnes	Pallister(7) Hodge(8)
Wright	Robson	Platt	Beardsley	Lineker*	J Barnes	Sharpe(4) I Wright(10)
Pallister	Platt	G Thomas	A Smith	Lineker*	J Barnes	Hodge(8)
Wright*	Platt[2]	G Thomas	A Smith[1]	I Wright	J Barnes	Batty(4) Beardsley(10)
Wright	Platt[1]	G Thomas	A Smith	Lineker*[1]	J Barnes	Clough(11)
Wright	Platt	G Thomas	Clough	Lineker*	Hirst	† Wise(10) Salako(11)
Barrett	Platt	G Thomas	Wise	Lineker*[1]	Walters	Deane(4) Salako(11)
Wright	Platt	G Thomas	Deane	I Wright	Salako	Hirst(9)[1]
Wright	Platt	G Thomas	Clough	Lineker*[4]	Salako	
Parker	Platt	Steven	A Smith	Lineker*	Salako	Stewart(8)Merson(11)
Mabbutt	Robson	Platt	A Smith[1]	Lineker*	Waddle	
Mabbutt	Platt	G Thomas	Rocastle	Lineker*[1]	Sinton	A Smith(4)Daley(11)
Wright	Webb	G Thomas	Clough	Shearer[1]	Hirst	Lineker(11)[1]
Mabbutt	Platt	Merson[1]	Clough	Hateley	J Barnes	Dixon(4)Lineker(6) Stewart(9)Dorigo(11)
Keown	Platt	Steven[1]	Shearer	Lineker*[1]	Daley	Martyn(1)Curle(3) Stewart(8)Clough(9)
Keown	Webb[1]	Palmer	Merson	Lineker*	Daley	Seaman(1)Sinton(4)Batty(7) A Smith(9)I Wright(10)
Keown	Daley	Steven	Platt[1]	Lineker*	Sinton	Pearce(3)Merson(7)Webb(8) Rocastle(11)
Wright	Platt[2]	Steven	Webb	Lineker*	J Barnes	Palmer(2)Daley(8)Merson(11)
Keown	Platt	Steven	A Smith	Lineker*	Merson	Daley(2)Webb(11)
Keown	Platt	Steven	Shearer	Lineker*	Palmer	
Palmer	Platt[1]	Webb	Sinton	Lineker*	Daley	Merson(9)A Smith(10)

versus	venue	Result	1	2	3	4	5
1992–93							
Spain	A	0–1	Woods	Dixon	Pearce*	Ince	Walker
Norway	H	1–1	Woods	Dixon	Pearce*	Batty	Walker
Turkey	H	4–0	Woods	Dixon	Pearce*[1]	Palmer	Walker
San Marino	H	6–0	Woods	Dixon	Dorigo	Palmer[1]	Walker
Turkey	A	2–0	Woods	Dixon	Sinton	Palmer	Walker
Holland	H	2–2	Woods	Dixon	Keown	Palmer	Walker
Poland	A	1–1	Woods	Bardsley	Dorigo	Palmer	Walker
Norway	A	0–2	Woods	Dixon	Pallister	Palmer	Walker
United States	A	0–2	Woods	Dixon	Dorigo	Palmer	Pallister
Brazil	N	1–1	Flowers	Barrett	Dorigo	Walker	Pallister
Germany	N	1–2	Martyn	Barrett	Sinton	Walker	Pallister
1993–94							
Poland	H	3–0	Seaman	Jones	Pearce*[1]	Ince	Pallister
Holland	A	0–2	Seaman	Parker	Dorigo	Ince	Pallister
San Marino	A	7–1	Seaman	Dixon	Pearce*	Ince[2]	Pallister
Denmark	H	1–0	Seaman	Parker	Le Saux	Ince	Adams
Greece	H	5–0	Flowers	Jones	Le Saux	Richardson	Bould
Norway	H	0–0	Seaman	Jones	Le Saux	Ince	Bould

‡West Germany won 4–3 on penalties

6	7	8	9	10	11	*Substitutes*
Wright	White	Platt	Clough	Shearer	Sinton	Bardsley(2)Palmer(2) Merson(7)Deane(11)
Adams	Platt[1]	Gascoigne	Shearer	I Wright	Ince	Palmer(2)Merson(10)
Adams	Platt	Gascoigne[2]	Shearer[1]	I Wright	Ince	
Adams	Platt*[4]	Gascoigne	Ferdinand[1]	J Barnes	Batty	
Adams	Platt*[1]	Gascoigne[1]	J Barnes	I Wright	Ince	Clough(2)Sharpe(10)
Adams	Plat*[1]	Gascoigne	Ferdinand	J Barnes[1]	Ince	Merson(8)
Adams	Platt*	Gascoigne	Sheringham	J Barnes	Ince	I Wright(4)[1]Clough(8)
Adams	Platt*	Gascoigne	Ferdinand	Sheringham	Sharpe	Clough(5)I Wright(10)
Batty	Ince*	Clough	Sharpe	Ferdinand	J Barnes	Walker(4)I Wright(10)
Batty	Ince*	Clough	I Wright	Sinton	Sharpe	Platt(6)[1]Palmer(7)Merson(8)
Ince	Platt*[1]	Clough	Sharpe	J Barnes	Merson	Keown(5)I Wright(8) Winterburn(9)
Adams	Platt	Gascoigne[1]	Ferdinand[1]	Wright	Sharpe	
Adams	Platt*	Palmer	Shearer	Merson	Sharpe	Sinton(8)Wright(10)
Walker	Platt	Ripley	Ferdinand[1]	Wright[4]	Sinton	
Pallister	Platt*[1]	Gascoigne	Shearer	Beardsley	Anderton	Batty(4)Le Tissier(8)
Adams	Platt*[2]	Merson	Shearer[1]	Beardsley[1]	Anderton[1]	Pearce(2)Wright(10) Le Tissier(11)
Adams	Platt*	Wise	Shearer	Beardsley	Anderton	Le Tissier(4)Wright(11)

PUTTING THE FANS FIRST FOR
UEFA euro 96 ™

THE EVENT

In June 1996 the European Championship Finals will be held in England for the very first time. With sixteen nations competing for the trophy, dramatically won by Denmark in 1992, the tournament will not only be the largest European Championship ever, but will also be the greatest sporting event held in England since the 1966 World Cup. Hosting the tournament is a great honour for the English game after some challenging times and is a great reward for all genuine football fans in this country.

TICKETS

Euro 96 will offer a feast of football from many of the world's best players. The ticketing strategy for Euro 96 breaks new ground in terms of both availability and pricing and provides a great opportunity for football supporters throughout the country. Unusually for a major international football tournament, it will be possible to buy a ticket for an individual match. Previously supporters have had to buy packages of tickets for several matches. However, tickets for the knock-out stages of the tournament (Quarters, Semis and Final) will be allocated on a 'loyalty' basis. This means that priority will be given to fans who have supported Euro 96 in its early stages (by buying tickets to at least three group games).

PRICES

A single match ticket to witness the excitement of Euro 96 can cost as little as £15. It is also possible

to see, for example, six matches during Euro 96 (three group games, a Quarter-Final, a Semi-Final and the Final) for just £160. This is good value by any standards and exceptional when compared with a similar package on offer at this year's World Cup currently costing more than £300.

A direct debit scheme specially created for Euro 96 will also enable football fans to spread the cost of tickets over a period of six months.

'FOOTBALL FAMILY'

Euro 96 will capture the imagination of football fans everywhere. To enable as many supporters as possible to be part of the experience, a 'Football Family' has been created. This Football Family includes season ticket holders and members at all FA Premier League and Football League Clubs who will be offered priority to apply for EURO 96 tickets before they go on sale to the general public in the summer of 1994.

APPLICATION FORMS AND INFORMATION

Ticket application forms for Euro 96 are available now from all FA Premier League Club and Football League Club ticket offices for season ticket holders and club members. For further information telephone Euro 96 on **078 274 1996**.

EURO 96 is a department of The Football Association

International Matches 1872–1994

WCQ = World Cup Qualifier
WCF = World Cup Finals
ECQ = European Championship Qualifier
ECF = European Championship Finals
RC = Rous Cup
BJT = Brazilian Jubilee Tournament
USBT = US Bicentennial Tournament
USC = US Cup

v Albania

1989	8/3	Tirana	W2–0 (WCQ)
1989	26/4	Wembley	W5–0 (WCQ)

P2, W2, D0, L0, F7, A0

v Argentina

1951	9/5	Wembley	W2–1
1953	17/5	Buenos Aires	D0–0 *
1962	2/6	Rancagua	W3–1 (WCF)
1964	6/6	Rio de Janeiro	L0–1 (BJT)
1966	23/7	Wembley	W1–0 (WCF)
1974	22/5	Wembley	D2–2
1977	12/6	Buenos Aires	D1–1
1980	13/5	Wembley	W3–1
1986	22/6	Mexico City	L1–2 (WCF)
1991	25/5	Wembley	D2–2

P10, W4, D4, L2, F15, A11
*Abandoned after 21 minutes

v Australia

1980	31/5	Sydney	W2–1
1983	12/6	Sydney	D0–0
1983	15/6	Brisbane	W1–0
1983	19/6	Melbourne	D1–1
1991	1/6	Sydney	W1–0

P5, W3, D2, L0, F5, A2

v Austria

1908	6/6	Vienna	W6–1
1908	8/6	Vienna	W11–1
1909	1/6	Vienna	W8–1
1930	14/5	Vienna	D0–0
1932	7/12	Chelsea	W4–3
1936	6/5	Vienna	L1–2
1951	28/11	Wembley	D2–2
1952	25/5	Vienna	W3–2
1958	15/6	Boras	D2–2 (WCF)
1961	27/5	Vienna	L1–3
1962	4/4	Wembley	W3–1
1965	20/10	Wembley	L2–3
1967	27/5	Vienna	W1–0
1973	26/9	Wembley	W7–0
1979	13/6	Vienna	L3–4

P15, W8, D3, L4, F54, A25

v Belgium

1921	21/5	Brussels	W2–0
1923	19/3	Arsenal	W6–1
1923	1/11	Antwerp	D2–2
1924	8/12	West Bromwich	W4–0
1926	24/5	Antwerp	W5–3
1927	11/5	Brussels	W9–1
1928	19/5	Antwerp	W3–1
1929	11/5	Brussels	W5–1
1931	16/5	Brussels	W4–1
1936	9/5	Brussels	L2–3
1947	21/9	Brussels	W5–2
1950	18/5	Brussels	W4–1
1952	26/11	Wembley	W5–0
1954	17/6	Basle	D4–4 (WCF)
1964	21/10	Wembley	D2–2
1970	25/2	Brussels	W3–1
1980	12/6	Turin	D1–1 (ECF)
1990	26/6	Bologna	W1–0 (WCF)

P18, W13, D4, L1, F67, A24

v Bohemia

1908	13/6	Prague	W4–0

P1, W1, D0, L0, F4, A0

v Brazil

1956	9/5	Wembley	W4–2
1958	11/6	Gothenburg	D0–0 (WCF)
1959	13/5	Rio de Janeiro	L0–2
1962	10/6	Vina del Mar	L1–3 (WCF)
1963	8/5	Wembley	D1–1
1964	30/5	Rio de Janeiro	L1–5 (BJT)
1969	12/6	Rio de Janeiro	L1–2
1970	7/6	Guadalajara	L0–1 (WCF)
1976	23/5	Los Angeles	L0–1 (USBT)
1977	8/6	Rio de Janeiro	D0–0
1978	19/4	Wembley	D1–1
1981	12/5	Wembley	L0–1
1984	10/6	Rio de Janeiro	W2–0
1987	19/5	Wembley	D1–1 (RC)
1990	28/3	Wembley	W1–0
1992	17/5	Wembley	D1–1
1993	13/6	Washington	D1–1 (USC)

P17, W3, D7, L7, F15, A22

v Bulgaria

1962	7/6	Rancagua	D0–0 (WCF)
1968	11/12	Wembley	D1–1
1974	1/6	Sofia	W1–0
1979	6/6	Sofia	W3–0 (ECQ)
1979	22/11	Wembley	W2–0 (ECQ)

P5, W3, D2, L0, F7, A1

v Cameroon

1990	1/7	Naples	W3–2 (WCF)
1991	6/2	Wembley	W2–0

P2, W2, D0, L0, F5, A2

v Canada

1986	24/5	Vancouver	W1–0

P1, W1, D0, L0, F1, A0

v Chile

1950	25/6	Rio de Janeiro	W2–0 (WCF)
1953	24/5	Santiago	W2–1
1984	17/6	Santiago	D0–0
1989	23/5	Wembley	D0–0 (RC)

P4, W2, D2, L0, F4, A1

v CIS

1992	29/4	Moscow	D2–2

P1, W0, D1, L0, F2, A2

v Colombia

1970	20/5	Bogota	W4–0
1988	24/5	Wembley	D1–1 (RC)

P2, W1, D1, L0, F5, A1

v Cyprus

1975	16/4	Wembley	W5–0 (ECQ)
1975	11/5	Limassol	W1–0 (ECQ)

P2, W2, D0, L0, F6, A0

v Czechoslovakia

1934	16/5	Prague	L1–2
1937	1/12	Tottenham	W5–4
1963	29/5	Bratislava	W4–2
1966	2/11	Wembley	D0–0
1970	11/6	Guadalajara	W1–0 (WCF)
1973	27/5	Prague	D1–1
1974	30/10	Wembley	W3–0 (ECF)
1975	30/10	Bratislava	L1–2 (ECF)
1978	29/11	Wembley	W1–0
1982	20/6	Bilbao	W2–0 (WCF)
1990	25/4	Wembley	W4–2
1992	25/3	Prague	D2–2

P12, W7, D3, L2, F25, A15

v Denmark

1948	26/9	Copenhagen	D0–0
1955	2/10	Copenhagen	W5–1
1956	5/12	Wolverhampton	W5–2 (WCQ)
1957	15/5	Copenhagen	W4–1 (WCQ)
1966	3/7	Copenhagen	W2–0
1978	20/9	Copenhagen	W4–3 (ECQ)
1979	12/9	Wembley	W1–0 (ECQ)
1982	22/9	Copenhagen	D2–2 (ECQ)
1983	21/9	Wembley	L0–1 (ECQ)
1988	14/9	Wembley	W1–0
1989	7/6	Copenhagen	D1–1
1990	15/5	Wembley	W1–0
1992	11/6	Malmö	D0–0 (ECF)
1994	9/3	Wembley	W1–0

P14, W9, D4, L1, F27, A11

v Ecuador

1970	24/5	Quito	W2–0

P1, W1, D0, L0, F2, A0

v Egypt

1986	29/1	Cairo	W4–0
1990	21/6	Cagliari	W1–0 (WCF)

P2, W2, D0, L0, F5, A0

v FIFA

1953	21/10	Wembley	D4–4

P1, W0, D1, L0, F4, A4

v Finland

1937	20/5	Helsinki	W8–0
1956	20/5	Helsinki	W5–1
1966	26/6	Helsinki	W3–0
1976	13/6	Helsinki	W4–1 (WCQ)
1976	13/10	Wembley	W2–1 (WCQ)
1982	3/6	Helsinki	W4–1
1984	17/10	Wembley	W5–0 (WCQ)
1985	22/5	Helsinki	D1–1 (WCQ)
1992	3/6	Helsinki	W2–1

P9, W8, D1, L0, F34, A6

v France

1923	10/5	Paris	W4–1
1924	17/5	Paris	W3–1
1925	21/5	Paris	W3–2
1927	26/5	Paris	W6–0
1928	17/5	Paris	W5–1
1929	9/5	Paris	W4–1
1931	14/5	Paris	L2–5
1933	6/12	Tottenham	W4–1
1938	26/5	Paris	W4–2
1947	3/5	Arsenal	W3–0
1949	22/5	Paris	W3–1
1951	3/10	Arsenal	D2–2
1955	15/5	Paris	L0–1
1957	27/11	Wembley	W4–0
1962	3/10	Sheffield	D1–1 (ECQ)
1963	27/2	Paris	L2–5 (ECQ)
1966	20/7	Wembley	W2–0 (WCF)

1969	12/3	Wembley	W5–0
1982	16/6	Bilbao	W3–1 (WCF)
1984	29/2	Paris	L0–2
1992	19/2	Wembley	W2–0
1992	14/6	Malmö	D0–0 (ECF)

P22, W15, D3, L4, F62, A27

v East Germany

1963	2/6	Leipzig	W2–1
1970	25/11	Wembley	W3–1
1974	29/5	Leipzig	D1–1
1984	12/9	Wembley	W1–0

P4, W3, D1, L0, F7, A3

v West Germany

1930	10/5	Berlin	D3–3 †
1935	4/12	Tottenham	W3–0 †
1938	14/5	Berlin	W6–3 †
1954	1/12	Wembley	W3–1
1956	26/5	Berlin	W3–1
1965	12/5	Nuremberg	W1–0
1966	23/2	Wembley	W1–0
1966	30/7	Wembley	W4–2 (WCF)
1968	1/6	Hanover	L0–1
1970	14/6	Leon	L2–3 (WCF)
1972	29/4	Wembley	L1–3 (ECQ)
1972	13/5	Berlin	D0–0 (ECQ)
1975	12/3	Wembley	W2–0
1978	22/2	Munich	L1–2
1982	29/6	Madrid	D0–0 (WCF)
1982	13/10	Wembley	L1–2
1985	12/6	Mexico City	W3–0
1987	9/9	Düsseldorf	L1–3
1990	4/7	Turin	D1–1 *(WCF)

P19, W9, D3, L7, F36, A25

† *as Germany*
* *After extra time (England lost 3–4 on penalties)*

v Germany

| 1991 | 11/9 | Wembley | L0–1 |
| 1993 | 19/6 | Detroit | L1–2 (USC) |

P2, W0, D0, L2, F1, A3

v Greece

1971	21/4	Wembley	W3–0 (ECQ)
1971	1/12	Athens	W2–0 (ECQ)
1982	17/11	Salonika	W3–0 (ECQ)
1983	30/3	Wembley	D0–0 (ECQ)
1989	8/2	Athens	W2–1
1994	17/5	Wembley	W5–0

P6, W5, D1, L0, F15, A1

v Holland

1935	18/5	Amsterdam	W1–0
1946	27/11	Huddersfield	W8–2
1964	9/12	Amsterdam	D1–1
1969	5/11	Amsterdam	W1–0
1970	14/1	Wembley	D0–0
1977	9/2	Wembley	L0–2
1982	25/5	Wembley	W2–0
1988	23/3	Wembley	D2–2
1988	15/6	Düsseldorf	L1–3 (ECF)
1990	16/6	Cagliari	D0–0 (WCF)
1993	28/4	Wembley	D2–2 (WCQ)
1993	13/10	Rotterdam	L0–2 (WCQ)

P12, W4, D5, L3, F18, A14

v Hungary

1908	10/6	Budapest	W7–0
1909	29/5	Budapest	W4–2
1909	31/5	Budapest	W8–2
1934	10/5	Budapest	L1–2
1936	2/12	Arsenal	W6–2
1953	25/11	Wembley	L3–6
1954	23/5	Budapest	L1–7
1960	22/5	Budapest	L0–2
1962	31/5	Rancagua	L1–2 (WCF)
1965	5/5	Wembley	W1–0
1978	24/5	Wembley	W4–1
1981	6/6	Budapest	W3–1 (WCQ)
1981	18/11	Wembley	W1–0 (WCQ)
1983	27/4	Wembley	W2–0 (ECQ)
1983	12/10	Budapest	W3–0 (ECQ)
1988	27/4	Budapest	D0–0
1990	12/9	Wembley	W1–0
1992	12/5	Budapest	W1–0

P18, W12, D1, L5, F47, A27

v Iceland

| 1982 | 2/6 | Reykjavik | D1–1 |

P1, W0, D1, L0, F1, A1

v Ireland

1882	18/2	Belfast	W13–0
1883	24/2	Liverpool	W7–0
1884	23/2	Belfast	W8–1
1885	28/2	Manchester	W4–0
1886	13/3	Belfast	W6–1
1887	5/2	Sheffield	W7–0
1888	31/3	Belfast	W5–1
1889	2/3	Everton	W6–1
1890	15/3	Belfast	W9–1
1891	7/3	Wolverhampton	W6–1
1892	5/3	Belfast	W2–0
1893	25/2	Birmingham	W6–1
1894	3/3	Belfast	D2–2
1895	9/3	Derby	W9–0
1896	7/3	Belfast	W2–0

Year	Date	Venue	Result
1897	20/2	Nottingham	W6–0
1898	5/3	Belfast	W3–2
1899	18/2	Sunderland	W13–2
1900	17/3	Dublin	W2–0
1901	9/3	Southampton	W3–0
1902	22/3	Belfast	W1–0
1903	14/2	Wolverhampton	W4–0
1904	12/3	Belfast	W3–1
1905	25/2	Middlesbrough	D1–1
1906	17/2	Belfast	W5–0
1907	16/2	Everton	W1–0
1908	15/2	Belfast	W3–1
1909	13/2	Bradford	W4–0
1910	12/2	Belfast	D1–1
1911	11/2	Derby	W2–1
1912	10/2	Dublin	W6–1
1913	15/2	Belfast	L1–2
1914	14/2	Middlesbrough	L0–3
1919	25/10	Belfast	D1–1
1920	23/10	Sunderland	W2–0
1921	22/10	Belfast	D1–1
1922	21/10	West Bromwich	W2–0
1923	20/10	Belfast	L1–2
1924	22/10	Everton	W3–1
1925	24/10	Belfast	D0–0
1926	20/10	Liverpool	D3–3
1927	22/10	Belfast	L0–2
1928	22/10	Everton	W2–1
1929	19/10	Belfast	W3–0
1930	20/10	Sheffield	W5–1
1931	17/10	Belfast	W6–2
1932	17/10	Blackpool	W1–0
1933	14/10	Belfast	W3–0
1935	6/2	Everton	W2–1
1935	19/10	Belfast	W3–1
1936	18/11	Stoke	W3–1
1937	23/10	Belfast	W5–1
1938	16/11	Manchester	W7–0
1946	28/9	Belfast	W7–2
1947	5/11	Everton	D2–2
1948	9/10	Belfast	W6–2
1949	16/11	Manchester	W9–2 (WCQ)
1950	7/10	Belfast	W4–1
1951	14/11	Aston Villa	W2–0
1952	4/10	Belfast	D2–2
1953	11/11	Everton	W3–1 (WCQ)
1954	2/10	Belfast	W2–0
1955	2/11	Wembley	W3–0
1956	6/10	Belfast	D1–1
1957	6/11	Wembley	L2–3
1958	4/10	Belfast	D3–3
1959	18/11	Wembley	W2–1
1960	8/10	Belfast	W5–2
1961	22/11	Wembley	D1–1
1962	20/10	Belfast	W3–1
1963	20/11	Wembley	W8–3
1964	3/10	Belfast	W4–3
1965	10/11	Wembley	W2–1
1966	20/10	Belfast	W2–0 (ECQ)
1967	22/11	Wembley	W2–0 (ECQ)
1969	3/5	Belfast	W3–1
1970	21/4	Wembley	W3–1
1971	15/5	Belfast	W1–0
1972	23/5	Wembley	L0–1
1973	12/5	Everton	W2–1
1974	15/5	Wembley	W1–0
1975	17/5	Belfast	D0–0
1976	11/5	Wembley	W4–0
1977	28/5	Belfast	W2–1
1978	16/5	Wembley	W1–0
1979	7/2	Wembley	W4–0 (ECQ)
1979	19/5	Belfast	W2–0
1979	17/10	Belfast	W5–1 (ECQ)
1980	20/5	Wembley	D1–1
1982	23/2	Wembley	W4–0
1983	28/5	Belfast	D0–0
1984	4/4	Wembley	W1–0
1985	27/2	Belfast	W1–0 (WCQ)
1985	13/11	Wembley	D0–0 (WCQ)
1986	15/10	Wembley	W3–0 (ECQ)
1987	1/4	Belfast	W2–0 (ECQ)

P96, W74, D16, L6, F319, A80

v Israel

1986	26/2	Tel Aviv	W2–1
1988	17/2	Tel Aviv	D0–0

P2, W1, D1, L0, F2, A1

v Italy

1933	13/5	Rome	D1–1
1934	14/11	Arsenal	W3–2
1939	13/5	Milan	D2–2
1948	16/5	Turin	W4–0
1949	30/11	Tottenham	W2–0
1952	18/5	Florence	D1–1
1959	6/5	Wembley	D2–2
1961	24/5	Rome	W3–2
1973	14/6	Turin	L0–2
1973	14/11	Wembley	L0–1
1976	28/5	New York	W3–2 (USBT)
1976	17/11	Rome	L0–2 (WCQ)
1977	16/11	Wembley	W2–0 (WCQ)
1980	15/6	Turin	L0–1 (ECF)
1985	6/6	Mexico City	L1–2
1989	15/11	Wembley	D0–0
1990	7/7	Bari	L1–2 (WCF)

P17, W6, D5, L6, F25, A22

v Kuwait

1982	25/6	Bilbao	W1–0 (WCF)

P1, W1, D0, L0, F1, A0

v Luxembourg

1927	21/5	Luxembourg	W5–2

1960	19/10	Luxembourg	W9–0 (WCQ)
1961	28/9	Arsenal	W4–1 (WCQ)
1977	30/3	Wembley	W5–0 (WCQ)
1977	12/10	Luxembourg	W2–0 (WCQ)
1982	15/12	Wembley	W9–0 (ECQ)
1983	16/11	Luxembourg	W4–0 (ECQ)

P7, W7, D0, L0, F38, A3

v Malaysia

1991	12/6	Kuala Lumpur	W4–2

P1, W1, D0, L0, F4, A2

v Malta

1971	3/2	Valletta	W1–0 (ECQ)
1971	12/5	Wembley	W5–0 (ECQ)

P2, W2, D0, L0, F6, A0

v Mexico

1959	24/5	Mexico City	L1–2
1961	10/5	Wembley	W8–0
1966	16/7	Wembley	W2–0 (WCF)
1969	1/6	Mexico City	D0–0
1985	9/6	Mexico City	L0–1
1986	17/5	Los Angeles	W3–0

P6, W3, D1, L2, F14, A3

v Morocco

1986	6/6	Monterrey	D0–0 (WCF)

P1, W0, D1, L0, F0, A0

v New Zealand

1991	3/6	Auckland	W1–0
1991	8/6	Wellington	W2–0

P2, W2, D0, L0, F3, A0

v Northern Ireland (see Ireland)

v Norway

1937	14/5	Oslo	W6–0
1938	9/11	Newcastle	W4–0
1949	18/5	Oslo	W4–1
1966	29/6	Oslo	W6–1
1980	10/9	Wembley	W4–0 (WCQ)
1981	9/9	Oslo	L1–2 (WCQ)
1992	14/10	Wembley	D1–1 (WCQ)
1993	2/6	Oslo	L0–2 (WCQ)
1994	22/5	Wembley	D0–0

P9, W5, D2, L2, F26, A7

v Paraguay

1986	18/6	Mexico City	W3–0 (WCF)

P1, W1, D0, L0, F3, A0

v Peru

1959	17/5	Lima	L1–4
1962	20/5	Lima	W4–0

P2, W1, D0, L1, F5, A4

v Poland

1966	5/1	Everton	D1–1
1966	5/7	Chorzow	W1–0
1973	6/6	Chorzow	L0–2 (WCQ)
1973	17/10	Wembley	D1–1 (WCQ)
1986	11/6	Monterrey	W3–0 (WCF)
1989	3/6	Wembley	W3–0 (WCQ)
1989	11/10	Katowice	D0–0 (WCQ)
1990	17/10	Wembley	W2–0 (ECQ)
1991	13/11	Poznan	D1–1 (ECQ)
1993	29/5	Katowice	D1–1 (WCQ)
1993	8/9	Wembley	W3–0 (WCQ)

P11, W5, D5, L1, F16, A6

v Portugal

1947	25/5	Lisbon	W10–0
1950	14/5	Lisbon	W5–3
1951	19/5	Everton	W5–2
1955	22/5	Oporto	L1–3
1958	7/5	Wembley	W2–1
1961	21/5	Lisbon	D1–1 (WCQ)
1961	25/10	Wembley	W2–0 (WCQ)
1964	17/5	Lisbon	W4–3
1964	4/6	São Paolo	D1–1 (BJT)
1966	26/7	Wembley	W2–1 (WCF)
1969	10/12	Wembley	W1–0
1974	3/4	Lisbon	D0–0
1974	20/11	Wembley	D0–0 (ECQ)
1975	19/11	Lisbon	D1–1 (ECQ)
1986	3/6	Monterrey	L0–1 (WCF)

P15, W8, D5, L2, F35, A17

v Republic of Ireland

1946	30/9	Dublin	W1–0
1949	21/9	Everton	L0–2
1957	8/5	Wembley	W5–1 (WCQ)
1957	19/5	Dublin	D1–1 (WCQ)
1964	24/5	Dublin	W3–1
1976	8/9	Wembley	D1–1
1978	25/10	Dublin	D1–1 (ECQ)
1980	6/2	Wembley	W2–0 (ECQ)
1985	26/3	Wembley	W2–1
1988	12/6	Stuttgart	L0–1 (ECF)
1990	11/6	Cagliari	D1–1 (WCF)
1990	14/11	Dublin	D1–1 (ECQ)
1991	27/3	Wembley	D1–1 (ECQ)

P13, W5, D6, L2, F19, A12

v Rest of Europe

1938	26/10	Arsenal	W3–0

P1, W1, D0, L0, F3, A0

v Rest of the World

| 1963 | 23/10 | Wembley | W2–1 |

P1, W1, D0, L0, F2, A1

v Romania

1939	24/5	Bucharest	W2–0
1968	6/11	Bucharest	D0–0
1969	15/1	Wembley	D1–1
1970	2/6	Guadalajara	W1–0 (WCF)
1980	15/10	Bucharest	L1–2 (WCQ)
1981	29/4	Wembley	D0–0 (WCQ)
1985	1/5	Bucharest	D0–0 (WCQ)
1985	11/9	Wembley	D1–1 (WCQ)

P8, W2, D5, L1, F6, A4

v San Marino

| 1993 | 17/2 | Wembley | W6–0 (WCQ) |
| 1993 | 17/11 | Bologna | W7–1 (WCQ) |

P2, W2, D0, L0, F13, A1

v Saudi Arabia

| 1988 | 16/11 | Riyadh | D1–1 |

P1, W0, D1, L0, F1, A1

v Scotland

1872	30/11	Glasgow	D0–0
1873	8/3	Kennington	W4–2
1874	7/3	Glasgow	L1–2
1875	6/3	Kennington	D2–2
1876	4/3	Glasgow	L0–3
1877	3/3	Kennington	L1–3
1878	2/3	Glasgow	L2–7
1879	5/4	Kennington	W5–4
1880	13/3	Glasgow	L4–5
1881	12/3	Kennington	L1–6
1882	11/3	Glasgow	L1–5
1883	10/3	Sheffield	L2–3
1884	15/3	Glasgow	L0–1
1885	21/3	Kennington	D1–1
1886	31/3	Glasgow	D1–1
1887	19/3	Blackburn	L2–3
1888	17/3	Glasgow	W5–0
1889	13/4	Kennington	L2–3
1890	5/4	Glasgow	D1–1
1891	6/4	Blackburn	W2–1
1892	2/4	Glasgow	W4–1
1893	1/4	Richmond	W5–2
1894	7/4	Glasgow	D2–2
1895	6/4	Everton	W3–0
1896	4/4	Glasgow	L1–2
1897	3/4	Crystal Palace	L1–2
1898	2/4	Glasgow	W3–1
1899	8/4	Birmingham	W2–1
1900	7/4	Glasgow	L1–4
1901	30/3	Crystal Palace	D2–2
1902	3/3	Birmingham	D2–2
1903	4/4	Sheffield	L1–2
1904	9/4	Glasgow	W1–0
1905	1/4	Crystal Palace	W1–0
1906	7/4	Glasgow	L1–2
1907	6/4	Newcastle	D1–1
1908	4/4	Glasgow	D1–1
1909	3/4	Crystal Palace	W2–0
1910	2/4	Glasgow	L0–2
1911	1/4	Everton	D1–1
1912	23/3	Glasgow	D1–1
1913	5/4	Chelsea	W1–0
1914	14/4	Glasgow	L1–3
1920	10/4	Sheffield	W5–4
1921	9/4	Glasgow	L0–3
1922	8/4	Aston Villa	L0–1
1923	14/4	Glasgow	D2–2
1924	12/4	Wembley	D1–1
1925	4/4	Glasgow	L0–2
1926	17/4	Manchester	L0–1
1927	2/4	Glasgow	W2–1
1928	31/3	Wembley	L1–5
1929	13/4	Glasgow	L0–1
1930	5/4	Wembley	W5–2
1931	28/3	Glasgow	L0–2
1932	9/4	Wembley	W3–0
1933	1/4	Glasgow	L1–2
1934	14/4	Wembley	W3–0
1935	6/4	Glasgow	L0–2
1936	4/4	Wembley	D1–1
1937	17/4	Glasgow	L1–3
1938	9/4	Wembley	L0–1
1939	15/4	Glasgow	W2–1
1947	12/4	Wembley	D1–1
1948	10/4	Glasgow	W2–0
1949	9/4	Wembley	L1–3
1950	15/4	Glasgow	W1–0 (WCQ)
1951	14/4	Wembley	L2–3
1952	5/4	Glasgow	W2–1
1953	18/4	Wembley	D2–2
1954	3/4	Glasgow	W4–2 (WCQ)
1955	2/4	Wembley	W7–2
1956	14/4	Glasgow	D1–1
1957	6/4	Wembley	W2–1
1958	19/4	Glasgow	W4–0
1959	11/4	Wembley	W1–0
1960	19/4	Glasgow	D1–1
1961	15/4	Wembley	W9–3
1962	14/4	Glasgow	L0–2
1963	6/4	Wembley	L1–2
1964	11/4	Glasgow	L0–1
1965	10/4	Wembley	D2–2
1966	2/4	Glasgow	W4–3
1967	15/4	Wembley	L2–3 (ECQ)
1968	24/2	Glasgow	D1–1 (ECQ)
1969	10/5	Wembley	W4–1
1970	25/4	Glasgow	D0–0
1971	22/5	Wembley	W3–1
1972	27/5	Glasgow	W1–0

1973	14/2	Glasgow	W5–0
1973	19/5	Wembley	W1–0
1974	18/5	Glasgow	L0–2
1975	24/5	Wembley	W5–1
1976	15/5	Glasgow	L1–2
1977	4/6	Wembley	L1–2
1978	20/5	Glasgow	W1–0
1979	26/5	Wembley	W3–1
1980	24/5	Glasgow	W2–0
1981	23/5	Wembley	L0–1
1982	29/5	Glasgow	W1–0
1983	1/6	Wembley	W2–0
1984	26/5	Glasgow	D1–1
1985	25/5	Glasgow	L0–1 (RC)
1986	23/4	Wembley	W2–1 (RC)
1987	23/5	Glasgow	D0–0 (RC)
1988	21/5	Wembley	W1–0 (RC)
1989	27/5	Glasgow	W2–0 (RC)

P107, W43, D24, L40, F188, A168

v Spain

1929	15/5	Madrid	L3–4
1931	9/12	Arsenal	W7–1
1950	2/7	Rio de Janeiro	L0–1 (WCF)
1955	18/5	Madrid	D1–1
1955	30/11	Wembley	W4–1
1960	15/5	Madrid	L0–3
1960	26/10	Wembley	W4–2
1965	8/12	Madrid	W2–0
1967	24/5	Wembley	W2–0
1968	3/4	Wembley	W1–0 (ECQ)
1968	8/5	Madrid	W2–1 (ECQ)
1980	26/3	Barcelona	W2–0
1980	18/6	Naples	W2–1 (ECF)
1981	25/3	Wembley	L1–2
1982	5/7	Madrid	D0–0 (WCF)
1987	18/2	Madrid	W4–2
1992	9/9	Santander	L0–1

P17, W10, D2, L5, F35, A20

v Sweden

1923	21/5	Stockholm	W4–2
1923	24/5	Stockholm	W3–1
1937	17/5	Stockholm	W4–0
1947	19/11	Arsenal	W4–2
1949	13/5	Stockholm	L1–3
1956	16/5	Stockholm	D0–0
1959	28/10	Wembley	L2–3
1965	16/5	Gothenburg	W2–1
1968	22/5	Wembley	W3–1
1979	10/6	Stockholm	D0–0
1986	10/6	Stockholm	L0–1
1988	19/10	Wembley	D0–0 (WCQ)
1989	6/9	Stockholm	D0–0 (WCQ)
1992	17/6	Stockholm	L1–2 (ECF)

P14, W6, D4, L4, F24, A16

v Switzerland

1933	29/5	Berne	W4–0
1938	21/5	Zurich	L1–2
1947	18/5	Zurich	L0–1
1948	2/12	Arsenal	W6–0
1952	28/5	Zurich	W3–0
1954	20/6	Berne	W2–0 (WCF)
1962	9/5	Wembley	W3–1
1963	5/6	Basle	W8–1
1971	13/10	Basle	W3–2 (ECQ)
1971	10/11	Wembley	D1–1 (ECQ)
1975	3/9	Basle	W2–1
1977	7/9	Wembley	D0–0
1980	19/11	Wembley	W2–1 (WCQ)
1981	30/5	Basle	L1–2 (WCQ)
1988	28/5	Lausanne	W1–0

P15, W10, D2, L3, F37, A12

v Tunisia

1990	2/6	Tunis	D1–1

P1, W0, D1, L0, F1, A1

v Turkey

1984	14/11	Istanbul	W8–0 (WCQ)
1985	16/10	Wembley	W5–0 (WCQ)
1987	29/4	Izmir	D0–0 (ECQ)
1987	14/10	Wembley	W8–0 (ECQ)
1991	1/5	Izmir	W1–0 (ECQ)
1991	16/10	Wembley	W1–0 (ECQ)
1992	18/11	Wembley	W4–0 (WCQ)
1993	31/3	Izmir	W2–0 (WCQ)

P8, W7, D1, L0, F29, A0

v USA

1950	29/6	Belo Horizonte	L0–1 (WCF)
1953	8/6	New York	W6–3
1959	28/5	Los Angeles	W8–1
1964	27/5	New York	W10–0
1985	16/6	Los Angeles	W5–0
1993	9/6	Boston	L0–2 (USC)

P6, W4, D0, L2, F29, A7

v USSR (see also CIS)

1958	18/5	Moscow	D1–1
1958	8/6	Gothenburg	D2–2 (WCF)
1958	17/6	Gothenburg	L0–1 (WCF)
1958	22/10	Wembley	W5–0
1967	6/12	Wembley	D2–2
1968	8/6	Rome	W2–0 (ECF)
1973	10/6	Moscow	W2–1
1984	2/6	Wembley	L0–2
1986	26/3	Tbilisi	W1–0
1988	18/6	Frankfurt	L1–3 (ECF)
1991	21/5	Wembley	W3–1

P11, W5, D3, L3, F19, A13

v Uruguay

1953	31/5	Montevideo	L1–2
1954	26/6	Basle	L2–4 (WCF)
1964	6/5	Wembley	W2–1
1966	11/7	Wembley	D0–0 (WCF)
1969	8/6	Montevideo	W2–1
1977	15/6	Montevideo	D0–0
1984	13/6	Montevideo	L0–2
1990	22/5	Wembley	L1–2

P8, W2, D2, L4, F8, A12

v Wales

1879	18/1	Kennington	W2–1
1880	15/3	Wrexham	W3–2
1881	26/2	Blackburn	L0–1
1882	13/3	Wrexham	L3–5
1883	3/2	Kennington	W5–0
1884	17/3	Wrexham	W4–0
1885	14/3	Blackburn	D1–1
1886	29/3	Wrexham	W3–1
1887	26/2	Kennington	W4–0
1888	4/2	Crewe	W5–1
1889	23/2	Stoke	W4–1
1890	15/3	Wrexham	W3–1
1891	7/5	Sunderland	W4–1
1892	5/3	Wrexham	W2–0
1893	13/3	Stoke	W6–0
1894	12/3	Wrexham	W5–1
1895	18/3	Kensington	D1–1
1896	16/3	Cardiff	W9–1
1897	29/3	Sheffield	W4–0
1898	28/3	Wrexham	W3–0
1899	20/3	Bristol	W4–0
1900	26/3	Cardiff	D1–1
1901	18/3	Newcastle	W6–0
1902	3/3	Wrexham	D0–0
1903	2/3	Portsmouth	W2–1
1904	29/2	Wrexham	D2–2
1905	27/3	Liverpool	W3–1
1906	19/3	Cardiff	W1–0
1907	18/3	Fulham	D1–1
1908	16/3	Wrexham	W7–1
1909	15/3	Nottingham	W2–0
1910	14/3	Cardiff	W1–0
1911	13/3	Millwall	W3–0
1912	11/3	Wrexham	W2–0
1913	17/3	Bristol	W4–3
1914	16/3	Cardiff	W2–0
1920	15/3	Arsenal	L1–2
1921	14/3	Cardiff	D0–0
1922	13/3	Liverpool	W1–0
1923	5/3	Cardiff	D2–2
1924	3/3	Blackburn	L1–2
1925	28/2	Swansea	W2–1
1926	1/3	Crystal Palace	L1–3
1927	12/2	Wrexham	D3–3
1927	28/11	Burnley	L1–2
1928	17/11	Swansea	W3–2

1929	20/11	Chelsea	W6–0
1930	22/11	Wrexham	W4–0
1931	18/11	Liverpool	W3–1
1932	16/11	Wrexham	D0–0
1933	15/11	Newcastle	L1–2
1934	29/9	Cardiff	W4–0
1936	5/2	Wolverhampton	L1–2
1936	17/10	Cardiff	L1–2
1937	17/11	Middlesbrough	W2–1
1938	22/10	Cardiff	L2–4
1946	13/11	Manchester	W3–0
1947	18/10	Cardiff	W3–0
1948	10/11	Aston Villa	W1–0
1949	15/10	Cardiff	W4–1 (WCQ)
1950	15/11	Sunderland	W4–2
1951	20/10	Cardiff	D1–1
1952	12/11	Wembley	W5–2
1953	10/10	Cardiff	W4–1 (WCQ)
1954	10/11	Wembley	W3–2
1955	22/10	Cardiff	L1–2
1956	14/11	Wembley	W3–1
1957	19/10	Cardiff	W4–0
1958	26/11	Aston Villa	D2–2
1959	17/10	Cardiff	D1–1
1960	23/11	Wembley	W5–1
1961	14/10	Cardiff	D1–1
1962	21/11	Wembley	W4–0
1963	12/10	Cardiff	W4–0
1964	18/11	Wembley	W2–1
1965	2/10	Cardiff	D0–0
1966	16/11	Wembley	W5–1 (ECQ)
1967	21/10	Cardiff	W3–0 (ECQ)
1969	7/5	Wembley	W2–1
1970	18/4	Cardiff	D1–1
1971	19/5	Wembley	D0–0
1972	20/5	Cardiff	W3–0
1972	15/11	Cardiff	W1–0 (WCQ)
1973	24/1	Wembley	D1–1 (WCQ)
1973	15/5	Wembley	W3–0
1974	11/5	Cardiff	W2–0
1975	21/5	Wembley	D2–2
1976	24/3	Wrexham	W2–1
1976	8/5	Cardiff	W1–0
1977	31/5	Wembley	L0–1
1978	3/5	Cardiff	W3–1
1979	23/5	Wembley	D0–0
1980	17/5	Wrexham	L1–4
1981	20/5	Wembley	D0–0
1982	27/4	Cardiff	W1–0
1983	23/2	Wembley	W2–1
1984	2/5	Wrexham	L0–1

P97, W62, D21, L14, F239, A90

v Yugoslavia

1939	18/5	Belgrade	L1–2
1950	22/11	Highbury	D2–2
1954	16/5	Belgrade	L0–1
1956	28/11	Wembley	W3–0

84

1958	11/5	Belgrade	L0–5	1974	5/6	Belgrade	D2–2
1960	11/5	Wembley	D3–3	1986	12/11	Wembley	W2–0 (ECQ)
1965	9/5	Belgrade	D1–1	1987	11/11	Belgrade	W4–1 (ECQ)
1966	4/5	Wembley	W2–0	1989	13/12	Wembley	W2–1
1968	5/6	Florence	L0–1 (ECF)				
1972	11/10	Wembley	D1–1	P14, W5, D5, L4, F23, A20			

Terry Venables – the new England coach.

Semi-Professional International/FA Representative Matches 1993–1994

FA XI 6   Herefordshire FA 2
29th September 1993, Hereford United FC

FA XI: Cooksey (Bromsgrove Rovers), Bloomfield (Gloucester City), Vickers (Worcester City), Richardson (Bromsgrove Rovers), Clark (Cheltenham Town), Webb (Bromsgrove Rovers), Purdie (Kidderminster Harriers), Hodges (Worcester City), Davies (Kidderminster Harriers), Cook (Gloucester City), Smith G. (Worcester City).
Subs.: Preedy (Hereford United) for Hodges, Watkins A. (Solihull Borough) for Cooksey, Watkins J. (Hereford United) for Purdie.
Scorers: Cook 2, Purdie 2, Webb, Preedy.
Team Manager: John Layton.

FA XI 1   Western League 4
19th October 1993, Tiverton Town FC

FA XI: Teasdale (Trowbridge Town), Bowles (Cinderford Town), Meacham (Shortwood United), Thorpe (Trowbridge Town), Kilgour (Trowbridge Town), Gillard (Clevedon Town), Knight (Trowbridge Town), Batty (Bath City), McPherson (Yeovil Town), Dann (Wadebridge Town), Harrower (Yeovil Town).
Subs.: Bush (Trowbridge Town) for Teasdale, Rutter (Yeovil Town) for Dann.
Scorer: Batty.
Team Manager: Tony Passey.

FA XI 1   Southern League 4
3rd November 1993, Nuneaton Borough FC

FA XI: Cooksey (Bromsgrove Rovers), Hodson (Kidderminster Harriers), Parrish (Telford United), Weir and Brindley (Kidderminster Harriers), Butterworth (Dagenham & Redbridge), Williams (Stafford Rangers), Bignot (Telford United), Burr (Stafford Rangers), Davies and Purdie (Kidderminster Harriers).
Subs.: Bodkin (Stafford Rangers) for Bignot, Pritchard (Telford United) for Hodson, Carrington (Kidderminster Harriers) for Cooksey.
Scorer: Burr.
Team Manager: Graham Allner.

FA XI 0   Northern Premier League 2
16th November 1993, Chorley FC

FA XI: Mason (Witton Albion), Shepherd and Bimson (Macclesfield Town), Butler and Parker (Northwich Victoria), Mooney (Southport), Constable (Halifax Town), Alford and Askey (Macclesfield Town), Burke (Witton Albion), Gamble (Southport).
Subs.: Brabin (Runcorn) for Gamble, Hughes (Stalybridge Celtic) for Mason, Dove (Southport) for Mooney.
Team Manager: Peter Wragg.

FA XI 1   Isthmian League 2
7th December 1993, Enfield FC

FA XI: Williams (Welling United), Stebbing and Watts (Dagenham & Redbridge), Hone (Welling United), Conner (Dagenham & Redbridge), Biggins (Woking), Jackson (Dover Athletic), Broom (Dagenham & Redbridge), Abbott (Welling United), Leworthy (Dover Athletic), Fiore (Slough Town).
Subs.: Keen (Chelmsford City) for Stebbing, Batty (Woking) for Williams, Fielder (Woking) for Abbott, Milton (Dover Athletic) for Biggins.
Scorer: Broom.
Team Manager: John Still.

FA XI 2   Combined Services 2
11th January 1994, Spennymoor United FC

FA XI: Popple (Billingham Synthonia), Atkinson (Guiseley), O'Brien (Billingham Synthonia), Ainsley (Spennymoor United), Wrightson (Gateshead), Alcide (Emley), Farrey (Gateshead), Ord (Durham City), Lamb (Gateshead), Suddick (Whitley Bay), Saunders (Spennymoor United).
Subs.: Race (Durham City) for Popple, Peattie (Blyth Spartans) for Saunders, Parkinson (Gateshead) for Ainsley, Saunders for O'Brien.
Scorers: Lamb, Ord.
Team Managers: Ron Reid, Colin Richardson.

Wales 1   England 2
22nd February 1994, Bangor City FC

England: Benstead (Kettering Town), Hodson (Kidderminster Harriers), Brighton and Richardson (Bromsgrove Rovers), Holden (Kettering Town), Brabin (Runcorn), Humphreys (Kidderminster Harriers), Webb (Bromsgrove Rovers), Robbins (Welling United), Leworthy (Dover Athletic), Collins (Enfield).
Subs.: Hone (Welling United) for Hodson, Ross (Marine) for Leworthy, Venables (Stevenage Borough) for Collins.
Scorers: Webb, Humphreys.
Team Manager: Tony Jennings.

Guernsey 1   England 3
14th March 1994, St Martins FC

England: Rose (Kettering Town), Simpson (Stafford Rangers), Brighton (Bromsgrove Rovers), Hone (Welling United), Richardson (Bromsgrove Rovers), Brabin (Runcorn), Venables (Stevenage Borough), Brown D. (Woking), Robbins (Welling United), Browne C. and Milton (Dover Athletic).
Subs.: Hodson (Kidderminster Harriers) for Richardson, Williams (Welling United) for Rose, Webb (Bromsgrove Rovers) for Brabin, Bartlett (Dover Athletic) for Brighton.
Scorers: Browne 2, Venables.
Team Manager: Tony Jennings.

Finland U-21 2   England 0
30th May 1994, Aanekoski FC

England: Benstead (Kettering Town), Simpson (Stafford Rangers), Ashby and Holden (Kettering Town), Richardson and Webb (Bromsgrove Rovers), Milton (Dover Athletic), Humphreys (Kidderminster Harriers), Robbins (Welling United), Collins (Enfield), Brabin (Runcorn).
Subs.: Hodson (Kidderminster Harriers) for Simpson, Rose (Kidderminster Harriers) for Benstead, Hone (Welling United) for Holden, Browne C. (Dover Athletic) for Webb, Brown D. (Woking) for Robbins.
Team Manager: Tony Jennings.

Norway U-21 2   England 1
1st June 1994, Slemmenstad

England: Rose and Hodson (Kidderminster Harriers), Ashby (Kettering Town), Hone (Welling United), Richardson (Bromsgrove Rovers), Brown D. (Woking), Milton (Dover Athletic), Humphreys (Kidderminster Harriers), Robbins (Welling United), Collins (Enfield), Brabin (Runcorn).
Subs.: Holden (Kettering Town) for Hone, Browne C. (Dover Athletic) for Robbins, Simpson (Stafford Rangers) for Milton, Benstead (Kettering Town) for Rose, Webb (Bromsgrove Rovers) for Collins.
Scorer: Browne C.
Team Manager: Tony Jennings.

FA Challenge Cup Winners 1872–1994

Final venues:

1872 & 1874–92	Kennington Oval	1895–1914	Crystal Palace
1873	Lillie Bridge, London	1915	Old Trafford, Manchester
1893	Fallowfield, Manchester	1920–22	Stamford Bridge, London
1894	Goodison Park, Liverpool	1923 to date	Wembley Stadium

Year	Winners		Runners-up	Result	
1872	Wanderers	v	Royal Engineers	1–0	
1873	Wanderers	v	Oxford University	2–0	
1874	Oxford University	v	Royal Engineers	2–0	
1875	Royal Engineers	v	Old Etonians	2–0	after 1–1 draw
1876	Wanderers	v	Old Etonians	3–0	after 0–0 draw
1877	Wanderers	v	Oxford University	2–0	after extra time
1878	*Wanderers	v	Royal Engineers	3–1	
1879	Old Etonians	v	Clapham Rovers	1–0	
1880	Clapham Rovers	v	Oxford University	1–0	
1881	Old Carthusians	v	Old Etonians	3–0	
1882	Old Etonians	v	Blackburn Rovers	1–0	
1883	Blackburn Olympic	v	Old Etonians	2–1	after extra time
1884	Blackburn Rovers	v	Queen's Park, Glasgow	2–1	
1885	Blackburn Rovers	v	Queen's Park, Glasgow	2–0	
1886	†Blackburn Rovers	v	West Bromwich Albion	2–0	after 0–0 draw
1887	Aston Villa	v	West Bromwich Albion	2–0	
1888	West Bromwich Albion	v	Preston North End	2–1	
1889	Preston North End	v	Wolverhampton Wanderers	3–0	
1890	Blackburn Rovers	v	Sheffield Wednesday	6–1	
1891	Blackburn Rovers	v	Notts County	3–1	
1892	West Bromwich Albion	v	Aston Villa	3–0	
1893	Wolverhampton Wanderers	v	Everton	1–0	
1894	Notts County	v	Bolton Wanderers	4–1	
1895	Aston Villa	v	West Bromwich Albion	1–0	
1896	Sheffield Wednesday	v	Wolverhampton Wanderers	2–1	
1897	Aston Villa	v	Everton	3–2	
1898	Nottingham Forest	v	Derby County	3–1	
1899	Sheffield United	v	Derby County	4–1	
1900	Bury	v	Southampton	4–0	
1901	Tottenham Hotspur	v	Sheffield United	3–1	after 2–2 draw
1902	Sheffield United	v	Southampton	2–1	after 1–1 draw
1903	Bury	v	Derby County	6–0	
1904	Manchester City	v	Bolton Wanderers	1–0	
1905	Aston Villa	v	Newcastle United	2–0	
1906	Everton	v	Newcastle United	1–0	
1907	Sheffield Wednesday	v	Everton	2–1	
1908	Wolverhampton Wanderers	v	Newcastle United	3–1	
1909	Manchester United	v	Bristol City	1–0	
1910	Newcastle United	v	Barnsley	2–0	after 1–1 draw
1911	Bradford City	v	Newcastle United	1–0	after 0–0 draw
1912	Barnsley	v	West Bromwich Albion	1–0	after 0–0 draw
1913	Aston Villa	v	Sunderland	1–0	
1914	Burnley	v	Liverpool	1–0	
1915	Sheffield United	v	Chelsea	3–0	
1920	Aston Villa	v	Huddersfield Town	1–0	after extra time
1921	Tottenham Hotspur	v	Wolverhampton Wanderers	1–0	

* *Won outright but restored to The Association*
† *A special trophy was awarded for third consecutive win*

Year	Winners		Runners-up	Result	
1922	Huddersfield Town	v	Preston North End	1–0	
1923	Bolton Wanderers	v	West Ham United	2–0	
1924	Newcastle United	v	Aston Villa	2–0	
1925	Sheffield United	v	Cardiff City	1–0	
1926	Bolton Wanderers	v	Manchester City	1–0	
1927	Cardiff City	v	Arsenal	1–0	
1928	Blackburn Rovers	v	Huddersfield Town	3–1	
1929	Bolton Wanderers	v	Portsmouth	2–0	
1930	Arsenal	v	Huddersfield Town	2–0	
1931	West Bromwich Albion	v	Birmingham City	2–1	
1932	Newcastle United	v	Arsenal	2–1	
1933	Everton	v	Manchester City	3–0	
1934	Manchester City	v	Portsmouth	2–1	
1935	Sheffield Wednesday	v	West Bromwich Albion	4–2	
1936	Arsenal	v	Sheffield United	1–0	
1937	Sunderland	v	Preston North End	3–1	
1938	Preston North End	v	Huddersfield Town	1–0	after extra time
1939	Portsmouth	v	Wolverhampton Wanderers	4–1	
1946	Derby County	v	Charlton Athletic	4–1	after extra time
1947	Charlton Athletic	v	Burnley	1–0	after extra time
1948	Manchester United	v	Blackpool	4–2	
1949	Wolverhampton Wanderers	v	Leicester City	3–1	
1950	Arsenal	v	Liverpool	2–0	
1951	Newcastle United	v	Blackpool	2–0	
1952	Newcastle United	v	Arsenal	1–0	
1953	Blackpool	v	Bolton Wanderers	4–3	
1954	West Bromwich Albion	v	Preston North End	3–2	
1955	Newcastle United	v	Manchester City	3–1	
1956	Manchester City	v	Birmingham City	3–1	
1957	Aston Villa	v	Manchester United	2–1	
1958	Bolton Wanderers	v	Manchester United	2–0	
1959	Nottingham Forest	v	Luton Town	2–1	
1960	Wolverhampton Wanderers	v	Blackburn Rovers	3–0	
1961	Tottenham Hotspur	v	Leicester City	2–0	
1962	Tottenham Hotspur	v	Burnley	3–1	
1963	Manchester United	v	Leicester City	3–1	
1964	West Ham United	v	Preston North End	3–2	
1965	Liverpool	v	Leeds United	2–1	after extra time
1966	Everton	v	Sheffield Wednesday	3–2	
1967	Tottenham Hotspur	v	Chelsea	2–1	
1968	West Bromwich Albion	v	Everton	1–0	after extra time
1969	Manchester City	v	Leicester City	1–0	
1970	Chelsea	v	Leeds United	2–1	after 2–2 draw both games extra time
1971	Arsenal	v	Liverpool	2–1	after extra time
1972	Leeds United	v	Arsenal	1–0	
1973	Sunderland	v	Leeds United	1–0	
1974	Liverpool	v	Newcastle United	3–0	
1975	West Ham United	v	Fulham	2–0	
1976	Southampton	v	Manchester United	1–0	
1977	Manchester United	v	Liverpool	2–1	
1978	Ipswich Town	v	Arsenal	1–0	
1979	Arsenal	v	Manchester United	3–2	
1980	West Ham United	v	Arsenal	1–0	
1981	Tottenham Hotspur	v	Manchester City	3–2	after 1–1 draw after extra time

Year	Winners		Runners-up	Result
1982	Tottenham Hotspur	v	Queens Park Rangers	1–0 after 1–1 draw after extra time
1983	Manchester United	v	Brighton & Hove Albion	4–0 after 2–2 draw after extra time
1984	Everton	v	Watford	2–0
1985	Manchester United	v	Everton	1–0 after extra time
1986	Liverpool	v	Everton	3–1
1987	Coventry City	v	Tottenham Hotspur	3–2 after extra time
1988	Wimbledon	v	Liverpool	1–0
1989	Liverpool	v	Everton	3–2 after extra time
1990	Manchester United	v	Crystal Palace	1–0 after 3–3 draw after extra time
1991	Tottenham Hotspur	v	Nottingham Forest	2–1 after extra time
1992	Liverpool	v	Sunderland	2–0
1993	Arsenal	v	Sheffield Wednesday	2–1 after 1–1 draw both games extra time
1994	Manchester United	v	Chelsea	4–0

Paul Ince and Mark Stein in a determined chase for the ball.

FA Challenge Cup – Final Tie 1994

Manchester United 4   Chelsea 0

The 113th FA Cup Final saw Manchester United become the fourth team this century – and the sixth in history – to achieve the League and Cup 'double' in one season. They equalled Tottenham's record of eight Final victories and their 4–0 win was the biggest in the Final since United beat Brighton by the same score in the replay of 1983. Eric Cantona, the first Frenchman to feature in the annual Wembley showpiece, also became the first player ever to score a brace of goals from the penalty mark.

United began the match as clear favourites. Yet they had been a mere 40 seconds from defeat when Hughes' spectacular volley at Wembley forced a semi-final replay with Oldham. And Chelsea had already beaten United twice in the Premiership (1–0, Peacock scoring, both times).

Chelsea arguably shaded the first half in the Final, which had Johnsen yellow-carded in only the second minute for upending Giggs in full flight and United skipper Bruce disciplined in similar fashion for a late tackle on the tricky Spencer after 15 minutes. The highlight of the half was certainly a Peacock left-footer from outside the box which flew over Schmeichel and thudded against the face of the crossbar. Agony for the Londoners in their first Final for 24 years.

Wembley was as colourful as ever, with reds and blues everywhere, but the sky was an unremitting grey. There was drizzly rain throughout the match and the floodlights were on for the second half. Things got even greyer for Chelsea as a nightmare spell of nine minutes around the middle of the second half saw them, incredibly, three goals in arrears and virtually out of contention.

First Eddie Newton, who had a busy, impressive first half in which he never seemed to lose possession in midfield, was much too late as he attempted to block Irwin's progress after Giggs had toe-ended the ball into his path. The United full-back was scythed down well into the box and the referee, himself almost on top of the incident, only had one option. Cantona sent Kharine the wrong way for 1–0 (60 minutes 48 seconds).

Six minutes later the Frenchman completed his unique penalty double after Sinclair had given Kanchelskis a substantial nudge as he hurtled into the box to meet Hughes' astute pass. The award was less clear-cut than the previous one and Chelsea looked stunned. Cantona, unmoved, stepped up to strike the ball cleanly into exactly the same part of Kharine's goal. Player-manager Glenn Hoddle, a veteran of three FA Cup Finals, decided it was time to enter the fray – but, for the Blues, the game was up.

Any doubt about that was removed within three minutes as Hughes took clinical advantage of Sinclair's slip to run on and blast a low shot into the far corner. Chelsea ended with a flourish, forcing United's Danish goalkeeper Schmeichel to save brilliantly from Wise, Peacock and Spencer, but there was no consolation goal. Just the sight of Ince rounding Kharine and unselfishly rolling the ball across the face of the goal for substitute McClair to side-foot into an unguarded net. Chelsea had hardly deserved to lose by four.

Manchester United: Schmeichel, Parker, Irwin (Sharpe), Bruce, Pallister, Keane, Kanchelskis (McClair), Ince, Cantona, Hughes, Giggs.
Chelsea: Kharine, Clarke, Sinclair, Kjeldbjerg, Johnsen, Newton, Spencer, Burley (Hoddle), Stein (Cascarino), Peacock, Wise.
Referee: D. Elleray (Harrow).
Chief Guest: HRH The Duchess of Kent.
Attendance: 79,634.

FA Cup 1993–1994

PRELIMINARY ROUND   28th August 1993

(replays in italics)

			Result	Att
Consett	v	Willington	5–2	44
Billingham Town	v	Alnwick Town	1–1	78
Alnwick	v	*Billingham Town*	*1–2*	85
Yorkshire Amateur	v	Brandon United	2–1	82
Billingham Synthonia	v	Darlington CS	3–0	75
Harrogate Town	v	Peterlee Newtown	5–2	249
Evenwood Town	v	Ferryhill Athletic	3–1	71
Esh Winning	v	Gretna	0–1	35
Horden CW	v	Hebburn	4–4	100
Hebburn	v	*Horden CW*	*2–1*	260
Ryhope CA	v	Prudhoe East End	0–3	25
Shildon	v	South Shields		
(walkover for Shildon – South Shields removed from the competition)				
Pickering Town	v	Penrith	5–2	92
Workington	v	Crook Town	0–2	234
Tow Law Town	v	West Auckland Town	1–0	118
Lancaster City	v	Whickham	3–1	90
Murton	v	Durham City	3–2	130
Atherton LR	v	Blackpool (Wren) Rovers	1–1	100
Blackpool (Wren) Rovers	v	*Atherton LR*	*1–6*	170
Alfreton Town	v	Armthorpe Welfare	3–2	100
Blidworth MW	v	Arnold Town	1–4	120
Belper Town	v	Bamber Bridge	1–2	159
Caernarfon Town	v	Burscough	0–0	59
Burscough	v	*Caernarfon Town*	*2–0*	150
Clitheroe	v	Congleton Town	1–0	111

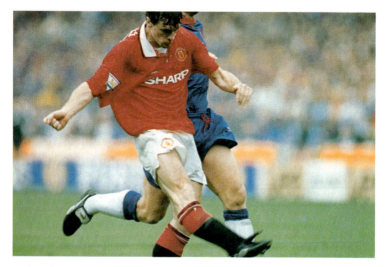

Mark Hughes slams home United's third goal.

			Result	Att
Warrington Town	v	Bradford Park Avenue	5–0	248
Flixton	v	Farsley Celtic	2–0	115
Glasshoughton Welfare	v	Glossop North End	0–2	110
Eccleshill United	v	Denaby United	2–2	90
Denaby United	v	*Eccleshill United*	*2–1*	90
Hucknall Town	v	Chadderton	4–0	260
Great Harwood Town	v	Guiseley	1–5	210
Ossett Town	v	Harworth CI	5–3	120
Immingham Town	v	Ilkeston Town	1–3	112
Newcastle Town	v	Ossett Albion	1–1	55
Ossett Albion	v	*Newcastle Town*	*1–2*	111
Maine Road	v	Maltby MW	0–1	63
Lincoln United	v	Mossley	4–2	150
Oldham Town	v	North Ferriby United	1–3	72
Skelmersdale United	v	Thackley	0–1	100
Rossendale United	v	Rossington Main	3–0	184
Radcliffe Borough	v	Salford City	1–3	145
Stocksbridge Park Steels	v	St Helens Town	1–2	192
Wednesfield	v	Eastwood Town	1–0	66
West Bromwich Town	v	Willenhall Town	1–3	92
Winterton Rangers	v	Prescot	2–0	70
Bilston Town	v	Bridgnorth Town	0–2	88
Armitage	v	Banbury United	1–0	60
Chasetown	v	Barwell	2–1	89
Boldmere St Michaels	v	Blakenall	2–0	101
Halesowen Harriers	v	Leicester United	2–4	70
Dudley Town	v	Eastwood Hanley	2–1	127
Desborough Town	v	Evesham United	1–0	69
Hinckley Town	v	Hinckley Athletic	2–1	303
Long Buckby	v	Redditch United	2–2	85
Redditch United	v	*Long Buckby*	*3–1*	122
Lye Town	v	Northampton Spencer	1–2	142
Daventry Town	v	Oldbury United	0–3	49
Racing Club Warwick	v	Pershore Town	1–2	136
Stewarts & Lloyds	v	Stratford Town	1–3	33
Rothwell Town	v	Rushall Olympic	2–0	120
Rocester	v	Rushden & Diamonds	0–1	169
Stourport Swifts	v	Stourbridge	0–0	128
Stourbridge	v	*Stourport Swifts*	*2–1*	173
Brightlingsea United	v	Canvey Island	1–3	143
Bishop's Stortford	v	Boston	4–0	354
Billericay Town	v	Bourne Town	5–2	233
Bury Town	v	Burnham Ramblers	1–2	184
Haverhill Rovers	v	Eynesbury Rovers	1–2	109
Felixstowe Town	v	Gorleston	1–1	63
Gorleston	v	*Felixstowe*	*0–2*	112
(At Diss Town FC)				
Fakenham Town	v	Great Yarmouth Town	2–2	90
Great Yarmouth Town	v	*Fakenham Town*	*3–1*	126
Histon	v	Heybridge Swifts	0–9	73
Stamford	v	Tiptree United	4–1	94
Mirrlees Blackstone	v	Kings Lynn	0–1	175
March Town United	v	Saffron Walden Town	3–2	143
Sudbury Town	v	Stowmarket Town	4–1	285
Watton United	v	Barking	3–1	120
(at Diss Town FC)				
Wisbech Town	v	Brimsdown Rovers	3–1	302
Lowestoft Town	v	Tamworth	3–2	266

			Result	Att
Brook House	v	Boreham Wood	2–1	55
Chatteris Town	v	Cornard United	2–3	66
Biggleswade Town	v	Barton Rovers	0–3	87
(at Letchworth GC FC)				
Dunstable	v	Collier Row	2–2	87
Collier Row	v	*Dunstable*	*0–1*	121
Edgware Town	v	Feltham & Hounslow Borough	3–0	100
Clapton	v	Cheshunt	1–1	61
Cheshunt	v	*Clapton*	*2–1*	85
Hertford Town	v	Kempston Rovers	0–1	85
Hanwell Town	v	Harefield United	1–2	70
Ford United	v	Haringey Borough	1–1	27
Haringey Borough	v	*Ford United*	*2–0*	85
Hornchurch	v	Hoddesdon Town	1–1	79
Hoddesdon Town	v	*Hornchurch*	*0–3*	60
(At Ware FC)				
Northwood	v	Royston Town	3–0	128
Langford	v	Leighton Town	2–1	168
Ruislip Manor	v	Letchworth Garden City	4–3	125
Rainham Town	v	Purfleet	1–5	92
Walthamstow Pennant	v	Wingate & Finchley	2–3	65
Tilbury	v	Tring Town	1–1	31
Tring Town	v	*Tilbury*	*0–4*	59
Staines Town	v	Uxbridge	1–0	203
Southall	v	Ware	1–0	41
Bracknell Town	v	Bognor Regis Town	3–3	106
Bognor Regis Town	v	*Bracknell Town*	*5–0*	289
Burgess Hill Town	v	Arundel	3–0	157
Bedfont	v	Beckenham Town		
(walkover for Bedfont – Beckenham Town withdrawn)				
Horsham YMCA	v	Croydon Athletic	2–2	44
Croydon Athletic	v	*Horsham YMCA*	*5–2*	42
Eastbourne United	v	Egham Town	5–1	100
Croydon	v	Corinthian Casuals	5–0	52
Hailsham Town	v	Epsom & Ewell	1–4	142
Faversham Town	v	Fisher	3–0	150
(tie awarded to Fisher – Faversham Town removed for playing an ineligible player)				
Erith & Belvedere	v	Godalming & Guildford	2–1	86
Horsham	v	Herne Bay	1–2	200
Merstham	v	Pagham	1–4	38
Lewes	v	Littlehampton Town	3–1	127
Langney Sports	v	Malden Vale	2–1	150
Oakwood	v	Metropolitan Police	1–1	43
Metropolitan Police	v	*Oakwood*	*3–1*	76
Portfield	v	Steyning Town	1–0	50
Redhill	v	Ringmer	1–2	122
Ramsgate	v	Selsey	1–1	61
Selsey	v	*Ramsgate*	*0–1*	150
(tie awarded to Selsey – Ramsgate removed for playing an ineligible player)				
Southwick	v	Slade Green	2–1	159
Whyteleafe	v	Three Bridges	5–1	100
Tooting & Mitcham Utd	v	Tunbridge Wells	7–0	203
Tonbridge	v	Whitehawk	4–1	344
Windsor & Eton	v	Wick	1–4	134
Cove	v	Walton & Hersham	2–1	109
Bournemouth	v	Brockenhurst	0–1	120
Shoreham	v	Buckingham Town	0–2	56

			Result	Att
Fareham Town	v	Eastleigh	1–1	113
Eastleigh	v	*Fareham Town*	*4–1*	208
Newbury Town	v	Lancing	6–1	164
Gosport Borough	v	Hungerford Town	0–3	146
Peacehaven & Telscombe	v	Fleet Town	2–1	124
Oxford City	v	Newport (IOW)	0–7	242
Totton	v	Ryde Sports	1–1 aet	63
Ryde Sports	v	*Totton*	*1–3*	65
Poole Town	v	Swanage Town & Herston	5–0	192
Petersfield United	v	Thame United		
(walkover for Thame United – Petersfield United removed from the Competition)				
Wimborne Town	v	Westbury United	5–0	311
Barnstaple Town	v	Exmouth Town	4–0	123
Bridport	v	Bristol Manor Farm	4–0	209
Bideford	v	Chippenham Town	2–2	130
Chippenham Town	v	*Bideford*	*3–0*	145
Elmore	v	Devizes Town	2–1	61
Melksham Town	v	Falmouth Town	1–0	110
Frome Town	v	Glastonbury	3–3	113
Glastonbury	v	*Frome Town*	*0–1* aet	133
Odd Down	v	Ilfracombe Town	1–1	85
Ilfracombe	v	*Odd Down*	*2–2* aet	110
Odd Down	v	*Ilfracombe*	*1–0*	61
Moreton Town	v	Minehead	2–0	93
Torrington	v	Yate Town	1–4	140
Shortwood United	v	St Blazey	3–2	85
Dawlish Town	v	Taunton Town	0–12	152
Weston-super-Mare	v	Welton Rovers	6–1	300

FIRST QUALIFYING ROUND   11th September 1993

(replays in italics)

			Result	Att
Billingham Town	v	Billingham Synthonia	0–3	310
Yorkshire Amateur	v	Dunston Fed Brewery	1–3	90
Gateshead	v	Blyth Spartans	4–0	728
Chester-le-Street Town	v	Consett	2–3	102
Evenwood Town	v	Hebburn	0–0	76
Hebburn	v	*Evenwood Town*	*0–3*	201
Gretna	v	Seaham Red Star	3–1	101
Barrow	v	Guisborough Town	3–1	826
Harrogate Railway	v	Harrogate Town	1–2	634
Shildon	v	Easington Colliery	0–1	90
Pickering Town	v	Northallerton Town	0–2	147
Bishop Auckland	v	Netherfield	1–4	208
Newcastle Blue Star	v	Prudhoe East End	3–2	85
Tow Law Town	v	Murton	3–3	146
Murton	v	*Tow Law Town*	*1–2*	85
Lancaster City	v	Stockton	2–1	73
Whitley Bay	v	Spennymoor United	1–6	320
Whitby Town	v	Crook Town	5–1	208
Alfreton Town	v	Bamber Bridge	2–3	133
Arnold Town	v	Leek Town	1–3	347
Northwich Victoria	v	Emley	2–2	709
Emley	v	*Northwich Victoria*	*2–0*	358
Ashton United	v	Atherton LR	4–0	201

			Result	Att
Clitheroe	v	Curzon Ashton	2–2	123
Curzon Ashton	v	*Clitheroe*	*0–1*	113
Warrington Town	v	Matlock Town	3–0	302
Stalybridge Celtic	v	Fleetwood Town	6–0	517
Bootle	v	Burscough	5–1	94
Glossop North End	v	Goole Town	2–2	200
Goole Town	v	*Glossop North End*	*1–0*	184
Denaby United	v	Morecambe	0–4	124
Bridlington Town	v	Frickley Athletic	2–0	335
Darwen	v	Flixton	1–1	97
Flixton	v	*Darwen*	*3–0*	158
Guiseley	v	Ilkeston Town	3–1	563
Ossett Town	v	Winsford United	1–1	210
Winsford United	v	*Ossett Town*	*3–1*	184
Buxton	v	Gainsborough Trinity	2–1	282
Heanor Town	v	Hucknall Town	1–2	218
Maltby MW	v	North Ferriby United	1–1	90
North Ferriby United	v	*Maltby MW*	*4–2*	100
Lincoln United	v	Nantwich Town	2–0	174
Chorley	v	Horwich RMI	3–1	407
Liversedge	v	Newcastle Town	3–2	77
Rossendale United	v	St Helens Town	1–1	212
St Helens Town	v	*Rossendale United*	*1–0*	120
Salford City	v	Knowsley United	1–1	120
Knowsley United	v	*Salford City*	*6–0*	127
Colwyn Bay	v	Hyde United	4–1	209
Sheffield	v	Thackley	1–4	147
Willenhall Town	v	West Midlands Police	1–2	100
Winterton Rangers	v	Nuneaton Borough	1–7	305
Droylsden	v	Brigg Town	1–1	136
Brigg Town	v	*Droylsden*	*0–1*	89
Worksop Town	v	Wednesfield	1–1	233
Wednesfield	v	*Worksop Town*	*0–2*	110
Armitage 90	v	Boldmere St Michaels	3–0	60
Chasetown	v	Solihull Borough	0–1	181
Bromsgrove Rovers	v	Gresley Rovers	1–1	902
Gresley Rovers	v	*Bromsgrove Rovers*	*0–1*	1222
Bedworth United	v	Bridgnorth Town	2–1	161
Dudley Town	v	Hinckley Town	1–1	175
Hinckley Town	v	*Dudley Town*	*2–3 aet*	101
Desborough Town	v	Raunds Town	1–3	112
Telford United	v	Halesowen Town	4–0	903
Grantham Town	v	Leicester United	3–1	320
Northampton Spencer	v	Pershore Town	0–1	90
Oldbury United	v	Pelsall Villa	1–1	107
Pelsall Villa	v	*Oldbury United*	*3–0*	241
Atherstone United	v	Hednesford Town	2–1	514
Paget Rangers	v	Redditch United	1–1	106
Redditch United	v	*Paget Rangers*	*2–1*	144
Rothwell Town	v	Stourbridge	7–1	143
Rushden & Diamonds	v	Sutton Coldfield Town	2–0	536
Burton Albion	v	Moor Green	2–1	508
Sandwell Borough	v	Stratford Town	5–0	42
Bishop's Stortford	v	Burnham Ramblers	2–0	479
Billericay Town	v	Aveley	1–1	301
Aveley	v	*Billericay Town*	*1–3 aet*	232
Boston United	v	Braintree Town	1–1	802
Braintree Town	v	*Boston United*	*1–2*	420

			Result	*Att*
Basildon United	v	Canvey Island	1–1	240
Canvey Island	v	*Basildon United*	*1–0*	405
Felixstowe Town	v	Heybridge Swifts	1–1	110
Heybridge Swifts	v	*Felixstowe Town*	*5–1*	153
Great Yarmouth Town	v	Hendon	2–2	215
Hendon	v	*Great Yarmouth Town*	*4–2*	232
Cambridge City	v	Berkhamsted Town	4–1	223
Harwich & Parkeston	v	Eynesbury Rovers	4–1	203
Kings Lynn	v	Sudbury Town	2–1	909
March Town United	v	Wivenhoe Town	3–6	144
Chelmsford City	v	Newmarket Town	0–0	438
Newmarket Town	v	*Chelmsford City*	*1–1* aet	321
Chelmsford City	v	*Newmarket Town*	*3–0*	489
Spalding United	v	Stamford	1–2	204
Wisbech Town	v	East Thurrock United	1–1	348
East Thurrock United	v	*Wisbech Town*	*1–0*	161
Lowestoft Town	v	Witham Town	1–0	184
Stevenage Borough	v	Wembley	2–2	557
Wembley	v	*Stevenage Borough*	*1–1* aet	260
Wembley	v	*Stevenage Borough*	*0–1*	282
Corby Town	v	Watton United	4–0	202
Cornard United	v	Halstead Town	0–1	190
Barton Rovers	v	Arlesey Town	1–0	138
Dagenham & Redbridge	v	Hitchin Town	1–0	600
Baldock Town	v	Brook House	6–0	138
Edgware Town	v	Flackwell Heath	2–0	116
Cheshunt	v	Burnham	0–2	70
Chesham United	v	St Albans City	5–0	1004
Chalfont St Peter	v	Dunstable	1–0	70
Harefield United	v	Hornchurch	1–2	+
Haringey Borough	v	Hampton	0–0	50
Hampton	v	*Haringey Borough*	*1–2*	155
Enfield	v	Welling United	4–1	938
Hemel Hempstead	v	Kempston Rovers	2–1	67
Langford	v	Purfleet	1–4	114
Ruislip Manor	v	Leyton	3–1	163
Grays Athletic	v	Yeading	0–2	183
Kingsbury Town	v	Northwood	2–1	93
Tilbury	v	Southall	3–2	42
Staines Town	v	Chertsey Town	1–2	393
Harrow Borough	v	Wealdstone	3–1	555
Viking Sports	v	Wingate & Finchley	3–0	47
Burgess Hill Town	v	Chatham Town	0–1	151
Bedfont	v	Canterbury City	0–1	75
Kingstonian	v	Ashford Town	2–1	429
Banstead Athletic	v	Bognor Regis Town	0–3	114
Eastbourne United	v	Greenwich Borough	0–2	85
Croydon	v	Chipstead	4–1	70
Hastings Town	v	Molesey	1–5	336
Corinthian	v	Croydon Athletic	3–0	23
Fisher	v	Herne Bay	3–3	124
Herne Bay	v	*Fisher*	*3–2*	409
Erith & Belvedere	v	Deal Town	4–3	93
Sittingbourne	v	Dover Athletic	1–1	3583
Dover Athletic	v	*Sittingbourne*	*1–2*	3016
Gravesend & Northfleet	v	Epsom & Ewell	3–0	350
Lewes	v	Metropolitan Police	1–1	98
Metropolitan Police	v	*Lewes*	*3–2*	94

			Result	Att
Langney Sports	v	Leatherhead	3–8	168
Bromley	v	Dulwich Hamlet	3–1	541
Margate	v	Pagham	6–0	343
Ringmer	v	Southwick	1–0	106
Selsey	v	Basingstoke Town	2–3	82
Carshalton Athletic	v	Havant Town	2–0	371
Sheppey United	v	Portfield	1–1	41
Portfield	v	*Sheppey United*	*0–3*	49
Tooting & Mitcham Utd	v	Wick	3–1	216
Tonbridge	v	Bemerton Heath Harlequins	3–0	412
Dorking	v	Worthing	4–1	298
Whitstable Town	v	Whyteleafe	2–1	160
Brockenhurst	v	Eastleigh	1–4	133
Buckingham Town	v	Andover	0–1	118
Bashley	v	Abingdon Town	2–1	240
Calne Town	v	Cove	5–1	71
Hungerford Town	v	Newport (IOW)	0–2	137
Peacehaven & Telscombe	v	Lymington	1–1	152+
Lymington	v	*Peacehaven & Telscombe*	*2–0*	76
Dorchester Town	v	Wokingham Town	1–0	489
Maidenhead United	v	Newbury Town	1–2	222
Poole Town	v	Wimborne Town	0–0	456
Wimborne Town	v	*Poole Town*	*2–0*	710
Thame United	v	Witney Town	1–1	152
Witney Town	v	*Thame United*	*1–2* aet	172
Waterlooville	v	Salisbury City	1–0	295
Thatcham Town	v	Totton	4–2	128
Bridport	v	Elmore	2–3	252
Chippenham Town	v	Weymouth	0–5	332
Gloucester City	v	Clevedon Town	1–2	436
Cinderford Town	v	Barnstaple Town	1–1	105
Barnstaple Town	v	*Cinderford Town*	*3–1*	218
Frome Town	v	Moreton Town	0–0	128
Moreton Town	v	*Frome Town*	*1–0*	123
Odd Down	v	Forest Green Rovers	2–2	87
Forest Green Rovers	v	*Odd Down*	*1–3*	108
Trowbridge Town	v	Newport AFC	1–1	477
Newport AFC	v	*Trowbridge Town*	*0–5*	244
Mangotsfield United	v	Melksham Town	3–0	138
Shortwood United	v	Weston-super-Mare	1–3	110
Taunton Town	v	Saltash United	3–0	253
Worcester City	v	Tiverton Town	1–1	823
Tiverton Town	v	*Worcester City*	*4–2*	580
Paulton Rovers	v	Yate Town	2–1	104

SECOND QUALIFYING ROUND   25th September 1993

(replays in italics)

			Result	Att
Dunston FB	v	Billingham Synthonia	1–1	125
Billingham Synthonia	v	*Dunston FB*	*1–0*	128
Gateshead	v	Consett	3–1	365
Gretna	v	Evenwood Town	8–1	65
Barrow	v	Harrogate Town	6–1	998
Northallerton Town	v	Easington Colliery	4–1	124
Netherfield	v	Newcastle Blue Star	3–2	184

			Result	*Att*
Lancaster City	v	Tow Law Town	3–2	155
Spennymoor United	v	Whitby Town	2–3	417
Leek Town	v	Bamber Bridge	5–3	394
Emley	v	Ashton United	2–0	407
Warrington Town	v	Clitheroe	2–2	259
Clitheroe	v	*Warrington Town*	*0–2*	270
Stalybridge Celtic	v	Bootle	2–2	426
Bootle	v	*Stalybridge Celtic*	*1–3*	313
Morecambe	v	Goole Town	3–2	354
Bridlington Town	v	Flixton	2–1	121
Winsford United	v	Guiseley	2–1	271
Buxton	v	Hucknall Town	2–0	320
Lincoln United	v	North Ferriby United	1–5	115
Chorley	v	Liversedge	2–1	273
Knowsley United	v	St Helens Town	2–1	191
Colwyn Bay	v	Thackley	4–1	188
Nuneaton Borough	v	West Midlands Police	3–3 aet	1073
West Midlands Police	v	*Nuneaton Borough*	*0–3*	300
Droylsden	v	Worksop Town	1–1	254
Worksop Town	v	*Droylsden*	*3–0*	276
Solihull Borough	v	Armitage 90	2–2	146
Armitage 90	v	*Solihull Borough*	*2–3 aet*	125
Bromsgrove Rovers	v	Bedworth United	2–0	701
Raunds Town	v	Dudley Town	3–1	78
Telford United	v	Grantham Town	2–2	665
Grantham Town	v	*Telford United*	*1–3*	557
Pelsall Villa	v	Pershore Town	1–2	292
Atherstone United	v	Redditch United	0–0	290
Redditch United	v	*Atherstone United*	*1–1*	302
Redditch United	v	*Atherstone United*	*1–3*	445
Rushden & Diamonds	v	Rothwell Town	1–1	990
Rothwell Town	v	*Rushden & Diamonds*	*0–2*	929
Burton Albion	v	Sandwell Borough	3–2	425
Billericay Town	v	Bishop's Stortford	1–3	567
Boston United	v	Canvey Island	2–3	855
Hendon	v	Heybridge Swifts	5–2	171
Cambridge City	v	Harwich & Parkeston	3–0	327
Wivenhoe Town	v	Kings Lynn	2–2	324
Kings Lynn	v	*Wivenhoe Town*	*1–4*	1019
Chelmsford City	v	Stamford AFC	5–2	468
Lowestoft Town	v	East Thurrock United	1–2	285
Stevenage Borough	v	Corby Town	4–3	707
Barton Rovers	v	Halstead Town	1–2	153
Dagenham & Redbridge	v	Baldock Town	2–1	677
Burnham	v	Edgware Town	1–3	118
Chesham United	v	Chalfont St Peter	5–0	538
Haringey Borough	v	Hornchurch	1–3	63
Enfield	v	Hemel Hempstead	1–0	623
Ruislip Manor	v	Purfleet	1–1	172
Purfleet	v	*Ruislip Manor*	*1–0*	97
Yeading	v	Kingsbury Town	5–2	130
Chertsey Town	v	Tilbury	2–0	268
Harrow Borough	v	Viking Sports	6–0	185
Canterbury City	v	Chatham Town	1–4	104
Kingstonian	v	Bognor Regis Town	1–1	458
Bognor Regis Town	v	*Kingstonian*	*1–6*	450
Croydon	v	Greenwich Borough	0–1	70
Molesey	v	Corinthian	2–0	109

			Result	Att
Erith & Belvedere	v	Herne Bay	2–1	187
Sittingbourne	v	Gravesend & Northfleet	0–2	2044
Leatherhead	v	Metropolitan Police	3–5	140
Bromley	v	Margate	0–3	343
Basingstoke Town	v	Ringmer	3–0	185
Carshalton Athletic	v	Sheppey United	5–1	474
Tonbridge	v	Tooting & Mitcham United	0–2	542
Dorking	v	Whitstable Town	4–0	215
Andover	v	Eastleigh	3–0	221
Bashley	v	Calne Town	3–1	263
Lymington	v	Newport (IOW)	0–1	215
Dorchester Town	v	Newbury Town	0–3	449
Thame United	v	Wimborne Town	2–3	189
Waterlooville	v	Thatcham Town	3–0	140
Weymouth	v	Elmore	3–0	699
Clevedon Town	v	Barnstaple Town	2–2	474
Barnstaple Town	v	*Clevedon Town*	*2–1*	410
Odd Down	v	Moreton Town	0–2	213
Trowbridge Town	v	Mangotsfield United	0–0	432
Mangotsfield United	v	*Trowbridge Town*	*2–2* aet	420
Trowbridge Town	v	*Mangotsfield Town*	*2–3*	497
Taunton Town	v	Weston-super-Mare	2–4	493
Tiverton Town	v	Paulton Rovers	2–1	454

THIRD QUALIFYING ROUND   9th October 1993

(replays in italics)

			Result	Att
Billingham Synthonia	v	Gateshead	1–1	409
Gateshead	v	*Billingham Synthonia*	*0–1*	383
Gretna	v	Barrow	2–1	732
Northallerton Town	v	Netherfield	4–3	226
Lancaster City	v	Whitby Town	1–2	213
Leek Town	v	Emley	1–0	572
Warrington Town	v	Stalybridge Celtic	0–1	654
Morecambe	v	Bridlington Town	2–0	405
Winsford United	v	Buxton	6–1	322
North Ferriby United	v	Chorley	1–1	284
Chorley	v	*North Ferriby United*	*2–1*	347
Knowsley United	v	Colwyn Bay	3–0	254
Nuneaton Borough	v	Worksop Town	4–1	1382
Solihull Borough	v	Bromsgrove Rovers	1–2	821
Raunds Town	v	Telford United	0–4	354
Pershore Town	v	Atherstone United	1–0	709
Rushden & Diamonds	v	Burton Albion	4–0	1201
Bishop's Stortford	v	Canvey Island	0–1	921
Hendon	v	Cambridge City	0–1	382
Wivenhoe Town	v	Chelmsford City	2–0	706
East Thurrock United	v	Stevenage Borough	1–5	622
Halstead Town	v	Dagenham & Redbridge	1–3	850
Edgware Town	v	Chesham United	1–2	631
Hornchurch	v	Enfield	1–4	554
Purfleet	v	Yeading	1–2	153
Chertsey Town	v	Harrow Borough	1–3	556
Chatham Town	v	Kingstonian	1–2	498
Greenwich Borough	v	Molesey	0–4	280

			Result	Att
Erith & Belvedere	v	Gravesend & Northfleet	0–1	742
Metropolitan Police	v	Margate	5–2	217
Basingstoke Town	v	Carshalton Athletic	1–3	417
Tooting & Mitcham Utd	v	Dorking	2–0	524
Andover	v	Bashley	0–2	517
Newport (IOW)	v	Newbury Town	4–2	548
Wimborne Town	v	Waterlooville	0–1	495
Weymouth	v	Barnstaple Town	2–1	707
Moreton Town	v	Mangotsfield United	1–1	155
Mangotsfield United	v	*Moreton Town*	*1–2*	324
Weston-super-Mare	v	Tiverton Town	0–0	845
Tiverton Town	v	*Weston-super-Mare*	*0–2*	891

FOURTH QUALIFYING ROUND   23rd October 1993

(replays in italics)

			Result	Att
Witton Albion	v	Northallerton Town	2–1	706
Winsford United	v	Gretna	0–0	347
Gretna	v	*Winsford United*	*5–0*	754
Macclesfield Town	v	Southport	5–3	1253
Altrincham	v	Accrington Stanley	0–2	956
Stalybridge Celtic	v	Whitby Town	0–0	740
Whitby Town	v	*Stalybridge Celtic*	*0–1*	887
Stafford Rangers	v	Knowsley United	1–1	973
Knowsley United	v	*Stafford Rangers*	*2–2 aet*	612
Knowsley United	v	*Stafford Rangers*	*1–0*	951
Billingham Synthonia	v	Leek Town	1–1	469
Leek Town	v	*Billingham Synthonia*	*2–1*	876
Chorley	v	Marine	0–2	740
Telford United	v	Morecambe	2–0	901
Wivenhoe Town	v	Enfield	1–2	532
Hayes	v	Slough Town	0–2	877
Cambridge City	v	Dagenham & Redbridge	2–2	1026
Dagenham & Redbridge	v	*Cambridge City*	*0–2*	1410
Stevenage Borough	v	Nuneaton Borough	1–2	2187
Kettering Town	v	Canvey Island	3–1	2190
VS Rugby	v	Harrow Borough	2–2	826
Harrow Borough	v	*VS Rugby*	*1–2*	640
Aylesbury United	v	Marlow	1–2	926
Pershore Town	v	Yeading	1–3	1356
Rushden & Diamonds	v	Bromsgrove Rovers	1–3	1512
Chesham United	v	Kidderminster Harriers	1–4	1144
Kingstonian	v	Metropolitan Police	0–1	689
Waterlooville	v	Gravesend & Northfleet	1–3	686
Crawley Town	v	Merthyr Tydfil	2–1	1623
Cheltenham Town	v	Bath City	1–1	1020
Bath City	v	*Cheltenham Town*	*4–2*	1166
Bashley	v	Carshalton Athletic	1–1	615
Carshalton Athletic	v	*Bashley*	*4–2*	971
Sutton United	v	Moreton Town	0–0	804
Moreton Town	v	*Sutton United*	*0–2*	706
Molesey	v	Tooting & Mitcham United	0–0	461
Tooting & Mitcham Utd	v	*Molesey*	*1–2*	702
Weymouth	v	Farnborough Town	1–4	1283
Weston-super-Mare	v	Newport (IOW)	2–0	700

FIRST ROUND   13th November 1993

(replays in italics)

			Result	Att
Crewe Alexandra	v	Darlington	4–2	3489
Leek Town	v	Wigan Athletic	2–2	2785
Wigan Athletic	v	*Leek Town*	*3–0*	1807
Port Vale	v	Blackpool	2–0	8211
Witton Albion	v	Lincoln City	0–2	1450
Runcorn	v	Hull City *(at Witton Albion FC)*	0–2	1883
(1st tie abandoned after 29 mins, 0–1 due to collapsed wall)				
Halifax Town	v	West Bromwich Albion	2–1	4250
Telford United	v	Huddersfield Town	1–1	2257
Huddersfield Town	v	*Telford United*	*1–0*	3517
Wrexham	v	Walsall	1–1	4907
Walsall	v	*Wrexham*	*2–0*	3971
Rotherham United	v	Stockport County	1–2	4836
Mansfield Town	v	Preston North End	1–2	4119
Chesterfield	v	Rochdale	0–1	3457
Scarborough	v	Bury	1–0	2194
Macclesfield Town	v	Hartlepool United	2–0	2747
Bradford City	v	Chester City	0–0	6240
Chester City	v	*Bradford City*	*1–0*	3707
Gretna	v	Bolton Wanderers	2–3	6447
(at Bolton Wanderers FC)				
Accrington Stanley	v	Scunthorpe United	2–3	5846
(at Burnley FC)				
Shrewsbury Town	v	Doncaster Rovers	1–1	3408
Doncaster Rovers	v	*Shrewsbury Town*	*1–2* aet	3524
Knowsley United	v	Carlisle United	1–4	5015
(at Everton FC)				
Burnley	v	York City	0–0	10198
York City	v	*Burnley*	*2–3*	5720
Stalybridge Celtic	v	Marine	1–1	1525
Marine	v	*Stalybridge Celtic*	*4–4* aet	853
(Stalybridge Celtic won 4–2 on kicks from the penalty mark)				
Colchester United	v	Sutton United	3–4	3051
Enfield	v	Cardiff City	0–0	2374
Cardiff City	v	*Enfield*	*1–0*	3232
Slough Town	v	Torquay United	1–2	2371
Yeading	v	Gillingham	0–0	2285
(at Hayes FC)				
Gillingham	v	*Yeading*	*3–1*	3231
Northampton Town	v	Bromsgrove Rovers	1–2	3382
VS Rugby	v	Brentford	0–3	3006
Marlow	v	Plymouth Argyle	0–2	2700
Metropolitan Police	v	Crawley Town	0–2	1561
Bristol Rovers	v	Wycombe Wanderers	1–2	6355
Yeovil Town	v	Fulham	1–0	6180
Molesey	v	Bath City	0–4	913
Swansea City	v	Nuneaton Borough	1–1	3532
Nuneaton Borough	v	*Swansea City*	*2–1* aet	4443
Cambridge United	v	Reading	0–0	4594
Reading	v	*Cambridge United*	*1–2*	4725
Kidderminster Harriers	v	Kettering Town	3–0	3775
Woking	v	Weston-super-Mare	2–2	2766
Weston-super-Mare	v	*Woking*	*0–1*	2623
Cambridge City	v	Hereford United	0–1	2325

			Result	Att
Barnet	v	Carshalton Athletic	2–1	2690
AFC Bournemouth	v	Brighton & Hove Albion	4–2	5559
Farnborough Town	v	Exeter City	1–3	2069
Leyton Orient	v	Gravesend & Northfleet	2–1	5461

SECOND ROUND   4th December 1993

(replays in italics)

			Result	Att
Lincoln City	v	Bolton Wanderers	1–3	6250
Wigan Athletic	v	Scarborough	1–0	1837
Shrewsbury Town	v	Preston North End	0–1	5018
Burnley	v	Rochdale	4–1	11388
Chester City	v	Hull City	2–0	4333
Stockport County	v	Halifax Town	5–1	5496
Port Vale	v	Huddersfield Town	1–0	8602
Carlisle United	v	Stalybridge Celtic	3–1	5546
Walsall	v	Scunthorpe United	1–1	4962
Scunthorpe United	v	*Walsall*	*0–0* aet	3300
(Scunthorpe United won from kicks from the penalty mark 7–6)				
Crewe Alexandra	v	Macclesfield Town	2–1	6007
Brentford	v	Cardiff City	1–3	4845
Torquay United	v	Sutton United	0–1	3414
Kidderminster Harriers	v	Woking	1–0	4411
Leyton Orient	v	Exeter City	1–1	4366
Exeter City	v	*Leyton Orient*	*2–2* aet	3628
(Exeter City won from kicks from the penalty mark 5–4)				
Plymouth Argyle	v	Gillingham	2–0	6051
Crawley Town	v	Barnet	1–2	4104
Bath City	v	Hereford Utd	2–1	3086
Yeovil Town	v	Bromsgrove Rovers	0–2	5462
AFC Bournemouth	v	Nuneaton Borough	1–1	5485
Nuneaton Borough	v	*AFC Bournemouth*	*0–1*	4127
Wycombe Wanderers	v	Cambridge United	1–0	6313

THIRD ROUND   8th January 1994

(replays in italics)

			Result	Att
Swindon Town	v	Ipswich Town	1–1	12105
Ipswich Town	v	*Swindon Town*	*2–1* aet	12796
Oxford United	v	Tranmere Rovers	2–0	5283
Preston North End	v	AFC Bournemouth	2–1	8457
Luton Town	v	Southend United	1–0	7955
Stockport County	v	Queens Park Rangers	2–1	7569
West Ham United	v	Watford	2–1	19802
Cardiff City	v	Middlesbrough	2–2	13750
Middlesbrough	v	*Cardiff City*	*1–2* aet	10769
Wycombe Wanderers	v	Norwich City	0–2	7802
Bromsgrove Rovers	v	Barnsley	1–2	4893
Wolverhampton Wanderers	v	Crystal Palace	1–0	25047
Sheffield Wednesday	v	Nottingham Forest	1–1	32488
Nottingham Forest	v	*Sheffield Wednesday*	*0–2*	25268
Millwall	v	Arsenal	0–1	20093

			Result	Att
Newcastle United	v	Coventry City	2–0	35444
Charlton Athletic	v	Burnley	3–0	8336
Stoke City	v	Bath City	0–0	14159
Bath City	v	*Stoke City*	*1–4*	6213
Bolton Wanderers	v	Everton	1–1	21702
Everton	v	*Bolton Wanderers*	*2–3 aet*	34642
Plymouth Argyle	v	Chester City	1–0	9170
Wimbledon	v	Scunthorpe United	3–0	4944
Grimsby Town	v	Wigan Athletic	1–0	4488
Barnet	v	Chelsea	0–0	23200
(At Chelsea FC)				
Chelsea	v	*Barnet*	*4–0*	16209
Bristol City	v	Liverpool	1–1	21718
(Match abandoned after 65 minutes due to floodlight failure, 1–1)				
Liverpool	v	*Bristol City*	*0–1*	36720
Birmingham City	v	Kidderminster Harriers	1–2	19666
Exeter City	v	Aston Villa	0–1	10570
Manchester City	v	Leicester City	4–1	22613
Sheffield United	v	Manchester United	0–1	22019
Southampton	v	Port Vale	1–1	11086
Port Vale	v	*Southampton*	*1–0*	12042
Leeds United	v	Crewe Alexandra	3–1	23475
Notts County	v	Sutton United	3–2	6805
Oldham Athletic	v	Derby County	2–1	12810
Blackburn Rovers	v	Portsmouth	3–3	17219
Portsmouth	v	*Blackburn Rovers*	*1–3*	23035
Sunderland	v	Carlisle United	1–1	23587
Carlisle United	v	*Sunderland*	*0–1aet*	12771
Peterborough United	v	Tottenham Hotspur	1–1	19169
Tottenham Hotspur	v	*Peterborough United*	*1–1aet*	24893
(Tottenham Hotspur won on kicks from the penalty mark, 5–4)				

FOURTH ROUND   29th January 1994

(replays in italics)

			Result	Att
Port Vale	v	Wolverhampton Wanderers	0–2	21999
Grimsby Town	v	Aston Villa	1–2	15771
Newcastle United	v	Luton Town	1–1	32216
Luton Town	v	*Newcastle United*	*2–0*	12503
Wimbledon	v	Sunderland	2–1	10477
Stockport County	v	Bristol City	0–4	7691
Norwich City	v	Manchester United	0–2	21060
Plymouth Argyle	v	Barnsley	2–2	12760
Barnsley	v	*Plymouth Argyle*	*1–0*	10913
Ipswich Town	v	Tottenham Hotspur	3–0	22539
Oldham Athletic	v	Stoke City	0–0	14465
Stoke City	v	*Oldham Athletic*	*0–1*	19871
Chelsea	v	Sheffield Wednesday	1–1	26094
Sheffield Wednesday	v	*Chelsea*	*1–3 aet*	26144
Kidderminster Harriers	v	Preston North End	1–0	7000
Notts County	v	West Ham United	1–1	14952
West Ham United	v	*Notts County*	*1–0 aet*	23373
Cardiff City	v	Manchester City	1–0	20486
Charlton Athletic	v	Blackburn	0–0	8532
Blackburn	v	*Charlton Athletic*	*0–1*	15438

			Result	Att
Oxford United	v	Leeds United	2–2	11029
Leeds United	v	*Oxford United*	*2–3* aet	22167
Bolton Wanderers	v	Arsenal	2–2	18891
Arsenal	v	*Bolton Wanderers*	*1–3* aet	33863

FIFTH ROUND   19th February 1994

(replays in italics)

			Result	Att
Cardiff City	v	Luton Town	1–2	17296
Oldham Athletic	v	Barnsley	1–0	15685
Kidderminster Harriers	v	West Ham United	0–1	7850
Wolverhampton Wanderers	v	Ipswich Town	1–1	26244
Ipswich Town	v	*Wolverhampton Wanderers*	*1–2*	19385
Bolton Wanderers	v	Aston Villa	1–0	18817
Oxford United	v	Chelsea	1–2	10787
Wimbledon	v	Manchester United	0–3	27511
Bristol City	v	Charlton Athletic	1–1	20416
Charlton Athletic	v	*Bristol City*	*2–0*	8205

SIXTH ROUND   12th March 1994

(replays in italics)

			Result	Att
West Ham United	v	Luton Town	0–0	27331
Luton Town	v	*West Ham United*	*3–2*	13166
Manchester United	v	Charlton Athletic	3–1	44547
Chelsea	v	Wolverhampton Wanderers	1–0	29340
Bolton Wanderers	v	Oldham Athletic	0–1	20321

SEMI–FINAL   9th/10th April 1994

Wembley

			Result	Att
Chelsea	v	Luton Town	2–0	59989
Oldham Athletic	v	Manchester United	1–1	56399

Replay at Maine Road   13th April 1994

			Result	Att
Manchester United	v	Oldham Athletic	4–1	32211

FA Challenge Cup Competition 1994–1995

LIST OF 116 CLUBS RECEIVING EXEMPTION

44 Clubs to the Third Round Proper*

Arsenal
Aston Villa
Barnsley
Blackburn Rovers
Bolton Wanderers
Bristol City
Charlton Athletic
Chelsea
Coventry City
Crystal Palace
Derby County
Everton
Grimsby Town
Ipswich Town
Leeds United

Leicester City
Liverpool
Luton Town
Manchester City
Manchester United
Middlesbrough
Millwall
Newcastle United
Norwich City
Nottingham Forest
Notts County
Oldham Athletic
Portsmouth
Queens Park Rangers
Reading

Sheffield United
Sheffield Wednesday
Southampton
Southend United
Stoke City
Sunderland
Swindon Town
Tottenham Hotspur
Tranmere Rovers
Watford
West Bromwich Albion
West Ham United
Wimbledon
Wolverhampton Wanderers

Correct at 1st June 1994, i.e. prior to Disciplinary Commission concerning Tottenham Hotspur FC

52 Clubs to the First Round Proper

Barnet
Bath City*
Birmingham City
Blackpool
Bournemouth AFC
Bradford City
Brentford
Brighton & Hove Albion
Bristol Rovers
Burnley
Bury
Cambridge United
Cardiff City
Carlisle United
Chester City
Chesterfield
Colchester United
Crewe Alexandra

Darlington
Doncaster Rovers
Exeter City
Fulham
Gillingham
Hartlepool United
Hereford United
Huddersfield Town
Hull City
Kidderminster Harriers*
Leyton Orient
Lincoln City
Mansfield Town
Northampton Town
Oxford United
Peterborough United
Plymouth Argyle
Port Vale

Preston North End
Rochdale
Rotherham United
Runcorn†
Scarborough
Scunthorpe United
Shrewsbury Town
Stockport County
Swansea City
Torquay United
Walsall
Wigan Athletic
Woking†
Wrexham
Wycombe Wanderers
York City

† Trophy Finalists   * Clubs outside The Football League considered most appropriate

20 Clubs to the Fourth Round Qualifying

Accrington Stanley
Altrincham
Bromsgrove Rovers
Cheltenham Town
Crawley Town
Farnborough Town
Halifax Town

Kettering Town
Macclesfield Town
Marine
Marlow
Nuneaton Borough
Slough Town
Southport

Stafford Rangers
Stalybridge Celtic
Sutton United
VS Rugby
Witton Albion
Yeovil Town

FA Challenge Trophy – Final Tie 1994

Woking 2 Runcorn 1

Runcorn were back at Wembley twelve months after comprehensive defeat against Wycombe (now Endsleigh League) in the 1993 Trophy final. On another rain-spattered afternoon – this year's Challenge Cup and Vase finals had been similarly afflicted – the Cheshire team lost out again. Woking, also the of the GM Vauxhall Conference, got their hands on the Trophy for the first time in their first Wembley visit for four decades. They had beaten Ilford 3–0 to win the old FA Amateur Cup in 1958.

Woking were very much on the back foot in the early part of the 25th Trophy final. Runcorn started more positively in the difficult conditions – the Wembley pitch had surely never seen so much surface water – and they forced a succession of corners as the ball flopped around the Woking box. Then a free-kick from Runcorn skipper Andy Lee hit the defensive wall and deflected narrowly wide of Batty's right-hand post. But the Surrey outfit's first shot on target was a telling one: Scott Steele took swift advantage of a defensive slip on 20 minutes to cross the ball instantly from the left and Dereck Brown stabbed it home inside Williams' near post.

Ten minutes later it was 2–0 and last year's losing finalists were in trouble. Woking, still on a high after Brown's strike, pushed forward again and Steele chased an apparently lost cause as the ball skidded towards the advertising hoardings behind the Runcorn goal. He stopped it a yard short of the line and laid it back, Brown slightly mis-hit it along the ground in the general direction of the far post and Darran Hay flicked it in with his heel.

Neither of the Woking scorers took any part in the second half – perhaps a Wembley 'first' – with Brown straining a muscle in a tackle on 33 minutes and Hay also limping out of the action at the end of the half. Woking played with two old campaigners in attack after the break – Clive Walker and Dave Puckett – and they showed themselves to be adroit at keeping possession, though they failed to engineer a clear-out scoring chance because of a poor final ball. For Walker, 36, it was ultimately a case of 'third time lucky', as he had already played and lost at Wembley with Sunderland (Milk Cup) and Brighton (Second Division Play-Off).

Runcorn left-back Paul Robertson, solid throughout, skimmed the bar with a long-range effort on the hour and, with nothing to lose by going forward, the 'Linnets' pushed for the goal that would be sure to set up a frantic finale. It duly arrived on 75 minutes, as the ball and Gwynne Berry's forearm came into fleeting contact inside the box and Nigel Shaw planted a perfect penalty-kick into the corner. But the Woking defence remained unbreached to the end, with Berry outstanding in the middle, and at the final whistle the massive Woking contingent in the crowd cheered like mad.

Woking: Batty, Tucker, Wye, Berry, Brown K., Clement, Brown D. (Rattray), Fielder, Steele, Hay (Puckett), Walker.
Runcorn: Williams, Bates, Robertson, Shaw, Lee, Anderson, Thomas, Connor, McInerney (Hill), McKenna, Brabin.
Referee: P Durkin (Portland).
Chief Guest: Steve Coppell.
Attendance: 15,818.

Jubilant Woking celebrate their Trophy success.

FA Trophy 1993–1994

FIRST QUALIFYING ROUND   18th September 1993

(replays in italics)

			Result	Att
Bridlington Town	v	Ferryhill Athletic	4–0	63
Peterlee Newtown	v	Workington	0–2	46
Ashton United	v	Chester-le-Street Town	1–2	223
Dunston FB	v	Easington Colliery	3–0	105
Fleetwood Town	v	Great Harwood Town	0–6	141
Durham City	v	Tow Law Town	0–1	150
Whitley Bay	v	Chorley	1–1	184
Chorley	v	*Whitley Bay*	*3–1* aet	266
Shildon	v	Harrogate Town	1–1	126
Harrogate Town	v	*Shildon*	*4–2* aet	202
Consett	v	Hebburn	2–2	49
Hebburn	v	*Consett*	*1–2*	131
Brandon United	v	Seaham Red Star	0–2	46
Matlock Town	v	Knowsley United	0–0	351
Knowsley United	v	*Matlock Town*	*1–1* aet	128
Matlock Town	v	*Knowsley United*	*3–0*	376
Tamworth	v	Worksop Town	3–2	480
Buxton	v	Curzon Ashton	0–0	268
Curzon Ashton	v	*Buxton*	*2–4*	136
Dudley Town	v	Mossley	3–2	192
Grantham Town	v	Bedworth United	5–2	335
Burton Albion	v	Caernarfon Town	3–0	398
Horwich RMI	v	Congleton Town	0–2	67
Gainsborough Trinity	v	Eastwood Town	5–3	337

Gresley Rovers	v	Goole Town	1–2	701
Sutton Coldfield Town	v	Colwyn Bay	1–1	138
Colwyn Bay	v	*Sutton Coldfield Town*	*4–0*	177
Atherstone United	v	Redditch United	1–1	305
Redditch United	v	*Atherstone United*	*2–0*	194
Leicester United	v	Moor Green	0–2	129
Droylsden	v	Solihull Borough	2–0	195
Barking	v	Billericay Town	0–1	133
Bishop's Stortford	v	Braintree Town	1–0	490
Hitchin Town	v	Boreham Wood	0–2	366
Hendon	v	Marlow	1–2	247
Ruislip Manor	v	Chelmsford City	1–4	203
Sudbury Town	v	Purfleet	3–3	352
Purfleet	v	*Sudbury Town*	*3–0* aet	191
Leyton	v	Chalfont St Peter	6–4	89
Berkhamsted Town	v	Yeading	1–1	105
Yeading	v	*Berkhamsted Town*	*2–0*	168
Uxbridge	v	Harrow Borough	1–2	225
Ashford Town	v	Windsor & Eton	3–1	354
Bromley	v	Molesey	0–2	365
Gravesend & Northfleet	v	Bognor Regis Town	3–0	448
Tooting & Mitcham Utd	v	Whyteleafe	3–1	222
Dorking	v	Sittingbourne	1–5	526
Margate	v	Worthing	0–2	360
Fisher 93	v	Walton & Hersham	1–0	73
Croydon	v	Canterbury City	3–0	30
Dulwich Hamlet	v	Hastings Town	2–1	232
Wokingham Town	v	Maidenhead United	1–0	275
Fareham Town	v	Weston-super-Mare	1–2	119
Salisbury City	v	Poole Town	1–3	256
Newport AFC	v	Havant Town	1–0	253
Basingstoke Town	v	Abingdon Town	0–2	192
Weymouth	v	Witney Town	0–2	799

SECOND QUALIFYING ROUND   16th October 1993

(replays in italics)

			Result	Att
Guiseley	v	Tow Law Town	4–3	486
Dunston FB	v	Newcastle Blue Star	2–1	98
Harrogate Town	v	Chorley	3–1	244
Stockton	v	Great Harwood Town	2–1	79
Workington	v	Bridlington Town	0–2	282
Seaham Red Star	v	West Auckland Town	3–1	95
Consett	v	Chester-le-Street Town	3–0	59
Gainsborough Trinity	v	Matlock Town	1–2	362
Goole Town	v	Dudley Town	3–1	156
Alfreton Town	v	Congleton Town	2–0	111
Redditch United	v	Moor Green	2–1	218
Stourbridge	v	Halesowen Town	0–1	835
Grantham Town	v	Droylsden	3–2	343
Buxton	v	Colwyn Bay	1–6	215
Rushden & Diamonds	v	Burton Albion	0–1	812
Tamworth	v	Emley	2–2	562
Emley	v	*Tamworth*	*4–0*	409
Baldock Town	v	Purfleet	2–3	176

109

			Result	Att
Marlow	v	Hayes	1–1	260
Hayes	v	*Marlow*	*2–3*	197
Yeading	v	Leyton	1–1	68
Leyton	v	*Yeading*	*1–3*	110
Cambridge City	v	Chelmsford City	1–1	344
Chelmsford City	v	*Cambridge City*	*3–2*	452
Bishop's Stortford	v	Billericay Town	1–2	449
Wembley	v	Staines Town	1–1	73
Staines Town	v	*Wembley*	*1–0*	202
Harrow Borough	v	Boreham Wood	0–0	233
Boreham Wood	v	*Harrow Borough*	*1–2*	122
Tooting & Mitcham Utd	v	Erith & Belvedere	1–2	187
Molesey	v	Sittingbourne	0–4	342
Ashford Town	v	Gravesend & Northfleet	1–1	633
Gravesend & Northfleet	v	*Ashford Town*	*2–0*	721
Croydon	v	Worthing	1–7	90
Fisher 93	v	Dulwich Hamlet	0–2	210
Witney Town	v	Dorchester Town	0–1	121
Weston-super-Mare	v	Newport AFC	2–0	405
Abingdon Town	v	Wokingham Town	1–1	238
Wokingham Town	v	*Abingdon Town*	*2–1*	206
Poole Town	v	Waterlooville	1–1	153
Waterlooville	v	*Poole Town*	*2–0*	168

THIRD QUALIFYING ROUND   27th November 1993

(replays in italics)

			Result	Att
Harrogate Town	v	Guiseley	3–4	505
Consett	v	Billingham Synthonia	1–3	37
Bishop Auckland	v	Murton	2–2	279
Murton	v	*Bishop Auckland*	*1–4*	190
Stockton	v	Spennymoor United	0–3	121
Seaham Red Star	v	Gretna	0–3	119
Alfreton Town	v	Bridlington Town	4–1	148
Goole Town	v	Northallerton Town	1–1	147
Northallerton Town	v	*Goole Town*	*1–0*	227
Colwyn Bay	v	Guisborough Town	2–2	114
Guisborough Town	v	*Colwyn Bay*	*2–3*	281
Hyde United	v	Accrington Stanley	2–0	355
Matlock Town	v	Blyth Spartans	1–3	534
Dunston FB	v	Frickley Athletic	1–5	281
Barrow	v	Emley	2–2	1020
Emley	v	*Barrow*	*2–1*	408
Enfield	v	Corby Town	2–1	414
Billericay Town	v	Yeading	2–0	283
Purfleet	v	Heybridge Swifts	3–2	138
VS Rugby	v	Chelmsford City	0–3	426
Staines Town	v	St Albans City	0–3	321
Nuneaton Borough	v	Aylesbury United	2–2	1375
Aylesbury United	v	*Nuneaton Borough*	*1–2*	537
Wivenhoe Town	v	Grantham Town	1–2	138
Burton Albion	v	Halesowen Town	1–2	709
Redditch United	v	Hednesford Town	1–1	163
Hednesford Town	v	*Redditch United*	*1–0*	224

			Result	Att
Leek Town	v	Stevenage Borough	0–2	485
Wealdstone	v	Harrow Borough	2–2	364
Harrow Borough	v	*Wealdstone*	*3–0*	557
Erith & Belvedere	v	Weston-super-Mare	1–4	110
Dulwich Hamlet	v	Gloucester City	2–1	312
Dorchester Town	v	Bashley	0–0	372
Bashley	v	*Dorchester Town*	*3–0*	214
Sittingbourne	v	Kingstonian	1–2	1248
Worcester City	v	Crawley Town	1–1	612
Crawley Town	v	*Worcester City*	*1–2*	445
Waterlooville	v	Wokingham Town	3–0	233
Trowbridge Town	v	Cheltenham Town	1–1	467
Cheltenham Town	v	*Trowbridge Town*	*1–0*	489
Worthing	v	Carshalton Athletic	3–0	432
Gravesend & Northfleet	v	Marlow	1–4	604

FIRST ROUND   22nd January 1994

(replays in italics)

			Result	Att
Alfreton Town	v	Runcorn	0–5	502
Gretna	v	Warrington Town	1–1	102
Warrington Town	v	*Gretna*	*2–3*	244
Halifax Town	v	Emley	2–1	1579
Halesowen Town	v	Gateshead	0–2	936
Stalybridge Celtic	v	Colwyn Bay	1–1	422
Colwyn Bay	v	*Stalybridge Celtic*	*2–2 aet*	220
Colwyn Bay	v	*Stalybridge Celtic*	*2–1 aet*	138
Winsford United	v	Guiseley	0–1	302
Grantham Town	v	Witton Albion	3–2	527
Billingham Synthonia	v	Frickley Athletic	2–1	238
Spennymoor United	v	Hyde United	2–1	529
Blyth Spartans	v	Bishop Auckland	1–3	622
Hednesford Town	v	Whitby Town	1–0	517
Boston United	v	Macclesfield Town	1–1	1559
Macclesfield Town	v	*Boston United*	*1–0*	590
Morecambe	v	Northwich Victoria	2–1	693
Telford United	v	Northallerton Town	2–1	926
Marine	v	Southport	0–0	1179
Southport	v	*Marine*	*3–1*	878
Altrincham	v	Stafford Rangers	0–2	790
Cheltenham Town	v	Nuneaton Borough	1–0	1118
Dulwich Hamlet	v	Kingstonian	1–2	487
Welling United	v	Chelmsford City	6–1	1108
Kettering Town	v	Stevenage Borough	2–1	2414
St Albans City	v	Merthyr Tydfil	4–5	1017
Billericay Town	v	Slough Town	0–2	709
Kidderminster Harriers	v	Dagenham & Redbridge	0–2	1587
Waterlooville	v	Bromsgrove Rovers	1–1	300
Bromsgrove Rovers	v	*Waterlooville*	*2–1*	1026
Farnborough Town	v	Grays Athletic	1–1	521
Grays Athletic	v	*Farnborough Town*	*2–0*	277
Bashley	v	Woking	2–4	1102
Weston-super-Mare	v	Dover Athletic	0–2	575
Yeovil Town	v	Bath City	3–3	2611
Bath City	v	*Yeovil Town*	*4–0*	1148

			Result	Att
Sutton United	v	Chesham United	2–0	1027
Enfield	v	Purfleet	2–0	703
Harrow Borough	v	Worcester City	3–3	489
Worcester City	v	*Harrow Borough*	*5–3*	1021
Worthing	v	Marlow	3–0	564

SECOND ROUND   12th February 1994

(replays in italics)

			Result	Att
Runcorn	v	Telford United	2–1	844
Grantham Town	v	Bishop Auckland	1–2	815
Colwyn Bay	v	Southport	0–3	660
Dagenham & Redbridge	v	Woking	1–2	1711
Worcester City	v	Macclesfield Town	0–0	1578
Macclesfield Town	v	*Worcester City*	*3–2*	704
Worthing	v	Enfield	1–1	837
Enfield	v	*Worthing*	*2–0*	583
Spennymoor United	v	Halifax Town	1–2	1426
Kettering Town	v	Billingham Synthonia	2–2	2076
Billingham Synthonia	v	*Kettering Town*	*3–1*	842
Guiseley	v	Stafford Rangers	3–2	1209
Kingstonian	v	Merthyr Tydfil	0–2	853
Sutton United	v	Bath City	6–1	1188
Grays Athletic	v	Bromsgrove Rovers	1–2	494
Welling United	v	Dover Athletic	1–3	1726
Gateshead	v	Gretna	0–0	402
Gretna	v	*Gateshead*	*0–1aet*	205
Cheltenham Town	v	Hednesford Town	1–0	965
Morecambe	v	Slough Town	1–0	831

THIRD ROUND   5th March 1994

(replays in italics)

			Result	Att
Macclesfield Town	v	Billingham Synthonia	0–1	909
Cheltenham Town	v	Guiseley	0–0	1117
Guiseley	v	*Cheltenham Town*	*1–0*	1139
Gateshead	v	Merthyr Tydfil	3–2	502
Sutton United	v	Dover Athletic	0–0	1989
Dover Athletic	v	*Sutton United*	*2–3 aet*	2207
Runcorn	v	Halifax Town	1–1	1302
Halifax Town	v	*Runcorn*	*0–2*	1406
Bishop Auckland	v	Enfield	2–2	830
Enfield	v	*Bishop Auckland*	*2–1*	850
Woking	v	Bromsgrove Rovers	3–2	2342
Morecambe	v	Southport	2–1	2246

FOURTH ROUND 26th March 1994

(replays in italics)

			Result	Att
Gateshead	v	Runcorn	0–3	1807
Sutton United	v	Enfield	1–1	1813
Enfield	v	*Sutton United*	*1–0*	1255
Woking	v	Billingham Synthonia	1–1	2767
Billingham Synthonia	v	*Woking*	*1–2*	1776
Guiseley	v	Morecambe	3–2	1805

SEMI-FINAL First Leg 16th April 1994

(replays in italics)

			Result	Att
Woking	v	Enfield	1–1	3841
Runcorn	v	Guiseley	1–1	1595
(At Chester City FC)				

Second Leg 23rd April 1994

			Result	Att
Enfield	v	Woking	0–0 aet	3310
Guiseley	v	Runcorn	0–1 aet	2176

Replay 26th April 1994

			Result	Att
Woking	v	Enfield	3–0	2674
(at Wycombe Wanderers FC)				

FINAL 21 May 1994

			Result	Att
Woking	v	Runcorn	2–1	15818

FA Challenge Trophy Winners 1970–1994

Year/venue	Winners		Runners-up	Result
1970 Wembley	Macclesfield Town	v	Telford United	2–0
1971 Wembley	Telford United	v	Hillingdon Borough	3–2
1972 Wembley	Stafford Rangers	v	Barnet	3–0
1973 Wembley	Scarborough	v	Wigan Athletic	2–1*
1974 Wembley	Morecambe	v	Dartford	2–1
1975 Wembley	Matlock Town	v	Scarborough	4–0
1976 Wembley	Scarborough	v	Stafford Rangers	3–2*
1977 Wembley	Scarborough	v	Dagenham	2–1
1978 Wembley	Altrincham	v	Leatherhead	3–1
1979 Wembley	Stafford Rangers	v	Kettering Town	2–0

Year/venue	Winners		Runners-up	Result
1980 Wembley	Dagenham	v	Mossley	2–1
1981 Wembley	Bishop's Stortford	v	Sutton United	1–0
1982 Wembley	Enfield	v	Altrincham	1–0*
1983 Wembley	Telford United	v	Northwich Victoria	2–1
1984 Wembley	Northwich Victoria	v	Bangor City	1–1
Stoke	Northwich Victoria	v	Bangor City	2–1
1985 Wembley	Wealdstone	v	Boston United	2–1
1986 Wembley	Altrincham	v	Runcorn	1–0
1987 Wembley	Kidderminster Harriers	v	Burton Albion	0–0
West Bromwich	Kidderminster Harriers	v	Burton Albion	2–1
1988 Wembley	Enfield	v	Telford United	0–0
West Bromwich	Enfield	v	Telford United	3–2
1989 Wembley	Telford United	v	Macclesfield Town	1–0*
1990 Wembley	Barrow	v	Leek Town	3–0
1991 Wembley	Wycombe Wanderers	v	Kidderminster Harriers	2–1
1992 Wembley	Colchester United	v	Witton Albion	3–1
1993 Wembley	Wycombe Wanderers	v	Runcorn	4–1
1994 Wembley	Woking	v	Runcorn	2–1

* After extra time

FA Challenge Trophy Competition 1994–1995

LIST OF 64 CLUBS RECEIVING EXEMPTION

32 Clubs to the First Round Proper

Altrincham
Bath City
Billingham Synthonia
Bishop Auckland
Bromsgrove Rovers
Dagenham & Redbridge
Dover Athletic
Durham City
Enfield
Farnborough Town
Gateshead

Guiseley
Halifax Town
Kettering Town
Kidderminster Harriers
Macclesfield Town
Marine
Merthyr Tydfil
Morecambe
Northwich Victoria
Runcorn
Slough Town

Southport
Stafford Rangers
Stalybridge Celtic
Stevenage Borough
Sutton United
Telford United
Welling United
Witton Albion
Woking
Yeovil Town

32 Clubs to the Third Round Qualifying

Atherstone United
Barrow
Blyth Spartans
Boston United
Carshalton Athletic
Chelmsford City
Cheltenham Town
Chesham United
Colwyn Bay
Crawley Town
Frickley Athletic

Grantham Town
Grays Athletic
Gretna
Halesowen Town
Hednesford Town
Hitchin Town
Hyde United
Kingstonian
Leek Town
Marlow
Northallerton Town

Seaham Red Star
Spennymoor United
St Albans City
Trowbridge Town
Warrington Town
Weston-super-Mare
Whitby Town
Winsford United
Worcester City
Worthing

FA Challenge Vase – Final Tie 1994

Diss Town 2   Taunton Town 1
(after extra time)

DissTown, the Jewson Eastern Counties League side from Norfolk, were ultimately able to celebrate victory after an extraordinary Vase final which looked to be slipping away from them, as Taunton fought bravely to hold on to a one-goal lead deep into injury time. The break Diss deserved – they virtually ran the game after conceding a goal on 12 minutes to Derek Fowler's close-range header – came when Taunton goalkeeper Kevin Maloy was adjudged to have brought down Paul Gibbs as he attempted to dribble round him, and the Diss No. 11 (he actually played left-back) got up to convert a nerveless penalty. This equalising goal was scored after nine minutes of added time!

From that traumatic moment for the Somerset team – so near and yet so far – Taunton were a beaten side. In extra time a buoyant Diss scored through Peter Mendham (109 minutes), a vastly experienced player who had enjoyed ten successful seasons with Norwich City before being forced to retire with a pelvic injury. The highlight of his Carrow Road career had been the 1985 Milk Cup triumph against Sunderland – now the 34-year-old midfielder was a Wembley winner once again.

Taunton impressed early on and almost scored in the first fifteen seconds as Woodcock plunged to his left to stop John Durham's stinging right-foot volley from just inside the box. The goalkeeper's momentum took him over the line, inches from his left-hand post, for a corner-kick to Taunton. Andy Perrett, a prolific marksman with the Great Mills Western League outfit, proved an enigma: a player who had already scored 60 goals in the season, including six in an FA Cup tie at Dawlish, wore strapping on his left knee and seemed to struggle from the start. He finally limped out of the action after 54 minutes, but he had helped to fashion Taunton's goal, heading the ball on for Fowler to nod it just out of Woodcock's reach and into the far corner off the post.

The abiding memory of a very sporting final, with several players shaking opponents' hands as they prepared to start the second period of extra time, was of match-winner Mendham stripping off his tangerine shirt at the finish and whirling it around his head before thousands of ecstatic Diss supporters.

Diss Town: Woodcock, Carter, Wolsey (Musgrave), Casey (Bugg), Hartle, Smith G., Barth, Mendham, Miles, Warne, Gibbs.
Taunton Town: Maloy, Morris, Walsh, Ewens, Graddon, Palfrey, West (Hendy), Fowler, Durham, Perrett (Ward), Jarvis.
Referee: K. Morton (Bury St. Edmunds).
Chief Guest: Sir Walter Winterbottom, C.B.E.
Attendance: 13,450.

Peter Mendham, scorer of the winning goal, moves in to challenge Taunton's Palfrey.

FA Vase 1993–1994

EXTRA PRELIMINARY ROUND 4th September 1993

(replays in italics)

			Result	Att
Shotton Comrades	v	Ponteland United	0–5	25
Heaton Stannington	v	Cleator Moor Celtic	1–6	14
West Allotment Celtic	v	Bedlington Terriers	4–1	101
Sunderland Kennet Roker	v	Walker	2–4	26
Marske United	v	Holker Old Boys	0–2	50
Wolviston	v	Seaton Delaval Amateurs	2–6	30
Seaton Delaval Seaton Terr	v	Newton Aycliffe	1–3	17
Mickleover RBL	v	North Trafford	0–5	62
(at North Trafford FC)				
Hall Road Rangers	v	Heswall	2–1	42
Clipstone Welfare	v	Westhoughton Town	5–0	75
Priory (Eastwood)	v	Ayone	5–2	55
Christleton	v	Waterloo Dock	1–3	35
(at Upton AA FC)				
Poulton Victoria	v	Rainworth MW	3–3 aet	46
Rainworth MW	v	*Poulton Victoria*	*1–2*	94
Maghull	v	General Chemicals	1–1 aet	55
General Chemicals	v	*Maghull*	*1–3*	55
Nettleham	v	Merseyside Police	2–3	52
Borrowash Victoria	v	Wythenshawe Amateur	1–0	42
Grove United	v	Ashfield United	0–1	40
Kimberley Town	v	Worsbro Bridge MW	3–2	42
Shirebrook Town	v	Hallam	1–5 aet	140
RES Parkgate	v	Cheadle Town	3–1	30

			Result	Att
St Dominics	v	Vauxhall Motors (WC)	1–4	38
Lucas Sports	v	Ashville	5–1	56
(at Ashville FC)				
Louth United	v	Castleton Gabriels	1–0	34
Atherton Collieries	v	Liversedge	1–2	55
Blackpool Mechanics	v	Ellesmere Port Town	1–4	+
Walsall Wood	v	Lutterworth Town	1–0	48
Holwell Sports	v	Barwell	3–1	100
Alvechurch	v	Meir KA	3–0	79
St Andrews	v	Bolehall Swifts	0–0 aet	40
Bolehall Swifts	v	*St Andrews*	*0–4*	45
Pegasus Juniors	v	Westfields	2–2 aet	148
(at Hereford United FC)				
Westfields	v	*Pegasus Juniors*	*5–2*	126
Dunkirk	v	Cradley Town	6–1	42
Stapenhill	v	Brierley Hill Town	2–1 aet	80
Knowle	v	Kings Heath	4–1	38
Oadby Town	v	Anstey Nomads	1–1 aet	104
Anstey Nomads	v	*Oadby Town*	*1–3 aet*	187
Gedling Town	v	Birstall United	2–1	50
Sawbridgeworth Town	v	Hadleigh United	5–3 aet	68
Clacton Town	v	Brightlingsea United	1–0	104
Warboys Town	v	Brantham Athletic	1–2 aet	92
Somersham Town	v	Stanway Rovers	1–0	46
Ely City	v	Downham Town	7–0	54
Woodbridge Town	v	Ipswich Wanderers	0–3	143
Long Sutton Athletic	v	Great Wakering Rovers	1–5	92
Beaconsfield United	v	Brook House	1–3 aet	40
St Margaretsbury	v	London Colney	1–2	34
(at Hertford Town FC)				
Wootton Blue Cross	v	Tower Hamlets	1–5	74
Concord Rangers	v	Bowers United	3–0	60
Totternhoe	v	Luton Old Boys'	2–0	29
Hillingdon Borough	v	Welwyn Garden City	3–1	32
Stansted	v	East Ham United	0–2 aet	38
Romford	v	Potton United	1–2	145
(at East Ham United FC)				
Leverstock Green	v	Potters Bar Town	3–1	57
Barkingside	v	Cockfosters	3–1	18
Rayners Lane	v	Harpenden Town	2–1	62
Slade Green	v	Eastbourne United	2–1	46
Cray Wanderers	v	Ashford Town (Middx)	2–3 aet	72
Furness	v	Cranleigh	1–0	40
Broadbridge Heath	v	Hartley Wintney	3–1	55
Newhaven	v	St Andrews (London)	4–2	100
Crowborough Athletic	v	Worthing United	3–1	98
West Wickham	v	Alma Swanley	1–4	51
Farleigh Rovers	v	Eastbourne Town	2–0	39
Folkestone Invicta	v	Ash United	3–2	156
Shoreham	v	Cobham	0–3	35
Arundel	v	Ditton	2–1	57
Thamesmead Town	v	Beckenham Town	4–0	33
Petersfield United	v	Christchurch		
(walkover for Christchurch – Petersfield United removed from the Competition)				
Swindon Supermarine	v	Clanfield	5–1	35
Sandhurst Town	v	Flight Refuelling	1–1 aet	57
Flight Refuelling	v	*Sandhurst Town*	*0–1*	28
BAT Sports	v	Sherborne Town	1–2	53

			Result	Att
Sholing Sports	v	North Leigh		
(walkover for North Leigh – Sholing Sports withdrawn from the Competition)				
Whitchurch United	v	Peppard	1–3	74
Tuffley Rovers	v	Keynsham Town	1–4	84
DRG	v	Bishop Sutton	0–1	70
Almondsbury Town	v	Larkhall Athletic	1–3	42
Patchway Town	v	Brislington	0–5	30
Old Georgians	v	Wotton Rovers	1–0	45
Clyst Rovers	v	Cirencester Town	0–1	48
Porthleven	v	Newquay	0–2	111
Hallen	v	Ellwood	2–1	79
Moreton Town	v	Backwell United	1–0	50
Crediton United	v	Bridgwater Town	2–0	129

PRELIMINARY ROUND   2nd October 1993

(replays in italics)

			Result	Att
Walker	v	Eppleton CW	1–3	65
Horden CW	v	Penrith	0–3	30
Darlington Cleveland Social	v	Evenwood Town	1–2	14
Pickering Town	v	Holker Old Boys	7–3	81
Billingham Town	v	Cleator Moor Celtic	4–0	46
Newton Aycliffe	v	Crook Town	1–4	30
Whickham	v	Netherfield	1–0	60
Prudhoe East End	v	Norton & Stockton Ancients	4–3 aet	23
Ponteland United	v	Alnwick Town	2–0	26
Harrogate Railway	v	West Allotment Celtic	3–0	61
Annfield Plain	v	Seaton Delaval Amateurs	0–2	28
Langley Park S&S United	v	Willington	0–1	33
Esh Winning	v	Ryhope CA	2–1	35
Nantwich Town	v	Ossett Town	2–0	128
Clitheroe	v	Maine Road	1–0	110
Tadcaster Albion	v	Louth United	1–3	33
Chadderton	v	Ossett Albion	0–4	163
Blidworth MW	v	Kimberley Town	2–4	27
Lincoln United	v	Skelmersdale United	3–2	114
Belper Town	v	Bradford Park Avenue	1–0	185
Armthorpe Welfare	v	Harworth CI	4–1	58
Hallam	v	St Helens Town	2–0	117
Lancaster City	v	Ilkeston Town	0–1	151
Garforth Town	v	Maghull	1–1 aet	61
Maghull	v	*Garforth Town*	*2–1*	78
Selby Town	v	Bacup Borough	2–4 aet	36
Prescot	v	Hucknall Town	3–1	82
Thackley	v	Clipstone Welfare	3–0	180
Salford City	v	Poulton Victoria	2–0	100
Heanor Town	v	Stocksbridge Park Steels	1–3 aet	137
Priory (Eastwood)	v	Rossendale United	2–5	102
Merseyside Police	v	Farsley Celtic	2–1	150
Glossop North End	v	Hatfield Main	2–1	195
Borrowash Victoria	v	Eccleshill United	1–2	54
Immingham Town	v	Maltby MW	2–6	55
Liversedge	v	Winterton Rangers	3–0	88
North Trafford	v	Lucas Sports	2–1	82
Sheffield	v	Hall Road Rangers	2–0	13

			Result	Att
Bootle	v	Ellesmere Port Town	3–1	41
Waterloo Dock	v	RES Parkgate	0–2	32
Rossington Main	v	Pontefract Collieries	0–1 aet	36
Oldham Town	v	Darwen	1–3	34
Formby	v	Radcliffe Borough	1–2	62
Ashfield United	v	Vauxhall	0–4	91
Yorkshire Amateur	v	Blackpool (Wren) Rovers	2–0	45
Glasshoughton Welfare	v	Denaby United	2–3 aet	90
St Andrews	v	Boldmere St Michaels	0–1	40
Northampton Spencer	v	Banbury United	3–2	81
Gedling Town	v	Walsall Wood	3–3 aet	22
Walsall Wood	v	*Gedling Town*	*3–0*	43
Stapenhill	v	Pershore Town	3–1	83
Long Buckby	v	Knowle	3–1	57
Rushall Olympic	v	Sandwell Borough	1–0	42
Alvechurch	v	Halesowen Harriers	4–2 aet	84
Chasetown	v	Stourport Swifts	4–1	102
Highgate United	v	Holwell Sports	1–2	42
Daventry Town	v	Dunkirk	0–3	24
Racing Club Warwick	v	Wellingborough Town	3–0	90
Raunds Town	v	Wednesfield	4–2	86
Lye Town	v	Stratford Town	1–0	71
Willenhall Town	v	West Bromwich Town	0–3	80
Westfields	v	Mile Oak Rovers & Youth	4–2 aet	62
Cogenhoe United	v	Northfield Town	6–1	35
Paget Rangers	v	Desborough Town	3–2	76
Blakenall	v	Oadby Town	1–1 aet	45
Oadby Town	v	*Blakenall*	*6–0*	144
Hinckley Town	v	Stewarts & Lloyds	5–1	50
Rocester	v	Newport Pagnell Town	4–0	137
Watton United	v	Witham Town	1–3	95
Sawbridgeworth Town	v	Bury Town	2–1	80
Fakenham Town	v	Boston	5–5 aet	199
Boston	v	*Fakenham Town*	*2–1*	65
Halstead Town	v	Norwich United	4–0	150
Spalding United	v	Holbeach United	1–1 aet	221
Holbeach United	v	*Spalding United*	*3–4*	306
Great Wakering Rovers	v	Gorleston	4–1	109
Cornard United	v	Felixstowe Town	1–1 aet	47
Felixstowe Town	v	*Cornard United*	*0–2*	85
Brantham Athletic	v	Ely City	5–4 aet	46
Histon	v	Tiptree United	3–0	30
Soham Town Rangers	v	Basildon United	5–3 aet	125
Mirrlees Blackstone	v	Sudbury Wanderers	3–1	67
abandoned after 45 minutes due to waterlogged pitch, 0–1)				
March Town United	v	Bourne Town	1–0	121
Kings Lynn	v	Clacton Town	1–0	458
Stowmarket Town	v	Ipswich Wanderers	5–2	131
Chatteris Town	v	Stamford	2–2 aet	70
Stamford	v	*Chatteris Town*	*1–2*	128
Eynesbury Rovers	v	Haverhill Rovers	2–3 aet	71
Newmarket Town	v	Somersham Town	4–0	78
Arlesey Town	v	Flackwell Heath	2–0	45
Hornchurch	v	East Ham United	2–0	94
Hemel Hempstead	v	Haringey Borough	4–2	67
Kingsbury Town	v	Cheshunt	1–2	53
East Thurrock United	v	Concord Rangers	2–4	178
Ware	v	Tower Hamlets	3–2	44

			Result	*Att*
Kempston Rovers	v	Ford United	0–2	
Wingate & Finchley	v	Hatfield Town	2–10	40+
Brook House	v	Royston Town	2–4	65
Viking Sports	v	Leverstock Green	3–4 aet	40
Letchworth Garden City	v	Hertford Town	4–0	49
Hillingdon Borough	v	Potton United	1–1 aet	62
Potton United	v	*Hillingdon Borough*	*1–0*	140
London Colney	v	Feltham & Hounslow Borough	1–2	50
Stotfold	v	Barkingside	6–2	90
Biggleswade Town	v	Rayners Lane	1–3	51
Leighton Town	v	Totternhoe	2–0	177
Southall	v	Burnham	1–5	16
(at Burnham FC)				
Rainham Town	v	Hanwell Town	2–5 aet	38
Shillington	v	Langford	2–1 aet	92
Hampton	v	Collier Row	0–1	102
Clapton	v	Dunstable	2–1	58
Three Bridges	v	Horsham YMCA	2–2	89

(tie awarded to Horsham YMCA – Three Bridges removed from the Competition for playing an ineligible player)

Burgess Hill Town	v	Pagham	3–1	168
Bracknell Town	v	Steyning Town	6–0	108
Bedfont	v	Egham Town	2–1	60
Merstham	v	Arundel	1–1 aet	89
Arundel	v	*Merstham*	*3–1*	57
Leatherhead	v	Whitehawk	0–1	160
(at Whitehawk FC)				
Epsom & Ewell	v	Ashford Town (Middx)	1–1 aet	52
Ashford Town (Middx)	v	*Epsom & Ewell*	*3–1 aet*	94
(at Walton & Hersham FC)				
Newhaven	v	Furness	2–1	105
Farleigh Rovers	v	Corinthian	0–3	55
Cobham	v	Crowborough Athletic	0–2	35
Chipstead	v	Chichester City	1–0	21
Lancing	v	Horsham	2–1	171
Faversham Town	v	Croydon Athletic	1–3	70
Chatham Town	v	Southwick	2–1	102
Greenwich Borough	v	Alma Swanley	1–4	86
Corinthian Casuals	v	Broadbridge Heath	4–0	29
Redhill	v	Godalming & Guildford	1–3	66
Portfield	v	Ramsgate	3–1	85
Whitstable Town	v	Wick	2–3	146
Selsey	v	Herne Bay	0–1	105
Slade Green	v	Ringmer	3–2	53
Thamesmead Town	v	Folkestone Invicta	2–4 aet	50
Sheppey United	v	Langney Sports	8–0	56
Oakwood	v	Deal Town	3–0	28
Swindon Supermarine	v	Eastleigh	1–2	40
Sandhurst Town	v	Totton	1–0	34
Swanage Town & Herston	v	North Leigh	1–3	101
Bournemouth	v	First Tower United	0–1	60
Newbury Town	v	Westbury United	4–1	257
Thatcham Town	v	Brockenhurst	1–1 aet	48
Brockenhurst	v	*Thatcham Town*	*1–1*	98
Brockenhurst	v	*Thatcham Town*	*0–3*	172
Aldershot Town	v	Gosport Borough	7–0	1701
Thame United	v	Kintbury Rangers	9–0	85

			Result	Att
Sherborne Town	v	Horndean	2–2 aet	79
Horndean	v	*Sherborne Town*	*1–3*	62
Calne Town	v	Bicester Town	1–0	38
Bemerton Heath Harlequins	v	Christchurch	1–2	47
Abingdon United	v	Cove	2–5	37
Hamworthy United	v	Ryde Sports	1–5	101
Milton United	v	Wantage Town	1–0	72
Peppard	v	Fleet Town	5–2	135
Frome Town	v	Ilfracombe Town	3–1	70
Chard Town	v	Cinderford Town	2–1	76
Crediton United	v	Torpoint Athletic	1–2	118
Mangotsfield United	v	Brislington	3–0	153
Moreton Town	v	Taunton Town	0–2	130
Liskeard Athletic	v	Melksham Town	1–2	130
Fairford Town	v	Bridport	1–2	40
Glastonbury	v	Falmouth Town	1–3	95
Cirencester Town	v	Wellington Town	3–1	35
Bristol Manor Farm	v	Keynsham Town	0–2	30
Dawlish Town	v	Torrington	1–5	48
Odd Down	v	Chippenham Town	2–2 aet	71
Chippenham Town	v	*Odd Down*	*2–1*	155
Minehead	v	Hallen	5–2	80
Shortwood United	v	St Blazey	1–2	70
Exmouth Town	v	Bishop Sutton	0–2	89
Elmore	v	Newquay	4–3	129
Larkhall Athletic	v	Devizes Town	2–0 aet	58
Old Georgians	v	Barnstaple Town	0–2	55

FIRST ROUND   30th October 1993

(replays in italic)

			Result	Att
Whickham	v	Billingham Town	3–2	50
Harrogate Railway	v	Pickering Town	1–4	92
Penrith	v	Eppleton CW	2–1 aet	114
Esh Winning	v	South Shields	2–7	35
Willington	v	Prudhoe East End	0–1	23
Ponteland United	v	Seaton Delaval Amateurs	2–1 aet	20
Crook Town	v	Evenwood Town	1–0	79
Eccleshill United	v	Belper Town	1–2	37
Prescot AFC	v	Hallam	2–0	90
Rossendale United	v	Bootle	2–4	168
Vauxhall	v	Denaby United	2–1	38
Salford City	v	RES Parkgate	0–0 aet	60
RES Parkgate	v	*Salford City*	*4–1*	51
Liversedge	v	North Ferriby United	4–1	74
Thackley	v	Stocksbridge Park Steels	0–0 aet	85
Stocksbridge Park Steels	v	*Thackley*	*0–2*	81
Pontefract Collieries	v	Maltby MW	2–4	48
Merseyside Police	v	Louth United	4–5	50
Ossett Albion	v	Sheffield	1–1 aet	112
Sheffield	v	*Ossett Albion*	*4–0*	80
Bacup Borough	v	Clitheroe	1–1 aet	110
Clitheroe	v	*Bacup Borough*	*1–2*	250
Lincoln United	v	Darwen	2–0	121

Kimberley Town	v	Nantwich Town	1–2 aet	70
Yorkshire Amateur	v	Armthorpe Welfare	1–0	48
Newcastle Town	v	Glossop North End	3–4	53
(at Eastwood Hanley FC)				
Radcliffe Borough	v	North Trafford	2–0	118
Maghull	v	Ilkeston Town	0–1	164
Friar Lane OB	v	Cogenhoe United	1–1 aet	141
Cogenhoe United	v	*Friar Lane OB*	*2–0*	129
Northampton Spencer	v	Walsall Wood	3–0	64
Arnold Town	v	Boldmere St Michaels	3–0	170
Bridgnorth Town	v	Lye Town	1–0	133
Westfields	v	Racing Club Warwick	1–0	81
Armitage 90	v	Chatteris Town	1–2	42
Raunds Town	v	Stapenhill	5–2	110
Chasetown	v	Long Buckby	3–1	98
Dunkirk	v	Rushall Olympic	4–4 aet	40
Rushall Olympic	v	*Dunkirk*	*2–3 aet*	80
Rocester	v	West Bromwich Town	4–2	122
Hinckley Town	v	Oadby Town	0–3	83
Holwell Sports	v	Paget Rangers	1–1 aet	120
Paget Rangers	v	*Holwell Sports*	*2–4*	48
Oldbury United	v	Alvechurch	3–3 aet	102
Alvechurch	v	*Oldbury United*	*1–0*	62
March Town United	v	Witham Town	4–0	100
Spalding United	v	Sawbridgeworth Town	1–4	162
Lowestoft Town	v	Brantham Athletic	10–1	147
Harwich & Parkeston	v	Newmarket Town	2–3 aet	178
Boston	v	Mirrlees Blackstone	2–1	49
Haverhill Rovers	v	Tilbury	2–1	122
Kings Lynn	v	Great Yarmouth Town	2–1 aet	492
Stowmarket Town	v	Soham Town Rangers	2–5	134
Halstead Town	v	Histon	5–0	220
Great Wakering Rovers	v	Cornard United	4–1	159
Edgware Town	v	Feltham & Hounslow Borough	1–0	128
Tring Town	v	Hatfield Town	5–2	56
Leverstock Green	v	Brimsdown Rovers	1–2	57
Burnham	v	Hemel Hempstead	0–1 aet	87
Concord Rangers	v	Letchworth Garden City	0–2	90
Ware	v	Arlesey Town	0–1 aet	69
Cheshunt	v	Royston Town	1–1 aet	114
Royston Town	v	*Cheshunt*	*0–2*	72
Hornchurch	v	Leighton Town	4–0	76
Harefield United	v	Aveley	0–3	+
Shillington	v	Burnham Ramblers	2–0	60
Clapton	v	Barton Rovers	0–1	73
Northwood	v	Stotfold	1–0	157
Collier Row	v	Rayners Lane	4–1 aet	95
Potton United	v	Ford United	0–0aet	156
Ford United	v	*Potton United*	*1–1 aet*	63
Ford United	v	*Potton United*	*1–0*	47
Ashford Town (Middx)	v	Bedfont	0–2	85
Burgess Hill Town	v	Chatham Town	2–0	113
Newhaven	v	Tonbridge	2–3	320
Croydon Athletic	v	Littlehampton Town	3–1 aet	85
Arundel	v	Lewes	0–3	53
Sheppey United	v	Corinthian Casuals	0–2	101
Portfield	v	Oakwood	2–0	31
Alma Swanley	v	Tunbridge Wells	0–1	60

			Result	Att
Crowborough Athletic	v	Slade Green	2–0	90
Hanwell Town	v	Lancing	2–3	41
Corinthian	v	Whitehawk	0–3	31
Wick	v	Hailsham Town	3–1	143
Godalming & Guildford	v	Chipstead	2–2 aet	44
Chipstead	v	*Godalming & Guildford*	2–3	40
Bracknell Town	v	Folkestone Invicta	3–0	115
Herne Bay	v	Horsham YMCA	3–0	225
Cove	v	Eastleigh	1–3	102
Newbury Town	v	Sandhurst Town	2–0	210
Lymington	v	Thame United	0–2	94
Hungerford Town	v	Melksham Town	2–3	89
North Leigh	v	Christchurch	3–1	101
Peppard	v	Oxford City	1–0	113

(Peppard removed from the Competition and Oxford City awarded the tie due to a protest received from Oxford City regarding the incorrect pitch dimensions at Peppard)

Ryde Sports	v	Andover	0–3	32
Milton United	v	Calne Town	4–2	49
First Tower United	v	Sherborne Town	1–0 aet	100
Thatcham Town	v	Aldershot Town	0–1	1138
St Blazey	v	Chard Town	3–1 aet	105
Chippenham Town	v	Torpoint Athletic	2–2 aet	129
Torpoint Athletic	v	*Chippenham Town*	3–0	121
Yate Town	v	Cirencester Town	2–1	109
Saltash United	v	Barnstaple Town	1–1 aet	132
Barnstaple Town	v	*Saltash United*	2–1	208
Mangotsfield United	v	Minehead	3–1	115
Larkhall Athletic	v	Frome Town	0–1	62
Bishop Sutton	v	Bideford	1–2	73
Elmore	v	Torrington	2–1	75
Taunton Town	v	Keynsham Town	2–0	302
Bridport	v	Falmouth Town	1–2	303

SECOND ROUND   20th November 1993

(replays in italics)

			Result	Att
Atherton LR	v	Prudhoe East End	3–0	120
Ponteland United	v	Liversedge	3–1	50
Yorkshire Amateur	v	Sheffield	3–2	77
Burscough	v	Penrith	2–3	120
Cammell Laird	v	Bootle	6–2	150
Brigg Town	v	Flixton	3–1	126
Bamber Bridge	v	Vauxhall	4–2	346
South Shields	v	Maltby MW	2–3	160
Thackley	v	Prescot AFC	2–1	127
Pickering Town	v	Bacup Borough	0–1	89
RES Parkgate	v	Whickham	0–3	49
Radcliffe Borough	v	Crook Town	3–1	133
Chasetown	v	Oadby Town	3–4 aet	108
Arnold Town	v	Lincoln United	1–2	267
Cogenhoe United	v	Evesham United	0–0 aet	105
Evesham United	v	*Cogenhoe United*	1–2	164
Belper Town	v	Ilkeston Town	1–0	404
Dunkirk	v	Louth United	4–2	94
Pelsall Villa	v	Alvechurch	1–1 aet	162

			Result	Att
Alvechurch	v	*Pelsall Villa*	2–3	103
Bridgnorth Town	v	Chatteris Town	5–1	104
Westfields	v	Northampton Spencer	1–1 aet	91
Northampton Spencer	v	*Westfields*	3–0	71
Holwell Sports	v	Nantwich Town	1–6	143
Rothwell Town	v	Eastwood Hanley	1–1 aet	127
Eastwood Hanley	v	*Rothwell Town*	2–1	121
Hinckley Athletic	v	West Midlands Police	2–1	169
Rocester	v	Glossop North End	1–2	147
Bilston Town	v	Raunds Town	2–2 aet	102
Raunds Town	v	*Bilston Town*	4–0	102
Walthamstow Pennant	v	Saffron Walden Town	1–4	77
Arlesey Town	v	Haverhill Rovers	2–1	100
Brimsdown Rovers	v	Shillington	2–1	28
Edgware Town	v	Wisbech Town	1–2	208
Tring Town	v	Diss Town	0–0 aet	95
Diss Town	v	*Tring Town*	2–0	248
Collier Row	v	Newmarket Town	3–2	118
Lowestoft Town	v	Buckingham Town	0–2	126
Letchworth Garden City	v	Soham Town Rangers	2–3	85
Hoddesdon Town	v	Cheshunt	1–4	175
Hemel Hempstead	v	Ford United	0–1	90
Kings Lynn	v	Hornchurch	7–1	398
Halstead Town	v	Sawbridgeworth Town	3–1	250
Boston	v	Barton Rovers	3–1	64
March Town United	v	Great Wakering Rovers	0–2	175
Aveley	v	Canvey Island	2–4	320
Godalming & Guildford	v	Bracknell Town	2–4 aet	142
Wick	v	Malden Vale	0–1 aet	140
Burgess Hill Town	v	Metropolitan Police	0–3	164
Thame United	v	North Leigh	2–1	99
Aldershot Town	v	Herne Bay	2–1	1965
Whitehawk	v	Portfield	4–1	83
Eastleigh	v	Peacehaven & Telscombe	1–2 aet	93
Crowborough Athletic	v	Corinthian Casuals	1–4	134
Chertsey Town	v	Newbury Town	0–3	306
Tunbridge Wells	v	Lewes	2–0	148
Bedfont	v	Northwood	1–1 aet	75
Northwood	v	*Bedfont*	1–2 aet	101
Newport (IOW)	v	Banstead Athletic	2–2 aet	297
Banstead Athletic	v	*Newport (IOW)*	0–0 aet	55
Banstead Athletic	v	*Newport (IOW)*	1–1 aet	
Newport (IOW)	v	*Banstead Athletic*	1–6	213
Lancing	v	Tonbridge	3–4	246
Croydon Athletic	v	Oxford City	2–0	91
Forest Green Rovers	v	Barnstaple Town	0–0 aet	112

(Forest Green Rovers removed from the Competition and the tie awarded to Barnstaple Town as Forest Green Rovers played an ineligible player)

Torpoint Athletic	v	First Tower United	2–0	205
Melksham Town	v	Taunton Town	0–6	170
Welton Rovers	v	Wimborne Town	0–1	134
Mangotsfield United	v	Tiverton Town	0–5	318
Yate Town	v	Elmore	1–2	125
Andover	v	Bideford	6–2	204
Milton United	v	Falmouth Town	1–4	119
Clevedon Town	v	St Blazey	4–0	372
Paulton Rovers	v	Frome Town	2–1	128

THIRD ROUND   11th December 1993

(replays in italics)

			Result	Att
Thackley	v	Lincoln United	2–1	213
Cammell Laird	v	Glossop North End	2–3	155
Oadby Town	v	Ponteland United	2–0 aet	170
Nantwich Town	v	Bacup Borough	2–0	220
Belper Town	v	Brigg Town	2–1	202
Radcliffe Borough	v	Yorkshire Amateur	2–0	149
Penrith	v	Atherton LR	0–1	89
Whickham	v	Bamber Bridge	1–0	135
Dunkirk	v	Maltby MW	2–1	103
Wisbech Town	v	Collier Row	1–2	410
Great Wakering Rovers	v	Hinckley Athletic	3–3 aet	159
Hinckley Athletic	v	*Great Wakering Town*	*2–1*	323
Northampton Spencer	v	Cogenhoe United	1–2	185
Boston	v	Bedfont	6–1	55
Ford United	v	Diss Town	1–2 aet	72
Saffron Walden Town	v	Raunds Town	1–4	137
Bridgnorth Town	v	Cheshunt	3–1	145
Soham Town Rangers	v	Brimsdown Rovers	3–0	155
Buckingham Town	v	Kings Lynn	1–2	260
Pelsall Villa	v	Halstead Town	2–4	61
(abandoned after 57 minutes, 0–0)				
Eastwood Hanley	v	Arlesey Town	1–2	120
Canvey Island	v	Corinthian Casuals	2–1	381
Taunton Town	v	Barnstaple Town	2–0	284
Elmore	v	Thame United	1–2	120
Croydon Athletic	v	Paulton Rovers	0–2	120
Tonbridge	v	Tiverton Town	0–1	536+
Aldershot Town	v	Malden Vale	1–0 aet	1697
Tunbridge Wells	v	Torpoint Athletic	2–6	181
Clevedon Town	v	Wimborne Town	3–4 aet	392
Bracknell Town	v	Newbury Town	1–2	165
Banstead Athletic	v	Peacehaven & Telscombe	1–0 aet	45
Falmouth Town	v	Andover	3–1 aet	418
Whitehawk	v	Metropolitan Police	3–2 aet	175

FOURTH ROUND   15th January 1994

(replays in italics)

			Result	Att
Radcliffe Borough	v	Boston	3–3 aet	216
Boston	v	*Radcliffe Borough*	*2–1*	160
Atherton LR	v	Thackley	0–0 aet	320
Thackley	v	*Atherton LR*	*2–3 aet*	250
Raunds Town	v	Belper Town	1–2 aet	330
Whickham	v	Dunkirk	0–0 aet	356
Dunkirk	v	*Whickham*	*1–0*	380
Kings Lynn	v	Nantwich Town	1–0	886
Bridgnorth Town	v	Glossop North End	3–2	310
Oadby Town	v	Cogenhoe United	5–1	400
Halstead Town	v	Wimborne Town	1–5	463
Canvey Island	v	Newbury Town	1–2	782
Taunton Town	v	Banstead Athletic	1–1 aet	479
Banstead Athletic	v	*Taunton Town*	*0–2*	135

			Result	Att
Whitehawk	v	Thame United	3–2	285
Torpoint Athletic	v	Diss Town	0–3	329
Aldershot Town	v	Soham Town Rangers	5–0	2284
Tiverton Town	v	Paulton Rovers	5–0	810
Hinckley Athletic	v	Collier Row	4–2	440
Arlesey Town	v	Falmouth Town	5–3	350

FIFTH ROUND   5th February 1994

(replays in italics)

			Result	Att
Hinckley Athletic	v	Newbury Town	0–3	636
Atherton LR	v	Bridgnorth Town	1–0	567
Oadby Town	v	Arlesey Town	1–2 aet	600
Dunkirk	v	Tiverton Town	0–2	814
Diss Town	v	Kings Lynn	2–0	1492
Whitehawk	v	Boston	2–3	485
Aldershot	v	Wimborne Town	1–0	3420
Belper Town	v	Taunton Town	1–3	1050

SIXTH ROUND   26th February 1994

(replays in italics)

			Result	Att
Aldershot Town	v	Atherton LR	0–0 aet	4246
Atherton LR	v	*Aldershot Town*	*0–0 aet*	1856
Aldershot Town	v	*Atherton LR*	*0–2*	4439
Arlesey Town	v	Boston	2–3	1159
Diss Town	v	Tiverton Town	1–0	1256
Taunton Town	v	Newbury Town	2–0	1472

SEMI–FINAL First Leg   19th March 1994

(replays in italics)

			Result	Att
Taunton Town	v	Boston	1–0	1369
Diss Town	v	Atherton LR	3–1	1731

Second Leg   26–27th March 1994

			Result	Att
Atherton LR	v	Diss Town	2–0 aet	1720
Boston	v	Taunton Town	0–1	1785

Replay 30th March 1994

			Result	Att
Diss Town	v	*Atherton LR*	*2–1*	768
(at VS Rugby FC)				

FINAL   7 May 1994

			Result	Att
Diss Town	v	Taunton	2–1 aet	13450

FA Challenge Vase Winners 1975–1994

Year/venue		Winners		Runners-up	Result
1975	Wembley	Hoddesdon Town	v	Epsom & Ewell	2–1
1976	Wembley	Billericay Town	v	Stamford	1–0*
1977	Wembley	Billericay Town	v	Sheffield	1–1*
	Nottingham	Billericay Town	v	Sheffield	2–1
1978	Wembley	Blue Star	v	Barton Rovers	2–1
1979	Wembley	Billericay Town	v	Almondsbury Greenway	4–1
1980	Wembley	Stamford	v	Guisborough Town	2–0
1981	Wembley	Whickham	v	Willenhall Town	3–2*
1982	Wembley	Forest Green Rovers	v	Rainworth Miners' Welfare	3–0
1983	Wembley	VS Rugby	v	Halesowen Town	1–0
1984	Wembley	Stansted	v	Stamford	3–2
1985	Wembley	Halesowen Town	v	Fleetwood Town	3–1
1986	Wembley	Halesowen Town	v	Southall	3–0
1987	Wembley	St Helens Town	v	Warrington Town	3–2
1988	Wembley	Colne Dynamoes	v	Emley	1–0*
1989	Wembley	Tamworth	v	Sudbury Town	1–1*
	Peterborough	Tamworth	v	Sudbury Town	3–0
1990	Wembley	Yeading	v	Bridlington Town	0–0*
	Leeds	Yeading	v	Bridlington Town	1–0
1991	Wembley	Guiseley	v	Gresley Rovers	4–4*
	Sheffield	Guiseley	v	Gresley Rovers	3–1
1992	Wembley	Wimborne Town	v	Guiseley	5–3
1993	Wembley	Bridlington Town	v	Tiverton Town	1–0
1994	Wembley	Diss Town	v	Taunton Town	2–1*

* After extra time

FA Challenge Vase Competition 1994–1995

List of 64 clubs receiving exemption
32 Clubs to the Second Round

Arlesey Town
Banstead Athletic
Belper Town
Boston
Brandon United
Brigg Town
Burscough
Cammell Laird
Canvey Island
Chalfont St Peter
Croydon

Diss Town
Dunkirk
Eastwood Hanley
Hinckley Athletic
Hoddesdon Town
Malden Vale
Metropolitan Police
Oadby Town
Paulton Rovers
Peacehaven & Telscombe
Pelsall Villa

Saffron Walden Town
Stockton
Taunton Town
Tiverton Town
Tunbridge Wells
Walthamstow Pennant
Whitehawk
Wimborne Town
Windsor & Eton
Wisbech Town

32 Clubs to the First Round

Andover
Arnold Town
Aveley
Barton Rovers
Basildon United
Bideford
Brimsdown Rovers
Cogenhoe United
Collier Row
Falmouth Town
Flixton

Glossop North End
Hailsham Town
Halstead Town
Herne Bay
Lewes
Lowestoft Town
Moreton Town
Nantwich Town
Oxford City
Pershore Town
Raunds Town

Soham Town Rangers
South Shields
Stocksbridge Park Steels
Thackley
Thame United
Torpoint Athletic
Tring Town
Welton Rovers
West Midlands Police
Whickham

FA Youth Challenge Cup Winners 1953–1994

The FA Youth Cup Final is played on a two-leg basis but the 1978 final between Crystal Palace and Aston Villa was a single match. The only final which needed a replay was the 1983 contest between Norwich and Everton.

Year	Winners		Runners-up	Result
1953	Manchester United	v	Wolverhampton Wanderers	9–3
1954	Manchester United	v	Wolverhampton Wanderers	5–4
1955	Manchester United	v	West Bromwich Albion	7–1
1956	Manchester United	v	Chesterfield	4–3
1957	Manchester United	v	West Ham United	8–2
1958	Wolverhampton Wanderers	v	Chelsea	7–6
1959	Blackburn Rovers	v	West Ham United	2–1
1960	Chelsea	v	Preston North End	5–2
1961	Chelsea	v	Everton	5–3
1962	Newcastle United	v	Wolverhampton Wanderers	2–1
1963	West Ham United	v	Liverpool	6–5
1964	Manchester United	v	Swindon Town	5–2
1965	Everton	v	Arsenal	3–2
1966	Arsenal	v	Sunderland	5–3
1967	Sunderland	v	Birmingham City	2–0
1968	Burnley	v	Coventry City	3–2
1969	Sunderland	v	West Bromwich Albion	6–3
1970	Tottenham Hotspur	v	Coventry City	4–3
1971	Arsenal	v	Cardiff City	2–0
1972	Aston Villa	v	Liverpool	5–2
1973	Ipswich Town	v	Bristol City	4–1
1974	Tottenham Hotspur	v	Huddersfield Town	2–1
1975	Ipswich Town	v	West Ham United	5–1
1976	West Bromwich Albion	v	Wolverhampton W anderers	5–0
1977	Crystal Palace	v	Everton	1–0
1978	Crystal Palace	v	Aston Villa	1–0
1979	Millwall	v	Manchester City	2–0
1980	Aston Villa	v	Manchester City	3–2
1981	West Ham United	v	Tottenham Hotspur	2–1
1982	Watford	v	Manchester United	7–6
1983	Norwich City	v	Everton	6–5*
1984	Everton	v	Stoke City	4–2
1985	Newcastle United	v	Watford	4–1
1986	Manchester City	v	Manchester United	3–1
1987	Coventry City	v	Charlton Athletic	2–1
1988	Arsenal	v	Doncaster Rovers	6–1
1989	Watford	v	Manchester City	2–1
1990	Tottenham Hotspur	v	Middlesbrough	3–2
1991	Millwall	v	Sheffield Wednesday	3–0
1992	Manchester United	v	Crystal Palace	6–3
1993	Leeds United	v	Manchester United	4–1
1994	Arsenal	v	Millwall	5–3

* aggregate score after replay

FA County Youth Challenge Cup Winners 1945–1994

From 1945 to 1969 the FA County Youth Cup final was played over two legs. Since 1970 it has been a one-match final and only twice (in 1988 and 1990) has a replay been required.

Year				Result
1945	Staffordshire	v	Wiltshire	3–2
1946	Berks & Bucks	v	Durham	4–3
1947	Durham	v	Essex	4–2
1948	Essex	v	Liverpool	5–3
1949	Liverpool	v	Middlesex	4–3
1950	Essex	v	Middlesex	4–3
1951	Middlesex	v	Leicestershire & Rutland	3–1
1952	Sussex	v	Liverpool	3–1
1953	Sheffield & Hallam	v	Hampshire	5–3
1954	Liverpool	v	Gloucestershire	4–1
1955	Bedfordshire	v	Sheffield & Hallam	2–0
1956	Middlesex	v	Staffordshire	3–2
1957	Hampshire	v	Cheshire	4–3
1958	Staffordshire	v	London	8–0
1959	Birmingham	v	London	7–5
1960	London	v	Birmingham	6–4
1961	Lancashire	v	Nottinghamshire	6–3
1962	Middlesex	v	Nottinghamshire	3–2
1963	Durham	v	Essex	3–2
1964	Sheffield & Hallam	v	Birmingham	1–0
1965	Northumberland	v	Middlesex	7–4
1966	Leics & Rutland	v	London	6–5
1967	Northamptonshire	v	Hertfordshire	5–4
1968	North Riding	v	Devon	7–4
1969	Northumberland	v	Sussex	1–0
1970	Hertfordshire	v	Cheshire	2–1
1971	Lancashire	v	Gloucestershire	2–0
1972	Middlesex	v	Liverpool	2–0
1973	Hertfordshire	v	Northumberland	3–0
1974	Nottinghamshire	v	London	2–0
1975	Durham	v	Bedfordshire	2–1
1976	Northamptonshire	v	Surrey	7–1
1977	Liverpool	v	Surrey	3–0
1978	Liverpool	v	Kent	3–1
1979	Hertfordshire	v	Liverpool	4–1
1980	Liverpool	v	Lancashire	2–0
1981	Lancashire	v	East Riding	3–1
1982	Devon	v	Kent	3–2*
1983	London	v	Gloucestershire	3–0
1984	Cheshire	v	Manchester	2–1
1985	East Riding	v	Middlesex	2–1
1986	Hertfordshire	v	Manchester	4–0
1987	North Riding	v	Gloucestershire	3–1
1988	East Riding	v	Middlesex	1–1
	East Riding	v	*Middlesex*	5–3
1989	Liverpool	v	Hertfordshire	2–1
1990	Staffordshire	v	Hampshire	1–1
	Staffordshire	v	*Hampshire*	2–1
1991	Lancashire	v	Surrey	6–0
1992	Nottinghamshire	v	Surrey	1–0
1993	Durham	v	Liverpool	4–0
1994	West Riding	v	Sussex	3–1

* after extra time

FA Youth Cup 1993–1994

EXTRA PRELIMINARY ROUND

(replays in italics)

			Result	Att
Sutton Coldfield Town	v	Bedworth United	4–0	59
Petersfield United	v	Woking		

(walkover for Woking – Petersfield United removed from the Competition)

PRELIMINARY ROUND   on or before 11th September 1993

(replays in italics)

			Result	Att
Darlington	v	Blackpool Mechanics	7–1	30
Guisborough Town	v	Huddersfield Town	1–5	67
Prudhoe East End	v	Atherton LR	3–2	36
Hartlepool United	v	Carlisle United	1–3	117
Bolton Wanderers	v	Marine	3–1	129
Burscough	v	Grimsby Town	0–5	21
Chadderton	v	Rochdale	1–4	124
(at Rochdale FC)				
Bury	v	Altrincham	7–1	105
Wrexham	v	Southport	7–1	45
Wigan Athletic	v	Prescot AFC	5–2	98
Stockport County	v	Warrington Town	2–3	91
Stalybridge Celtic	v	Lincoln City	1–6	204
Mansfield Town	v	Hinckley Athletic	9–1	82
Port Vale	v	Hednesford Town	3–2	200
Burton Albion	v	Lutterworth Town	6–1	51
Bridgnorth Town	v	Worksop Town	0–3	60
Stratford Town	v	Corby Town	4–0	57
Boldmere St Michaels	v	Hinckley Town	3–5	37
Chasetown	v	Rothwell Town	0–1	55
Bromsgrove Rovers	v	Sutton Coldfield Town	2–1	105
Nuneaton Borough	v	Wednesfield	4–1	35
Brierley Hill Town	v	Redditch United	2–4	46
Pershore Town	v	Willenhall Town	3–1	35
Pelsall Villa	v	Lye Town	2–5	52
Stewarts & Lloyds	v	Leighton Town	0–1	22
Banbury United	v	Dunstable	3–0	40
Baldock Town	v	Kempston Rovers	1–2	
Eynesbury Rovers	v	Rushden & Diamonds	1–6	29
Braintree Town	v	Peterborough United	2–8	103
Canvey Island	v	March Town United	1–7	80
Kings Lynn	v	Saffron Walden Town	1–2	87
Great Yarmouth Town	v	Bishop's Stortford	2–1	59
Wivenhoe Town	v	Stevenage Borough	1–2	29
Barkingside	v	Leyton	5–1	43
Grays Athletic	v	Waltham Abbey	1–3	60
East Thurrock United	v	Wisbech Town	4–0	37
Brook House	v	Wingate & Finchley	1–1	33

130

				Result	Att
Wingate & Finchley	v	*Brook House*		4–3 aet	60
Edgware Town	v	Uxbridge		4–0	33
Royston Town	v	Northwood		5–0	24
Enfield	v	Beaconsfield United		10–0	45
Hanwell Town	v	Ruislip Manor		3–4	
Harefield United	v	Marlow		5–0	35
Kingsbury Town	v	Staines Town		1–1	62
Staines Town	v	*Kingsbury Town*		3–4	51
Hillingdon Borough	v	Hampton		1–3	38
Dover Athletic	v	Herne Bay		5–0	55
Newhaven	v	Faversham Town		3–0	40
Corinthian	v	Gillingham		0–7	27
Ringmer	v	Ashford Town		2–3	35
Bracknell Town	v	Peacehaven & Telscombe			
(walkover for Bracknell Town – Peacehaven removed from the Competition)					
Chatham Town	v	Egham Town		2–0	28
Croydon Athletic	v	Thamesmead Town		7–1	38
Chipstead	v	Bedfont		3–2	22
Kingstonian	v	Whitehawk		10–0	40
Malden Vale	v	Three Bridges		2–4	46
Oakwood	v	Whitstable Town		1–6	28
Molesey	v	Farnborough Town			
(walkover for Farnborough Town – Molesey removed from the Competition)					
Shoreham	v	Welling United			
(walkover for Welling United – Shoreham removed from the Competition)					
Slough Town	v	Worthing		0–1	56
Walton & Hersham	v	Whyteleafe			
(walkover for Whyteleafe – Walton & Hersham removed from the Competition)					
Steyning Town	v	Redhill		5–1	20
Wick	v	Thatcham Town		2–1	37
Fleet Town	v	Maidenhead United		3–5	25
Basingstoke Town	v	Wokingham Town		1–4	39
Aldershot Town	v	Woking		6–1	117
Havant Town	v	Frome Town		3–0	62
Newbury Town	v	Chippenham Town		2–4	31
Romsey Town	v	Yate Town		3–5 aet	29
Oxford City	v	Dorchester Town		1–1	55
Dorchester Town	v	*Oxford City*		1–3	33
Cheltenham Town	v	Worcester City		1–1	94
Worcester City	v	*Cheltenham Town*		4–2 aet	63
Gloucester City	v	Weston-super-Mare		3–0	58
Torquay United	v	Yeovil Town		2–1	234
Hereford United	v	Bristol Rovers		1–1	62
Bristol Rovers	v	*Hereford United*		5–3	44

FIRST QUALIFYING ROUND   on or before 2nd October 1993

(replays in italics)

				Result	Att
Huddersfield Town	v	Carlisle United		2–1	100
Darlington	v	Prudhoe East End		9–0	60
Grimsby Town	v	Bury		4–1	68
Bolton Wanderers	v	Rochdale		1–2	141

			Result	Att
Wigan Athletic	v	Lincoln City	3–4	31
Wrexham	v	Warrington Town	1–2	43
Port Vale	v	Worksop Town	5–0	
Mansfield Town	v	Burton Albion	1–1	153
Burton Albion	v	*Mansfield Town*	*2–1*	110
Hinckley Town	v	Bromsgrove Rovers	1–1	30
Bromsgrove Rovers	v	*Hinckley Town*	*0–2*	57
Stratford Town	v	Rothwell Town	3–1	39
Redditch United	v	Lye Town	0–1	44
Nuneaton Borough	v	Pershore Town	6–3	37
Banbury United	v	Rushden & Diamonds	2–1	45
Leighton Town	v	Kempston Rovers	5–0	111
March Town United	v	Great Yarmouth Town	0–0	55
Great Yarmouth Town	v	*March Town*	*5–1*	30
Peterborough United	v	Saffron Walden Town	6–1	491
Barkingside	v	East Thurrock United	0–5	51
Stevenage Borough	v	Waltham Abbey	3–1	54
Edgware Town	v	Enfield	1–2	35
Wingate & Finchley	v	Royston Town	0–4	45
Harefield United	v	Hampton	4–1	27
Ruislip Manor	v	Kingsbury Town	1–2	39
Newhaven	v	Ashford Town	3–1	56

(first tie abandoned after 45 minutes, 3–2 due to waterlogged pitch)

			Result	Att
Dover Athletic	v	Gillingham	0–5	35
Chatham Town	v	Chipstead	1–3	35

(first tie abandoned after 45 minutes, 0–3 due to waterlogged pitch)

			Result	Att
Bracknell Town	v	Croydon Athletic	1–3	22
Three Bridges	v	Farnborough Town	3–1	26
Kingstonian	v	Whitstable Town	4–1	42
Worthing	v	Steyning Town	3–1	45
Welling United	v	Whyteleafe	3–0	50
Maidenhead United	v	Aldershot Town	4–4	39
Aldershot Town	v	*Maidenhead United*	*4–0*	58
Wick	v	Wokingham Town	2–5	28
Chippenham Town	v	Oxford City	4–3	57
Havant Town	v	Yate Town	1–0 aet	65
Gloucester City	v	Bristol Rovers	1–6	125
Worcester	v	Torquay United	1–2	172

SECOND QUALIFYING ROUND   on or before 16th October 1993

(replays in italics)

			Result	Att
Huddersfield Town	v	Darlington	5–1	99
Grimsby Town	v	Rochdale	1–0	174
Lincoln City	v	Warrington Town	2–2	77
Warrington Town	v	*Lincoln City*	*1–3*	218
Port Vale	v	Burton Albion	1–1	134
Burton Albion	v	*Port Vale*	*0–2*	168
Hinckley Town	v	Stratford Town	0–2	48
Lye Town	v	Nuneaton Borough	0–1	72
Banbury United	v	Leighton Town	1–3	47

			Result	Att
Great Yarmouth Town	v	Peterborough United	2–2 aet	53
Peterborough United	v	*Great Yarmouth Town*	*8–0*	549
East Thurrock United	v	Stevenage Borough	1–1	94
Stevenage Borough	v	*East Thurrock United*	*1–2*	65
Enfield	v	Royston Town	4–3	53
Harefield United	v	Kingsbury Town	5–0	43
Newhaven	v	Gillingham	0–4	30
Chipstead	v	Croydon Athletic	1–4	21
Three Bridges	v	Kingstonian	1–5	18
Worthing	v	Welling United	1–2	72
Aldershot Town	v	Wokingham Town	0–2	69
Chippenham Town	v	Havant Town	0–1	50
Bristol Rovers	v	Torquay United	0–0	38
Torquay United	v	*Bristol Rovers*	*3–1*	256

FIRST ROUND   on or before 13th November 1993

(replays in italics)

			Result	Att
Tranmere Rovers	v	Huddersfield Town	1–1	491
Huddersfield Town	v	*Tranmere Rovers*	*3–1*	160
Doncaster Rovers	v	Lincoln City	2–0	190
Rotherham United	v	Preston North End	2–1	127
Bradford City	v	Barnsley	2–1	95
Blackburn Rovers	v	Sheffield Wednesday	1–0	201
Newcastle United	v	Burnley	1–1	628
Burnley	v	*Newcastle United*	*3–0*	
Oldham Athletic	v	Hull City	3–2	361
Blackpool	v	Grimsby Town	0–1	124
Scunthorpe United	v	Sunderland	0–3	183
Stratford Town	v	Nuneaton Borough	2–2	54
Nuneaton Borough	v	*Stratford Town*	*2–1*	115
Kidderminster Harriers	v	Peterborough United	0–2	30
Stoke City	v	Shrewsbury Town	3–1	229
Cambridge United	v	Aston Villa	1–4	268
Birmingham City	v	Wolverhampton Wanderers	4–1	70
Luton Town	v	Derby County	1–1	149
Derby County	v	*Luton Town*	*1–1* aet	256
Luton Town	v	*Derby County*	*0–1*	168
Northampton Town	v	Leicester City	1–3	142
Cambridge City	v	Leighton Town	3–3	75
Leighton Town	v	*Cambridge City*	*1–0*	100
Walsall	v	Port Vale	0–1	151
Ipswich Town	v	Carshalton Athletic	8–0	227
Gillingham	v	Lewes	3–0	49
Dulwich Hamlet	v	East Thurrock United	2–2	141
East Thurrock United	v	*Dulwich Hamlet*	*2–4* aet	141
Brighton & Hove Albion	v	Fulham	3–1	115
Harefield United	v	St Albans City	1–1	51
St Albans City	v	*Harefield United*	*0–1*	135
Boreham Wood	v	Enfield	1–2	70
Croydon Athletic	v	Epsom & Ewell	3–1	85

			Result	Att
Sutton United	v	Wycombe Wanderers	0–2	47
Reading	v	Charlton Athletic	2–2	50
Charlton Athletic	v	*Reading*	2–3 aet	512
Kingstonian	v	Welling United	2–5	100
Portsmouth	v	Bashley	4–0	155
Southampton	v	AFC Bournemouth	1–0	251
Torquay United	v	Oxford United	3–2	305
Cardiff City	v	Witney Town	5–0	105
Havant Town	v	Wokingham Town	0–0	107
Wokingham Town	v	*Havant Town*	2–1	83
Exeter City	v	Swansea City	4–2	275

SECOND ROUND   on or before 11th December 1993

(replays in italics)

			Result	Att
Middlesbrough	v	Oldham Athletic	2–0	266
Burnley	v	Leeds United	3–0	1084
Bradford City	v	Manchester United	2–0	739
Crewe Alexandra	v	Huddersfield Town	4–2	307
York City	v	Blackburn Rovers	0–0	149
Blackburn Rovers	v	*York City*	1–1 aet	165
York City	v	*Blackburn Rovers*	1–2	144
Doncaster Rovers	v	Manchester City	1–4	181
Everton	v	Grimsby Town	0–2	362
Rotherham United	v	Sunderland	2–4	124
Sheffield United	v	Liverpool	1–2	214
Coventry City	v	Leicester City	2–1	208
Ipswich Town	v	Queens Park Rangers	3–1	252
Tottenham Hotspur	v	Stoke City	1–2	229
West Bromwich Albion	v	Leighton Town	2–1	265
West Ham United	v	Leyton Orient	6–0	611
Watford	v	Aston Villa	1–3	232
Birmingham City	v	Peterborough United	1–1	61
Peterborough United	v	*Birmingham City*	1–1 aet	290
Birmingham City	v	*Peterborough United*	1–2	150
Port Vale	v	Southend United	1–3	112
Chelsea	v	Norwich City	1–1	88
Norwich City	v	*Chelsea*	1–0	269
Nottingham Forest	v	Nuneaton Borough	3–1	154
Notts County	v	Derby County	0–3	233
Colchester United	v	Arsenal	2–3	345
Southampton	v	Wimbledon	2–6	89
Torquay United	v	Enfield	3–1	449
Croydon Athletic	v	Wycombe Wanderers	2–3	89
Reading	v	Bristol City	0–1	161
Gillingham	v	Swindon Town	1–2	54
Dulwich Hamlet	v	Crystal Palace	0–5	
Cardiff City	v	Harefield United	2–0	
Welling United	v	Portsmouth	4–6	227
Brighton & Hove Albion	v	Wokingham Town	1–0	124

			Result	Att
Brentford	v	Exeter City	5–1	151
Plymouth Argyle	v	Millwall	3–3	158
Millwall	v	*Plymouth Argyle*	*2–1*	312

THIRD ROUND   on or before 15th January 1994

(replays in italics)

			Result	Att
Manchester City	v	Norwich City	0–2	227
Bristol City	v	Aston Villa	1–4	
Middlesbrough	v	Nottingham Forest	2–2	706
Nottingham Forest	v	*Middlesbrough*	*3–3*	
Middlesbrough	v	*Nottingham Forest*	*2–1* aet	888
Blackburn Rovers	v	Bradford City	1–1	896
Bradford City	v	*Blackburn Rovers*	*4–0*	521
Wimbledon	v	Burnley	3–4	247
Ipswich Town	v	Peterborough United	1–1	472
Peterborough Town	v	*Ipswich Town*	*0–0*	1489
Ipswich Town	v	*Peterborough United*	*1–0*	880
Grimsby Town	v	Torquay United	3–1	340
West Bromwich Albion	v	Crewe Alexandra	2–1	114
Liverpool	v	West Ham United	2–2	347
West Ham United	v	*Liverpool*	*3–2*	1740
Brentford	v	Arsenal	1–1	493
Arsenal	v	*Brentford*	*3–1*	322
Swindon Town	v	Brighton & Hove Albion	0–1	172
Sunderland	v	Derby County	0–1	333
Cardiff City	v	Coventry City	1–2	177
Millwall	v	Wycombe Wanderers	2–2	392
Wycombe Wanderers	v	*Millwall*	*0–5*	
Southend United	v	Stoke City	0–4	102
Portsmouth	v	Crystal Palace	0–2	100

FOURTH ROUND   on or before 5th February 1994

(replays in italics)

			Result	Att
Coventry City	v	Norwich City	0–2	1076
Brighton & Hove Albion	v	Millwall	3–4	540
Middlesbrough	v	West Bromwich Albion	2–0	984
Ipswich Town	v	Portsmouth	2–4	480
Grimsby Town	v	Bradford City	1–1	406
Bradford City	v	*Grimsby Town*	*2–0*	354
Aston Villa	v	West Ham United	1–2	405
Stoke City	v	Derby County	3–1	1198
Burnley	v	Arsenal	0–1	4943

FIFTH ROUND   on or before 5th March 1994

(replays in italics)

			Result	Att
Arsenal	v	Stoke City	3–1	302
West Ham United	v	Bradford City	0–1	780
Middlesbrough	v	Portsmouth	5–0	1522
Millwall	v	Norwich City	2–0	345

SEMI-FINAL   on or before 2nd April 1994
First Leg

Middlesbrough	v	Millwall	2–2	6111
Bradford City	v	Arsenal	0–1	2746

Second Leg

Millwall	v	Middlesbrough	3–1	2342
Arsenal	v	Bradford City	1–0	959

FINAL   on or before 7th May 1994
First Leg

Millwall	v	Arsenal	3–2	6098

Second Leg

Arsenal	v	Millwall	3–0	4705

FA County Youth Challenge Cup 1993–1994

FIRST ROUND   on or before 16th October 1994

(replays in italics)

			Result
Nottinghamshire	v	Manchester	2–3 aet
Derbyshire	v	West Riding	0–5
Birmingham	v	Cheshire	1–2
Staffordshire	v	Westmorland	9–1
Shropshire	v	Northamptonshire	3–6
Oxfordshire	v	Herefordshire	4–1
Berks & Bucks	v	Cambridgeshire	1–0
Bedfordshire	v	Kent	0–2
Surrey	v	Hampshire	7–2
Dorset	v	Royal Navy	1–0
Somerset & Avon	v	Army	3–1
Gloucestershire	v	Devon	0–3
Sussex	v	Wiltshire	4–0

19 Counties receiving byes to the Second Round

Cornwall	Liverpool
Cumberland	London
Durham	Middlesex
East Riding	Norfolk
Essex	North Riding
Hertfordshire	Northumberland
Huntingdonshire	Sheffield & Hallamshire
Lancashire	Suffolk
Leicestershire & Rutland	Worcestershire
Lincolnshire	

SECOND ROUND   on or before 27th November 1993

(replays in italics)

			Result
Cumberland	v	Manchester	0–2
Lincolnshire	v	Durham	0–4
East Riding	v	Liverpool	3–4
Northumberland	v	West Riding	3–5
North Riding	v	Cheshire	3–2
Lancashire	v	Staffordshire	2–3
Sheffield & Hallamshire	v	Northamptonshire	3–2
Leicestershire & Rutland	v	Oxfordshire	2–0
Worcestershire	v	Berks & Bucks	1–1
Berks & Bucks	v	*Worcestershire*	*0–2*
Norfolk	v	Kent	0–3
Hertfordshire	v	Suffolk	1–1
Suffolk	v	*Hertfordshire*	*5–3*
Essex	v	Surrey	2–4
London	v	Dorset	1–0
Huntingdonshire	v	Somerset & Avon	1–3
Middlesex	v	Devon	3–3 aet
Devon	v	*Middlesex*	*1–3*
Cornwall	v	Sussex	0–2

THIRD ROUND   on or before 15th January 1994

(replays in italics)

			Result
Liverpool	v	North Riding	4–2
Durham	v	Manchester	0–1
Sheffield & Hallamshire	v	West Riding	1–3 aet
Leicestershire & Rutland	v	Staffordshire	0–3
Suffolk	v	London	1–2
Kent	v	Worcestershire	1–0 aet
Middlesex	v	Surrey	0–3
Sussex	v	Somerset & Avon (South)	1–0

FOURTH ROUND   on or before 19th February 1994

(replays in italics)

			Result
Surrey	v	West Riding	0–1
Staffordshire	v	Manchester	2–1
Kent	v	London	2–2 aet
London	v	*Kent*	*1–2*
Sussex	v	Liverpool	3–2

SEMI–FINAL   on or before 19th March 1994

(replays in italics)

			Result
Sussex *(at Lancing FC)*	v	Kent	2–1
Staffordshire *(at Stafford Rangers FC)*	v	West Riding	0–4

FINAL   30th April 1994

			Result
West Riding *(at Bradford City FC)*	v	Sussex	3–1

Youth International Matches 1993–1994

Under-18

Date	Venue				Result
24.8.93	Port Vale	England	v	Republic of Ireland	2–2
7.9.93	Port Vale	England	v	Romania	1–1*
13.10.93	Bucharest	Romania	v	England	1–1*
27.10.93	Besançon	France	v	England	2–0*
16.11.93	Yeovil	England	v	France	3–3*

* *UEFA Championship*

Under-16

Date	Venue				Result
4.8.93	Faroe Islands	Denmark	v	England	3–4†
5.8.93	Faroe Islands	Norway	v	England	2–1†
7.8.93	Faroe Islands	Sweden	v	England	2–2†
8.8.93	Faroe Islands	Finland	v	England	0–1†
30.10.93	Lilleshall	England	v	Republic of Ireland	2–0
24.11.93	Zwolle	Holland	v	England	1–1*
8.12.93	Pula	Italy	v	England	0–2*
2.2.94	Walsall	England	v	Italy	0–0*
8.3.94	Hereford	England	v	Holland	1–0*
26.4.94	Dublin	Portugal	v	England	0–1*
28.4.94	Dublin	Rep. of Ireland	v	England	1–1*
30.4.94	Dublin	Czech Republic	v	England	1–2*
3.5.94	Dublin	Ukraine**	v	England	2–2

† *Nordic Championship*
* *UEFA Championship*
** *won on penalty-kicks*

England Youth (Under-18) Caps 1993–1994

	Republic of Ireland	Romania	Romania	France	France
P. Pettinger (Leeds United)	1	1	1	1	1
D. Hinshlewood (Nottingham Forest)	2	2	2	2	
G. Strong (Wigan Athletic)	3				
M. Ford (Leeds United)	4	4	4	4	4*
R. Bowman (Leeds United)	5		5	5	
B. Thatcher (Millwall)	6	6			6
C. Holland (Preston North End)	7	7	7*	7	3
J. Walker (Nottingham Forest)	8				
R. Irving (Manchester United)	9	9	9*	11*	
K. Gallen (Queens Park Rangers)	10	10	10	10	10
J. Cureton (Norwich City)	11	11		3*	11
P. Stamp (Middlesbrough)	2*		11	8	7
B. Worrall (Swindon Town)	3*				
T. Challis (Queens Park Rangers)		3	3		
D. Faulkner (Sheffield Wednesday)		5			
R. Appleby (Newcastle United)		8			
T. Bennett (Barnsley)		8*			
J. O'Connor (Everton)			6	6	5
M. Hewlett (Bristol City)			7		
G. McGowan (Arsenal)			8	11	
C. Jackson (Barnsley)			9	9	
M. Burrows (Sheffield Wednesday)				3	
P. Neville (Manchester United)					2
I. Frodsham (Liverpool)					8
R. Simpson (Tottenham Hotspur)					9
J. Wright (Millwall)					11*

* *substitute*

England Youth (Under-16) Caps 1993–1994

R. Moore (Everton)
N. Harrison
M. Broomes (Blackburn Rovers)
D. Hilton (Manchester United)
J. Shore (Norwich City)
P. Teather (Manchester United)
S. Clemence (Tottenham Hotspur)
J. Cassidy (Liverpool)
L. Richardson (Oldham Athletic)
J. Carragher (Liverpool)
D. Hilton (Manchester United)
A. Futcher (Wimbledon)
L. Crooks (Manchester City)

A. Ducros (Coventry City)
G. McGann (Everton)
L. Darnborough (Oldham Athletic)
R. Wallwork (Manchester United)
R. Wright (Ipswich Town)
M. Millett (Wigan Athletic)
J. Curtis (FA National School)
N. Quashie (Queens Park Rangers)
D. Thompson (Liverpool)
C. Atkinson (Nottingham Forest)
I. Rankin (Arsenal)
E. Heskey (Leicester City)
S. Heath (Leeds United)

England Teams

v Denmark:
Moore, Harrison, Broomes, Hilton, Shore, Teather, Clemence, Cassidy, Richardson, Carragher, Wallwork (subs used: Futcher, Crooks, Ducros, McGann).

v Norway:
Darnborough, Futcher, Wallwork, Broomes, Hilton, Crooks, McGann, Clemence, Ducros, Richardson, Cassidy (subs used: Harrison, Teather, Shore, Carragher).

v Sweden:
Moore, Harrison, Broomes, Wallwork, Hilton, Shore, Teather, Clemence, Richardson, Cassidy, Carragher.

v Finland:
Darnborough, Futcher, Broomes, Wallwork, Hilton, Crooks, McGann, Clemence, Carragher, Cassidy, Ducros.

v Republic of Ireland:
Wright (Moore), Millett, Hilton, Curtis, Wallwork (Futcher), Broomes, Quashie (Thompson), Clemence (Atkinson), Richardson (Carragher), Ducros, Cassidy.

v Holland:
Wright, Millett, Hilton, Broomes, Wallwork, Thompson, Richardson (Carragher), Curtis, Ducros (Quashie), Clemence, Cassidy.

v Italy:
Wright, Millett, Hilton, Broomes, Wallwork, Thompson (Rankin), Richardson (Curtis), Clemence, Ducros, Carragher, Cassidy.

v Italy:
Darnborough, Millett, Hilton, Broomes, Wallwork, Thompson, Richardson, Clemence, Ducros, Carragher, Cassidy (Quashie).

v Holland:
Wright, Millett, Hilton, Broomes, Wallwork, Thompson (Quashie), Richardson, Clemence, Ducros, Carragher (Rankin), Cassidy.

v Portugal:
Wright, Millett, Hilton, Broomes, Wallwork, Richardson, Clemence, Carragher (Heskey), Ducros, Cassidy (Quashie), Shore.

v Republic of Ireland:
Wright, Millett, Hilton, Broomes, Wallwork, Quashie (Shore), Richardson, Clemence, Ducros (Heath), Cassidy, Heskey.

v Czech Republic:
Wright, Millett, Hilton, Broomes, Richardson, Clemence, Carragher, Cassidy, Heath (Quashie), Shore, Crooks (Heskey).

v Ukraine:
Wright, Millett, Hilton, Broomes, Wallwork, Richardson, Clemence, Carragher (Quashie), Ducros (Heskey), Cassidy, Shore.

European Under-16 Championship Finals

THE REPUBLIC OF IRELAND – 24th April to 9th May 1994
First Stage

Group A

Date	Venue				Result
26.4.94	Dundalk	Austria	v	Albania	1-0
26.4.94	Drogheda	Spain	v	Belarus	0-1
28.4.94	Dundalk	Spain	v	Austria	1-1
28.4.94	Drogheda	Albania	v	Belarus	1-1
30.4.94	Dundalk	Albania	v	Spain	0-4
30.4.94	Drogheda	Belarus	v	Austria	1-1

Belarus and Austria qualified for quarter-finals

Group B

Date	Venue				Result
26.4.94	Dublin	Czech Rep	v	Rep. of Ireland	1-0
26.4.94	Dublin	England	v	Portugal	1-0
28.4.94	Dublin	England	v	Rep. of Ireland	1-1
28.4.94	Dublin	Portugal	v	Czech Rep.	2-0
30.4.94	Dublin	England	v	Czech Rep.	2-1
30.4.94	Dublin	Rep. of Ireland	v	Portugal	0-3

England and Portugal qualified for quarter-finals

Group C

Date	Venue				Result
26.4.94	Cobh	Germany	v	Russia	0-2
26.4.94	Cork	Switzerland	v	Denmark	3-4
28.4.94	Limerick	Denmark	v	Russia	3-2
28.4.94	Tipperary	Switzerland	v	Germany	1-5
30.4.94	Cork	Denmark	v	Germany	3-4
30.4.94	Cork	Russian	v	Switzerland	5-1

Russia and Denmark qualified for quarter-finals

Group D

Date	Venue				Result
26.4.94	Dublin	Turkey	v	Iceland	2-1
26.4.94	Dublin	Ukraine	v	Belgium	2-1
28.4.94	Dublin	Iceland	v	Belgium	1-2
28.4.94	Dublin	Turkey	v	Ukraine	1-1
30.4.94	Dublin	Belgium	v	Turkey	0-4
30.4.94	Dublin	Iceland	v	Ukraine	1-2

Turkey and Ukraine qualified for quarter-finals

Quarter-Finals

Date	Venue				Result
3.5.94	Dublin	England	v	Ukraine*	2-2
3.5.94	Dundalk	Turkey*	v	Portugal	0-0
3.5.94	Dublin	Belarus	v	Denmark	1-3
3.5.94	Dublin	Russia	v	Austria	0-2

Semi-Finals

Date	Venue				Result
5.5.94	Dublin	Austria	v	Turkey	0-1
5.5.94	Dublin	Denmark	v	Ukraine	2-2*

Third/Fourth Place

Date	Venue				Result
8.5.94	Dublin	Ukraine	v	Austria	2-0

Final

Date	Venue				Result
8.5.94	Dublin	Turkey	v	Denmark	1-0

* won on penalty-kicks

Youth International Matches 1947–1994

WYC = World Youth Championship
IYT = International Youth Tournament
* Qualifying Competition
† Professionals   § Abandoned

v Algeria

| † 1984 | 22/4 | Cannes | W3–0 | |

v Argentina

| † 1981 | 5/10 | Sydney | D1–1 | (WYC) |

v Australia

| † 1981 | 8/10 | Sydney | D1–1 | (WYC) |
| | 1993 | 20/3 | Sydney | W2–1 | (WYC) |

v Austria

	1949	19/4	Zeist	W4–2	(IYT)
	1952	17/4	Barcelona	D5–5	(IYT)
	1957	16/4	Barcelona	L0–3	(IYT)
	1958	4/3	Highbury	W3–2	
	1958	1/6	Graz	W4–3	
	1960	20/4	Vienna	L0–1	(IYT)
† 1964	1/4	Rotterdam	W2–1	(IYT)
† 1980	6/9	Pazin	L0–1	
† 1981	29/5	Bonn	W7–0	(IYT)
† 1981	3/9	Umag	W3–0	
† 1984	6/9	Izola	D2–2	

v Belgium

	1948	16/4	West Ham	W3–1	(IYT)
	1951	22/3	Cannes	D1–1	(IYT)
	1953	31/3	Brussels	W2–0	(IYT)
§ 1956	7/11	Brussels	W3–2	
	1957	13/11	Sheffield	W2–0	
† 1965	15/4	Ludwigshafen	W3–0	(IYT)
	1969	11/3	West Ham	W1–0	(IYT*)
† 1969	26/3	Waregem	W2–0	(IYT)
	1972	13/5	Palma	D0–0	(IYT*)
† 1973	4/6	Viareggio	D0–0	(IYT)
† 1977	19/5	Lokeren	W1–0	(IYT)
† 1979	17/1	Brussels	W4–0	
† 1980	8/9	Labia	W6–1	
† 1983	13/4	Birmingham	D1–1	
† 1988	20/5	Chatel	D0–0	
† 1990	24/7	Nyiregyhaza	D1–1	(IYT)
† 1990	16/10	Sunderland	D0–0	(IYT*)
† 1991	16/10	Eernegem	L0–1	(IYT*)

v Brazil

† 1986	29/3	Cannes	D0–0	
† 1986	13/5	Peking	L1–2	
† 1987	2/6	Niteroi	L0–2	

v Bulgaria

	1956	28/3	Salgotarjan	L1–2	(IYT)
	1960	16/4	Graz	L0–1	(IYT)
	1962	24/4	Ploesti	D0–0	(IYT)
† 1968	7/4	Nimes	D0–0	(IYT)
† 1969	26/3	Waregem	W2–0	(IYT)
† 1972	13/5	Palma	D0–0	(IYT)
† 1979	31/5	Vienna	L0–1	(IYT)

v Cameroon

| † 1981 | 3/10 | Sydney | W2–0 | (WYC) |
| † 1985 | 1/6 | Toulon | W1–0 | |

v China

† 1983	31/3	Cannes	W5–1	
† 1985	26/8	Baku	L0–2	(WYC)
† 1986	5/5	Peking	W1–0	

v Czechoslovakia

	1955	7/4	Lucca	L0–1	(IYT)
† 1966	21/5	Rijeka	L2–3	(IYT)
† 1969	20/5	Leipzig	W3–1	(IYT)
	1979	24/5	Bischofshofen	W3–0	(IYT)
† 1979	8/9	Pula	L1–2	
† 1982	11/4	Cannes	L0–1	
† 1983	20/5	Highbury	D1–1	(IYT)
† 1989	26/4	Bystrica	L0–1	(IYT*)
† 1989	14/11	Portsmouth	W1–0	(IYT*)
† 1990	25/4	Wembley	D1–1	

v Denmark

† 1955	1/10	Plymouth	W9–2	
	1956	20/5	Esbjerg	W2–1	
† 1979	31/10	Esbjerg	W3–1	(IYT*)
	1980	26/3	Coventry	W4–0	(IYT*)
† 1982	15/7	Stjordal	W5–2	
† 1983	16/7	Holbeck	L0–1	
† 1987	16/2	Manchester	W2–1	
† 1990	28/3	Wembley	D0–0	
† 1991	6/2	Oxford	L1–5	
† 1993	30/3	Stoke	W4–2	
† 1993	7/7	Nykobing	W5–0	

v Egypt

| † 1981 | 11/10 | Sydney | W4–2 | (WYC) |
| † 1992 | 13/10 | Bournemouth | W2–1 | |

v Finland

| † 1975 | 19/5 | Berne | D1–1 | (IYT) |

v France

| | 1957 | 24/3 | Fontainebleau | W1–0 | |
| | 1958 | 22/3 | Eastbourne | L0–1 | |

† 1966	23/5	Rijeka	L1–2	(IYT)
† 1967	11/5	Istanbul	W2–0	(IYT)
† 1968	25/1	Paris	L0–1	
1978	8/2	C Palace	W3–1	(IYT*)
1978	1/3	Paris	D0–0	(IYT*)
† 1979	2/6	Vienna	D0–0	(IYT)
† 1982	12/4	Cannes	L0–1	
† 1983	2/4	Cannes	L0–2	
1984	1/3	Watford	W4–0	
† 1984	23/4	Cannes	L1–2	
† 1985	7/6	Toulon	L1–3	
† 1986	31/3	Cannes	L1–2	
† 1986	11/5	Peking	D1–1	
† 1988	22/5	Monthey	L1–2	
† 1988	15/11	Bradford	D1–1	(IYT*)
† 1989	11/10	Martigues	D0–0	(IYT*)
† 1990	22/5	Wembley	L1–3	
† 1992	7/10	Boulogne	L0–2	
1993	18/7	Stoke	W2–0	(IYT)
† 1993	27/10	Besançon	L0–2	(IYT*)
† 1993	16/11	Yeovil	D3–3	(IYT*)

v East Germany

1958	7/4	Neunkirchen	W1–0	(IYT)
1959	8/3	Zwickau	L3–4	
1960	2/4	Portsmouth	D1–1	
† 1965	25/4	Essen	L2–3	(IYT)
† 1969	22/5	Magdeburg	L0–4	(IYT)
† 1973	10/6	Florence	W3–2	(IYT)
† 1984	25/5	Moscow	D1–1	(IYT)
† 1988	21/5	Monthey	W1–0	

v West Germany

1953	4/4	Boom	W3–1	(IYT)
1954	15/4	Gelsenkirchen	D2–2	(IYT)
1956	1/4	Sztalinvaros	W2–1	(IYT)
1957	31/3	Oberhausen	W4–1	
1958	12/3	Bolton	L1–2	
1961	12/3	Flensberg	L0–2	
† 1962	31/3	Northampton	W1–0	
† 1967	14/2	Mönchengladbach		
			W1–0	
† 1972	22/5	Barcelona	W2–0	(IYT)
† 1975	25/1	Las Palmas	W4–2	
† 1976	14/11	Monte Carlo	D1–1	
† 1979	28/5	Salzburg	W2–0	(IYT)
† 1979	1/9	Pula	D1–1	
† 1983	5/9	Pazin	W2–0	

v Ghana

1993	17/3	Sydney	L1–2	(IYT)

v Greece

1957	18/4	Barcelona	L2–3	(IYT)
1959	2/4	Dimitrovo	W4–0	(IYT)
† 1977	23/5	Beveren	D1–1	(IYT)
† 1983	28/6	Puspokladany	W1–0	

† 1988	26/10	Tranmere	W5–0	(IYT*)
† 1989	8/3	Xanthi	W5–0	(IYT*)

v Holland

1948	17/4	Tottenham	W3–2	(IYT)
1951	26/3	Cannes	W2–1	(IYT)
† 1954	21/11	Arnhem	L2–3	
† 1955	5/11	Norwich	W3–1	
1957	2/3	Brentford	D5–5	
1957	14/4	Barcelona	L1–2	(IYT)
1957	2/10	Amsterdam	W3–2	
1961	9/3	Utrecht	L0–1	
† 1962	31/1	Brighton	W4–0	
† 1962	22/4	Ploesti	L0–3	(IYT)
† 1963	13/4	Wimbledon	W5–0	(IYT)
1968	9/4	Nîmes	W1–0	(IYT)
† 1974	13/2	West Brom	D1–1	(IYT*)
† 1974	27/2	The Hague	W1–0	(IYT*)
† 1980	23/5	Halle	W1–0	(IYT*)
† 1982	9/4	Cannes	W1–0	
† 1985	7/4	Cannes	L1–3	
† 1987	1/8	Wembley	W3–1	
† 1993	20/7	Walsall	W4–1	(IYT)

v Hungary

1954	11/4	Düsseldorf	L1–3	(IYT)
1956	31/3	Tatabanya	L2–4	(IYT)
1956	23/10	Tottenham	W2–1	
† 1956	25/10	Sunderland	W2–1	
† 1965	21/4	Wuppertal	W5–0	(IYT)
† 1975	16/5	Olten	W3–1	(IYT)
† 1977	16/10	Las Palmas	W3–0	(IYT)
† 1979	5/9	Pula	W2–0	
† 1980	11/9	Pula	L1–2	
† 1981	7/9	Porec	W4–0	
† 1983	29/7	Debrecen	L1–2	
† 1983	3/9	Umag	W3–2	
† 1986	30/3	Cannes	W2–0	

v Iceland

† 1973	31/5	Viareggio	W2–0	(IYT)
† 1977	21/5	Turnhout	D0–0	(IYT)
† 1983	7/9	Reykjavik	W3–0	(IYT*)
1983	19/9	Blackburn	W4–0	(IYT*)
1983	12/10	Reykjavik	W3–0	
† 1983	1/11	Crystal Palace	W3–0	
† 1984	16/10	Manchester	W5–3	(IYT*)
† 1985	11/9	Reykjavik	W5–0	(IYT*)
† 1990	12/9	Reykjavik	W3–2	(IYT*)
† 1991	12/9	Crystal Palace	W2–1	(IYT*)

v Israel

† 1962	20/5	Tel Aviv	W3–1	
† 1962	22/5	Haifa	L1–2	

v Italy

1958	13/4	Luxembourg	L0–1	(IYT)
1959	25/3	Sofia	L1–3	(IYT)
1961	4/4	Braga	L2–3	(IYT)
† 1965	23/4	Marl–Huels	W3–1	(IYT)
† 1966	25/5	Rijeka	D1–1	(IYT)
† 1967	5/5	Izmir	W1–0	(IYT)
† 1973	14/2	Cava Dei Tirreni		
			L0–1	
† 1973	14/3	Highbury	W1–0	
† 1973	7/6	Viareggio	W1–0	(IYT)
† 1978	19/11	Monte Carlo	L1–2	
† 1979	28/2	Rome	W1–0	(IYT*)
† 1979	4/4	Birmingham	W2–0	(IYT*)
† 1983	22/5	Watford	D1–1	(IYT)
† 1984	20/4	Cannes	W1–0	
† 1985	5/4	Cannes	D2–2	

v Luxembourg

1950	25/5	Vienna	L1–2	(IYT)
1954	17/4	Bad Neuenahr	L0–2	(IYT)
1957	2/2	West Ham	W7–1	
1957	17/11	Luxembourg	W3–0	
1958	9/4	Esch sur Alzette		
			W5–0	(IYT)
† 1984	29/5	Moscow	W2–0	(IYT)

v Malta

† 1969	18/5	Wolfen	W6–0	(IYT)
† 1979	26/5	Salzburg	W3–0	(IYT)

v Mexico

† 1984	18/4	Cannes	W4–0	
† 1985	5/6	Toulon	W2–0	
† 1985	29/8	Baku	L0–1	(WYC)
† 1991	27/3	Port of Spain	L1–3	
† 1993	14/3	Melbourne	D0–0	(WYC)

v Northern Ireland

1948	15/5	Belfast	D2–2	
1949	18/4	Haarlem	D3–3	(IYT)
1949	14/5	Hull	W4–2	
1950	6/5	Belfast	L0–1	
1951	5/5	Liverpool	W5–2	
1952	19/4	Belfast	L0–2	
1953	11/4	Wolverhampton		
			D0–0	
1954	10/4	Bruehl	W5–0	(IYT)
1954	8/5	Newtonards	D2–2	
1955	14/5	Watford	W3–0	
1956	12/5	Belfast	D0–1	
1957	11/5	Leyton	W6–2	
1958	10/5	Bangor	L2–4	
1959	9/5	Liverpool	W5–0	
1960	14/5	Belfast	W5–2	
1961	13/5	Manchester	W2–0	
1962	12/5	Londonderry	L1–2	

† 1963	23/4	Wembley	W4–0	(IYT)
1963	11/5	Oldham	D1–1	
1964	25/1	Belfast	W3–1	
1965	22/1	Birkenhead	L2–3	
1966	26/2	Belfast	W4–0	
1967	25/2	Stockport	W3–0	
1968	23/2	Belfast	L0–2	
1969	28/2	Birkenhead	L0–2	
1970	28/2	Lurgan	L1–3	
1971	6/3	Blackpool	D1–1	(IYT)
1972	11/3	Chester	D1–1	
1972	17/5	Sabadell	W4–0	(IYT)
1973	24/3	Wellington	W3–0	
1974	19/4	Birkenhead	L1–2	
† 1975	13/5	Kriens	W3–0	(IYT)
† 1980	16/5	Arnstadt	W1–0	(IYT)
† 1981	11/2	Walsall	W1–0	(IYT*)
† 1981	11/3	Belfast	W3–0	(IYT*)

v Norway

† 1982	13/7	Levanger	L1–4	
† 1983	14/7	Korsor	W1–0	
1992	24/7	Amberg	D1–1	

v Paraguay

† 1985	24/8	Baku	D2–2	(WYC)

v Poland

1960	18/4	Graz	W4–2	(IYT)
† 1964	26/3	Breda	D1–1	(IYT)
† 1971	26/5	Presov	D0–0	(IYT)
† 1972	20/5	Valencia	W1–0	(IYT)
† 1975	21/1	Las Palmas	D1–1	
1978	9/5	Chorzow	L0–2	(IYT)
† 1979	3/9	Porec	L0–1	
† 1980	25/5	Leipzig	W2–1	(IYT)
† 1982	17/7	Steinkver	W3–2	
† 1983	12/7	Slagelse	W1–0	
† 1990	15/5	Wembley	W3–0	
† 1992	20/7	Regensburg	W6–1	(IYT)

v Portugal

1954	18/4	Bonn	L0–2	(IYT)
1961	2/4	Lisbon	L0–4	(IYT)
† 1964	3/4	The Hague	W4–0	(IYT)
† 1971	30/5	Prague	W3–0	(IYT)
† 1978	13/11	Monte Carlo	W2–0	
† 1980	18/5	Rosslau	D1–1	(IYT)
† 1982	7/4	Cannes	W3–0	
† 1992	22/7	Schweinfurt	D1–1	(IYT)

v Qatar

† 1981	14/10	Sydney	L1–2	(WYC)
† 1983	4/4	Cannes	D1–1	

v Republic of Ireland

1953	5/4	Leuven	W2–0	(IYT)
†1964	30/3	Middleburg	W6–0	(IYT)
†1968	7/2	Dublin	D0–0	(IYT*)
†1968	28/2	Portsmouth	W4–1	(IYT*)
†1970	14/1	Dublin	W4–1	(IYT*)
†1970	4/2	Luton	W10–0	(IYT*)
†1975	9/5	Brunnen	W1–0	(IYT)
†1985	26/2	Dublin	L0–1	(IYT*)
†1986	25/2	Leeds	W2–0	(IYT*)
†1988	17/2	Stoke	W2–0	
†1988	20/9	Dublin	W2–0	
†1993	24/8	Port Vale	D2–2	

v Romania

1957	15/10	Tottenham	W4–2	
1958	11/4	Luxembourg	W1–0	(IYT)
1959	31/3	Pazardijc	L1–2	(IYT)
†1963	15/4	Highbury	W3–0	(IYT)
†1981	17/10	Adelaide	L0–1	(WYC)
†1993	7/9	Port Vale	D1–1	(IYT*)
†1993	13/10	Bucharest	D1–1	(IYT*)

v Saar

1954	13/4	Dortmund	D1–1	(IYT)
1955	9/4	Prato	W3–1	(IYT)

v Scotland

1947	25/10	Doncaster	W4–2	
1948	30/10	Aberdeen	L1–3	
1949	21/4	Utrecht	L0–1	(IYT)
1950	4/2	Carlisle	W7–1	
1951	3/2	Kilmarnock	W6–1	
1952	15/3	Sunderland	W3–1	
1953	7/2	Glasgow	W4–3	
1954	6/2	Middlesbrough	W2–1	
1955	5/3	Kilmarnock	L3–4	
1956	3/3	Preston	D2–2	
1957	9/3	Aberdeen	W3–1	
1958	1/3	Hull	W2–0	
1959	28/2	Aberdeen	D1–1	
1960	27/2	Newcastle	D1–1	
1961	25/2	Elgin	W3–2	
1962	24/2	Peterborough	W4–2	
†1963	19/4	White City	W1–0	(IYT)
1963	18/5	Dumfries	W3–1	
1964	22/2	Middlesbrough	D1–1	
1965	27/2	Inverness	L1–2	
1966	5/2	Hereford	W5–3	
1967	4/2	Aberdeen	L0–1	
†1967	1/3	Southampton	W1–0	(IYT*)
†1967	15/3	Dundee	D0–0	(IYT*)
1968	3/2	Walsall	L0–5	
1969	1/2	Stranraer	D1–1	
1970	31/1	Derby	L1–2	
1971	30/1	Greenock	L1–2	
1972	29/1	Bournemouth	W2–0	
1973	20/1	Kilmarnock	W3–2	
1974	26/1	Brighton	D2–2	
†1981	27/5	Aachen	L0–1	(IYT)
†1982	23/2	Glasgow	L0–1	(IYT*)
†1982	23/3	Coventry	D2–2	(IYT*)
†1983	15/5	Birmingham	W4–2	(IYT)
1983	5/10	Middlesbrough	W3–1	
1983	19/10	Motherwell	W4–0	
†1984	27/11	Fulham	L1–0	(IYT*)
1985	8/4	Cannes	W1–0	(IYT*)
†1986	25/3	Aberdeen	L1–4	(IYT*)

v South Korea

†1993	7/3	Melbourne	D1–1	(WYC)

v Spain

1952	15/4	Barcelona	L1–4	(IYT)
1957	26/9	Birmingham	D4–4	
1958	5/4	Saarbrücken	D2–2	(IYT)
†1958	8/10	Madrid	W4–2	
1961	30/3	Lisbon	D0–0	(IYT)
†1964	27/2	Murcia	W2–1	
†1964	5/4	Amsterdam	W4–0	(IYT)
†1965	17/4	Heilbronn	D0–0	(IYT)
†1966	30/3	Swindon	W3–0	
†1967	7/5	Manisa	W2–1	(IYT)
†1971	31/3	Pamplona	L2–3	
†1971	20/4	Luton	D1–1	
†1972	9/2	Alicante	D0–0	
†1972	15/3	Sheffield	W4–1	(IYT*)
†1975	25/2	Bristol	D1–1	(IYT*)
†1975	18/3	Madrid	W1–0	(IYT*)
†1976	12/11	Monte Carlo	W3–0	
†1978	7/5	Bukowas	W1–0	(IYT)
†1978	17/11	Monte Carlo	D1–1	
†1981	25/5	Siegen	L1–2	(IYT)
†1983	13/5	Stoke	W1–0	(IYT)
†1990	29/7	Gyula	L0–1	(IYT)
†1991	25/5	Wembley	D1–1	
†1991	15/6	Faro	L0–1	(WYC)
†1993	17/2	Alicante	D1–1	
†1993	22/7	Walsall	W5–1	(IYT)

v Sweden

†1971	24/5	Poprad	W1–0	(IYT)
†1981	5/9	Pazin	W3–2	
†1984	10/9	Rovinj	D1–1	
†1986	10/11	West Brom	D3–3	

v Switzerland

1950	26/5	Stockerau	W2–1	(IYT)
1951	27/3	Nice	W3–1	(IYT)
1952	13/4	Barcelona	W4–0	(IYT)
1955	11/4	Florence	D0–0	(IYT)
1956	11/3	Schaffhausen	W2–0	
1956	13/10	Brighton	D2–2	
1958	26/5	Zurich	W3–0	

<table>
<tr><td>† 1960</td><td>8/10</td><td>Leyton</td><td>W4–3</td><td></td></tr>
<tr><td>1962</td><td>22/11</td><td>Coventry</td><td>W1–0</td><td></td></tr>
<tr><td>† 1963</td><td>21/3</td><td>Bienne</td><td>W7–1</td><td></td></tr>
<tr><td>† 1973</td><td>2/6</td><td>Forte Dei Marmi</td><td></td><td></td></tr>
<tr><td></td><td></td><td></td><td>W2–0</td><td>(IYT)</td></tr>
<tr><td>† 1975</td><td>11/5</td><td>Buochs</td><td>W4–0</td><td>(IYT)</td></tr>
<tr><td>† 1980</td><td>4/9</td><td>Rovinj</td><td>W3–0</td><td></td></tr>
<tr><td>† 1982</td><td>6/9</td><td>Porec</td><td>W2–0</td><td></td></tr>
<tr><td>† 1983</td><td>26/7</td><td>Hajduboszormeny</td><td></td><td></td></tr>
<tr><td></td><td></td><td></td><td>W4–0</td><td></td></tr>
<tr><td>† 1983</td><td>1/9</td><td>Porec</td><td>W4–2</td><td></td></tr>
<tr><td>† 1988</td><td>19/5</td><td>Sion</td><td>W2–0</td><td></td></tr>
<tr><td>† 1992</td><td>17/11</td><td>Port Vale</td><td>W7–2</td><td></td></tr>
</table>

v Syria

† 1991	18/6	Faro	D3–3	(WYC)

v Thailand

† 1986	7/5	Peking	L1–2

v Trinidad & Tobago

† 1991	25/3	Port of Spain	W4–0

v Turkey

1959	29/3	Dimitrovo	D1–1	(IYT)
† 1978	5/5	Wodzislaw	D1–1	(IYT)
† 1992	17/11	High Wycombe		
			W2–1	
† 1993	11/3	Melbourne	W1–0	(WYC)
† 1993	25/7	Nottingham	W1–0	(IYT)

v Uruguay

† 1977	9/10	Las Palmas	D1–1	
† 1987	10/6	Montevideo	D2–2	
† 1991	20/6	Faro	D0–0	(WYC)

v USA

† 1993	9/3	Melbourne	W1–0	(WYC)

v USSR

† 1963	17/4	Tottenham	W2–0	(IYT)
† 1967	13/5	Istanbul	L0–1	(IYT)
† 1968	11/4	Nîmes	D1–1	(IYT)
† 1971	28/5	Prague	D1–1	(IYT)
† 1978	10/10	Las Palmas	W1–0	
† 1982	4/9	Umag	W1–0	
† 1983	29/3	Cannes	D0–0	
† 1983	17/5	Aston Villa	L0–2	(IYT)
1984	3/5	Ludwigsburg	L0–2	
† 1984	27/5	Moscow	D1–1	(IYT)
† 1984	8/9	Porec	W1–0	
† 1985	3/4	Cannes	W2–1	
† 1985	3/6	Toulon	L0–2	
† 1990	26/7	Debrecen	L1–3	(IYT)

v Wales

1948	28/2	High Wycombe		
			W4–3	
1948	15/4	London	W4–0	
1949	26/2	Swansea	D0–0	
1950	25/2	Worcester	W1–0	
1951	17/2	Wrexham	D1–1	
1952	23/2	Plymouth	W6–0	
1953	21/2	Swansea	W4–2	
1954	20/2	Derby	W2–1	
1955	19/2	Milford Haven	W7–2	
1956	18/2	Shrewsbury	W5–1	
1957	9/2	Cardiff	W7–1	
1958	15/2	Reading	W8–2	
1959	14/2	Portmadoc	W3–0	
1960	19/3	Canterbury	D1–1	
1961	18/3	Newtown	W4–0	
1962	17/3	Swindon	W4–0	
1963	16/3	Haverfordwest	W1–0	
1964	14/3	Leeds	W2–1	
1965	20/3	Newport	D2–2	
1966	19/3	Northampton	W4–1	
1967	18/3	Cwmbran	D3–3	
1968	16/3	Watford	L2–3	
1969	15/3	Haverfordwest	W3–1	
† 1970	25/2	Newport	D0–0	(IYT*)
† 1970	18/3	Leyton	L1–2	
1970	20/4	Reading	D0–0	
1971	20/2	Aberystwyth	L1–2	
1972	19/2	Swindon	W4–0	
1973	24/2	Portmadoc	W4–1	
† 1974	9/1	West Brom	W1–0	(IYT*)
1974	2/3	Shrewsbury	W2–1	
† 1974	13/3	Cardiff	L0–1	(IYT*)
† 1976	11/2	Cardiff	W1–0	(IYT*)
† 1976	3/3	Manchester	L2–3	(IYT*)
† 1977	9/3	West Brom	W1–0	(IYT*)
† 1977	23/3	Cardiff	D1–1	(IYT*)
† 1991	30/4	Wrexham	W1–0	(IYT*)
† 1991	22/5	Yeovil	W3–0	(IYT*)

v Yugoslavia

1953	2/4	Liège	D1–1	(IYT)
1958	4/2	Chelsea	D2–2	
1962	20/4	Ploesti	L0–5	(IYT)
† 1967	9/5	Izmir	D1–1	(IYT)
† 1971	22/5	Bardejor	W1–0	(IYT)
† 1972	17/5	Barcelona	W1–0	(IYT)
† 1976	16/11	Monte Carlo	L0–3	
1978	15/11	Monte Carlo	D1–1	
† 1980	20/5	Altenberg	W2–0	(IYT)
† 1981	10/9	Pula	W5–0	
† 1982	9/9	Pula	W1–0	
† 1983	25/7	Debrecen	D4–4	
† 1983	8/9	Pula	D2–2	
1984	5/5	Boblingen	W1–0	
† 1984	12/9	Buje	L1–4	

FA Premier League Champions 1992–1994

Season	Winners	Pts	Max	Season	Winners	Pts	Max
1992–93	Manchester United	84	126	1993–94	Manchester United	92	126

Football League Champions 1888–1992

First Division 1888–1992

Season	Winners	Pts	Max	Season	Winners	Pts	Max
1888–89	Preston North End	40	44	1946–47	Liverpool	57	84
1889–90	Preston North End	33	44	1947–48	Arsenal	59	84
1890–91	Everton	29	44	1948–49	Portsmouth	58	84
1891–92	Sunderland	42	52	1949–50*	Portsmouth	53	84
1892–93	Sunderland	48	60	1950–51	Tottenham Hotspur	60	84
1893–94	Aston Villa	44	60	1951–52	Manchester United	57	84
1894–95	Sunderland	47	60	1952–53*	Arsenal	54	84
1895–96	Aston Villa	45	60	1953–54	Wolverhampton Wanderers	57	84
1896–97	Aston Villa	47	60	1954–55	Chelsea	52	84
1897–98	Sheffield United	42	60	1955–56	Manchester United	60	84
1898–99	Aston Villa	45	68	1956–57	Manchester United	64	84
1899–1900	Aston Villa	50	68	1957–58	Wolverhampton Wanderers	64	84
1900–01	Liverpool	45	68	1958–59	Wolverhampton Wanderers	61	84
1901–02	Sunderland	44	68	1959–60	Burnley	55	84
1902–03	Sheffield Wednesday	42	68	1960–61	Tottenham Hotspur	66	84
1903–04	Sheffield Wednesday	47	68	1961–62	Ipswich Town	56	84
1904–05	Newcastle United	48	68	1962–63	Everton	61	84
1905–06	Liverpool	51	76	1963–64	Liverpool	57	84
1906–07	Newcastle United	51	76	1964–65*	Manchester United	61	84
1907–08	Manchester United	52	76	1965–66	Liverpool	61	84
1908–09	Newcastle United	53	76	1966–67	Manchester United	60	84
1909–10	Aston Villa	53	76	1967–68	Manchester City	58	84
1910–11	Manchester United	52	76	1968–69	Leeds United	67	84
1911–12	Blackburn Rovers	49	76	1969–70	Everton	66	84
1912–13	Sunderland	54	76	1970–71	Arsenal	65	84
1913–14	Blackburn Rovers	51	76	1971–72	Derby County	53	84
1914–15	Everton	46	76	1972–73	Liverpool	60	84
1919–20	West Bromwich Albion	60	84	1973–74	Leeds United	62	84
1920–21	Burnley	59	84	1974–75	Derby County	58	84
1921–22	Liverpool	57	84	1975–76	Liverpool	60	84
1922–23	Liverpool	60	84	1976–77	Liverpool	57	84
1923–24*	Huddersfield Town	57	84	1977–78	Nottingham Forest	64	84
1924–25	Huddersfield Town	58	84	1978–79	Liverpool	68	84
1925–26	Huddersfield Town	57	84	1979–80	Liverpool	60	84
1926–27	Newcastle United	56	84	1980–81	Aston Villa	60	84
1927–28	Everton	53	84	1981–82	Liverpool	87	126
1928–29	Sheffield Wednesday	52	84	1982–83	Liverpool	82	126
1929–30	Sheffield Wednesday	60	84	1983–84	Liverpool	80	126
1930–31	Arsenal	66	84	1984–85	Everton	90	126
1931–32	Everton	56	84	1985–86	Liverpool	88	126
1932–33	Arsenal	58	84	1986–87	Everton	86	126
1933–34	Arsenal	59	84	1987–88	Liverpool	90	120
1934–35	Arsenal	58	84	1988–89*	Arsenal	76	114
1935–36	Sunderland	56	84	1989–90	Liverpool	79	114
1936–37	Manchester City	57	84	1990–91	Arsenal	83	114
1937–38	Arsenal	52	84	1991–92	Leeds United	82	126
1938–39	Everton	59	84				

Won on goal average/difference   *No competition 1915–19 and 1939–46*

Football League Champions 1888–1994

First Division 1992–1994 (Second Division 1892–1992)

Season	Winners	Pts	Max	Season	Winners	Pts	Max
1892–93	Small Heath	36	44	1948–49	Fulham	57	84
1893–94	Liverpool	50	56	1949–50	Tottenham Hotspur	61	84
1894–95	Bury	48	60	1950–51	Preston North End	57	84
1895–96*	Liverpool	46	60	1951–52	Sheffield Wednesday	53	84
1896–97	Notts County	42	60	1952–53	Sheffield United	60	84
1897–98	Burnley	48	60	1953–54*	Leicester City	56	84
1898–99	Manchester City	52	68	1954–55*	Birmingham City	54	84
1899–1900	Sheffield Wednesday	54	68	1955–56	Sheffield Wednesday	55	84
1900–01	Grimsby Town	49	68	1956–57	Leicester City	61	84
1901–02	West Bromwich Albion	55	68	1957–58	West Ham United	57	84
1902–03	Manchester City	54	68	1958–59	Sheffield Wednesday	62	84
1903–04	Preston North End	50	68	1959–60	Aston Villa	59	84
1904–05	Liverpool	58	68	1960–61	Ipswich Town	59	84
1905–06	Bristol City	66	76	1961–62	Liverpool	62	84
1906–07	Nottingham Forest	60	76	1962–63	Stoke City	53	84
1907–08	Bradford City	54	76	1963–64	Leeds United	63	84
1908–09	Bolton Wanderers	52	76	1964–65	Newcastle United	57	84
1909–10	Manchester City	54	76	1965–66	Manchester City	59	84
1910–11	West Bromwich Albion	53	76	1966–67	Coventry City	59	84
1911–12	Derby County	54	76	1967–68	Ipswich Town	59	84
1912–13	Preston North End	53	76	1968–69	Derby County	63	84
1913–14	Notts County	53	76	1969–70	Huddersfield Town	60	84
1914–15	Derby County	53	76	1970–71	Leicester City	59	84
1919–20	Tottenham Hotspur	70	76	1971–72	Norwich City	57	84
1920–21	Birmingham	58	76	1972–73	Burnley	62	84
1921–22	Nottingham Forest	56	76	1973–74	Middlesbrough	65	84
1922–23	Notts County	53	76	1974–75	Manchester United	61	84
1923–24	Leeds United	54	76	1975–76	Sunderland	56	84
1924–25	Leicester City	59	76	1976–77	Wolverhampton Wanderers	57	84
1925–26	Sheffield Wednesday	60	76	1977–78	Bolton Wanderers	58	84
1926–27	Middlesbrough	62	76	1978–79	Crystal Palace	57	84
1927–28	Manchester City	59	76	1979–80	Leicester City	55	84
1928–29	Middlesbrough	55	76	1980–81	West Ham United	66	84
1929–30	Blackpool	58	76	1981–82	Luton Town	88	126
1930–31	Everton	61	76	1982–83	Queens Park Rangers	85	126
1931–32	Wolverhampton Wanderers	56	76	1983–84*	Chelsea	88	126
1932–33	Stoke City	56	76	1984–85	Oxford United	84	126
1933–34	Grimsby Town	59	76	1985–86	Norwich City	84	126
1934–35	Brentford	61	76	1986–87	Derby County	84	126
1935–36	Manchester United	56	76	1987–88	Millwall	82	132
Season	Winners	Pts	Max	1988–89	Chelsea	99	138
1936–37	Leicester City	56	76	1989–90	Leeds United	85	138
1937–38	Aston Villa	57	76	1990–91	Oldham Athletic	88	138
1938–39	Blackburn Rovers	55	84	1991–92	Ipswich Town	84	138
1946–47	Manchester City	62	84	1992–93	Newcastle United	96	138
1947–48	Birmingham City	59	84	1993–94	Crystal Palace	90	138

* Won on goal average/difference   No competition 1915–19 and 1939–46

Third Division (S) 1920–1958

Season	Winners	Pts	Max	Season	Winners	Pts	Max
1920–21	Crystal Palace	59	84	1936–37	Luton Town	58	84
1921–22*	Southampton	61	84	1937–38	Millwall	56	84
1922–23	Bristol City	59	84	1938–39	Newport County	55	84
1923–24	Portsmouth	59	84	1946–47	Cardiff City	66	84
1924–25	Swansea Town	57	84	1947–48	Queens Park Rangers	61	84
1925–26	Reading	57	84	1948–49	Swansea Town	62	84
1926–27	Bristol City	62	84	1949–50	Notts County	58	84
1927–28	Millwall	65	84	1950–51	Nottingham Forest	70	92
1928–29*	Charlton Athletic	54	84	1951–52	Plymouth Argyle	66	92
1929–30	Plymouth Argyle	68	84	1952–53	Bristol Rovers	64	92
1930–31	Notts County	59	84	1953–54	Ipswich Town	64	92
1931–32	Fulham	57	84	1954–55	Bristol City	70	92
1932–33	Brentford	62	84	1955–56	Leyton Orient	66	92
1933–34	Norwich City	61	84	1956–57*	Ipswich Town	59	92
1934–35	Charlton Athletic	61	84	1957–58	Brighton and Hove Albion	60	92
1935–36	Coventry City	57	84				

Third Division (N) 1921–1958

Season	Winners	Pts	Max	Season	Winners	Pts	Max
1921–22	Stockport County	56	76	1936–37	Stockport County	60	84
1922–23	Nelson	51	76	1937–38	Tranmere Rovers	56	84
1923–24	Wolverhampton Wanderers	63	84	1938–39	Barnsley	67	84
1924–25	Darlington	58	84	1946–47	Doncaster Rovers	72	84
1925–26	Grimsby Town	61	84	1947–48	Lincoln City	60	84
1926–27	Stoke City	63	84	1948–49	Hull City	65	84
1927–28	Bradford	63	84	1949–50	Doncaster Rovers	55	84
1928–29	Bradford City	63	84	1950–51	Rotherham United	71	92
1929–30	Port Vale	67	84	1951–52	Lincoln City	69	92
1930–31	Chesterfield	58	84	1952–53	Oldham Athletic	59	92
1931–32*	Lincoln City	57	80	1953–54	Port Vale	69	92
1932–33	Hull City	59	84	1954–55	Barnsley	65	92
1933–34	Barnsley	62	84	1955–56	Grimsby Town	68	92
1934–35	Doncaster Rovers	57	84	1956–57	Derby County	63	92
1935–36	Chesterfield	60	84	1957–58	Scunthorpe United	66	92

Second Division 1992–1994 (Third Division 1958–1992)

Season	Winners	Pts	Max	Season	Winners	Pts	Max
1958–59	Plymouth Argyle	62	92	1976–77	Mansfield Town	64	92
1959–60	Southampton	61	92	1977–78	Wrexham	61	92
1960–61	Bury	68	92	1978–79	Shrewsbury Town	61	92
1961–62	Portsmouth	65	92	1979–80	Grimsby Town	62	92
1962–63	Northampton Town	62	92	1980–81	Rotherham United	61	92
1963–64*	Coventry City	60	92	1981–82	Burnley	80	92
1964–65	Carlisle United	60	92	1982–83	Portsmouth	91	138
1965–66	Hull City	69	92	1983–84	Oxford United	95	138
1966–67	Queens Park Rangers	67	92	1984–85	Bradford City	94	138
1967–68	Oxford United	57	92	1985–86	Reading	94	138
1968–69*	Watford	64	92	1986–87	AFC Bournemouth	97	138
1969–70	Orient	62	92	1987–88	Sunderland	93	138
1970–71	Preston North End	61	92	1988–89	Wolverhampton Wanderers	92	138
1971–72	Aston Villa	70	92	1989–90	Bristol Rovers	93	138
1972–73	Bolton Wanderers	61	92	1990–91	Cambridge United	86	138
1973–74	Oldham Athletic	62	92	1991–92	Brentford	82	138
1974–75	Blackburn Rovers	60	92	1992–93	Stoke City	93	138
1975–76	Hereford United	63	92	1993–94	Reading	89	138

* Won on goal average/difference   No competition 1939–46

Third Division 1992–1994 (Fourth Division 1958–1992)

Season	Winners	Pts	Max	Season	Winners	Pts	Max
1958–59	Port Vale	64	92	1976–77	Cambridge United	65	92
1959–60	Walsall	65	92	1977–78	Watford	71	92
1960–61	Peterborough United	66	92	1978–79	Reading	65	92
1961–62	Millwall	56	88	1979–80	Huddersfield Town	66	92
1962–63	Brentford	62	92	1980–81	Southend United	67	92
1963–64*	Gillingham	60	92	1981–82	Sheffield United	96	138
1964–65	Brighton and Hove Albion	63	92	1982–83	Wimbledon	98	138
1965–66	Doncaster Rovers	59	92	1983–84	York City	101	138
1966–67	Stockport County	64	92	1984–85	Chesterfield	91	138
1967–68	Luton Town	66	92	1985–86	Swindon Town	102	138
1968–69	Doncaster Rovers	59	92	1986–87	Northampton Town	99	138
1969–70	Chesterfield	64	92	1987–88	Wolverhampton Wanderers	90	138
1970–71	Notts County	69	92	1988–89	Rotherham United	82	138
1971–72	Grimsby Town	63	92	1989–90	Exeter City	89	138
1972–73	Southport	62	92	1990–91	Darlington	83	138
1973–74	Peterborough United	65	92	1991–92	Burnley	83	126
1974–75	Mansfield Town	68	92	1992–93	Cardiff City	83	126
1975–76	Lincoln City	74	92	1993–94	Shrewsbury Town	79	126

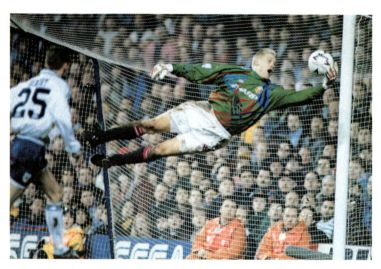

Peter Schmeichel makes a spectacular save against Tottenham.

Review of the League Season 1993–1994

Manchester United's 92 points was the highest total achieved in the top division since three points had been awarded for a win (1981). It gave them their ninth overall League championship, including a second successive Premiership title. United's 2–1 win at relegation-haunted Ipswich on 1 May left Blackburn Rovers – the only team capable of heading them – requiring all three points from a trip to Highfield Road on the following evening to stay in contention. Mid-table Coventry triumphed 2–1 and United were free to uncork the champagne. Their star performer during the season had been the French international, Eric Cantona, who was voted the PFA's Player of the Year. (Alan Shearer of Blackburn and England won the FWA award.)

It was nail-biting stuff at the bottom of the Premiership. Newly-promoted Swindon had an unhappy season, doomed to relegation after a 4–2 home defeat against Wimbledon on 23 April and eventually finishing ten points adrift of the rest. Five clubs – Everton, Southampton, Ipswich, Sheffield United and Oldham – were playing for their Premiership lives on the last Saturday of the season (7 May). The last two of these fell through the relegation trap-door: Sheffield lost in the last minute to a Mark Stein goal at Chelsea when a draw would have saved them. A match on the same day at Villa Park between Villa (10th) and Liverpool (8th) attracted 45,347, the best Premiership gate of the season.

Crystal Palace were First Division champions after a 3–2 victory in their penultimate match at Middlesbrough on 1 May, and despite losing their last match at home to Watford (before 28,000), they had accumulated 90 League points during the season. It was the fourth time Palace had reached the top flight, though the four seasons between 1969 and 1973 have been the longest they have remained there. Nottingham Forest, with Frank Clark in charge after 18 years under Clough, achieved automatic promotion back to the Premiership a year after demotion. Millwall, now at the 'New Den', clinched one of the play-off spots. Bobby Robson had brought his Sporting Lisbon team to play a pre-season friendly to officially open the London club's brand new stadium.

Two Midlands rivals, West Bromwich and Birmingham, went into their last respective First Division fixtures on 8 May knowing that three points were necessary – but not sufficient – for survival. City achieved a notable 2–1 success at Tranmere, the Merseysiders already installed in the play-offs, but Albion's Lee Ashcroft scored the goal at Fratton Park that kept them up and consigned City to the drop.

Reading were well clear at the top of the Second Division after completing a run of 15 matches without defeat in mid-season and they were never headed, despite being shadowed for most of the time by a Stockport team with games in hand. County stuttered at the end and, though they managed to secure a play-off place, it was Port Vale who were automatically promoted after a 3–1 win at Brighton in their final fixture (7 May). Shrewsbury went one better than Reading: they were unbeaten in 16 matches on the way to winning the Third Division title.

FA Carling Premiership – Final Table 1993–1994

		P	Home					Away					Total			
			W	D	L	F	A	W	D	L	F	A	F	A	GD	Pts
1	Manchester United	42	14	6	1	39	13	13	5	3	41	25	80	38	+42	92
2	Blackburn Rovers	42	14	5	2	31	11	11	4	6	32	25	63	36	+27	84
3	Newcastle United	42	14	4	3	51	14	9	4	8	31	27	82	41	+41	77
4	Arsenal	42	10	8	3	25	15	8	9	4	28	13	53	28	+25	71
5	Leeds United	42	13	6	2	37	18	5	10	6	28	21	65	39	+26	70
6	Wimbledon	42	12	5	4	35	21	6	6	9	21	32	56	53	+3	65
7	Sheffield Wednesday	42	10	7	4	48	24	6	9	6	28	30	76	54	+22	64
8	Liverpool	42	12	4	5	33	23	5	5	11	26	32	59	55	+4	60
9	Queens Park Rangers	42	8	7	6	32	29	8	5	8	30	32	62	61	+1	60
10	Aston Villa	42	8	5	8	23	18	7	7	7	23	32	46	50	−4	57
11	Coventry City	42	9	7	5	23	17	5	7	9	20	28	43	45	−2	56
12	Norwich City	42	4	9	8	26	29	8	8	5	39	32	65	61	+4	53
13	West Ham United	42	6	7	8	26	31	7	6	8	21	27	47	58	−11	52
14	Chelsea	42	11	5	5	31	20	2	7	12	18	33	49	53	−4	51
15	Tottenham Hotspur	42	4	8	9	29	33	7	4	10	25	26	54	59	−5	45
16	Manchester City	42	6	10	5	24	22	3	8	10	14	27	38	49	−11	45
17	Everton	42	8	4	9	26	30	4	4	13	16	33	42	63	−21	44
18	Southampton	42	9	2	10	30	31	3	5	13	19	35	49	66	−17	43
19	Ipswich Town	42	5	8	8	21	32	4	8	9	14	26	35	58	−23	43
20	Sheffield United	42	6	10	5	24	23	2	8	11	18	37	42	60	−18	42
21	Oldham Athletic	42	5	8	8	24	33	4	5	12	18	35	42	68	−26	40
22	Swindon Town	42	4	7	10	25	45	1	8	12	22	55	47	100	−53	30

Endsleigh Insurance League First Division – Final Table 1993–1994

		P	Home					Away					Total			
			W	D	L	F	A	W	D	L	F	A	F	A	GD	Pts
1	Crystal Palace	46	16	4	3	39	18	11	5	7	34	28	73	46	+27	90
2	Nottingham Forest	46	12	9	2	38	22	11	5	7	36	27	74	49	+25	83
3	Millwall	46	14	8	1	36	17	5	9	9	22	32	58	49	+9	74
4	Leicester City	46	11	9	3	45	30	8	7	8	27	29	72	59	+13	73*
5	Tranmere Rovers	46	15	3	5	48	23	6	6	11	21	30	69	53	+16	72
6	Derby County	46	15	3	5	44	25	5	8	10	29	43	73	68	+5	71
7	Notts County	46	16	3	4	43	26	4	5	14	22	43	65	69	−4	68
8	Wolverhampton Wanderers	46	10	10	3	34	19	7	7	9	26	28	60	47	+13	68
9	Middlesbrough	46	12	6	5	40	19	6	7	10	26	35	66	54	+12	67
10	Stoke City	46	14	4	5	35	19	4	9	10	22	40	57	59	−2	67
11	Charlton Athletic	46	14	3	6	39	22	5	5	13	22	36	61	58	+3	65
12	Sunderland	46	14	2	7	35	22	5	6	12	19	35	54	57	−3	65
13	Bristol City	46	11	7	5	27	18	5	9	9	20	32	47	50	−3	64
14	Bolton Wanderers	46	10	8	5	40	31	5	6	12	23	33	63	64	−1	59
15	Southend United	46	10	5	8	34	28	7	3	13	29	39	63	67	−4	59
16	Grimsby Town	46	7	14	2	26	16	6	6	11	26	31	52	47	+5	59
17	Portsmouth	46	10	6	7	29	22	5	7	11	23	36	52	58	−6	58
18	Barnsley	46	9	3	11	25	26	7	4	12	30	41	55	67	−12	55
19	Watford	46	10	5	8	39	35	5	4	14	27	45	66	80	−14	54
20	Luton Town	46	12	4	7	38	25	2	7	14	18	35	56	60	−4	53
21	West Bromwich Albion	46	9	7	7	38	31	4	5	14	22	38	60	69	−9	51
22	Birmingham City	46	9	7	7	28	29	4	5	14	24	40	52	69	−17	51
23	Oxford United	46	10	5	8	33	33	3	5	15	21	42	54	75	−21	49
24	Peterborough United	46	6	9	8	31	30	2	4	17	17	46	48	76	−28	37

* *Promoted via the play-offs*

154

Endsleigh Insurance League Second Division – Final Table 1993–1994

			Home					Away					Total			
		P	W	D	L	F	A	W	D	L	F	A	F	A	GD	Pts
1	Reading	46	15	6	2	40	16	11	5	7	41	28	81	44	+37	89
2	Port Vale	46	16	6	1	46	18	10	4	9	33	28	79	46	+33	88
3	Plymouth Argyle	46	16	4	3	46	26	9	6	8	42	30	88	56	+32	85
4	Stockport County	46	15	3	5	50	22	9	10	4	24	22	74	44	+30	85
5	York City	46	12	7	4	33	13	9	5	9	31	27	64	40	+24	75
6	Burnley	46	17	4	2	55	18	4	6	13	24	40	79	58	+21	73*
7	Bradford City	46	13	5	5	34	20	6	8	9	27	33	61	53	+8	70
8	Bristol Rovers	46	10	8	5	33	26	10	2	11	27	33	60	59	+1	70
9	Hull City	46	9	9	5	33	20	9	5	9	29	34	62	54	+8	68
10	Cambridge United	46	11	5	7	38	29	8	4	11	41	44	79	73	+6	66
11	Huddersfield Town	46	9	8	6	27	26	8	6	9	31	35	58	61	−3	65
12	Wrexham	46	13	4	6	45	33	4	7	12	21	44	66	77	−11	62
13	Swansea City	46	12	7	4	37	20	4	5	14	19	38	56	58	−2	60
14	Brighton & Hove Albion	46	10	7	6	38	29	5	7	11	22	38	60	67	−7	59
15	Rotherham United	46	11	4	8	42	30	4	9	10	21	30	63	60	+3	58
16	Brentford	46	7	10	6	30	28	6	9	8	27	27	57	55	+2	58
17	AFC Bournemouth	46	8	7	8	26	27	6	8	9	25	32	51	59	−8	57
18	Leyton Orient	46	11	9	3	38	26	3	5	15	19	45	57	71	−14	56
19	Cardiff City	46	10	7	6	39	33	3	8	12	27	46	66	79	−13	54
20	Blackpool	46	12	2	9	41	37	4	3	16	22	38	63	75	−12	53
21	Fulham	46	7	6	10	20	23	7	4	12	30	40	50	63	−13	52
22	Exeter City	46	8	7	8	38	37	3	5	15	14	46	52	83	−31	45
23	Hartlepool United	46	8	3	12	28	40	1	6	16	13	47	41	87	−46	36
24	Barnet	46	4	6	13	22	32	1	7	15	19	54	41	86	−45	28

Endsleigh Insurance League Third Division – Final Table 1993–1994

			Home					Away					Total			
		P	W	D	L	F	A	W	D	L	F	A	F	A	GD	Pts
1	Shrewsbury Town	42	10	8	3	28	17	12	5	4	35	22	63	39	+24	79
2	Chester City	42	13	5	3	35	18	8	6	7	34	28	69	46	+23	74
3	Crewe Alexandra	42	12	4	5	45	30	9	6	6	35	31	80	61	+19	73
4	Wycombe Wanderers	42	11	6	4	34	21	8	7	6	33	32	67	53	+14	70*
5	Preston North End	42	13	5	3	46	23	5	8	8	33	37	79	60	+19	67
6	Torquay United	42	8	10	3	30	24	9	6	6	34	32	64	56	+8	67
7	Carlisle United	42	10	4	7	35	23	8	6	7	22	19	57	42	+15	64
8	Chesterfield	42	8	8	5	32	22	8	6	7	23	26	55	48	+7	62
9	Rochdale	42	10	5	6	38	22	6	7	8	25	29	63	51	+12	60
10	Walsall	42	7	5	9	28	26	10	4	7	20	27	48	53	−5	60
11	Scunthorpe United	42	9	7	5	40	26	6	7	8	24	30	64	56	+8	59
12	Mansfield Town	42	9	3	9	28	30	6	7	8	25	32	53	62	−9	55
13	Bury	42	9	6	6	33	22	5	5	11	22	34	55	56	−1	53
14	Scarborough	42	8	4	9	29	28	7	4	10	26	33	55	61	−6	53
15	Doncaster Rovers	42	8	6	7	24	26	6	4	11	20	31	44	57	−13	52
16	Gillingham	42	8	8	5	27	23	4	7	10	17	28	44	51	−7	51
17	Colchester United	42	8	4	9	31	33	5	6	10	25	38	56	71	−15	49
18	Lincoln City	42	7	4	10	26	29	5	7	9	26	34	52	63	−11	47
19	Wigan Athletic	42	6	7	8	33	33	5	5	11	18	37	51	70	−19	45
20	Hereford United	42	6	4	11	34	33	6	2	13	26	46	60	79	−19	42
21	Darlington	42	7	5	9	24	28	3	6	12	18	36	42	64	−22	41
22	Northampton Town	42	6	7	8	25	23	3	4	14	19	43	44	66	−22	38

* Promoted via the play-offs

FA Carling Premiership: Results 1993–1994

Home \ Away	Arsenal	Aston Villa	Blackburn Rovers	Chelsea	Coventry City	Everton	Ipswich Town	Leeds United	Liverpool	Manchester City	Manchester United	Newcastle United	Norwich City	Oldham Athletic	Queens Park Rangers	Sheffield United	Sheffield Wednesday	Southampton	Swindon Town	Tottenham Hotspur	West Ham United	Wimbledon
Arsenal	•	1-2	1-0	1-0	0-3	2-0	4-0	2-1	1-0	0-0	2-2	2-1	0-0	1-1	0-0	3-0	1-0	1-0	1-1	1-1	0-2	1-1
Aston Villa	1-2	•	0-1	1-0	0-0	0-0	0-1	1-0	2-1	0-0	1-2	0-2	0-0	1-2	4-1	1-0	2-2	0-2	5-0	1-0	3-1	0-1
Blackburn Rovers	1-0	1-0	•	2-0	2-1	2-0	0-0	1-0	2-0	2-0	1-1	1-0	2-3	1-0	1-1	0-0	1-1	2-0	3-1	0-2	0-2	3-0
Chelsea	0-2	1-1	1-2	•	1-2	4-2	1-1	1-1	1-0	0-0	1-0	0-0	1-2	0-1	0-1	3-2	1-1	1-1	2-0	4-3	2-0	2-0
Coventry City	1-0	0-1	2-1	1-1	•	2-1	1-0	0-2	1-0	4-0	0-1	2-1	1-2	1-1	0-1	0-0	1-1	1-0	2-0	1-0	2-0	1-2
Everton	2-0	0-0	2-0	4-2	2-1	•	0-2	3-0	2-0	1-0	0-1	0-2	1-5	2-1	0-3	4-2	0-2	1-0	6-2	0-1	0-1	3-2
Ipswich Town	1-5	1-2	1-0	1-0	0-2	0-2	•	0-0	1-2	2-2	1-2	1-1	2-1	0-0	1-3	3-2	1-4	1-0	1-1	2-2	1-1	0-0
Leeds United	2-1	2-0	3-3	4-1	1-0	3-0	0-0	•	2-0	3-2	0-2	1-1	0-4	1-0	1-1	2-1	2-2	0-0	3-0	2-0	1-0	4-0
Liverpool	0-0	2-1	0-1	2-1	1-0	2-0	0-0	2-0	•	2-1	3-3	0-2	1-0	2-1	1-0	2-1	2-0	4-2	2-2	1-2	2-0	1-1
Manchester City	0-0	0-0	2-0	0-0	4-0	1-0	2-2	3-2	2-2	•	1-1	1-1	0-1	1-1	1-1	1-1	2-2	2-1	1-1	0-2	0-0	0-1
Manchester United	1-0	3-1	3-1	0-0	0-0	1-0	0-0	0-0	1-0	2-0	•	1-1	2-2	3-2	2-1	3-0	5-0	3-1	4-1	2-0	3-0	3-1
Newcastle United	2-0	5-1	1-0	0-0	4-0	0-2	1-1	1-1	0-2	2-0	1-1	•	3-0	2-1	1-0	0-0	4-0	2-1	2-2	1-0	2-0	4-0
Norwich City	0-0	0-0	1-1	2-1	0-1	1-1	0-0	1-2	2-1	1-1	2-2	1-2	•	3-2	1-1	1-1	1-1	2-1	3-3	1-3	0-0	3-1
Oldham Athletic	1-1	1-2	0-3	0-1	1-1	2-1	0-0	0-1	0-3	1-0	1-3	3-1	1-0	•	2-1	2-2	1-1	1-1	1-1	0-1	3-0	2-1
Queens Park Rangers	0-0	4-1	1-0	1-1	5-1	1-1	3-1	3-2	1-3	1-0	3-2	2-1	4-0	3-1	•	3-1	0-1	1-0	1-2	1-1	1-0	1-2
Sheffield United	1-1	2-0	0-0	1-0	0-0	2-0	2-1	2-2	1-1	1-0	1-2	2-0	1-2	1-0	1-1	•	1-1	0-2	2-2	2-1	0-0	2-2
Sheffield Wednesday	1-0	2-2	1-1	3-1	0-0	5-1	1-1	3-3	2-0	1-1	3-3	2-1	1-0	2-0	1-1	1-3	•	1-2	1-1	3-1	5-0	1-1
Southampton	1-0	4-1	3-1	1-1	2-1	2-0	4-3	2-1	4-2	0-1	0-1	0-0	1-0	1-0	1-2	3-3	2-0	•	1-0	0-1	0-2	2-4
Swindon Town	1-1	2-2	3-3	0-3	1-3	3-1	2-2	0-0	2-2	3-1	1-2	2-2	3-3	3-1	1-1	1-1	1-1	5-1	•	1-2	1-3	0-0
Tottenham Hotspur	1-1	1-1	0-1	1-1	1-2	3-2	1-3	1-1	3-3	1-0	0-1	2-1	1-3	1-2	1-1	2-0	3-1	3-0	1-1	•	1-3	1-1
West Ham United	0-0	0-0	2-0	1-0	3-2	0-1	2-1	0-0	1-2	3-1	2-2	2-4	3-3	2-2	4-0	0-0	2-0	3-3	0-0	3-1	•	0-2
Wimbledon	1-1	2-2	4-1	2-1	2-0	1-1	2-0	1-0	2-1	1-0	1-0	3-1	3-0	1-0	0-1	2-0	1-1	1-0	3-0	2-1	1-2	•

Endsleigh Insurance League First Division: Results 1993–1994

	Barnsley	Birmingham City	Bolton Wanderers	Bristol City	Charlton Athletic	Crystal Palace	Derby County	Grimsby Town	Leicester City	Luton Town	Middlesbrough	Millwall	Notts County	Nottingham Forest	Oxford United	Peterborough United	Portsmouth	Southend United	Stoke City	Sunderland	Tranmere Rovers	Watford	West Bromwich Albion	Wolverhampton Wanderers
Barnsley	•	2-3	1-1	1-1	0-1	1-3	0-1	1-2	0-1	1-0	1-4	0-1	0-3	1-0	1-0	1-0	2-0	1-3	3-0	4-0	1-0	0-1	1-1	2-0
Birmingham City	0-2	•	2-1	2-2	1-0	2-4	3-0	1-1	0-3	1-1	1-0	1-0	2-3	0-3	1-1	0-0	0-1	3-1	3-1	0-0	0-3	1-0	2-0	2-2
Bolton Wanderers	2-3	1-1	•	2-2	3-2	1-1	0-2	1-1	1-2	1-1	1-0	4-0	0-2	0-2	1-1	1-1	0-2	0-2	1-1	0-0	2-1	3-1	1-1	1-3
Bristol City	0-2	3-0	2-0	•	0-0	2-0	0-0	1-0	1-3	1-0	0-0	2-2	0-2	1-4	0-1	4-1	0-1	2-1	0-0	2-0	2-0	1-1	0-0	2-1
Charlton Athletic	1-0	1-0	3-0	0-0	•	0-0	1-2	0-1	2-1	1-0	0-0	0-0	5-1	0-1	1-0	5-1	5-1	4-3	4-1	0-0	3-1	0-2	2-1	0-1
Crystal Palace	2-0	1-1	1-1	2-0	2-0	•	1-1	2-1	2-1	3-2	2-5	0-0	1-2	2-0	2-1	3-2	5-1	1-3	4-1	5-0	4-0	0-2	1-0	1-1
Derby County	2-0	1-1	1-0	1-0	2-0	3-1	•	3-2	3-2	2-1	0-1	0-0	1-1	0-2	1-0	2-0	1-1	1-3	4-2	5-0	4-0	1-2	5-3	0-4
Grimsby Town	2-2	1-0	0-0	1-0	0-1	1-1	1-1	•	0-0	2-0	1-1	0-0	2-2	0-0	1-0	3-2	1-1	4-0	0-0	0-1	0-0	2-2	2-2	2-0
Leicester City	0-1	1-1	1-1	3-0	2-1	1-1	3-3	1-1	•	2-1	2-0	4-0	2-2	0-0	1-0	3-2	1-1	4-0	0-0	0-1	1-1	2-2	2-2	2-0
Luton Town	5-0	1-1	1-1	0-2	2-0	0-1	2-1	2-1	0-2	•	1-1	4-2	3-2	1-0	2-3	2-0	0-3	1-1	6-2	2-1	0-1	2-1	4-2	2-2
Middlesbrough	5-0	2-2	0-1	0-1	2-0	2-3	3-0	1-2	2-0	2-1	•	4-2	3-0	2-2	3-0	1-2	0-2	1-0	1-2	4-1	0-0	2-1	3-0	0-2
Millwall	2-0	2-1	1-0	0-0	2-1	3-0	0-0	1-0	0-0	0-0	1-1	•	2-0	1-0	2-2	1-0	0-0	1-4	2-0	2-1	3-1	4-1	2-1	1-0
Notts County	3-1	2-1	2-0	2-0	3-3	3-2	4-1	2-1	4-1	1-2	2-3	1-3	•	2-1	2-1	2-1	1-1	2-1	2-3	1-0	2-1	1-0	1-0	0-2
Nottingham Forest	2-1	1-0	3-2	0-0	1-1	1-1	1-1	5-3	4-0	4-0	1-1	1-0	1-0	•	2-1	2-0	1-1	2-1	2-3	2-2	2-1	2-1	1-0	0-2
Oxford United	1-1	2-0	0-2	4-2	0-4	1-3	2-0	2-2	2-2	0-1	1-1	0-2	2-1	1-0	•	1-2	3-2	3-1	1-1	0-3	1-0	2-3	1-1	4-0
Peterborough United	4-1	1-0	2-3	0-2	0-1	1-1	2-1	1-2	1-1	0-0	1-0	0-0	1-1	2-3	3-1	•	2-2	3-1	1-1	0-3	0-0	3-4	2-0	0-1
Portsmouth	2-1	0-2	2-0	0-0	1-2	0-1	3-2	3-1	0-1	0-0	2-0	2-2	0-0	1-1	0-2	0-2	•	3-1	3-3	0-1	1-2	2-0	2-0	1-1
Southend United	0-3	3-1	0-2	0-0	1-2	1-2	4-3	1-0	0-0	2-1	1-0	1-1	0-0	1-1	6-1	3-0	3-0	•	0-0	0-1	1-2	2-0	0-3	3-0
Stoke City	5-4	2-1	2-0	3-0	1-0	0-2	2-1	1-0	1-0	2-2	3-1	1-2	0-0	0-1	1-1	3-0	2-0	3-1	•	1-0	1-2	2-0	2-2	1-1
Sunderland	1-0	1-0	2-0	0-0	4-0	1-0	2-1	2-2	2-3	2-2	3-1	2-1	0-0	0-1	1-1	2-0	2-0	0-1	0-1	•	1-0	2-0	0-1	1-1
Tranmere Rovers	0-3	1-2	2-0	2-2	2-2	1-3	4-0	0-3	1-0	4-1	4-0	3-2	3-1	1-2	2-0	2-1	3-1	1-0	0-1	4-1	•	2-1	3-0	1-0
Watford	0-2	5-2	4-3	1-1	2-2	1-3	3-4	0-3	1-2	1-1	4-0	3-2	3-1	1-2	2-0	2-1	3-1	3-0	1-3	4-1	1-2	•	0-1	4-1
West Bromwich Albion	1-1	2-4	2-2	0-1	2-0	2-0	1-2	0-0	1-2	1-0	3-0	0-0	3-0	0-2	3-1	3-0	4-1	2-2	0-0	2-1	1-3	4-1	•	3-2
Wolverhampton Wanderers	1-1	3-0	1-0	3-1	1-1	2-0	2-2	0-0	1-1	1-0	2-3	2-0	3-0	1-1	2-1	1-1	1-1	0-1	1-1	1-1	2-1	2-0	1-2	•

Endsleigh Insurance League Second Division: Results 1993–1994

Home \ Away	Barnet	Blackpool	AFC Bournemouth	Bradford City	Brentford	Brighton & HA	Bristol Rovers	Burnley	Cambridge Utd	Cardiff City	Exeter City	Fulham	Hartlepool Utd	Huddersfield Town	Hull City	Leyton Orient	Plymouth Argyle	Port Vale	Reading	Rotherham Utd	Stockport County	Swansea City	Wrexham	York City
Barnet	•	0-1	1-2	1-2	0-0	1-1	1-2	1-1	2-3	0-0	3-0	0-2	3-2	0-1	1-2	3-1	0-0	2-3	0-1	2-1	0-0	0-1	1-2	1-3
Blackpool	0-1	•	2-1	1-3	3-0	3-2	0-1	3-1	3-2	0-2	1-0	2-0	1-1	2-1	2-0	4-1	2-0	2-0	1-0	0-4	2-0	1-1	4-1	0-5
AFC Bournemouth	1-1	0-0	•	0-1	0-3	1-0	3-0	4-0	1-2	3-2	0-2	1-3	1-2	1-2	0-2	0-0	0-1	2-1	0-1	0-0	1-1	0-1	1-2	3-1
Bradford City	2-1	2-1	0-0	•	1-0	2-0	0-1	0-1	1-2	2-0	6-0	1-1	2-1	3-0	1-1	0-0	1-5	1-2	2-4	2-1	1-2	2-1	1-0	0-0
Brentford	1-0	3-0	1-0	1-0	•	1-1	3-4	0-0	3-1	1-1	1-0	2-0	2-1	3-0	0-1	0-1	1-1	0-0	1-0	2-1	1-1	2-1	1-0	1-1
Brighton & Hove Albion	1-0	3-2	0-1	2-0	4-1	•	0-2	3-1	1-1	2-1	1-1	0-1	1-1	1-2	1-1	1-3	2-2	2-1	0-1	0-1	1-1	4-1	1-1	0-1
Bristol Rovers	5-2	1-0	0-1	4-3	3-1	1-0	•	3-1	2-1	2-1	1-1	2-1	1-1	0-3	3-1	4-1	2-1	0-0	1-1	0-2	1-1	1-2	3-1	0-1
Burnley	5-0	3-1	4-0	0-1	1-0	3-0	5-0	•	2-0	2-0	3-2	3-1	2-0	4-5	3-1	4-1	4-2	0-1	1-0	3-1	1-1	1-2	2-1	2-1
Cambridge United	2-3	2-0	1-2	2-0	3-3	4-1	3-1	3-0	•	2-0	2-0	1-2	1-0	2-3	3-4	2-1	4-2	2-7	1-1	0-0	1-2	1-0	2-2	0-2
Cardiff City	0-0	0-2	2-1	2-1	3-5	2-1	1-3	0-1	2-2	•	2-0	1-0	1-2	2-2	3-4	3-1	2-3	1-3	3-0	1-0	3-1	1-0	5-1	0-0
Exeter City	0-0	1-0	0-2	1-0	2-2	0-1	1-0	4-1	2-7	2-2	•	6-4	2-0	2-3	0-1	1-0	2-3	0-1	4-6	1-0	1-2	1-0	5-0	1-2
Fulham	3-0	1-0	1-1	1-1	0-0	0-1	0-1	3-2	4-1	1-3	0-2	•	2-0	1-1	0-1	2-3	0-2	1-4	1-4	2-0	0-1	3-1	0-0	0-2
Hartlepool United	3-2	2-0	0-0	2-1	1-0	1-1	1-1	2-0	1-0	1-2	2-0	1-1	•	1-4	0-2	1-0	1-0	1-0	0-3	2-0	1-0	1-1	3-0	0-2
Huddersfield Town	1-2	1-0	1-1	3-1	1-1	1-3	3-3	3-2	0-3	1-2	1-3	3-1	1-2	•	0-2	3-1	4-1	1-4	0-3	2-0	1-0	1-1	3-0	3-2
Hull City	4-4	0-0	1-1	3-1	1-0	0-0	3-0	1-2	1-0	1-0	5-1	2-2	1-0	2-1	•	0-1	2-2	1-0	1-2	4-1	0-1	0-1	0-0	1-1
Leyton Orient	2-1	2-0	1-1	1-2	0-1	2-2	2-1	4-1	0-2	2-2	1-1	2-2	1-2	1-0	3-1	•	2-1	2-3	3-1	2-0	0-0	2-1	2-2	2-0
Plymouth Argyle	4-2	2-0	0-0	2-1	1-1	1-3	1-0	3-1	0-3	1-2	1-1	3-1	1-2	2-0	3-1	3-1	•	2-3	3-1	4-2	2-3	2-1	1-1	2-0
Port Vale	6-0	2-0	2-1	0-0	1-0	4-0	2-0	2-1	0-3	1-2	3-0	2-2	1-0	2-0	2-1	3-1	2-1	•	2-3	4-2	1-1	8-0	3-0	2-1
Reading	1-1	0-2	3-0	1-1	1-1	0-1	1-1	2-1	3-2	5-2	3-0	1-2	4-0	0-0	1-1	3-2	3-2	1-2	•	0-4	0-0	2-1	0-1	2-1
Rotherham United	2-1	0-2	1-2	2-1	1-2	0-1	3-1	0-1	0-0	5-2	3-2	2-2	7-0	2-3	3-1	2-1	3-1	2-3	3-1	•	1-2	2-1	2-1	2-1
Stockport County	2-1	1-0	0-2	1-1	3-1	3-0	2-0	3-1	4-2	1-0	4-0	2-4	1-1	5-0	0-0	3-0	2-3	0-1	1-1	2-0	•	4-0	1-0	1-2
Swansea City	0-1	1-1	0-1	2-1	1-1	4-1	1-2	1-1	1-0	1-0	3-1	1-1	1-1	0-1	2-1	1-1	2-1	0-1	4-0	3-3	0-1	•	3-2	2-1
Wrexham	1-2	4-1	1-2	1-0	2-1	1-1	3-1	2-1	2-2	5-1	5-0	0-0	1-2	3-0	0-0	2-2	1-1	3-0	0-1	2-1	1-0	3-1	•	1-1
York City	1-3	0-5	3-1	0-0	1-1	0-1	0-1	2-1	0-2	0-0	1-2	0-1	0-2	3-2	1-1	2-0	2-1	2-1	2-1	2-1	1-2	1-2	1-1	•

Endsleigh Insurance League Third Division: Results 1993–1994

Home \ Away	Bury	Carlisle United	Chester City	Chesterfield	Colchester United	Crewe Alexandra	Darlington	Doncaster Rovers	Gillingham	Hereford United	Lincoln City	Mansfield Town	Northampton Town	Preston North End	Rochdale	Scarborough	Scunthorpe United	Shrewsbury Town	Torquay United	Walsall	Wigan Athletic	Wycombe Wanderers
Bury	•	2-1	1-1	2-1	0-1	1-0	5-1	4-0	0-0	5-3	1-0	2-2	0-0	1-1	0-1	0-2	1-0	2-3	1-1	1-2	3-0	1-2
Carlisle United	1-2	•	1-0	3-0	2-0	1-2	2-0	4-2	1-2	1-2	3-3	1-1	0-1	0-1	0-1	2-0	3-1	2-1	1-1	2-1	3-0	2-2
Chester City	3-0	0-0	•	3-1	2-1	1-2	0-0	0-1	1-0	3-1	1-1	0-2	1-0	3-2	3-1	4-1	0-2	1-0	3-1	2-1	2-1	3-1
Chesterfield	1-1	3-1	1-2	•	0-0	2-0	1-1	1-1	3-2	3-1	2-2	0-2	4-0	1-1	2-5	1-2	1-1	1-2	3-1	0-1	1-0	2-3
Colchester United	4-1	2-1	1-2	0-0	•	2-4	1-2	3-1	1-2	1-0	2-2	0-2	4-0	1-1	2-1	1-2	2-1	3-3	2-3	0-1	3-1	0-2
Crewe Alexandra	2-4	2-3	2-1	0-1	2-1	•	2-1	1-3	2-1	6-0	2-2	2-1	3-1	4-3	1-1	2-1	3-3	0-2	4-1	1-2	4-1	2-1
Darlington	1-0	1-3	1-2	0-0	2-1	1-0	•	1-3	2-1	1-3	3-2	2-0	0-1	0-2	1-1	1-1	2-1	0-0	1-2	0-0	0-0	0-0
Doncaster Rovers	1-3	0-0	3-4	0-0	2-1	1-0	0-0	•	2-1	1-0	3-2	2-0	0-1	0-2	2-1	0-4	3-1	0-2	0-2	4-0	3-1	0-3
Gillingham	1-0	2-0	3-4	0-2	1-0	1-3	0-0	2-0	•	0-2	1-1	1-0	1-0	2-2	1-2	2-2	1-0	0-2	2-2	1-1	0-2	0-1
Hereford United	3-0	0-0	0-3	0-3	3-0	1-2	2-0	2-0	2-0	•	3-1	1-2	1-1	2-2	5-1	2-2	1-2	0-1	2-2	0-1	3-0	3-4
Lincoln City	3-0	0-0	0-3	1-2	2-2	1-2	3-1	2-1	2-0	3-1	•	1-2	1-1	2-3	2-1	0-1	2-0	1-0	1-0	1-2	1-0	1-3
Mansfield Town	2-2	1-1	0-2	0-0	2-1	2-1	2-0	0-1	0-0	0-1	1-0	•	1-0	3-1	1-1	3-2	0-1	0-3	2-1	1-2	2-3	3-0
Northampton Town	0-0	1-1	1-0	4-0	3-2	3-1	0-1	2-1	1-0	4-3	1-1	1-0	•	2-0	2-0	2-1	4-0	6-1	0-1	0-1	0-2	1-1
Preston North End	1-1	0-1	3-2	1-1	1-1	4-3	2-1	3-1	2-1	3-4	2-0	5-1	2-1	•	3-4	1-1	2-2	1-2	3-1	2-0	3-0	2-3
Rochdale	0-1	0-1	3-1	2-5	2-1	1-2	1-1	2-1	1-2	5-1	2-1	1-1	2-0	3-4	•	1-1	2-3	1-4	4-1	0-0	1-2	2-2
Scarborough	0-2	2-0	4-1	1-2	1-2	2-1	1-1	0-4	2-2	2-2	0-1	3-2	2-1	1-1	1-0	•	0-1	1-1	1-2	1-0	4-1	3-1
Scunthorpe United	3-1	2-1	2-1	3-3	2-1	2-2	2-0	2-1	2-0	4-0	2-0	3-1	7-0	2-2	2-3	3-2	•	1-4	1-3	5-0	3-0	2-2
Shrewsbury Town	1-1	2-1	0-0	0-1	3-0	2-0	1-0	1-1	3-0	3-2	1-1	0-1	2-0	4-1	1-4	1-1	0-0	•	3-2	1-2	1-0	1-0
Torquay United	0-1	1-2	1-3	0-1	3-1	2-1	2-0	0-1	1-0	1-1	2-1	1-1	2-1	1-0	4-1	4-2	1-1	0-0	•	0-1	1-1	1-1
Walsall	0-1	2-1	1-1	0-2	3-3	2-2	2-0	2-0	0-1	3-3	5-2	0-2	1-3	2-0	0-0	1-0	1-2	0-1	0-1	•	1-1	4-2
Wigan Athletic	3-1	0-2	6-3	1-0	1-2	2-2	2-0	0-0	3-0	3-4	0-1	4-1	1-1	2-2	1-2	4-1	3-0	2-5	1-3	2-2	•	1-1
Wycombe Wanderers	2-1	2-0	1-0	0-1	2-5	3-1	1-0	1-0	1-1	3-2	2-3	1-0	1-1	1-1	2-2	4-0	2-2	1-1	1-1	3-0	0-1	•

159

League Cup Winners 1961–1994

Two-legged finals until 1966, all finals after 1966 played at Wembley

Year	Winners		Runners-up	Result
1961	Aston Villa	v	Rotherham United	3–2 (0–2, 3–0 after extra time)
1962	Norwich City	v	Rochdale	4–0 (3–0, 1–0)
1963	Birmingham City	v	Aston Villa	3–1 (3–1, 0–0)
1964	Leicester City	v	Stoke City	4–3 (1–1, 3–2)
1965	Chelsea	v	Leicester City	3–2 (3–2, 0–0)
1966	West Bromwich Albion	v	West Ham United	5–3 (1–2, 4–1)
1967	Queen's Park Rangers	v	West Bromwich Albion	3–2
1968	Leeds United	v	Arsenal	1–0
1969	Swindon Town	v	Arsenal	3–1 after extra time
1970	Manchester City	v	West Bromwich Albion	2–1 after extra time
1971	Tottenham Hotspur	v	Aston Villa	2–0
1972	Stoke City	v	Chelsea	2–1
1973	Tottenham Hotspur	v	Norwich City	1–0
1974	Wolverhampton Wanderers	v	Manchester City	1–0
1975	Aston Villa	v	Norwich City	1–0
1976	Manchester City	v	Newcastle United	2–1
1977	Aston Villa	v	Everton	0–0
	Aston Villa	v	Everton	1–1 after extra time replay at Hillsborough
	Aston Villa	v	Everton	3–2 after extra time; 2nd replay at Old Trafford
1978	Nottingham Forest	v	Liverpool	0–0 after extra time
	Nottingham Forest	v	Liverpool	1–0 replay at Old Trafford
1979	Nottingham Forest	v	Southampton	3–2
1980	Wolverhampton Wanderers	v	Nottingham Forest	1–0
1981	Liverpool	v	West Ham United	1–1 after extra time
	Liverpool	v	West Ham United	2–1 replay at Villa Park
as Milk Cup				
1982	Liverpool	v	Tottenham Hotspur	3–1 after extra time
1983	Liverpool	v	Manchester United	2–1 after extra time
1984	Liverpool	v	Everton	0–0 after extra time
	Liverpool	v	Everton	1–0 replay at Maine Road
1985	Norwich City	v	Sunderland	1–0
1986	Oxford United	v	Queens Park Rangers	3–0
as Littlewoods Cup				
1987	Arsenal	v	Liverpool	2–1
1988	Luton Town	v	Arsenal	3–2
1989	Nottingham Forest	v	Luton Town	3–1
1990	Nottingham Forest	v	Oldham Athletic	1–0
as Rumbelows Cup				
1991	Sheffield Wednesday	v	Manchester United	1–0
1992	Manchester United	v	Nottingham Forest	1–0
as Coca-Cola Cup				
1993	Arsenal	v	Sheffield Wednesday	2–1
1994	Aston Villa	v	Manchester United	3–1

Coca-Cola Cup 1993–1994

FIRST ROUND (Two Legs)

AFC Bournemouth	3 : 1	v	Cardiff City	1 : 1
Birmingham City	3 : 0	v	Plymouth Argyle	0 : 2
Bolton Wanderers	0 : 2*	v	Bury	2 : 0
Brentford	2 : 1	v	Watford	2 : 3
Bristol Rovers	1 : 0	v	West Bromwich Albion	4 : 0
Cambridge United	1 : 1	v	Luton Town	0 : 0
Chesterfield	3 : 1	v	Carlisle United	1 : 1
Crewe Alexandra	0 : 3	v	Wrexham	1 : 3
Darlington	1 : 0	v	Bradford City	5 : 6
Doncaster Rovers	0 : 3	v	Blackpool	1 : 3
Fulham	2 : 2	v	Colchester United	1 : 1
Gillingham	1 : 0	v	Brighton & Hove Albion	0 : 2
Hereford United	0 : 2*	v	Torquay United	2 : 0
Huddersfield Town	0 : 3	v	Scarborough	0 : 0
Leyton Orient	0 : 0	v	Wycombe Wanderers	2 : 1
Notts County	2 : 1†	v	Hull City	0 : 3
Port Vale	2 : 0	v	Lincoln City	2 : 0†
Preston North End	1 : 1	v	Burnley	2 : 4
Reading	3 : 2	v	Northampton Town	0 : 0
Rochdale	2 : 0	v	York City	0 : 0
Shrewsbury Town	1 : 1	v	Scunthorpe United	0 : 1
Southend United	0 : 1	v	Barnet	2 : 1
Stockport County	1 : 1	v	Hartlepool United	1 : 2
Stoke City	2 : 3	v	Mansfield Town	2 : 1
Sunderland	3 : 0	v	Chester City	1 : 0
Swansea City	0 : 2	v	Bristol City	1 : 0
Walsall	0 : 1	v	Exeter City	0 : 2
Wigan Athletic	0 : 2	v	Rotherham United	1 : 4

SECOND ROUND (Two Legs)

Barnet	1 : 0	v	Queens Park Rangers	2 : 4
Barnsley	1 : 1	v	Peterborough United	1 : 3
Birmingham City	0 : 0	v	Aston Villa	1 : 1
Blackburn Rovers	1 : 0	v	AFC Bournemouth	0 : 0
Blackpool	3 : 0	v	Sheffield United	0 : 2
Bolton Wanderers	1 : 0	v	Sheffield Wednesday	1 : 1
Bradford City	2 : 0	v	Norwich City	1 : 3
Burnley	0 : 1	v	Tottenham Hotspur	0 : 3
Coventry City	3 : 2	v	Wycombe Wanderers	0 : 4
Crystal Palace	3 : 1	v	Charlton Athletic	1 : 0
Exeter City	1 : 0	v	Derby County	3 : 2
Fulham	1 : 0	v	Liverpool	3 : 5
Grimsby Town	3 : 2	v	Hartlepool United	0 : 0
Hereford United	0 : 1	v	Wimbledon	1 : 4
Huddersfield Town	0 : 1	v	Arsenal	5 : 1
Ipswich Town	2 : 2	v	Cambridge United	1 : 0
Lincoln City	3 : 2	v	Everton	4 : 4
Manchester City	1 : 2	v	Reading	1 : 1
Middlesbrough	5 : 3	v	Brighton & Hove Albion	0 : 1
Newcastle United	4 : 7	v	Notts County	1 : 1

won on penalty-kicks   † won on away goals

Rochdale	1 : 1	v	Leicester City	6 : 2
Rotherham United	0 : 0	v	Portsmouth	0 : 5
Southampton	1 : 0	v	Shrewsbury Town	0 : 2
Stoke City	2 : 0	v	Manchester United	1 : 2
Sunderland	2 : 2	v	Leeds United	1 : 1
Swansea City	2 : 0	v	Oldham Athletic	1 : 2
Swindon Town	2 : 1	v	Wolverhampton Wanderers	0 : 2
Tranmere Rovers	5 : 1	v	Oxford United	1 : 1
Watford	0 : 3	v	Millwall	0 : 4
West Bromwich Albion	1 : 1	v	Chelsea	1 : 2
West Ham United	5 : 2	v	Chesterfield	1 : 0
Wrexham	3 : 1	v	Nottingham Forest	3 : 3

THIRD ROUND

(Replays in italics)

Arsenal	v	Norwich City	1 : 1
Norwich City	v	*Arsenal*	*0 : 3*
Blackburn Rovers	v	Shrewsbury Town	0 : 0
Shrewsbury Town	v	*Blackburn Rovers*	*3 : 4*
Blackpool	v	Peterborough United	2 : 2
Peterborough United	v	*Blackpool*	*2 : 1*
Derby County	v	Tottenham Hotspur	0 : 1
Everton	v	Crystal Palace	2 : 2
Crystal Palace	v	*Everton*	*1 : 4*
Liverpool	v	Ipswich Town	3 : 2
Manchester City	v	Chelsea	1 : 0
Manchester United	v	Leicester City	5 : 1
Middlesbrough	v	Sheffield Wednesday	1 : 1
Sheffield Wednesday	v	*Middlesbrough*	*2 : 1*
Nottingham Forest	v	West Ham United	2 : 1
Oldham Athletic	v	Coventry City	2 : 0
Portsmouth	v	Swindon Town	2 : 0
Queens Park Rangers	v	Millwall	3 : 0
Sunderland	v	Aston Villa	1 : 4
Tranmere Rovers	v	Grimsby Town	4 : 1
Wimbledon	v	Newcastle United	2 : 1

FOURTH ROUND

(Replays in italics)

Arsenal	v	Aston Villa	0 : 1
Everton	v	Manchester United	0 : 2
Liverpool	v	Wimbledon	1 : 1
Wimbledon	v	*Liverpool*	*2 : 2**
Nottingham Forest	v	Manchester City	0 : 0
Manchester City	v	*Nottingham Forest*	*1 : 2*
Peterborough United	v	Portsmouth	0 : 0
Portsmouth	v	*Peterborough United*	*1 : 0*
Queens Park Rangers	v	Sheffield Wednesday	1 : 2
Tottenham Hotspur	v	Blackburn Rovers	1 : 0
Tranmere Rovers	v	Oldham Athletic	3 : 0

FIFTH ROUND

(Replays in italics)

Manchester United	v	Portsmouth	2 : 2
Portsmouth	v	*Manchester United*	*0 : 1*
Nottingham Forest	v	Tranmere Rovers	1 : 1
Tranmere Rovers	v	*Nottingham Forest*	*2 : 0*
Tottenham Hotspur	v	Aston Villa	1 : 2
Wimbledon	v	Sheffield Wednesday	1 : 2

SEMI : FINAL (Two Legs)

Manchester United	1 : 4	v	Sheffield Wednesday	0 : 1
Tranmere Rovers	3 : 1	v	Aston Villa	1 : 3*

FINAL

Aston Villa	v	Manchester United	3 : 1

* won on penalty-kicks

FA Women's Challenge Cup – Final 1994

Doncaster Belles 1   Knowsley United 0

Many people still think of women's football as a new sport, though women have been playing the game in England for over a hundred years. It remained a low key activity until a boom just after the First World War which saw, for example, a 53,000 crowd present to see Dick Kerr's Ladies play St. Helens Ladies at Everton's ground on Boxing Day in 1920.

The women's game was to wait until England's success in the 1966 World Cup for the necessary stimulus for a major national surge to rival those of earlier periods. In 1969 the Women's FA was formed and three years later the FA at Lancaster Gate lifted its ban on women's football. Since the early 1970s there has been a gradual increase in the number of women in this country who play football: in Season 1992-93 there were as many as 12,000 players at 450 affiliated clubs.

In June 1993 The Football Association took over responsibility for the women's game. The first 'FA Women's Challenge Cup' attracted 147 entries and the first women's final staged by the FA was played on a Sunday afternoon (24 April) at Scunthorpe United FC. Doncaster Belles, who had appeared in ten finals of the old 'Women's FA Cup', beat Knowsley United 1–0 with Karen Walker's first-half strike and underlined their dominance of women's football in England. Their victory at Glanford Park kept them in line for the 'treble' of FA Cup, National League and League Cup.

Doncaster Belles' manager claimed after the match that his team's performance had been below par, but they were better organised defensively and their front line of Karen Walker and Gail Borman (both current England internationals) was more threatening. Knowsley, a Merseyside team formed just three years ago but with a sprinkling of internationals itself, had its chances and could have equalised a minute into injury time when Karen Burke hit the bar with a fierce right-footer.

Knowsley had knocked all-conquering Arsenal out of the competition at the quarter-final stage, and their hopes of winning the final must have been raised when the Belles captain, Gillian Coultard (holder of a record 75 England caps), was forced to withdraw after 34 minutes. But four minutes later Doncaster scored what proved to be the decisive goal, Walker heading in Joanne Broadhurst's corner. It rounded off a brilliant display by Walker, a 24-year-old civil servant, who was voted Player of the Match.

Doncaster Belles: Davison, Lowe, Ryde, Jackson, Woodhead, Goodman, Murray, Coultard (Lisseman) (Chipchase), Broadhurst, Walker, Borman.
Knowsley United: Thomas, Hayward, Taylor, Coughlin, McQuiggan, Baker (Holland), Davis, Gore, Gallimore, Burke, Harper.
Referee: I. Hemley (Ampthill).
Chief Guest: Lady Millichip.
Attendance: 1,674.

FA Women's Challenge Cup

FIRST ROUND   19th September 1993

(replays in italics)

			Result
Ashington East North	v	Newcastle	0–5
City Roses	v	Wigginton Grasshopers	3–0
Barnsley	v	Cleveland	2–3
Bradford City	v	Sheffield Utd & Hallam Univ	11–1
Wakefield	v	Brighouse	10–3
Huddersfield Town	v	Grimsby	22–0
Wigan	v	Liverpool Feds	10–0
Broadoak	v	Bolton	12–1
Runcorn	v	Newsham	1–7
Bury	v	Warrington Town	6–4
Haslingden	v	Vernon-Carus	2–0
Bangor City Girls	v	Preston Rangers	0–5
Tranmere Rovers	v	Stockport	8–2
Oldham Athletic	v	Manchester Belle Vue	3–4
Manchester City	v	Manchester United	2–0
Nottingham Forest	v	Birmingham City	1–9
Worcester City	v	Stratford	16–0
Rugby	v	Rainworth Miners Welfare	1–7
TNT Ladies	v	Derby City	3–1
Nettleham	v	Derby County	1–3
Leicester City	v	Highfield Rangers	3–2
St Germaine	v	Peterborough Pythons	2–0
Dunstable	v	Stevenage Town	9–0
Welwyn Garden City	v	Colchester Royals	1–10
Colchester United	v	Pye	0–5
Sutton Athletic	v	Abbey Rangers	1–2
Leyton Orient	v	Tonbridge Angels	23–0
Crowborough Athletic	v	Palace Eagles	2–5
Gillingham Girls	v	Brentford	2–17
Walton & Hersham	v	Teynham Gunners	4–0
Winchester All Stars	v	Charlton	0–7
Collier Row	v	Enfield	3–0
Tottenham Hotspur	v	Chislehurst United	4–0
Edenbridge Town	v	SE Rangers	0–4
Lambeth	v	Barnet	5–3
Carterton	v	Havant	0–3
Farnborough	v	Launton	0–1 aet
Isle of Wight	v	Binfield	0–9
Portsmouth	v	Gosport Borough	1–2
Pagham	v	Corematch	1–9
Bournemouth	v	Aylesbury United	3–2
Whitehawk	v	Reading	17–0
Reading Royals	v	Newbury	0–1
Swansea	v	Bristol City	4–6 aet
Cheltenham YMCA	v	Truro City	3–3 aet
Truro City	v	*Cheltenham YMCA*	*4–4 aet*
(Truro won on kicks from the penalty mark 2–0)			
Tongwynlais	v	Swindon Spitfires	2–1
Yate Town	v	Cardiff Institute	
(walkover for Yate Town – Cardiff Institute removed from the Competition)			
Plymouth Pilgrims	v	Clevedon Town	2–0
Inter Cardiff	v	Frome	2–1

19 Clubs receiving byes to the Second Round

Amble Town	Kilnhurst	Rochdale
Bedford Belles	Leek Town	Shoreham
Bristol Rovers	Leighton Linslade	Sittingbourne
Chailey	Liverpool	Sporting Kesteven
Chesterfield	Middlesbrough	Stockport County
Drayton	QPR	Torquay United
Hackney		

20 Clubs receiving exemption to the Second Round

Abbeydale/Alvechurch	Hassocks	Oxford United
Brighton & Hove Albion	Hemel Hempstead	Sheffield Wednesday
Bristol Backwell	Horsham	St Helens
Bromley Borough	Kidderminster Harriers	Town & Country
Bronte	Langford	Villa Aztecs
Cowgate Kestrels	Maidstone Tigresses	Wolverhampton
Epsom & Ewell	Nottingham Argyle	

10 Clubs receiving exemption to the Fourth Round

Arsenal	Millwall Lionesses
Doncaster Belles	Red Star Southampton
Ipswich Town	Stanton Rangers
Knowsley United	Wembley
Leasowe Pacific	Wimbledon

SECOND ROUND   17th October 1993

(replays in italics)

			Result
Amble Town	v	Sheffield Wednesday	0–6
Cowgate Kestrels	v	Newcastle	2–1
Cleveland	v	Wakefield	0–9
Bronte	v	Bradford City	4–2
City Roses	v	Kilnhurst	0–4
Huddersfield	v	Middlesbrough	14–1
Manchester Belle Vue	v	Broadoak	1–2
Preston Rangers	v	Leek Town	3–2
Liverpool District	v	Wigan	0–5
Haslingden	v	Tranmere Rovers	1–5
Bury	v	Manchester City	4–1
St Helens	v	Newsham	5–1
Stockport County	v	Rochdale	1–0
Abbeydale/Alvechurch	v	Wolverhampton	0–5
Nottingham Argyle	v	Birmingham City	3–2
Rainworth Miners Welfare	v	Derby County	5–0
Chesterfield	v	TNT Ladies	3–1
Kidderminster Harriers	v	Sporting Kesteven	13–0
Leicester City	v	Villa Aztecs	1–7
Colchester Royals	v	St Germaine	2–6
Town & County	v	Bedford Belles	9–0
Dunstable	v	Langford	4–1
Pye	v	Leighton Linslade	5–0
Collier Row	v	Sittingbourne	4–0
Lambeth	v	Palace Eagles	9–2
Abbey Rangers	v	Queens Park Rangers	1–7
Maidstone Tigresses	v	Epsom & Ewell	1–2
Leyton Orient	v	Drayton Wanderers	3–2

			Result
Walton & Hersham	v	Charlton	2–3
Hackney	v	Bromley Borough	2–3
SE Rangers	v	Tottenham Hotspur	1–13
Hemel Hempstead	v	Brentford	3–0
Newbury	v	Launton	5–2
Bournemouth	v	Chailey Mavericks	10–0
Hassocks	v	Havant	

(Havant withdrawn – tie awarded to Hassocks)

Corematch	v	Whitehawk	0–6
Gosport Borough	v	Brighton & Hove Albion	1–2
Oxford United	v	Binfield	3–0
Shoreham	v	Horsham	0–5
Inter Cardiff	v	Bristol City	3–1 aet
Bristol	v	Bristol Rovers	13–0
Yate Town	v	Tongwynlais	0–6
Torquay United	v	Truro City	2–5
Plymouth Pilgrims	v	Worcester City	4–5 aet

THIRD ROUND   14th November 1993

(replays in italics)

			Result
Stockport	v	Nottingham Argyle	2–1
Cowgate Kestrels	v	Kilnhurst	4–1
Bronte	v	Villa Aztecs	1–2
Broadoak	v	Wakefield	0–2
St Helens	v	Wolverhampton	2–10
Tranmere Rovers	v	Sheffield Wednesday	2–4
Wigan	v	Preston Rangers	2–5
Chesterfield	v	Bury	2–1
Rainworth Miners Welfare	v	Huddersfield Town	2–4
Pye	v	Dunstable	0–3
Town & County	v	Hemel Hempstead	5–4
Tottenham Hotspur	v	St Germaine	0–0 aet
St Germaine	v	*Tottenham Hotspur*	*1–3*
Bromley Borough	v	Collier Row	7–0
Leyton Orient	v	Queens Park Rangers	16–0
Lambeth	v	Charlton	0–1
Worcester City	v	Kidderminster Harriers	1–6
Newbury	v	Brighton & Hove Albion	1–2
Oxford United	v	Inter Cardiff	2–4 aet
Horsham	v	Bristol	3–2
Tongwynlais	v	Truro City	2–5
Epsom & Ewell	v	Bournemouth	2–1
Whitehawk	v	Hassocks	8–2

FOURTH ROUND   5th December 1993

(replays in italics)

			Result
Doncaster Belles	v	Millwall Lionesses	9–0
Truro City	v	Stockport County	1–0
Tottenham Hotspur	v	Inter Cardiff	1–3

			Result
Chesterfield	v	Wakefield	1–2
Red Star Southampton	v	Bromley Borough	1–3
Horsham	v	Brighton & Hove Albion	0–2 aet
Huddersfield Town	v	Whitehawk	6–0
Arsenal	v	Sheffield Wednesday	8–0
Kidderminster Harriers	v	Cowgate Kestrels	2–1 aet
Charlton	v	Leasowe Pacific	0–7
Town & County	v	Ipswich Town	4–1
Leyton Orient	v	Knowsley United	2–7
Wembley	v	Wolverhampton	2–0
Epsom & Ewell	v	Wimbledon	0–0 aet
Wimbledon	v	*Epsom & Ewell*	1–2
Preston Rangers	v	Villa Aztecs	6–2
Stanton Rangers	v	Dunstable	6–0

FIFTH ROUND   16th January 1994

(replays in italics)

			Result
Leasowe Pacific	v	Town & County	9–0
Epsom & Ewell	v	Inter Cardiff	7–0
Brighton & Hove Albion	v	Truro City	1–0
Doncaster Belles	v	Bromley Borough	10–1
Wembley	v	Arsenal	2–4
Wakefield	v	Stanton Rangers	1–3
Knowsley United	v	Huddersfield Town	5–2
Kidderminster Harriers	v	Preston Rangers	0–6

SIXTH ROUND   13th February 1994

(replays in italics)

			Result
Preston Rangers	v	Stanton Rangers	2–3 aet
Arsenal	v	Knowsley United	0–1
Doncaster Belles	v	Brighton & Hove Albion	5–1
Epsom & Ewell	v	Leasowe Pacific	2–3 aet

SEMI–FINAL   6th March 1994

(replays in italics)

			Result
Stanton Rangers *at Ilkeston Town FC*	v	Knowsley United	0–1
Leasowe Pacific *at Southport FC*	v	Doncaster Belles	0–6

FINAL   24th April 1994

			Result
Doncaster Belles *(at Scunthorpe United FC)*	v	Knowsley United	1–0

England Women's Caps 1993–1994

	Slovenia	Belgium	Spain	Spain	Belgium	Slovenia
Lesley Shipp (Arsenal)	1	1	1	1	1	1
Karen Burke (Knowsley United)	2	4*			11*	
Michelle Curley (Arsenal)	3	3				
Samantha Britton (Arsenal)	4		4		4	4
Clare Taylor (Knowsley United)	5	5	5	5	5	5
Gillian Coultard (Doncaster Belles)	6	6	6	6	6	6
Marieanne Spacey (Arsenal)	7	7	7	7	7	7
Debbie Bampton (Arsenal)	8	8	8	8	8	8
Karen Walker (Doncaster Belles)	9	9	9	9*	9	9
Gail Borman (Doncaster Belles)	10	10	10	10	10	10
Janice Murray (Doncaster Belles)	11	11	11	11		
Frances Carroll (Millwall Lionesses)	4*					
Kerry Davis (Knowsley United)	10*		3	9	11	11
Kirsty Pealling (Arsenal)		2		2	2	2
Hope Powell (Bromley Borough)		4	7*	4		8*
Louise Waller (Millwall Lionesses)		2*	2	3	3	3
Joanne Broadhurst (Doncaster Belles)			11*	4*		
Samantha Hayward (Knowsley United)					3*	
Tracy Davidson (Doncaster Belles)						1*

substitute

European Championship for Women's Teams 1993–1995

Qualifying Group 7 Table

	P	W	D	L	F	A	Pts
England*	6	4	2	0	29	0	10
Spain	6	3	3	0	29	0	9
Belgium	6	2	1	3	15	13	5
Slovenia	6	0	0	6	0	60	0

England qualify for quarter-finals (November 1994)

England's Results

25. 9.93   Slovenia   0   England   10   in Ljubljana
Scorers: Spacey 4, Walker 3, Taylor, Borman and Davis

6.11.93   Belgium   0   England   3   in Koksijde
Scorers: Walker 2 and Taylor

19.12.93   Spain   0   England   0   in Osuna

20. 2.94   England   0   Spain   0   at Bradford City FC

13. 3.94   England   6   Belgium   0   at Nottingham Forest FC
Scorers: Spacey 2, Walker 2, Davis and Coultard

17. 4.94   England   10   Slovenia   0   at Brentford FC
Scorers: Taylor 2, Walker 2, Britton 2, Coultard, Powell, Borman and Spacey

FA Sunday Cup Winners 1965–1994

Year/venue	Winners		Runners-up	Result
1965	London	v	Staffordshire	6–2†
1966 Dudley	Unique United	v	Aldridge Fabrications	1–0
1967 Hendon	Carlton United	v	Stoke Works	2–0
1968 Cambridge	Drovers	v	Brook United	2–0
1969 Romford	Leigh Park	v	Loke United	3–1
1970 Corby	Vention United	v	Unique United	1–0
1971 Leamington	Beacontree Rovers	v	Saltley United	2–0
1972 Dudley	Newton Unity	v	Springfield Colts	4–0
1973 Spennymoor	Carlton United	v	Wear Valley	2–1*
1974 Birmingham	Newton Unity	v	Brentford East	3–0
1975 High Wycombe	Fareham Town Centipedes	v	Players Athletic Engineers	1–0
1976 Spennymoor	Brandon United	v	Evergreen	2–1
1977 Spennymoor	Langley Park RH	v	Newton Unity	2–0
1978 Nuneaton	Arras	v	Lion Rangers	2–2
Bishop's Stortford	Arras	v	Lion Rangers	2–1
1979 Southport	Lobster	v	Carlton United	3–2
1980 Letchworth	Fantail	v	Twin Foxes	1–0
1981 Birkenhead	Fantail	v	Mackintosh	1–0
1982 Hitchin	Dingle Rail	v	Twin Foxes	2–1
1983 Walthamstow	Eagle	v	Lee Chapel North	2–1
1984 Runcorn	Lee Chapel North	v	Eagle	1–1
Dagenham	Lee Chapel North	v	Eagle	4–3*
1985 Norwich	Hobbies	v	Avenue	1–1
Birkenhead	Hobbies	v	Avenue	2–2
Nuneaton	Hobbies	v	Avenue	2–1
1986 Birkenhead	Avenue	v	Glenn Sports	1–0
1987 Birmingham	Lodge Cottrell	v	Avenue	1–0*
1988 Newcastle	Nexday	v	Sunderland Humb Plains	2–0
1989 Stockport	Almithak	v	East Levenshulme	3–1
1990 West Bromwich	Humbledon Plains Farm	v	Marston Sports	2–1
1991 Wigan	Nicosia	v	Ouzavich	3–2*
1992 Reading	Theale	v	Marston Sports	3–2
1993 Chester	Seymour	v	Bedfont Sunday	1–0
1994 Woking	Ranelagh Sports	v	Hartlepool Lion Hotel	2–0

* after extra time
† two legs

FA Sunday Cup

FIRST ROUND   31st October 1993

(replays in italics)

			Result	Att
Croxteth & Gilmoss RBL	v	Bedini Altone	3–0	30
Baildon Athletic	v	Newfield	2–3 aet	80
Carnforth	v	Almithak	1–0	50
Humbledon Plains Farm	v	Clubmoor Nalgo	1–1	120
Clubmoor Nalgo	v	*Humbledon Plains Farm*	*1–2*	150
Dudley & Weetslade	v	Framwellgate Moor & Pity Me	4–5 aet	80
East Levenshulme	v	East Bowling Unity	4–0	47
Littlewoods Athletic	v	Mitre	3–2	100
Green Man 88	v	Lion Hotel	0–2	74
Moorlands Hotel	v	Allerton	1–2	40
Hartlepool Lion Hotel	v	Iron Bridge	5–0	60
Woodlands 84	v	BRNESC	0–3	20
Royal Oak	v	Bolton Woods	0–1	48
Waterloo Social Club Blyth	v	Northwood	1–4	160
Sandon	v	Western Approaches	2–4 aet	43
Cork & Bottle	v	Berner United	2–1	96
Bournville Warriors	v	Broad Plain House (Sunday)	1–2	45
Dulwich	v	Sawston Keys	2–3	nil
Brookvale Athletic	v	Clifton Albion	2–0	30
Poringland Wanderers	v	Ford Basildon	2–4	85
Kenwick Dynamo	v	Courage	0–1	40
Olton Royale	v	Inter Volante	1–1 aet	60
Inter Volante	v	*Olton Royale*	*0–2*	40
Leicester City Bus	v	St Clements Hospital	2–3	27
Hobbies	v	Continental	1–0	25
Elliott Bull & Tiger	v	AD Bulwell	1–1	18
AD Bulwell	v	*Elliott Bull & Tiger*	*2–4*	21
Corby Phoenix	v	Ansells Stockland Star	4–1	76
BRSC Aidan	v	Ford United Supporters	1–1 aet	45
Ford United Supporters	v	*BRSC Aidan*	*2–1*	50
Caversham Park	v	Chapel United	2–0	40
Lebeq Tavern	v	Olympic Star	5–0	40
Hammer	v	Sandwell	3–0	48
Inter Royalle	v	Fryerns Community	2–2 aet	60
Fryerns Community	v	*Inter Royalle*	*3–2*	60
Hanham Sunday	v	Kerria Sports	2–4 aet	38
S&N Fairway	v	Leavesden Sports & Social	0–3	53
Oakwood Sports	v	Sheerness Steel United	4–0	94
Oxford Road Social	v	Northfield Rangers	1–2	60
Ouzavich	v	Poole Town Social	8–1	40
Tottenham Wine	v	Vosper	1–3 aet	35
Somerset Ambury V & E	v	Thorn Walk Tavern	3–0	48
Slade Celtic	v	London Boys	4–0	40
St Joseph's (Sth Oxhey)	v	St Joseph's AFC (Bristol)	2–0	40

9 Clubs receiving byes to the Second Round

Albion Sports	Forest Athletic	Hundred Acre
Dock	Gibraltar	Marine
Etnaward	Golden Eagle	Nenthead

16 Clubs receiving exemption to the Second Round

A3	Lodge Cottrell	Ranelagh Sports
B & A Scaffolding	Manfast Kirkby	Reading Borough
Bedfont Sunday	Marston Sports	Seymour
Bly Spartans	Nicosia	St Joseph's (Luton)
Heathfield	Oakenshaw	Theale
Lobster		

SECOND ROUND   21st November 1993

(replays in italics)

			Result	Att
Newfield	v	Croxteth & Gilmoss RBL	4–3 aet	50
Allerton	v	Western Approaches	4–0	50
Golden Eagle	v	Carnforth	1–3	10
Oakenshaw	v	Northwood	3–0	70
East Levenshulme	v	A3	3–0	52
Albion Sports	v	Hartlepool Lion Hotel	1–5	32
B&A Scaffolding	v	Bolton Woods	4–0	32
Dock	v	BRNESC	2–2 aet	43
BRNESC	v	*Dock*	*1–2 aet*	40
Lobster	v	Nicosia	1–2 aet	42
Nenthead	v	Lion Hotel	2–5	52
Marston Sports	v	Gibraltar	1–1 aet	55
Gibraltar	v	*Marston Sports*	*6–3 aet*	52
Seymour	v	Manfast Kirkby	2–1	100
Framwellgate Moor & Pity Me	v	Littlewoods Athletic	3–1	30
Etnaward	v	Humbledon Plains Farm	0–1	70
St Joseph's (Luton)	v	Olton Royale	2–1 aet	49
Elliott Bull & Tiger	v	Corby Phoenix	1–0	24
St Clements Hospital	v	Sawston Keys	9–1	48
Hobbies	v	Courage	5–3	40
Forest Athletic	v	Ford Basildon	2–1	16
Heathfield	v	Brookvale Athletic	3–1	18
Lodge Cottrell	v	Broad Plain House (Sunday)	3–3 aet	21
(tie awarded to Lodge Cottrell as Broad Plain House played an ineligible player)				
Cork & Bottle	v	Hundred Acre	5–1	nil
Bedfont Sunday	v	Lebeq Tavern	0–4	48
Hammer	v	Bly Spartans	3–2	29
Oakwood Sports	v	Northfield Rangers	2–0	78
St Joseph's (Sth Oxhey)	v	Fryerns Community	0–2	33
Marine (Sx)	v	Ouzavich	0–1	35
Vosper	v	Kerria Sports	1–0	52
Slade Celtic	v	Leavesden Sports & Social	2–1 aet	120
Reading Borough	v	Theale	0–1	166
Somerset Ambury V & E	v	Ranelagh Sports	1–4	10
Caversham Park	v	Ford United Supporters	1–2	40

THIRD ROUND   12th December 1993

(replays in italics)

			Result	Att
Seymour	v	Carnforth	5–1	70
Oakenshaw	v	Nicosia	1–0	50
East Levenshulme	v	Newfield	1–0	84
B&A Scaffolding	v	Gibraltar	5–3	20
Harlepool Lion Hotel	v	Humbledon Plains Farm	1–0	50
Allerton	v	Framwellgate Moor & Pity Me	2–1	80

			Result	Att
Dock	v	Lion Hotel	1–2	65
Hammer	v	St Clements Hospital	3–5	14
Slade Celtic	v	Ranelagh Sports	1–2	18
St Joseph's (Luton)	v	Vosper	2–0	46
Ouzavich	v	Forest Athletic	2–1	nil
Ford United Supporters	v	Hobbies	2–1	45
Oakwood Sports	v	Lodge Cottrell	1–3	84
Elliott Bull & Tiger	v	Theale	1–4	74
Cork & Bottle	v	Lebeq Tavern	1–3	nil
Fryerns Community	v	Heathfield	1–2	30

FOURTH ROUND   16th January 1994

(replays in italics)

			Result	Att
Seymour	v	Allerton	0–0 aet	100
Allerton	v	*Seymour*	*3–2 aet*	100
Hartlepool Lion Hotel	v	Oakenshaw	2–0	70
Lion Hotel	v	East Levenshulme	5–1	252
Lodge Cottrell	v	B&A Scaffolding	1–3 aet	
St Joseph's (Luton)	v	Heathfield	2–0	72
St Clements Hospital	v	Lebeq Tavern	3–2 aet	76
Ranelagh Sports	v	Theale	4–3	28
Ford United Supporters	v	Ouzavich	2–3	53

FIFTH ROUND   13th February 1994

(replays in italics)

			Result	Att
Lion Hotel	v	Hartlepool Lion Hotel	0–1	183
B&A Scaffolding	v	Ranelagh Sports	2–3	111
Allerton	v	Ouzavich	0–1	200
St Clements Hospital	v	St Joseph's (Luton)	2–3 aet	158

SEMI–FINAL   20th March1994

(replays in italics)

			Result	Att
St Joseph's (Luton)	v	Hartlepool Lion Hotel	1–1 aet	450
at Hitchin Town FC				
Hartlepool Lion Hotel	v	*St Joseph's (Luton)*	*4–1*	433
at Peterlee Newtown FC				
Ranelagh Sports	v	Ouzavich	3–1 aet	350
at Carshalton Athletic FC				

FINAL   8th May 1994

			Result	Att
Ranelagh Sports	v	Hartlepool Lion Hotel	2–0	522
(at Woking FC)				

FA Charity Shield Winners 1908–1993

Year	Winners		Runners-up	Result
1908	Manchester United	v	Queens Park Rangers	1–1
	Manchester United	v	*Queens Park Rangers*	*4–0*
1909	Newcastle United	v	Northampton Town	2–0
1910	Brighton and Hove Albion	v	Aston Villa	1–0
1911	Manchester United	v	Swindon Town	8–4
1912	Blackburn Rovers	v	Queens Park Rangers	2–1
1913	Professionals	v	Amateurs	7–2
1914–18		not played		
1920	West Bromwich Albion	v	Tottenham Hotspur	2–0
1921	Tottenham Hotspur	v	Burnley	2–0
1922	Huddersfield Town	v	Liverpool	1–0
1923	Professionals	v	Amateurs	2–0
1924	Professionals	v	Amateurs	3–1
1925	Amateurs	v	Professionals	6–1
1926	Amateurs	v	Professionals	6–3
1927	Cardiff City	v	Corinthians	2–1
1928	Everton	v	Blackburn Rovers	2–1
1929	Professionals	v	Amateurs	3–0
1930	Arsenal	v	Sheffield Wednesday	2–1
1931	Arsenal	v	West Bromwich Albion	1–0
1932	Everton	v	Newcastle United	5–3
1933	Arsenal	v	Everton	3–0
1934	Arsenal	v	Manchester City	4–0
1935	Sheffield Wednesday	v	Arsenal	1–0
1936	Sunderland	v	Arsenal	2–1
1937	Manchester City	v	Sunderland	2–0
1938	Arsenal	v	Preston North End	2–1
1939–47		not played		
1948	Arsenal	v	Manchester United	4–3
1949	Portsmouth	v	Wolverhampton Wanderers	1–1*
1950	World Cup Team	v	Canadian Touring Team	4–2
1951	Tottenham Hotspur	v	Newcastle United	2–1
1952	Manchester United	v	Newcastle United	4–2
1953	Arsenal	v	Blackpool	3–1
1954	Wolverhampton Wanderers	v	West Bromwich Albion	4–4*
1955	Chelsea	v	Newcastle United	3–0
1956	Manchester United	v	Manchester City	1–0
1957	Manchester United	v	Aston Villa	4–0
1958	Bolton Wanderers	v	Wolverhampton Wanderers	4–1
1959	Wolverhampton Wanderers	v	Nottingham Forest	3–1
1960	Burnley	v	Wolverhampton Wanderers	2–2*
1961	Tottenham Hotspur	v	FA XI	3–2
1962	Tottenham Hotspur	v	Ipswich Town	5–1
1963	Everton	v	Manchester United	4–0
1964	Liverpool	v	West Ham United	2–2*
1965	Manchester United	v	Liverpool	2–2*
1966	Liverpool	v	Everton	1–0
1967	Manchester United	v	Tottenham Hotspur	3–3*
1968	Manchester City	v	West Bromwich Albion	6–1
1969	Leeds United	v	Manchester City	2–1
1970	Everton	v	Chelsea	2–1
1971	Leicester City	v	Liverpool	1–0
1972	Manchester City	v	Aston Villa	1–0

* each club retained Shield for six months

Year	Winners		Runners-up	Result
1973	Burnley	v	Manchester City	1–0
1974	Liverpool	v	Leeds United	1–1†
1975	Derby County	v	West Ham United	2–0
1976	Liverpool	v	Southampton	1–0
1977	Liverpool	v	Manchester United	0–0*
1978	Nottingham Forest	v	Ipswich Town	5–0
1979	Liverpool	v	Arsenal	3–1
1980	Liverpool	v	West Ham United	1–0
1981	Aston Villa	v	Tottenham Hotspur	2–2*
1982	Liverpool	v	Tottenham Hotspur	1–0
1983	Manchester United	v	Liverpool	2–0
1984	Everton	v	Liverpool	1–0
1985	Everton	v	Manchester United	2–0
1986	Everton	v	Liverpool	1–1*
1987	Everton	v	Coventry City	1–0
1988	Liverpool	v	Wimbledon	2–1
1989	Liverpool	v	Arsenal	1–0
1990	Liverpool	v	Manchester United	1–1*
1991	Arsenal	v	Tottenham Hotspur	0–0*
1992	Leeds United	v	Liverpool	4–3
1993	Manchester United	v	Arsenal	1–1†

each club retained Shield for six months   † *won on penalty–kicks*

Attendances at League Matches

Season	Matches Played	Total (Millions)	Div. 1	Div. 2	Div. 3(S)	Div. 3 (N)
1946-47	1848	35.6	15.0	11.1	5.7	3.9
1947-48	1848	40.3	16.7	12.3	6.7	4.6
1948-49	1848	41.3	17.9	11.4	7.0	5.0
1949-50	1848	40.5	17.3	11.7	7.1	4.4
1950-51	2028	39.6	16.7	10.8	7.4	4.8
1951-52	2028	39.0	16.1	11.1	7.0	4.9
1952-53	2028	37.1	16.1	9.7	6.7	4.7
1953-54	2028	36.2	16.2	9.5	6.3	4.2
1954-55	2028	34.1	15.1	9.0	6.0	4.1
1955-56	2028	33.2	14.1	9.1	5.7	4.3
1956-57	2028	32.7	13.8	8.7	5.6	4.6
1957-58	2028	33.6	14.5	8.7	6.1	4.3
1958-59	2028	33.6	14.7	8.6	5.9	4.3
1959-60	2028	32.5	14.4	8.4	5.7	4.0
1960-61	2028	28.6	12.9	7.0	4.8	3.9
1961-62	2015	28.0	12.1	7.5	5.2	3.3
1962-63	2028	28.9	12.5	7.8	5.3	3.3
1963-64	2028	28.5	12.5	7.6	5.4	3.0
1964-65	2028	27.6	12.7	7.0	4.4	3.5
1965-66	2028	27.2	12.5	6.9	4.8	3.0
1966-67	2028	28.9	14.2	7.3	4.4	3.0
1967-68	2028	30.1	15.3	7.5	4.0	3.4
1968-69	2028	29.4	14.6	7.4	4.3	3.1
1969-70	2028	29.6	14.9	7.6	4.2	2.9
1970-71	2028	28.2	14.0	7.1	4.4	2.8
1971-72	2028	28.7	14.5	6.8	4.7	2.7
1972-73	2028	25.4	14.0	5.6	3.7	2.1
1973-74	2027	25.0	13.1	6.3	3.4	2.2
1974-75	2028	25.6	12.6	7.0	4.1	2.0
1975-76	2028	24.9	13.1	5.8	3.9	2.1
1976-77	2028	26.2	13.6	6.3	4.2	2.1
1977-78	2028	25.4	13.3	6.5	3.3	2.3
1978-79	2028	24.5	12.7	6.2	3.4	2.3
1979-80	2028	24.6	12.2	6.1	4.0	2.3
1980-81	2028	21.9	11.4	5.2	3.6	1.7
1981-82	2028	20.0	10.4	4.8	2.8	2.0
1982-83	2028	18.8	9.3	5.0	2.9	1.6
1983-84	2028	18.3	8.7	5.3	2.7	1.5
1984-85	2028	17.8	9.8	4.0	2.7	1.4
1985-86	2028	16.5	9.0	3.6	2.5	1.4
1986-87	2028	17.4	9.1	4.2	2.4	1.7
1987-88	2030	18.0	8.1	5.3	2.8	1.8
1988-89	2036	18.5	7.8	5.8	3.0	1.8
1989-90	2036	19.5	7.9	6.9	2.8	1.9
1990-91	2036	19.5	8.6	6.3	2.8	1.8
1991-92	2064*	20.5	10.0	5.8	3.0	1.7
1992-93	2028	20.7	9.8	5.9	3.5	1.5
1993-94	2028	21.7	10.6	6.5	3.0	1.6

NOTE: *From Season 1958-59 onwards for Div. 3(S) read Div. 3 and for Div. 3(N) read Div. 4. From Season 1992-93 onwards for Div. 1 read FA Premier League.*
* *Figures include matches played by Aldershot*

Football Association Fixture Programme
Season 1994–1995

JULY 1994

16	Saturday	Pre-Season commences

AUGUST 1994

10	Wednesday	Euro Competitions Preliminary Round – 1st Leg
13	Saturday	Football League Season commences
14	Sunday	FA Charity Shield
17	Wednesday	Coca-Cola Cup 1st Round – 1st Leg
20	Saturday	FA Premier League Season commences
24	Wednesday	Euro Comps Prel Round – 2nd Leg
		Coca-Cola Cup 1st Round – 2nd Leg
27	Saturday	FA Challenge Cup Preliminary Round
29	Monday	Bank Holiday

SEPTEMBER 1994

3	Saturday	FA Challenge Trophy Preliminary Round
		FA Challenge Vase Extra Preliminary Round
		FA Youth Challenge Cup Extra Preliminary Round*
6	Tuesday	England v Portugal (U-21)
7	Wednesday	International Date
10	Saturday	FA Challenge Cup 1st Round Qualifying
		FA Youth Challenge Cup Preliminary Round*
14	Wednesday	Euro Comps 1st Round – 1st Leg
17	Saturday	FA Challenge Trophy 1st Round Qualifying
		Holland v England (U-16)
18	Sunday	FA Women's Challenge Cup 1st Round
21	Wednesday	Coca-Cola 2nd Round – 1st Leg
24	Saturday	FA Challenge Cup 2nd Round Qualifying
25	Sunday	FA Sunday Cup Preliminary Round (*if required*)
28	Wednesday	Euro Comps 1st Round – 2nd Leg

OCTOBER 1994

1	Saturday	FA Challenge Vase Preliminary Round
		FA Youth Challenge Cup 1st Round Qualifying*
5	Wednesday	Coca-Cola Cup 2nd Round – 2nd Leg
8	Saturday	FA Challenge Cup 3rd Round Qualifying
11	Tuesday	Austria v England (U-21)
12	Wednesday	International Date
15	Saturday	FA Challenge Trophy 2nd Round Qualifying
		FA Youth Challenge Cup 2nd Round Qualifying*
		FA County Youth Challenge Cup 1st Round*
16	Sunday	FA Women's Challenge Cup 2nd Round
18	Tuesday	FA XI v Huntingdonshire FA
19	Wednesday	Euro Comps 2nd Round – 1st Leg
22	Saturday	FA Challenge Cup 4th Round Qualifying
26	Wednesday	Coca-Cola Cup 3rd Round
29	Saturday	FA Challenge Vase 1st Round
30	Sunday	FA Sunday Cup 1st Round

NOVEMBER 1994

2	Wednesday	Euro Comps 2nd Round – 2nd Leg
12	Saturday	FA Challenge Cup 1st Round Proper
		FA Youth Challenge Cup 1st Round Proper*
13	Sunday	FA Women's Challenge Cup 3rd Round
15	Tuesday	England v Republic of Ireland (U-21)
		FA XI v Northern Premier League
16	Wednesday	International Date
19	Saturday	FA Challenge Vase 2nd Round
20	Sunday	FA Sunday Cup 2nd Round
23	Wednesday	Euro Comps 3rd Rd – 1st Leg
26	Saturday	FA Challenge Trophy 3rd Round Qualifying
		FA County Youth Challenge Cup 2nd Round*
30	Wednesday	Coca-Cola Cup 4th Round

DECEMBER 1994

3	Saturday	FA Challenge Cup 2nd Round Proper
4	Sunday	FA Women's Challenge Cup 4th Round
7	Wednesday	Euro Comps 3rd Rd – 2nd Leg
		FA XI v Isthmian League
10	Saturday	FA Challenge Vase 3rd Round
		FA Youth Challenge Cup 2nd Round Proper*
11	Sunday	FA Sunday Cup 3rd Round
14	Wednesday	International Date
25	Sunday	Christmas Day
26	Monday	Boxing Day
27	Tuesday	Bank Holiday

JANUARY 1995

1	Sunday	New Year's Day
2	Monday	Bank Holiday
7	Saturday	FA Challenge Cup 3rd Round Proper
10	Tuesday	FA XI v British Students
11	Wednesday	Coca-Cola Cup 5th Round
14	Saturday	FA Challenge Vase 4th Round
		FA Youth Challenge Cup 3rd Round Proper*
		FA County Youth Challenge Cup 3rd Round*
15	Sunday	FA Women's Challenge Cup 5th Round
17	Tuesday	FA XI v Combined Services
21	Saturday	FA Challenge Trophy 1st Round Proper
22	Sunday	FA Sunday Cup 4th Round
28	Saturday	FA Challenge Cup 4th Round Proper

FEBRUARY 1995

4	Saturday	FA Challenge Vase 5th Round
		FA Youth Challenge Cup 4th Round Proper*
11	Saturday	FA Challenge Trophy 2nd Round Proper
12	Sunday	FA Women's Challenge Cup 6th Round
		Coca-Cola Cup Semi-Final – 1st Leg
18	Saturday	FA Challenge Cup 5th Round Proper
		FA County Youth Challenge Cup 4th Round*
19	Sunday	FA Sunday Cup 5th Round
22	Wednesday	Coca-Cola Cup Semi-Final – 2nd Leg
25	Saturday	FA Challenge Vase 6th Round
		Tournament in Greece (U–16) commences
28	Tuesday	England v Wales (Semi-Pro)

MARCH 1995

1	Wednesday	Euro Comps Quarter-Final – 1st Leg
4	Saturday	FA Challenge Trophy 3rd Round Proper
		FA Youth Challenge Cup 5th Round Proper*
11	Saturday	FA Challenge Cup 6th Round Proper
15	Wednesday	Euro Comps Quarter-Final – 2nd Leg
18	Saturday	FA Challenge Vase Semi-Final – 1st Leg
		FA County Youth Challenge Cup Semi-Final*
19	Sunday	FA Women's Challenge Cup Semi-Final
25	Saturday	FA Challenge Trophy 4th Round Proper
		FA Challenge Vase Semi-Final – 2nd Leg
28	Tuesday	Republic of Ireland v England (U-21)
29	Wednesday	International Date

APRIL 1995

1	Saturday	FA Youth Challenge Cup Semi-Final*
2	Sunday	FA Sunday Cup Semi-Final
		Coca-Cola Cup Final
5	Wednesday	Euro Comps Semi-Final – 1st Leg
8	Saturday	FA Challenge Trophy Semi-Final – 1st Leg
9	Sunday	FA Challenge Cup Semi-Final
14	Friday	Good Friday
15	Saturday	FA Challenge Trophy Semi-Final – 2nd Leg
17	Monday	Easter Monday
19	Wednesday	Euro Comps Semi-Final – 2nd Leg
25	Tuesday	Latvia v England (U-21)
26	Wednesday	International Date
29	Saturday	FA County Youth Final (*fixed date*)
30	Sunday	FA Women's Challenge Cup Final

MAY 1995

1	Monday	Bank Holiday
3	Wednesday	UEFA Cup Final – 1st Leg
6	Saturday	FA Youth Challenge Cup Final*
7	Sunday	FA Sunday Cup Final
10	Wednesday	European Cup Winners' Cup Final
13	Saturday	FA Challenge Vase Final
14	Sunday	FA Challenge Trophy Final
17	Wednesday	UEFA Cup Final – 2nd Leg
20	Saturday	FA Challenge Cup Final
24	Wednesday	European Champion Clubs' Cup Final
25	Thursday	FA Challenge Cup Final Possible Replay
27	Saturday	Football League Play-Off (Division 3)
28	Sunday	Football League Play-Off (Division 2)
29	Monday	Football League Play-Off (Division 1)
		Bank Holiday
31	Wednesday	Gibraltar FA v England XI (Semi-Pro)

JUNE 1995

6	Tuesday	England v Latvia (U-21)
7	Wednesday	International Date
10	Saturday	International Date

closing date of round

Fixtures – Season 1994–1995

SAT. 13th AUGUST

ENDSLEIGH LEAGUE FIRST DIVISION
Barnsley v Derby County
Bristol City v Sunderland
Grimsby Town v Bolton Wdrs
Luton Town v WBA
Middlesbrough v Newcastle
Millwall v Southend Utd
Oldham Athletic v Charlton Athletic
Portsmouth v Notts County
Sheffield Utd v Watford
Stoke City v Tranmere Rovers
Wolverhampton Wdrs v Reading

SECOND DIVISION
Blackpool v Huddersfield Town
Chester City v Bradford City
Leyton Orient v Birmingham City
Oxford Utd v Hull City
Peterborough Utd v Bristol Rovers
Plymouth Argyle v Brentford
Rotherham Utd v Shrewsbury Town
Stockport County v Cardiff City
Swansea City v Brighton
Wrexham v AFC Bournemouth
Wycombe Wdrs v Cambridge Utd
York City v Crewe Alexandra

THIRD DIVISION
Barnet v Scunthorpe Utd
Bury v Rochdale
Carlisle Utd v Wigan Athletic
Chesterfield v Scarborough
Colchester Utd v Torquay Utd
Darlington v Preston North End
Fulham v Walsall
Gillingham v Hartlepool Utd
Hereford Utd v Doncaster Rovers
Lincoln City v Exeter City

SUN. 14th AUGUST

ENDSLEIGH LEAGUE FIRST DIVISION
Swindon Town v Port Vale

SAT. 20TH AUGUST

FA CARLING PREMIERSHIP
Arsenal v Manchester City
Chelsea v Norwich City
Coventry City v Wimbledon
Crystal Palace v Liverpool
Everton v Aston Villa
Ipswich Town v Nottingham Forest
Manchester Utd v QPR
Sheffield Wed v Tottenham Hotspur
Southampton v Blackburn Rovers
West Ham Utd v Leeds Utd

ENDSLEIGH LEAGUE FIRST DIVISION
Bolton Wdrs v Bristol City
Burnley v Stoke City
Charlton Athletic v Barnsley
Derby County v Luton Town
Port Vale v Oldham Athletic
Reading v Portsmouth
Southend Utd v Middlesbrough
Sunderland v Millwall
Tranmere Rovers v Swindon Town

Watford v Grimsby Town
WBA v Sheffield Utd

SECOND DIVISION
AFC Bournemouth v Blackpool
Birmingham City v Chester City
Bradford City v Leyton Orient
Brentford v Peterborough Utd
Brighton v Plymouth Argyle
Bristol Rovers v York City
Cambridge Utd v Stockport County
Cardiff City v Oxford Utd
Crewe Alexandra v Rotherham Utd
Huddersfield Town v Wycombe Wdrs
Hull City v Swansea City
Shrewsbury Town v Wrexham

THIRD DIVISION
Doncaster Rovers v Northampton Town
Exeter City v Bury
Hartlepool Utd v Darlington
Hereford Utd v Preston North End
Mansfield Town v Colchester Utd
Rochdale v Chesterfield
Scarborough v Barnet
Scunthorpe Utd v Fulham
Torquay Utd v Carlisle Utd
Walsall v Lincoln City
Wigan Athletic v Gillingham

SUN. 21st AUGUST

FA CARLING PREMIERSHIP
Leicester City v Newcastle Utd

ENDSLEIGH LEAGUE FIRST DIVISION
Notts County v Wolverhampton Wdrs

MON. 22nd AUGUST

FA CARLING PREMIERSHIP
Nottingham Forest v Manchester Utd

TUES. 23rd AUGUST

FA CARLING PREMIERSHIP
Blackburn Rovers v Leicester City
Leeds Utd v Arsenal
Wimbledon v Ipswich Town

WED. 24th AUGUST

FA CARLING PREMIERSHIP
Aston Villa v Southampton
Manchester City v West Ham Utd
Newcastle Utd v Coventry City
Norwich City v Crystal Palace
QPR v Sheffield Wed
Tottenham Hotspur v Everton

SAT. 27th AUGUST

FA CARLING PREMIERSHIP
Aston Villa v Crystal Palace
Blackburn Rovers v Coventry City
Leeds Utd v Chelsea
Manchester City v Everton

Newcastle Utd v Southampton
Norwich City v West Ham Utd
Nottingham Forest v Leicester City
QPR v Ipswich Town
Tottenham Hotspur v Manchester Utd
Wimbledon v Sheffield Wed

ENDSLEIGH LEAGUE FIRST DIVISION
Barnsley v Reading
Bristol City v Port Vale
Grimsby Town v Tranmere Rovers
Luton Town v Southend Utd
Middlesbrough v Bolton Wdrs
Millwall v Derby County
Oldham Athletic v Burnley
Portsmouth v Charlton Athletic
Sheffield Utd v Notts County
Stoke City v Sunderland
Swindon Town v Watford

SECOND DIVISION
Blackpool v Shrewsbury Town
Chester City v Huddersfield Town
Leyton Orient v Hull City
Oxford Utd v Cambridge Utd
Peterborough Utd v Crewe Alexandra
Plymouth Argyle v Bradford City
Rotherham Utd v AFC Bournemouth
Stockport County v Brentford
Swansea City v Birmingham City
Wrexham v Brighton
Wycombe Wdrs v Bristol Rovers
York City v Cardiff City

THIRD DIVISION
Barnet v Preston North End
Bury v Hartlepool Utd
Carlisle Utd v Scarborough
Chesterfield v Mansfield Town
Colchester Utd v Doncaster Rovers
Darlington v Exeter City
Fulham v Wigan Athletic
Gillingham v Rochdale
Hereford Utd v Walsall
Lincoln City v Torquay Utd
Scunthorpe Utd v Northampton Town

SUN. 28TH AUGUST

FA CARLING PREMIERSHIP
Liverpool v Arsenal

ENDSLEIGH LEAGUE FIRST DIVISION
Wolverhampton Wdrs v WBA

MON. 29th AUGUST

FA CARLING PREMIERSHIP
Coventry City v Aston Villa

TUES. 30th AUGUST

FA CARLING PREMIERSHIP
Crystal Palace v Leeds Utd
Everton v Nottingham Forest
Ipswich Town v Tottenham Hotspur

ENDSLEIGH LEAGUE FIRST DIVISION
Bolton Wdrs v Millwall
Burnley v Bristol City

Charlton Athletic v Sheffield Utd
Notts County v Oldham Athletic
Port Vale v Barnsley
Reading v Stoke City
Southend Utd v Portsmouth
Sunderland v Grimsby Town
Tranmere Rovers v Luton Town
Watford v Wolverhampton Wdrs

SECOND DIVISION
AFC Bournemouth v Peterborough Utd
Birmingham City v Wycombe Wdrs
Bradford City v Oxford Utd
Brentford v Rotherham Utd
Cambridge Utd v Chester City
Cardiff City v Wrexham
Crewe Alexandra v Stockport County
Huddersfield Town v Leyton Orient
Hull City v Plymouth Argyle
Shrewsbury Town v Swansea City

THIRD DIVISION
Bury v Preston North End
Exeter City v Colchester Utd
Doncaster Rovers v Fulham
Hartlepool Utd v Barnet
Mansfield Town v Darlington
Rochdale v Lincoln City
Scarborough v Hereford Utd
Scunthorpe Utd v Gillingham
Torquay Utd v Northampton Town
Walsall v Carlisle Utd
Wigan Athletic v Chesterfield

WED. 31st AUGUST

FA CARLING PREMIERSHIP
Arsenal v Blackburn Rovers
Chelsea v Manchester City
Leicester City v QPR
Manchester Utd v Wimbledon
Sheffield Wed v Norwich City
Southampton v Liverpool
West Ham Utd v Newcastle Utd

ENDSLEIGH LEAGUE FIRST DIVISION
Derby County v Middlesbrough
WBA v Swindon Town

SECOND DIVISION
Brighton v York City
Bristol Rovers v Blackpool

SAT. 3rd SEPTEMBER

ENDSLEIGH LEAGUE FIRST DIVISION
Bolton Wdrs v Stoke City
Burnley v Barnsley
Charlton Athletic v Bristol City
Derby County v Grimsby Town
Notts County v Swindon Town
Port Vale v Luton Town
Reading v Millwall
Southend Utd v Oldham Athletic
Sunderland v Wolverhampton Wdrs
Tranmere Rovers v Sheffield Utd
Watford v Middlesbrough
WBA v Portsmouth

SECOND DIVISION
AFC Bournemouth v York City
Birmingham City v Plymouth Argyle
Bradford City v Wycombe Wdrs
Brentford v Wrexham

Brighton v Leyton Orient
Bristol Rovers v Stockport County
Cambridge Utd v Rotherham Utd
Cardiff City v Swansea City
Crewe Alexandra v Blackpool
Huddersfield Town v Oxford Utd
Hull City v Chester City
Shrewsbury Town v Peterborough Utd

THIRD DIVISION
Doncaster Rovers v Darlington
Exeter City v Gillingham
Hartlepool Utd v Chesterfield
Mansfield Town v Bury
Preston North End v Lincoln City
Rochdale v Hereford Utd
Scarborough v Colchester Utd
Scunthorpe Utd v Carlisle Utd
Torquay Utd v Fulham
Walsall v Northampton Town
Wigan Athletic v Barnet

SAT. 10th SEPTEMBER

FA CARLING PREMIERSHIP
Aston Villa v Ipswich Town
Blackburn Rovers v Everton
Liverpool v West Ham Utd
Manchester City v Crystal Palace
Newcastle Utd v Chelsea
Norwich City v Arsenal
Nottingham Forest v Sheffield Wed
QPR v Coventry City
Wimbledon v Leicester City

ENDSLEIGH LEAGUE FIRST DIVISION
Barnsley v Watford
Bristol City v Notts County
Grimsby Town v Charlton Athletic
Luton Town v Burnley
Middlesbrough v Sunderland
Millwall v WBA
Oldham Athletic v Reading
Portsmouth v Port Vale
Sheffield Utd v Bolton Wdrs
Stoke City v Southend Utd
Swindon Town v Derby County
Wolverhampton Wdrs v Tranmere
 Rovers

SECOND DIVISION
Blackpool v Cardiff City
Chester City v Brighton
Leyton Orient v Cambridge Utd
Oxford Utd v Birmingham City
Peterborough Utd v Hull City
Plymouth Argyle v Huddersfield
 Town
Rotherham Utd v Bristol Rovers
Stockport County v AFC Bournemouth
Swansea City v Bradford City
Wrexham v Crewe Alexandra
Wycombe Wdrs v Brentford
York City v Shrewsbury Town

THIRD DIVISION
Barnet v Doncaster Rovers
Bury v Scunthorpe Utd
Carlisle Utd v Exeter City
Chesterfield v Walsall
Colchester Utd v Hartlepool Utd
Darlington v Torquay Utd
Fulham v Preston North End
Gillingham v Scarborough
Hereford Utd v Wigan Athletic

Lincoln City v Mansfield Town
Northampton Town v Rochdale

SUN. 11th SEPTEMBER

FA CARLING PREMIERSHIP
Leeds Utd v Manchester Utd

MON. 12th SEPTEMBER

FA CARLING PREMIERSHIP
Tottenham Hotspur v Southampton

TUES. 13th SEPTEMBER

ENDSLEIGH LEAGUE FIRST DIVISION
Barnsley v Notts County
Bristol City v Derby County
Grimsby Town v Port Vale
Luton Town v Bolton Wdrs
Middlesbrough v WBA
Oldham Athletic v Watford
Sheffield Utd v Sunderland
Wolverhampton Wdrs v Southend Utd

SECOND DIVISION
Blackpool v Brighton
Chester City v Cardiff City
Leyton Orient v AFC Bournemouth
Oxford Utd v Crewe Alexandra
Peterborough Utd v Huddersfield Town
Plymouth Argyle v Cambridge Utd
Rotherham Utd v Birmingham City
Stockport County v Shrewsbury Town
Swansea City v Bristol Rovers
Wrexham v Bradford City
Wycombe Wdrs v Hull City
York City v Brentford

THIRD DIVISION
Barnet v Rochdale
Bury v Doncaster Rovers
Carlisle Utd v Mansfield Town
Chesterfield v Exeter City
Colchester Utd v Walsall
Darlington v Scunthorpe Utd
Fulham v Scarborough
Gillingham v Preston North End
Hereford Utd v Torquay Utd
Lincoln City v Wigan Athletic
Northampton Town v Hartlepool Utd

WED. 14th SEPTEMBER

ENDSLEIGH LEAGUE FIRST DIVISION
Millwall v Burnley
Portsmouth v Tranmere Rovers
Stoke City v Charlton Athletic
Swindon Town v Reading

FRI. 16th SEPTEMBER

ENDSLEIGH LEAGUE THIRD DIVISION
Doncaster Rovers v Hereford Utd

SAT. 17th SEPTEMBER

FA CARLING PREMIERSHIP
Coventry City v Leeds Utd
Crystal Palace v Wimbledon

Everton v QPR
Leicester City v Tottenham Hotspur
Manchester Utd v Liverpool
Sheffield Wed v Manchester City
Southampton v Nottingham Forest
West Ham Utd v Aston Villa

Bolton Wdrs v Portsmouth
Burnley v Wolverhampton Wdrs
Charlton Athletic v Swindon Town
Derby County v Oldham Athletic
Notts County v Stoke City
Port Vale v Middlesbrough
Reading v Sheffield Utd
Southend Utd v Bristol City
Sunderland v Barnsley
Tranmere Rovers v Millwall
Watford v Luton Town
WBA v Grimsby Town

SECOND DIVISION
AFC Bournemouth v Chester City
Birmingham City v Peterborough Utd
Bradford City v York City
Brentford v Blackpool
Brighton v Oxford Utd
Bristol Rovers v Wrexham
Cambridge Utd v Swansea City
Cardiff City v Plymouth Argyle
Crewe Alexandra v Wycombe Wdrs
Huddersfield Town v Stockport
  County
Hull City v Rotherham Utd
Shrewsbury Town v Leyton Orient

THIRD DIVISION
Exeter City v Lincoln City
Hartlepool Utd v Gillingham
Mansfield Town v Northampton Town
Preston North End v Darlington
Rochdale v Bury
Scarborough v Chesterfield
Scunthorpe Utd v Barnet
Torquay Utd v Colchester Utd
Walsall v Fulham
Wigan Athletic v Carlisle Utd

SUN. 18th SEPTEMBER

FA CARLING PREMIERSHIP
Arsenal v Newcastle Utd
Chelsea v Blackburn Rovers

MON. 19th SEPTEMBER

FA CARLING PREMIERSHIP
Ipswich Town v Norwich City

SAT. 24th SEPTEMBER

FA CARLING PREMIERSHIP
Blackburn Rovers v Aston Villa
Coventry City v Southampton
Crystal Palace v Chelsea
Everton v Leicester City
Ipswich Town v Manchester Utd
Manchester City v Norwich City
Newcastle Utd v Liverpool
QPR v Wimbledon
Tottenham Hotspur v Nottingham
  Forest

ENDSLEIGH LEAGUE FIRST DIVISION
Bristol City v Middlesbrough
Derby County v Stoke City
Millwall v Luton Town
Notts County v Charlton Athletic
Oldham Athletic v Barnsley
Port Vale v Sheffield Utd
Portsmouth v Wolverhampton Wdrs
Southend Utd v Bolton Wdrs
Swindon Town v Grimsby Town
Tranmere Rovers v Sunderland
Watford v Reading
WBA v Burnley

SECOND DIVISION
AFC Bournemouth v Cardiff City
Birmingham City v Hull City
Blackpool v Wrexham
Bradford City v Huddersfield Town
Brighton v Cambridge Utd
Crewe Alexandra v Brentford
Oxford Utd v Leyton Orient
Peterborough Utd v Rotherham Utd
Plymouth Argyle v Chester City
Shrewsbury Town v Bristol Rovers
Stockport County v Wycombe Wdrs
Swansea City v York City

THIRD DIVISION
Bury v Chesterfield
Darlington v Colchester Utd
Doncaster Rovers v Preston North End
Fulham v Hereford Utd
Hartlepool Utd v Lincoln City
Mansfield Town v Exeter City
Northampton Town v Carlisle Utd
Scarborough v Rochdale
Scunthorpe Utd v Wigan Athletic
Walsall v Gillingham

SUN. 25th SEPTEMBER

FA CARLING PREMIERSHIP
West Ham Utd v Arsenal

MON. 26th SEPTEMBER

FA CARLING PREMIERSHIP
Sheffield Wed v Leeds Utd

SAT. 1st OCTOBER

FA CARLING PREMIERSHIP
Arsenal v Crystal Palace
Aston Villa v Newcastle Utd
Leeds Utd v Manchester City
Liverpool v Sheffield Wed
Manchester Utd v Everton
Norwich City v Blackburn Rovers
Southampton v Ipswich Town
Wimbledon v Tottenham Hotspur

ENDSLEIGH LEAGUE FIRST DIVISION
Barnsley v Swindon Town
Bolton Wdrs v Derby County
Burnley v Tranmere Rovers
Charlton Athletic v Watford
Grimsby Town v Portsmouth
Luton Town v Bristol City
Middlesbrough v Millwall
Reading v Notts County
Sheffield Utd v Oldham Athletic
Stoke City v WBA

Sunderland v Southend Utd
Wolverhampton Wdrs v Port Vale

SECOND DIVISION
Brentford v Shrewsbury Town
Bristol Rovers v Crewe Alexandra
Cambridge Utd v Bradford City
Cardiff City v Peterborough Utd
Chester City v Oxford Utd
Huddersfield Town v Brighton
Hull City v AFC Bournemouth
Leyton Orient v Plymouth Argyle
Rotherham Utd v Blackpool
Wrexham v Birmingham City
Wycombe Wdrs v Swansea City
York City v Stockport County

THIRD DIVISION
Barnet v Fulham
Carlisle Utd v Darlington
Chesterfield v Torquay Utd
Colchester Utd v Bury
Exeter City v Hartlepool Utd
Gillingham v Mansfield Town
Hereford Utd v Scunthorpe Utd
Lincoln City v Northampton Town
Preston North End v Walsall
Rochdale v Doncaster Rovers
Wigan Athletic v Scarborough

SUN. 2nd OCTOBER

FA CARLING PREMIERSHIP
Chelsea v West Ham United
Nottingham Forest v QPR

MON. 3rd OCTOBER

FA CARLING PREMIERSHIP
Leicester City v Coventry City

SAT. 8th OCTOBER

FA CARLING PREMIERSHIP
Chelsea v Leicester City
Coventry City v Ipswich Town
Liverpool v Aston Villa
Manchester City v Nottingham Forest
Norwich City v Leeds Utd
Sheffield Wed v Manchester Utd
Southampton v Everton
Tottenham Hotspur v QPR
Wimbledon v Arsenal

ENDSLEIGH LEAGUE FIRST DIVISION
Barnsley v Southend Utd
Bristol City v Millwall
Burnley v Bolton Wdrs
Charlton Athletic v Reading
Derby County v Watford
Grimsby Town v Sheffield Utd
Middlesbrough v Tranmere Rovers
Notts County v Port Vale
Oldham Athletic v Portsmouth
Stoke City v Luton Town
Swindon Town v Wolverhampton Wdrs
WBA v Sunderland

SECOND DIVISION
Birmingham City v Huddersfield Town
Bradford City v Brighton
Brentford v Bristol Rovers

Cambridge Utd v Wrexham
Cardiff City v Crewe Alexandra
Chester City v Swansea City
Hull City v Blackpool
Oxford Utd v Plymouth Argyle
Shrewsbury Town v AFC Bournemouth
Stockport County v Rotherham Utd
Wycombe Wdrs v Leyton Orient
York City v Peterborough Utd

THIRD DIVISION
Barnet v Hereford Utd
Colchester Utd v Chesterfield
Darlington v Bury
Doncaster Rovers v Wigan Athletic
Exeter City v Northampton Town
Gillingham v Torquay Utd
Lincoln City v Carlisle Utd
Mansfield Town v Hartlepool Utd
Preston North End v Scunthorpe Utd
Rochdale v Fulham
Walsall v Scarborough

SUN. 9th OCTOBER

FA CARLING PREMIERSHIP
Newcastle Utd v Blackburn Rovers

MON. 10th OCTOBER

FA CARLING PREMIERSHIP
West Ham Utd v Crystal Palace

TUES. 11th OCTOBER

ENDSLEIGH LEAGUE THIRD DIVISION
Northampton Town v Mansfield Town

SAT. 15th OCTOBER

FA CARLING PREMIERSHIP
Arsenal v Chelsea
Aston Villa v Norwich City
Blackburn Rovers v Liverpool
Crystal Palace v Newcastle Utd
Everton v Coventry City
Leeds Utd v Tottenham Hotspur
Leicester City v Southampton
Manchester Utd v West Ham Utd
QPR v Manchester City

ENDSLEIGH LEAGUE FIRST DIVISION
Bolton Wdrs v Oldham Athletic
Luton Town v Middlesbrough
Millwall v Stoke City
Port Vale v Charlton Athletic
Portsmouth v Swindon Town
Reading v Bristol City
Sheffield Utd v Barnsley
Southend Utd v Derby County
Sunderland v Burnley
Tranmere Rovers v WBA
Watford v Notts County
Wolverhampton Wdrs v Grimsby Town

SECOND DIVISION
AFC Bournemouth v Brentford
Blackpool v Bradford City
Brighton v Birmingham City
Bristol Rovers v Cardiff City
Crewe Alexandra v Shrewsbury Town

Huddersfield Town v Cambridge Utd
Leyton Orient v Chester City
Peterborough Utd v Stockport County
Plymouth Argyle v Wycombe Wdrs
Rotherham Utd v York City
Swansea City v Oxford Utd
Wrexham v Hull City

THIRD DIVISION
Bury v Lincoln City
Carlisle Utd v Colchester Utd
Chesterfield v Darlington
Fulham v Exeter City
Hartlepool Utd v Preston North End
Hereford Utd v Gillingham
Northampton Town v Barnet
Scarborough v Doncaster Rovers
Scunthorpe Utd v Walsall
Torquay Utd v Mansfield Town
Wigan Athletic v Rochdale

SUN. 16th OCTOBER

FA CARLING PREMIERSHIP
Ipswich Town v Sheffield Wed

MON. 17th OCTOBER

FA CARLING PREMIERSHIP
Nottingham Forest v Wimbledon

SAT. 22nd OCTOBER

FA CARLING PREMIERSHIP
Arsenal v Coventry City
Aston Villa v Nottingham Forest
Chelsea v Ipswich Town
Crystal Palace v Everton
Leeds Utd v Leicester City
Liverpool v Wimbledon
Manchester City v Tottenham Hotspur
Newcastle Utd v Sheffield Wed
Norwich City v QPR

ENDSLEIGH LEAGUE FIRST DIVISION
Barnsley v WBA
Charlton Athletic v Burnley
Grimsby Town v Bristol City
Notts County v Derby County
Oldham Athletic v Stoke City
Port Vale v Bolton Wdrs
Portsmouth v Middlesbrough
Reading v Sunderland
Sheffield Utd v Luton Town
Swindon Town v Southend Utd
Watford v Tranmere Rovers
Wolverhampton Wdrs v Millwall

SECOND DIVISION
AFC Bournemouth v Bradford City
Blackpool v Swansea City
Brentford v Birmingham City
Bristol Rovers v Brighton
Cardiff City v Cambridge Utd
Crewe Alexandra v Huddersfield
  Town
Peterborough Utd v Wycombe Wdrs
Rotherham Utd v Leyton Orient
Shrewsbury Town v Hull City
Stockport County v Plymouth Argyle
Wrexham v Oxford Utd
York City v Chester City

THIRD DIVISION
Bury v Gillingham
Carlisle Utd v Barnet
Chesterfield v Fulham
Colchester Utd v Preston North End
Darlington v Hereford Utd
Exeter City v Scunthorpe Utd
Hartlepool Utd v Walsall
Lincoln City v Scarborough
Mansfield Town v Doncaster Rovers
Northampton Town v Wigan Athletic
Torquay Utd v Rochdale

SUN. 23rd OCTOBER

FA CARLING PREMIERSHIP
Blackburn Rovers v Manchester Utd

SAT. 29th OCTOBER

FA CARLING PREMIERSHIP
Coventry City v Manchester City
Everton v Arsenal
Ipswich Town v Liverpool
Leicester City v Crystal Palace
Manchester Utd v Newcastle Utd
Nottingham Forest v Blackburn
  Rovers
QPR v Aston Villa
Sheffield Wed v Chelsea
Southampton v Leeds Utd
Tottenham Hotspur v West Ham Utd

ENDSLEIGH LEAGUE FIRST DIVISION
Bolton Wdrs v Watford
Bristol City v Portsmouth
Burnley v Notts County
Derby County v Charlton Athletic
Luton Town v Barnsley
Middlesbrough v Swindon Town
Millwall v Sheffield Utd
Southend Utd v Grimsby Town
Stoke City v Wolverhampton Wdrs
Sunderland v Oldham Athletic
Tranmere Rovers v Port Vale
WBA v Reading

SECOND DIVISION
Birmingham City v Bristol Rovers
Bradford City v Cardiff City
Brighton v Rotherham Utd
Cambridge Utd v Brentford
Huddersfield Town v AFC
  Bournemouth
Hull City v Crewe Alexandra
Leyton Orient v Stockport County
Oxford Utd v Shrewsbury Town
Plymouth Argyle v Blackpool
Swansea City v Peterborough Utd
Wycombe Wdrs v York City

THIRD DIVISION
Barnet v Chesterfield
Doncaster Rovers v Torquay Utd
Fulham v Carlisle Utd
Gillingham v Darlington
Hereford Utd v Lincoln City
Preston North End v Exeter City
Rochdale v Mansfield Town
Scarborough v Northampton Town
Scunthorpe Utd v Hartlepool Utd
Walsall v Bury
Wigan Athletic v Colchester Utd

SUN. 30th OCTOBER

FA CARLING PREMIERSHIP
Wimbledon v Norwich City

ENDSLEIGH LEAGUE SECOND DIVISION
Chester City v Wrexham

MON. 31st OCTOBER

FA CARLING PREMIERSHIP
QPR v Liverpool

TUES. 1st NOVEMBER

FA CARLING PREMIERSHIP
Everton v West Ham Utd
Ipswich Town v Leeds Utd

ENDSLEIGH LEAGUE FIRST DIVISION
Bolton Wdrs v Swindon Town
Bristol City v Wolverhampton Wdrs
Burnley v Watford
Luton Town v Grimsby Town
Middlesbrough v Oldham Athletic
Southend Utd v Notts County
Sunderland v Charlton Athletic
Tranmere Rovers v Barnsley

SECOND DIVISION
Birmingham City v Crewe Alexandra
Bradford City v Brentford
Cambridge Utd v Bristol Rovers
Huddersfield Town v Wrexham
Hull City v York City
Leyton Orient v Cardiff City
Oxford Utd v Blackpool
Plymouth Argyle v Peterborough Utd
Swansea City v Rotherham Utd
Wycombe Wdrs v Shrewsbury Town

WED. 2nd NOVEMBER

FA CARLING PREMIERSHIP
Coventry City v Crystal Palace
Nottingham Forest v Newcastle Utd
Sheffield Wed v Blackburn Rovers
Southampton v Norwich City
Wimbledon v Aston Villa

ENDSLEIGH LEAGUE FIRST DIVISION
Derby County v Reading
Millwall v Portsmouth
Stoke City v Sheffield Utd
WBA v Port Vale

SECOND DIVISION
Brighton v AFC Bournemouth
Chester City v Stockport County

SAT. 5th NOVEMBER

FA CARLING PREMIERSHIP
Blackburn Rovers v Tottenham
  Hotspur
Chelsea v Coventry City
Crystal Palace v Ipswich Town
Leeds Utd v Wimbledon
Liverpool v Nottingham Forest
Manchester City v Southampton
Newcastle Utd v QPR

Norwich City v Everton
West Ham Utd v Leicester City

ENDSLEIGH LEAGUE FIRST DIVISION
Barnsley v Stoke City
Charlton Athletic v Bolton Wdrs
Grimsby Town v Middlesbrough
Notts County v Sunderland
Oldham Athletic v Tranmere Rovers
Port Vale v Southend Utd
Portsmouth v Derby County
Reading v Burnley
Sheffield Utd v Bristol City
Swindon Town v Millwall
Watford v WBA
Wolverhampton Wdrs v Luton Town

SECOND DIVISION
AFC Bournemouth v Cambridge Utd
Blackpool v Leyton Orient
Brentford v Hull City
Bristol Rovers v Bradford City
Cardiff City v Brighton
Crewe Alexandra v Swansea City
Peterborough Utd v Chester City
Rotherham Utd v Plymouth Argyle
Shrewsbury Town v Birmingham City
Stockport County v Oxford Utd
Wrexham v Wycombe Wdrs
York City v Huddersfield Town

THIRD DIVISION
Bury v Scarborough
Carlisle Utd v Rochdale
Chesterfield v Hereford Utd
Colchester Utd v Gillingham
Darlington v Walsall
Exeter City v Doncaster Rovers
Hartlepool Utd v Wigan Athletic
Lincoln City v Barnet
Mansfield Town v Preston North End
Northampton Town v Fulham
Torquay Utd v Scunthorpe Utd

SUN. 6th NOVEMBER

FA CARLING PREMIERSHIP
Arsenal v Sheffield Wed
Aston Villa v Manchester Utd

WED. 9th NOVEMBER

FA CARLING PREMIERSHIP
Liverpool v Chelsea

THURS. 10th NOVEMBER

FA CARLING PREMIERSHIP
Manchester Utd v Manchester City

SAT. 12th NOVEMBER

ENDSLEIGH LEAGUE FIRST DIVISION
Barnsley v Bristol City
Charlton Athletic v WBA
Grimsby Town v Millwall
Notts County v Tranmere Rovers
Oldham Athletic v Luton Town
Portsmouth v Stoke City
Reading v Middlesbrough
Sheffield Utd v Derby County

Watford v Southend Utd
Wolverhampton Wdrs v Bolton Wdrs

SAT. 19th NOVEMBER

FA CARLING PREMIERSHIP
Coventry City v Norwich City
Ipswich Town v Blackburn Rovers
Manchester Utd v Crystal Palace
Nottingham Forest v Chelsea
QPR v Leeds Utd
Sheffield Wed v West Ham Utd
Southampton v Arsenal
Tottenham Hotspur v Aston Villa
Wimbledon v Newcastle Utd

ENDSLEIGH LEAGUE FIRST DIVISION
Bolton Wdrs v Notts County
Bristol City v Swindon Town
Burnley v Sheffield Utd
Derby County v Port Vale
Luton Town v Portsmouth
Middlesbrough v Wolverhampton Wdrs
Millwall v Barnsley
Southend United v Reading
Stoke City v Grimsby Town
Sunderland v Watford
Tranmere Rovers v Charlton Athletic
WBA v Oldham Athletic

SECOND DIVISION
Birmingham City v AFC Bournemouth
Bradford City v Crewe Alexandra
Brighton v Peterborough Utd
Cambridge Utd v Shrewsbury Town
Chester City v Blackpool
Huddersfield Town v Brentford
Hull City v Bristol Rovers
Leyton Orient v York City
Oxford Utd v Rotherham Utd
Plymouth Argyle v Wrexham
Swansea City v Stockport County
Wycombe Wdrs v Cardiff City

THIRD DIVISION
Barnet v Bury
Doncaster Rovers v Hartlepool Utd
Fulham v Lincoln City
Gillingham v Chesterfield
Hereford Utd v Carlisle Utd
Preston North End v Northampton
  Town
Rochdale v Colchester Utd
Scarborough v Torquay Utd
Scunthorpe Utd v Mansfield Town
Walsall v Exeter City
Wigan Athletic v Darlington

SUN. 20th NOVEMBER

FA CARLING PREMIERSHIP
Leicester City v Manchester City

MON. 21st NOVEMBER

FA CARLING PREMIERSHIP
Everton v Liverpool

WED. 23rd NOVEMBER

FA CARLING PREMIERSHIP
Leicester City v Arsenal
Tottenham Hotspur v Chelsea

ENDSLEIGH LEAGUE FIRST DIVISION
Swindon Town v Burnley

FRI. 25th NOVEMBER

ENDSLEIGH LEAGUE SECOND DIVISION
Cardiff City v Hull City

SAT. 26th NOVEMBER

FA CARLING PREMIERSHIP
Arsenal v Manchester Utd
Aston Villa v Sheffield Wed
Blackburn Rovers v QPR
Chelsea v Everton
Crystal Palace v Southampton
Leeds Utd v Nottingham Forest
Liverpool v Tottenham Hotspur
Manchester City v Wimbledon
Newcastle Utd v Ipswich Town
Norwich City v Leicester City
West Ham Utd v Coventry City

ENDSLEIGH LEAGUE FIRST DIVISION
Barnsley v Bolton Wdrs
Charlton Athletic v Middlesbrough
Grimsby Town v Burnley
Notts County v WBA
Oldham Athletic v Bristol City
Port Vale v Millwall
Portsmouth v Sunderland
Reading v Tranmere Rovers
Sheffield Utd v Southend Utd
Swindon Town v Luton Town
Watford v Stoke City
Wolverhampton Wdrs v Derby County

SECOND DIVISION
AFC Bournemouth v Oxford Utd
Blackpool v Wycombe Wdrs
Brentford v Brighton
Bristol Rovers v Huddersfield Town
Crewe Alexandra v Cambridge Utd
Peterborough Utd v Leyton Orient
Rotherham Utd v Chester City
Shrewsbury Town v Bradford City
Stockport County v Birmingham City
Wrexham v Swansea City
York City v Plymouth Argyle

THIRD DIVISION
Bury v Fulham
Carlisle Utd v Doncaster Rovers
Chesterfield v Preston North End
Colchester Utd v Scunthorpe Utd
Darlington v Barnet
Exeter City v Scarborough
Hartlepool Utd v Rochdale
Lincoln City v Gillingham
Mansfield Town v Walsall
Northampton Town v Hereford Utd
Torquay Utd v Wigan Athletic

TUES. 29th NOVEMBER

ENDSLEIGH LEAGUE FIRST DIVISION
Port Vale v Sunderland

SAT. 3rd DECEMBER

FA CARLING PREMIERSHIP
Coventry City v Liverpool
Ipswich Town v Manchester City

Leicester City v Aston Villa
Manchester Utd v Norwich City
Nottingham Forest v Arsenal
QPR v West Ham Utd
Sheffield Wed v Crystal Palace
Southampton v Chelsea
Tottenham Hotspur v Newcastle Utd
Wimbledon v Blackburn Rovers

ENDSLEIGH LEAGUE FIRST DIVISION
Bolton Wdrs v Port Vale
Bristol City v Grimsby Town
Burnley v Charlton Athletic
Derby County v Notts County
Luton Town v Sheffield Utd
Middlesbrough v Portsmouth
Millwall v Wolverhampton Wdrs
Southend Utd v Swindon Town
Stoke City v Oldham Athletic
Sunderland v Reading
Tranmere Rovers v Watford
WBA v Barnsley

MON. 5th DECEMBER

FA CARLING PREMIERSHIP
Everton v Leeds Utd

SAT. 10th DECEMBER

FA CARLING PREMIERSHIP
Aston Villa v Everton
Blackburn Rovers v Southampton
Leeds Utd v West Ham Utd
Liverpool v Crystal Palace
Manchester City v Arsenal
Newcastle Utd v Leicester City
Norwich City v Chelsea
Nottingham Forest v Ipswich Town
QPR v Manchester Utd
Wimbledon v Coventry City

ENDSLEIGH LEAGUE FIRST DIVISION
Barnsley v Charlton Athletic
Bristol City v Bolton Wdrs
Grimsby Town v Watford
Luton Town v Derby County
Middlesbrough v Southend Utd
Millwall v Sunderland
Oldham Athletic v Port Vale
Portsmouth v Reading
Sheffield Utd v WBA
Stoke City v Burnley
Swindon Town v Tranmere Rovers
Wolverhampton Wdrs v Notts County

SECOND DIVISION
Blackpool v AFC Bournemouth
Chester City v Birmingham City
Leyton Orient v Bradford City
Oxford Utd v Cardiff City
Peterborough Utd v Brentford
Plymouth Argyle v Brighton
Rotherham Utd v Crewe Alexandra
Stockport County v Cambridge Utd
Swansea City v Hull City
Wrexham v Shrewsbury Town
Wycombe Wdrs v Huddersfield Town
York City v Bristol Rovers

THIRD DIVISION
Barnet v Scarborough
Bury v Exeter City
Carlisle Utd v Torquay Utd

Chesterfield v Rochdale
Colchester Utd v Mansfield Town
Darlington v Hartlepool Utd
Fulham v Scunthorpe Utd
Gillingham v Wigan Athletic
Hereford Utd v Preston North End
Walsall v Lincoln City
Northampton Town v Doncaster
Rovers

MON. 12th DECEMBER

FA CARLING PREMIERSHIP
Tottenham Hotspur v Sheffield Wed

FRI. 16th DECEMBER

FA CARLING PREMIERSHIP
Ipswich Town v Wimbledon

ENDSLEIGH LEAGUE SECOND DIVISION
AFC Bournemouth v Wrexham
Cambridge Utd v Wycombe Wdrs
Crewe Alexandra v York City

THIRD DIVISION
Doncaster Rovers v Colchester Utd
Northampton Town v Scunthorpe Utd

SAT. 17th DECEMBER

FA CARLING PREMIERSHIP
Arsenal v Leeds Utd
Chelsea v Liverpool
Coventry City v Newcastle Utd
Crystal Palace v Norwich City
Everton v Tottenham Hotspur
Leicester City v Blackburn Rovers
Manchester Utd v Nottingham Forest
Sheffield Wed v QPR
Southampton v Aston Villa
West Ham Utd v Manchester City

ENDSLEIGH LEAGUE FIRST DIVISION
Bolton Wdrs v Grimsby Town
Burnley v Middlesbrough
Charlton Athletic v Oldham Athletic
Derby County v Barnsley
Notts County v Portsmouth
Port Vale v Swindon Town
Reading v Wolverhampton Wdrs
Southend Utd v Millwall
Sunderland v Bristol City
Tranmere Rovers v Stoke City
Watford v Sheffield Utd

SECOND DIVISION
Birmingham City v Leyton Orient
Bradford City v Chester City
Brentford v Plymouth Argyle
Brighton v Swansea City
Bristol Rovers v Peterborough Utd
Cardiff City v Stockport County
Huddersfield Town v Blackpool
Hull City v Oxford Utd
Shrewsbury Town v Rotherham Utd

THIRD DIVISION
Exeter City v Darlington
Hartlepool Utd v Bury
Preston North End v Barnet
Rochdale v Gillingham

Scarborough v Carlisle Utd
Torquay Utd v Lincoln City
Walsall v Hereford Utd
Wigan Athletic v Fulham

SUN.18th DECEMBER

WBA v Luton Town

THIRD DIVISION
Mansfield Town v Chesterfield

WED. 21st DECEMBER

FA CARLING PREMIERSHIP
Newcastle United v Everton

MON. 26th DECEMBER

FA CARLING PREMIERSHIP
Arsenal v Aston Villa
Chelsea v Manchester Utd (12.00)
Coventry City v Nottingham Forest
Crystal Palace v QPR
Everton v Sheffield Wed
Leeds Utd v Newcastle Utd
Leicester City v Liverpool (11.30)
Manchester City v Blackburn Rovers
 (3.00)
Norwich City v Tottenham Hotspur
Southampton v Wimbledon (12.00)
West Ham Utd v Ipswich Town

ENDSLEIGH LEAGUE FIRST DIVISION
Barnsley v Grimsby Town
Burnley v Port Vale
Charlton Athletic v Southend Utd
Notts County v Millwall
Oldham Athletic v Wolverhampton
 Wdrs
Reading v Luton Town
Sheffield Utd v Middlesbrough
Stoke City v Swindon Town
Sunderland v Bolton Wdrs
Tranmere Rovers v Derby County
Watford v Portsmouth
WBA v Bristol City

SECOND DIVISION
Birmingham City v Cambridge Utd
Brentford v Leyton Orient
Bristol Rovers v AFC Bournemouth
Crewe Alexandra v Chester City
Hull City v Huddersfield Town
Peterborough Utd v Oxford Utd
Rotherham Utd v Bradford City
Shrewsbury Town v Cardiff City
Stockport County v Wrexham
Swansea City v Plymouth Argyle
Wycombe Wdrs v Brighton
York City v Blackpool

THIRD DIVISION
Bury v Wigan Athletic
Chesterfield v Doncaster Rovers
Colchester Utd v Northampton Town
Darlington v Scarborough
Exeter City v Torquay Utd
Gillingham v Fulham
Hartlepool Utd v Carlisle Utd
Mansfield Town v Hereford Utd

Preston North End v Rochdale
Scunthorpe Utd v Lincoln City
Walsall v Barnet

TUES. 27th DECEMBER

FA CARLING PREMIERSHIP
Nottingham Forest v Norwich City
Tottenham Hotspur v Crystal Palace

ENDSLEIGH LEAGUE FIRST DIVISION
Bolton Wdrs v Tranmere Rovers
Bristol City v Stoke City
Derby County v Burnley
Grimsby Town v Oldham Athletic
Luton Town v Sunderland
Millwall v Watford
Port Vale v Reading
Portsmouth v Barnsley
Southend Utd v WBA
Swindon Town v Sheffield Utd

SECOND DIVISION
AFC Bournemouth v Crewe Alexandra
Blackpool v Stockport County
Brighton v Shrewsbury Town
Chester City v Brentford
Huddersfield Town v Rotherham Utd
Leyton Orient v Swansea City
Oxford Utd v Wycombe Wdrs
Plymouth Argyle v Bristol Rovers
Wrexham v Peterborough Utd

THIRD DIVISION
Barnet v Gillingham
Carlisle Utd v Bury
Doncaster Rovers v Scunthorpe Utd
Fulham v Colchester Utd
Hereford Utd v Exeter City
Lincoln City v Darlington
Northampton Town v Chesterfield
Rochdale v Walsall
Scarborough v Mansfield Town
Torquay Utd v Hartlepool Utd

WED. 28th DECEMBER

FA CARLING PREMIERSHIP
Aston Villa v Chelsea
Blackburn Rovers v Leeds Utd
Ipswich Town v Arsenal
Liverpool v Manchester City
QPR v Southampton
Sheffield Wed v Coventry City
Wimbledon v West Ham Utd

ENDSLEIGH LEAGUE FIRST DIVISION
Middlesbrough v Notts County
Wolverhampton Wdrs v Charlton
 Athletic

SECOND DIVISION
Bradford City v Hull City
Cambridge Utd v York City
Cardiff City v Brimingham City

THIRD DIVISION
Wigan Athletic v Preston North End

SAT. 31st DECEMBER

FA CARLING PREMIERSHIP
Arsenal v QPR
Chelsea v Wimbledon

Coventry City v Tottenham Hotspur
Crystal Palace v Blackburn Rovers
Everton v Ipswich Town
Leeds Utd v Liverpool
Leicester City v Sheffield Wed
Manchester City v Aston Villa
Norwich City v Newcastle Utd
Southampton v Manchester Utd
West Ham Utd v Nottingham Forest

ENDSLEIGH LEAGUE FIRST DIVISION
Barnsley v Wolverhampton Wdrs
Burnley v Southend Utd
Charlton Athletic v Millwall
Notts County v Luton Town
Oldham Athletic v Swindon Town
Reading v Grimsby Town
Sheffield Utd v Portsmouth
Stoke City v Middlesbrough
Sunderland v Derby County
Tranmere Rovers v Bristol City
Watford v Port Vale
WBA v Bolton Wdrs

SECOND DIVISION
Birmingham City v Blackpool
Brentford v Oxford Utd
Bristol Rovers v Chester City
Crewe Alexandra v Leyton Orient
Hull City v Brighton
Peterborough Utd v Cambridge Utd
Rotherham Utd v Cardiff City
Shrewsbury Town v Plymouth Argyle
Stockport County v Bradford City
Swansea City v Huddersfield Town
Wycombe Wdrs v AFC Bournemouth
York City v Wrexham

THIRD DIVISION
Bury v Torquay Utd
Chesterfield v Lincoln City
Colchester Utd v Hereford Utd
Darlington v Northampton Town
Exeter City v Wigan Athletic
Gillingham v Carlisle Utd
Hartlepool Utd v Fulham
Mansfield Town v Barnet
Preston North End v Scarborough
Scunthorpe Utd v Rochdale
Walsall v Doncaster Rovers

MON. 2nd JANUARY

FA CARLING PREMIERSHIP
Aston Villa v Leeds Utd
Blackburn Rovers v West Ham Utd
Ipswich Town v Leicester City
Liverpool v Norwich City
Newcastle Utd v Manchester City
Nottingham Forest v Crystal Palace
Sheffield Wed v Southampton
Tottenham Hotspur v Arsenal
Wimbledon v Everton

ENDSLEIGH LEAGUE FIRST DIVISION
Bolton Wdrs v Reading
Bristol City v Watford
Derby County v WBA
Grimsby Town v Notts County
Luton Town v Charlton Athletic
Middlesbrough v Barnsley
Millwall v Oldham Athletic
Port Vale v Stoke City
Portsmouth v Burnley
Southend Utd v Tranmere Rovers

Swindon Town v Sunderland
Wolverhampton Wdrs v Sheffield Utd

SECOND DIVISION
AFC Bournemouth v Swansea City
Blackpool v Peterborough Utd
Bradford City v Birmingham City
Brighton v Stockport County
Cambridge Utd v Hull City
Cardiff City v Brentford
Chester City v Wycombe Wdrs
Huddersfield Town v Shrewsbury
Town
Leyton Orient v Bristol Rovers
Oxford Utd v York City
Plymouth Argyle v Crewe Alexandra
Wrexham v Rotherham Utd

THIRD DIVISION
Barnet v Exeter City
Carlisle Utd v Chesterfield
Doncaster Rovers v Gillingham
Fulham v Mansfield Town
Hereford Utd v Hartlepool Utd
Lincoln City v Colchester Utd
Northampton Town v Bury
Rochdale v Darlington
Scarborough v Scunthorpe Utd
Torquay Utd v Preston North End
Wigan Athletic v Walsall

TUES. 3rd JANUARY

FA CARLING PREMIERSHIP
Manchester United v Coventry City
QPR v Chelsea

SAT. 7th JANUARY

ENDSLEIGH LEAGUE SECOND DIVISION
Birmingham City v Brentford
Bradford City v AFC Bournemouth
Brighton v Bristol Rovers
Cambridge Utd v Cardiff City
Chester City v York City
Huddersfield Town v Crewe Alexandra
Hull City v Shrewsbury Town
Leyton Orient v Rotherham Utd
Oxford Utd v Wrexham
Plymouth Argyle v Stockport County
Swansea City v Blackpool
Wycombe Wdrs v Peterborough Utd

THIRD DIVISION
Barnet v Carlisle Utd
Doncaster Rovers v Mansfield Town
Fulham v Chesterfield
Gillingham v Bury
Hereford Utd v Darlington
Preston North End v Colchester Utd
Rochdale v Torquay Utd
Scarborough v Lincoln City
Scunthorpe Utd v Exeter City
Walsall v Hartlepool Utd
Wigan Athletic v Northampton Town

SAT. 14th JANUARY

FA CARLING PREMIERSHIP
Arsenal v Everton
Aston Villa v QPR
Blackburn Rovers v Nottingham Forest
Chelsea v Sheffield Wed

Crystal Palace v Leicester City
Leeds Utd v Southampton
Liverpool v Ipswich Town
Manchester City v Coventry City
Newcastle Utd v Manchester Utd
Norwich City v Wimbledon
West Ham Utd v Tottenham Hotspur

ENDSLEIGH LEAGUE FIRST DIVISION
Barnsley v Luton Town
Charlton Athletic v Derby County
Grimsby Town v Southend Utd
Notts County v Burnley
Oldham Athletic v Sunderland
Port Vale v Tranmere Rovers
Portsmouth v Bristol City
Reading v WBA
Sheffield Utd v Millwall
Swindon Town v Middlesbrough
Watford v Bolton Wdrs
Wolverhampton Wdrs v Stoke City

SECOND DIVISION
AFC Bournemouth v Plymouth Argyle
Blackpool v Cambridge Utd
Brentford v Swansea City
Bristol Rovers v Oxford Utd
Cardiff City v Huddersfield Town
Crewe Alexandra v Brighton
Peterborough Utd v Bradford City
Rotherham Utd v Wycombe Wdrs
Shrewsbury Town v Chester City
Stockport County v Hull City
Wrexham v Leyton Orient
York City v Birmingham City

THIRD DIVISION
Bury v Hereford Utd
Carlisle Utd v Preston North End
Chesterfield v Scunthorpe Utd
Colchester Utd v Barnet
Darlington v Fulham
Exeter City v Rochdale
Hartlepool Utd v Scarborough
Lincoln City v Doncaster Rovers
Mansfield Town v Wigan Athletic
Northampton Town v Gillingham
Torquay Utd v Walsall

SAT. 21st JANUARY

FA CARLING PREMIERSHIP
Coventry City v Arsenal
Everton v Crystal Palace
Ipswich Town v Chelsea
Leicester City v Leeds Utd
Manchester Utd v Blackburn Rovers
Nottingham Forest v Aston Villa
QPR v Norwich City
Sheffield Wed v Newcastle Utd
Southampton v West Ham Utd
Tottenham Hotspur v Manchester City
Wimbledon v Liverpool

ENDSLEIGH LEAGUE FIRST DIVISION
Bolton Wdrs v Charlton Athletic
Bristol City v Sheffield Utd
Burnley v Reading
Derby County v Portsmouth
Luton Town v Wolverhampton Wdrs
Middlesbrough v Grimsby Town
Millwall v Swindon Town
Southend Utd v Port Vale
Stoke City v Barnsley
Sunderland v Notts County

Tranmere Rovers v Oldham Athletic
WBA v Watford

SECOND DIVISION
Birmingham City v Shrewsbury Town
Bradford City v Bristol Rovers
Brighton v Cardiff City
Cambridge Utd v AFC Bournemouth
Chester City v Peterborough Utd
Huddersfield Town v York City
Hull City v Brentford
Leyton Orient v Blackpool
Oxford Utd v Stockport County
Plymouth Argyle v Rotherham Utd
Swansea City v Crewe Alexandra
Wycombe Wdrs v Wrexham

THIRD DIVISION
Barnet v Lincoln City
Doncaster Rovers v Exeter City
Fulham v Northampton Town
Gillingham v Colchester Utd
Hereford Utd v Chesterfield
Preston North End v Mansfield Town
Rochdale v Carlisle Utd
Scarborough v Bury
Scunthorpe Utd v Torquay Utd
Walsall v Darlington
Wigan Athletic v Hartlepool Utd

TUES. 24th JANUARY

FA CARLING PREMIERSHIP
Arsenal v Southampton
Blackburn Rovers v Ipswich Town
Crystal Palace v Manchester Utd
Leeds Utd v QPR
Liverpool v Everton

WED. 25th JANUARY

FA CARLING PREMIERSHIP
Aston Villa v Tottenham Hotspur
Chelsea v Nottingham Forest
Manchester City v Leicester City
Newcastle Utd v Wimbledon
Norwich City v Coventry City
West Ham Utd v Sheffield Wed

SAT. 28th JANUARY

ENDSLEIGH LEAGUE SECOND DIVISION
AFC Bournemouth v Huddersfield
Town
Blackpool v Plymouth Argyle
Brentford v Cambridge Utd
Bristol Rovers v Birmingham City
Cardiff City v Bradford City
Crewe Alexandra v Hull City
Peterborough Utd v Swansea City
Rotherham Utd v Brighton
Shrewsbury Town v Oxford Utd
Stockport County v Leyton Orient
Wrexham v Chester City
York City v Wycombe Wdrs

THIRD DIVISION
Bury v Walsall
Carlisle Utd v Fulham
Chesterfield v Barnet
Colchester Utd v Wigan Athletic
Darlington v Gillingham
Exeter City v Preston North End

Hartlepool Utd v Scunthorpe Utd
Lincoln City v Hereford Utd
Mansfield Town v Rochdale
Northampton Town v Scarborough
Torquay Utd v Doncaster Rovers

SAT. 4th FEBRUARY

FA CARLING PREMIERSHIP
Coventry City v Chelsea
Everton v Norwich City
Ipswich Town v Crystal Palace
Leicester City v West Ham Utd
Manchester Utd v Aston Villa
Nottingham Forest v Liverpool
QPR v Newcastle Utd
Sheffield Wed v Arsenal
Southampton v Manchester City
Tottenham Hotspur v Blackburn Rovers
Wimbledon v Leeds Utd

ENDSLEIGH LEAGUE FIRST DIVISION
Bolton Wdrs v Wolverhampton Wdrs
Bristol City v Barnsley
Burnley v Swindon Town
Derby County v Sheffield Utd
Luton Town v Oldham Athletic
Middlesbrough v Reading
Millwall v Grimsby Town
Southend Utd v Watford
Stoke City v Portsmouth
Sunderland v Port Vale
Tranmere Rovers v Notts County
WBA v Charlton Athletic

SECOND DIVISION
Birmingham City v Stockport County
Bradford City v Shrewsbury Town
Brighton v Brentford
Cambridge Utd v Crewe Alexandra
Chester City v Rotherham Utd
Huddersfield Town v Bristol Rovers
Hull City v Cardiff City
Leyton Orient v Peterborough Utd
Oxford Utd v AFC Bournemouth
Plymouth Argyle v York City
Swansea City v Wrexham
Wycombe Wdrs v Blackpool

THIRD DIVISION
Barnet v Darlington
Doncaster Rovers v Carlisle Utd
Fulham v Bury
Gillingham v Lincoln City
Hereford Utd v Northampton Town
Preston North End v Chesterfield
Rochdale v Hartlepool Utd
Scarborough v Exeter City
Scunthorpe Utd v Colchester Utd
Walsall v Mansfield Town
Wigan Athletic v Torquay Utd

SAT. 11th FEBRUARY

FA CARLING PREMIERSHIP
Arsenal v Leicester City
Aston Villa v Wimbledon
Blackburn Rovers v Sheffield Wed
Chelsea v Tottenham Hotspur
Crystal Palace v Coventry City
Leeds Utd v Ipswich Town
Liverpool v QPR
Manchester City v Manchester Utd

Newcastle Utd v Nottingham Forest
Norwich City v Southampton
West Ham Utd v Everton

ENDSLEIGH LEAGUE FIRST DIVISION
Barnsley v Tranmere Rovers
Charlton Athletic v Sunderland
Grimsby Town v Luton Town
Notts County v Southend Utd
Oldham Athletic v Middlesbrough
Port Vale v WBA
Portsmouth v Millwall
Reading v Derby County
Sheffield Utd v Stoke City
Swindon Town v Bolton Wdrs
Watford v Burnley
Wolverhampton Wdrs v Bristol City

SECOND DIVISION
AFC Bournemouth v Brighton
Blackpool v Oxford Utd
Brentford v Bradford City
Bristol Rovers v Cambridge Utd
Cardiff City v Leyton Orient
Crewe Alexandra v Birmingham City
Peterborough Utd v Plymouth Argyle
Rotherham Utd v Swansea City
Shrewsbury Town v Wycombe Wdrs
Stockport County v Chester City
Wrexham v Huddersfield Town
York City v Hull City

THIRD DIVISION
Bury v Barnet
Carlisle Utd v Hereford Utd
Chesterfield v Gillingham
Colchester Utd v Rochdale
Darlington v Wigan Athletic
Exeter City v Walsall
Hartlepool Utd v Doncaster Rovers
Lincoln City v Fulham
Mansfield Town v Scunthorpe Utd
Northampton Town v Preston North End
Torquay Utd v Scarborough

FRI.17th FEBRUARY

ENDSLEIGH LEAGUE SECOND DIVISION
Swansea City v Brentford

SAT. 18th FEBRUARY

FA CARLING PREMIERSHIP
Coventry City v West Ham Utd
Everton v Chelsea
Ipswich Town v Newcastle Utd
Leicester City v Norwich City
Manchester Utd v Arsenal
Nottingham Forest v Leeds Utd
QPR v Blackburn Rovers
Sheffield Wed v Aston Villa
Southampton v Crystal Palace
Tottenham Hotspur v Liverpool
Wimbledon v Manchester City

ENDSLEIGH LEAGUE FIRST DIVISION
Bolton Wdrs v Barnsley
Bristol City v Oldham Athletic
Burnley v Grimsby Town
Derby County v Wolverhampton Wdrs
Luton Town v Swindon Town
Middlesbrough v Charlton Athletic
Millwall v Port Vale

Southend Utd v Sheffield Utd
Stoke City v Watford
Sunderland v Portsmouth
Tranmere Rovers v Reading
WBA v Notts County

SECOND DIVISION
Birmingham City v York City
Bradford City v Peterborough Utd
Brighton v Crewe Alexandra
Cambridge Utd v Blackpool
Chester City v Shrewsbury Town
Huddersfield Town v Cardiff City
Hull City v Stockport County
Leyton Orient v Wrexham
Oxford Utd v Bristol Rovers
Plymouth Argyle v AFC Bournemouth
Wycombe Wdrs v Rotherham Utd

THIRD DIVISION
Barnet v Colchester Utd
Doncaster Rovers v Lincoln City
Fulham v Darlington
Gillingham v Northampton Town
Hereford Utd v Bury
Preston North End v Carlisle Utd
Rochdale v Exeter City
Scarborough v Hartlepool Utd
Scunthorpe Utd v Chesterfield
Walsall v Torquay Utd
Wigan Athletic v Mansfield Town

TUES. 21st FEBRUARY

FA CARLING PREMIERSHIP
Arsenal v Nottingham Forest
Blackburn Rovers v Wimbledon
Crystal Palace v Sheffield Wed
Leeds Utd v Everton

ENDSLEIGH LEAGUE FIRST DIVISION
Barnsley v Millwall
Charlton Athletic v Tranmere Rovers
Grimsby Town v Stoke City
Notts County v Bolton Wdrs
Oldham Athletic v WBA
Port Vale v Derby County
Reading v Southend Utd
Sheffield Utd v Burnley
Watford v Sunderland
Wolverhampton Wdrs v Middlesbrough

SECOND DIVISION
AFC Bournemouth v Birmingham City
Blackpool v Chester City
Brentford v Huddersfield Town
Cardiff City v Wycombe Wdrs
Crewe Alexandra v Bradford City
Peterborough Utd v Brighton
Rotherham Utd v Oxford Utd
Shrewsbury Town v Cambridge Utd
Stockport County v Swansea City
Wrexham v Plymouth Argyle
York City v Leyton Orient

WED. 22nd FEBRUARY

FA CARLING PREMIERSHIP
Aston Villa v Leicester City
Chelsea v Southampton
Liverpool v Coventry City
Manchester City v Ipswich Town

Newcastle Utd v Tottenham Hotspur
Norwich City v Manchester Utd
West Ham Utd v QPR

ENDSLEIGH LEAGUE FIRST DIVISION
Swindon Town v Bristol City
Portsmouth v Luton Town

SECOND DIVISION
Bristol Rovers v Hull City

SAT. 25th FEBRUARY

FA CARLING PREMIERSHIP
Blackburn Rovers v Norwich City
Coventry City v Leicester City
Crystal Palace v Arsenal
Everton v Manchester Utd
Ipswich Town v Southampton
Manchester City v Leeds Utd
Newcastle Utd v Aston Villa
QPR v Nottingham Forest
Sheffield Wed v Liverpool
Tottenham Hotspur v Wimbledon
West Ham Utd v Chelsea

ENDSLEIGH LEAGUE FIRST DIVISION
Bristol City v Luton Town
Derby County v Bolton Wdrs
Millwall v Middlesbrough
Notts County v Reading
Oldham Athletic v Sheffield Utd
Port Vale v Wolverhampton Wdrs
Portsmouth v Grimsby Town
Southend Utd v Sunderland
Swindon Town v Barnsley
Tranmere Rovers v Burnley
Watford v Charlton Athletic
WBA v Stoke City

SECOND DIVISION
AFC Bournemouth v Hull City
Birmingham City v Wrexham
Blackpool v Rotherham Utd
Bradford City v Cambridge Utd
Brighton v Huddersfield Town
Crewe Alexandra v Bristol Rovers
Oxford Utd v Chester City
Peterborough Utd v Cardiff City
Plymouth Argyle v Leyton Orient
Shrewsbury Town v Brentford
Stockport County v York City
Swansea City v Wycombe Wdrs

THIRD DIVISION
Bury v Colchester Utd
Darlington v Carlisle Utd
Doncaster Rovers v Rochdale
Fulham v Barnet
Hartlepool Utd v Exeter City
Mansfield Town v Gillingham
Northampton Town v Lincoln City
Scarborough v Wigan Athletic
Scunthorpe Utd v Hereford Utd
Torquay Utd v Chesterfield
Walsall v Preston North End

SAT. 4th MARCH

FA CARLING PREMIERSHIP
Aston Villa v Blackburn Rovers
Chelsea v Crystal Palace
Leeds Utd v Sheffield Wed
Leicester City v Everton

Liverpool v Newcastle Utd
Manchester Utd v Ipswich Town
Norwich City v Manchester City
Nottingham Forest v Tottenham
  Hotspur
Southampton v Coventry City
Wimbledon v QPR

ENDSLEIGH LEAGUE FIRST DIVISION
Barnsley v Oldham Athletic
Bolton Wdrs v Southend Utd
Burnley v WBA
Charlton Athletic v Notts County
Grimsby Town v Swindon Town
Luton Town v Millwall
Middlesbrough v Bristol City
Reading v Watford
Sheffield Utd v Port Vale
Stoke City v Derby County
Sunderland v Tranmere Rovers
Wolverhampton Wdrs v Portsmouth

SECOND DIVISION
Brentford v Crewe Alexandra
Bristol Rovers v Shrewsbury Town
Cambridge Utd v Brighton
Cardiff City v AFC Bournemouth
Chester City v Plymouth Argyle
Huddersfield Town v Bradford City
Hull City v Birmingham City
Leyton Orient v Oxford Utd
Rotherham Utd v Peterborough Utd
Wrexham v Blackpool
Wycombe Wdrs v Stockport County
York City v Swansea City

THIRD DIVISION
Barnet v Torquay Utd
Carlisle Utd v Northampton Town
Chesterfield v Bury
Colchester Utd v Darlington
Exeter City v Mansfield Town
Gillingham v Walsall
Hereford Utd v Fulham
Lincoln City v Hartlepool Utd
Preston North End v Doncaster Rovers
Rochdale v Scarborough
Wigan Athletic v Scunthorpe Utd

SUN. 5th MARCH

FA CARLING PREMIERSHIP
Arsenal v West Ham Utd (3.00)

TUES. 7th MARCH

FA CARLING PREMIERSHIP
Blackburn Rovers v Arsenal
Leeds Utd v Crystal Palace
Wimbledon v Manchester Utd

ENDSLEIGH LEAGUE FIRST DIVISION
Barnsley v Burnley
Bristol City v Charlton Athletic
Grimsby Town v Derby County
Luton Town v Port Vale
Middlesbrough v Watford
Oldham Athletic v Southend Utd
Sheffield Utd v Tranmere Rovers
Wolverhampton Wdrs v Sunderland

SECOND DIVISION
Blackpool v Crewe Alexandra
Chester City v Hull City

Leyton Orient v Brighton
Oxford Utd v Huddersfield Town
Peterborough Utd v Shrewsbury
  Town
Plymouth Argyle v Birmingham City
Rotherham Utd v Cambridge Utd
Stockport County v Bristol Rovers
Swansea City v Cardiff City
Wrexham v Brentford
Wycombe Wdrs v Bradford City
York City v AFC Bournemouth

WED. 8th MARCH

FA CARLING PREMIERSHIP
Aston Villa v Coventry City
Liverpool v Southampton
Manchester City v Chelsea
Newcastle Utd v West Ham Utd
Norwich City v Sheffield Wed
Nottingham Forest v Everton
QPR v Leicester City
Tottenham Hotspur v Ipswich Town

ENDSLEIGH LEAGUE FIRST DIVISION
Millwall v Reading
Portsmouth v WBA
Stoke City v Bolton Wdrs
Swindon Town v Notts County

SAT. 11th MARCH

FA CARLING PREMIERSHIP
Arsenal v Liverpool
Chelsea v Leeds Utd
Coventry City v Blackburn Rovers
Crystal Palace v Aston Villa
Everton v Manchester City
Ipswich Town v QPR
Leicester City v Nottingham Forest
Manchester Utd v Tottenham Hotspur
Sheffield Wed v Wimbledon
Southampton v Newcastle Utd
West Ham Utd v Norwich City

ENDSLEIGH LEAGUE FIRST DIVISION
Bolton Wdrs v Middlesbrough
Burnley v Oldham Athletic
Charlton Athletic v Portsmouth
Derby County v Millwall
Notts County v Sheffield Utd
Port Vale v Bristol City
Reading v Barnsley
Southend Utd v Luton Town
Sunderland v Stoke City
Tranmere Rovers v Grimsby Town
Watford v Swindon Town
WBA v Wolverhampton Wdrs

SECOND DIVISION
AFC Bournemouth v Rotherham Utd
Birmingham City v Swansea City
Bradford City v Plymouth Argyle
Brentford v Stockport County
Brighton v Wrexham
Bristol Rovers v Wycombe Wdrs
Cambridge Utd v Oxford Utd
Cardiff City v York City
Crewe Alexandra v Peterborough
  Utd
Huddersfield Town v Chester City
Hull City v Leyton Orient
Shrewsbury Town v Blackpool

THIRD DIVISION
Doncaster Rovers v Barnet
Exeter City v Carlisle Utd
Hartlepool Utd v Colchester Utd
Mansfield Town v Lincoln City
Preston North End v Fulham
Rochdale v Northampton Town
Scarborough v Gillingham
Scunthorpe Utd v Bury
Torquay Utd v Darlington
Walsall v Chesterfield
Wigan Athletic v Hereford Utd

FRI. 17th MARCH

ENDSLEIGH LEAGUE SECOND DIVISION
Swansea City v Shrewsbury Town

SAT. 18th MARCH

FA CARLING PREMIERSHIP
Aston Villa v West Ham Utd
Blackburn Rovers v Chelsea
Leeds Utd v Coventry City
Liverpool v Manchester Utd
Manchester City v Sheffield Wed
Newcastle Utd v Arsenal
Norwich City v Ipswich Town
Nottingham Forest v Southampton
QPR v Everton
Tottenham Hotspur v Leicester City
Wimbledon v Crystal Palace

ENDSLEIGH LEAGUE FIRST DIVISION
Barnsley v Port Vale
Bristol City v Burnley
Grimsby Town v Sunderland
Luton Town v Tranmere Rovers
Middlesbrough v Derby County
Millwall v Bolton Wdrs
Oldham Athletic v Notts County
Portsmouth v Southend Utd
Sheffield Utd v Charlton Athletic
Stoke City v Reading
Swindon Town v WBA
Wolverhampton Wdrs v Watford

SECOND DIVISION
Blackpool v Bristol Rovers
Chester City v Cambridge Utd
Leyton Orient v Huddersfield Town
Oxford Utd v Bradford City
Peterborough Utd v AFC Bournemouth
Plymouth Argyle v Hull City
Rotherham Utd v Brentford
Stockport County v Crewe Alexandra
Wrexham v Cardiff City
Wycombe Wdrs v Birmingham City
York City v Brighton

THIRD DIVISION
Barnet v Hartlepool Utd
Carlisle Utd v Walsall
Chesterfield v Wigan Athletic
Colchester Utd v Exeter City
Darlington v Mansfield Town
Fulham v Doncaster Rovers
Gillingham v Scunthorpe Utd
Hereford Utd v Scarborough
Lincoln City v Rochdale
Northampton Town v Torquay Utd
Preston North End v Bury

TUES. 21st MARCH

ENDSLEIGH LEAGUE FIRST DIVISION
Bolton Wdrs v Sheffield Utd
Burnley v Luton Town
Charlton Athletic v Grimsby Town
Notts County v Bristol City
Port Vale v Portsmouth
Reading v Oldham Athletic
Southend Utd v Stoke City
Sunderland v Middlesbrough
Tranmere Rovers v Wolverhampton
Wdrs
Watford v Barnsley

SECOND DIVISION
AFC Bournemouth v Stockport County
Birmingham City v Oxford Utd
Bradford City v Swansea City
Brentford v Wycombe Wdrs
Cambridge Utd v Leyton Orient
Cardiff City v Blackpool
Crewe Alexandra v Wrexham
Huddersfield Town v Plymouth Argyle
Hull City v Peterborough Utd
Shrewsbury Town v York City

WED. 22nd MARCH

ENDSLEIGH LEAGUE FIRST DIVISION
Derby County v Swindon Town
WBA v Millwall

SECOND DIVISION
Brighton v Chester City
Bristol Rovers v Rotherham Utd

SAT. 25th MARCH

ENDSLEIGH LEAGUE FIRST DIVISION
Barnsley v Sunderland
Bristol City v Southend Utd
Grimsby Town v WBA
Luton Town v Watford
Middlesbrough v Port Vale
Millwall v Tranmere Rovers
Oldham Athletic v Derby County
Portsmouth v Bolton Wdrs
Sheffield Utd v Reading
Stoke City v Notts County
Swindon Town v Charlton Athletic
Wolverhampton Wdrs v Burnley

SECOND DIVISION
Blackpool v Brentford
Chester City v AFC Bournemouth
Leyton Orient v Shrewsbury Town
Oxford Utd v Brighton
Peterborough Utd v Birmingham City
Plymouth Argyle v Cardiff City
Rotherham Utd v Hull City
Stockport County v Huddersfield Town
Swansea City v Cambridge Utd
Wrexham v Bristol Rovers
Wycombe Wdrs v Crewe Alexandra
York City v Bradford City

THIRD DIVISION
Barnet v Wigan Athletic
Bury v Mansfield Town
Carlisle Utd v Scunthorpe Utd
Chesterfield v Hartlepool Utd
Colchester Utd v Scarborough

Darlington v Doncaster Rovers
Fulham v Torquay Utd
Gillingham v Exeter City
Hereford Utd v Rochdale
Lincoln City v Preston North End
Northampton Town v Walsall

SAT. 1st APRIL

FA CARLING PREMIERSHIP
Arsenal v Norwich City
Chelsea v Newcastle Utd
Coventry City v QPR
Crystal Palace v Manchester City
Everton v Blackburn Rovers
Ipswich Town v Aston Villa
Leicester City v Wimbledon
Manchester Utd v Leeds Utd
Sheffield Wed v Nottingham Forest
Southampton v Tottenham Hotspur
West Ham Utd v Liverpool

ENDSLEIGH LEAGUE FIRST DIVISION
Bolton Wdrs v Luton Town
Burnley v Millwall
Charlton Athletic v Stoke City
Derby County v Bristol City
Notts County v Barnsley
Port Vale v Grimsby Town
Reading v Swindon Town
Southend Utd v Wolverhampton Wdrs
Sunderland v Sheffield Utd
Tranmere Rovers v Portsmouth
Watford v Oldham Athletic
WBA v Middlesbrough

SECOND DIVISION
AFC Bournemouth v Leyton Orient
Birmingham City v Rotherham Utd
Bradford City v Wrexham
Brentford v York City
Brighton v Blackpool
Bristol Rovers v Swansea City
Cambridge Utd v Plymouth Argyle
Cardiff City v Chester City
Crewe Alexandra v Oxford Utd
Huddersfield Town v Peterborough Utd
Hull City v Wycombe Wdrs
Shrewsbury Town v Stockport County

THIRD DIVISION
Doncaster Rovers v Bury
Exeter City v Chesterfield
Hartlepool Utd v Northampton Town
Mansfield Town v Carlisle Utd
Preston North End v Gillingham
Rochdale v Barnet
Scarborough v Fulham
Scunthorpe Utd v Darlington
Torquay Utd v Hereford Utd
Walsall v Colchester Utd
Wigan Athletic v Lincoln City

TUES. 4th APRIL

ENDSLEIGH LEAGUE SECOND DIVISION
Blackpool v Birmingham City

SAT. 8th APRIL

FA CARLING PREMIERSHIP
Aston Villa v Manchester City
Blackburn Rovers v Crystal Palace

Ipswich Town v Everton
Liverpool v Leeds Utd
Manchester Utd v Southampton
Newcastle Utd v Norwich City
Nottingham Forest v West Ham Utd
QPR v Arsenal
Sheffield Wed v Leicester City
Tottenham Hotspur v Coventry City
Wimbledon v Chelsea

Bolton Wdrs v WBA
Bristol City v Tranmere Rovers
Derby County v Sunderland
Grimsby Town v Reading
Luton Town v Notts County
Middlesbrough v Stoke City
Millwall v Charlton Athletic
Port Vale v Watford
Portsmouth v Sheffield Utd
Southend Utd v Burnley
Swindon Town v Oldham Athletic
Wolverhampton Wdrs v Barnsley

SECOND DIVISION
AFC Bournemouth v Wycombe Wdrs
Bradford City v Stockport County
Brighton v Hull City
Cambridge Utd v Peterborough Utd
Cardiff City v Rotherham Utd
Chester City v Bristol Rovers
Huddersfield Town v Swansea City
Leyton Orient v Crewe Alexandra
Oxford Utd v Brentford
Plymouth Argyle v Shrewsbury Town
Wrexham v York City

THIRD DIVISION
Barnet v Mansfield Town
Carlisle Utd v Gillingham
Doncaster Rovers v Walsall
Fulham v Hartlepool Utd
Hereford Utd v Colchester Utd
Lincoln City v Chesterfield
Northampton Town v Darlington
Rochdale v Scunthorpe Utd
Scarborough v Preston North End
Torquay Utd v Bury
Wigan Athletic v Exeter City

SAT. 15th APRIL

FA CARLING PREMIERSHIP
Arsenal v Ipswich Town
Chelsea v Aston Villa
Coventry City v Sheffield Wed
Crystal Palace v Tottenham Hotspur
Everton v Newcastle Utd
Leeds Utd v Blackburn Rovers
Leicester City v Manchester Utd
Manchester City v Liverpool
Norwich City v Nottingham Forest
Southampton v QPR
West Ham Utd v Wimbledon

ENDSLEIGH LEAGUE FIRST DIVISION
Barnsley v Portsmouth
Burnley v Derby County
Charlton Athletic v Wolverhampton
 Wdrs
Notts County v Middlesbrough
Oldham Athletic v Grimsby Town
Reading v Port Vale
Sheffield Utd v Swindon Town
Stoke City v Bristol City

Sunderland v Luton Town
Tranmere Rovers v Bolton Wdrs
Watford v Millwall
WBA v Southend Utd

SECOND DIVISION
Birmingham City v Cardiff City
Brentford v Chester City
Bristol Rovers v Plymouth Argyle
Crewe Alexandra v AFC Bournemouth
Hull City v Bradford City
Peterborough Utd v Wrexham
Rotherham Utd v Huddersfield Town
Shrewsbury Town v Brighton
Stockport County v Blackpool
Swansea City v Leyton Orient
Wycombe Wdrs v Oxford Utd
York City v Cambridge Utd

THIRD DIVISION
Bury v Carlisle Utd
Chesterfield v Northampton Town
Colchester Utd v Fulham
Darlington v Lincoln City
Exeter City v Hereford Utd
Gillingham v Barnet
Hartlepool Utd v Torquay Utd
Mansfield Town v Scarborough
Preston North End v Wigan Athletic
Scunthorpe Utd v Doncaster Rovers
Walsall v Rochdale

MON. 17th APRIL

FA CARLING PREMIERSHIP
Aston Villa v Arsenal
Blackburn Rovers v Manchester City
Ipswich Town v West Ham Utd
Liverpool v Leicester City
Manchester Utd v Chelsea
Newcastle Utd v Leeds Utd
Nottingham Forest v Coventry City
QPR v Crystal Palace
Sheffield Wed v Everton
Tottenham Hotspur v Norwich City
Wimbledon v Southampton

ENDSLEIGH LEAGUE FIRST DIVISION
Bolton Wdrs v Sunderland
Bristol City v WBA
Derby County v Tranmere Rovers
Grimsby Town v Barnsley
Luton Town v Reading
Middlesbrough v Sheffield Utd
Port Vale v Burnley
Portsmouth v Watford
Swindon Town v Stoke City
Wolverhampton Wdrs v Oldham
 Athletic

SECOND DIVISION
Bradford City v Rotherham Utd
Cambridge Utd v Birmingham City
Cardiff City v Shrewsbury Town
Chester City v Crewe Alexandra
Huddersfield Town v Hull City
Leyton Orient v Brentford
Oxford Utd v Peterborough Utd
Plymouth Argyle v Swansea City
Wrexham v Stockport County

THIRD DIVISION
Barnet v Walsall
Carlisle Utd v Hartlepool Utd
Doncaster Rovers v Chesterfield

Fulham v Gillingham
Hereford Utd v Mansfield Town
Lincoln City v Scunthorpe Utd
Northampton Town v Colchester Utd
Rochdale v Preston North End

TUES. 18th APRIL

ENDSLEIGH LEAGUE FIRST DIVISION
Southend Utd v Charlton Athletic

SECOND DIVISION
AFC Bournemouth v Bristol Rovers
Blackpool v York City

THIRD DIVISION
Scarborough v Darlington
Torquay Utd v Exeter City
Wigan Athletic v Bury

WED. 19th APRIL

ENDSLEIGH LEAGUE FIRST DIVISION
Millwall v Notts County

SECOND DIVISION
Brighton v Wycombe Wdrs

SAT. 22nd APRIL

ENDSLEIGH LEAGUE FIRST DIVISION
Barnsley v Middlesbrough
Burnley v Portsmouth
Charlton Athletic v Luton Town
Notts County v Grimsby Town
Oldham Athletic v Millwall
Reading v Bolton Wdrs
Sheffield Utd v Wolverhampton Wdrs
Stoke City v Port Vale
Sunderland v Swindon Town
Tranmere Rovers v Southend Utd
Watford v Bristol City
WBA v Derby County

SECOND DIVISION
Birmingham City v Bradford City
Brentford v Cardiff City
Bristol Rovers v Leyton Orient
Crewe Alexandra v Plymouth Argyle
Hull City v Cambridge Utd
Peterborough Utd v Blackpool
Rotherham Utd v Wrexham
Shrewsbury Town v Huddersfield
 Town
Stockport County v Brighton
Swansea City v AFC Bournemouth
Wycombe Wdrs v Chester City
York City v Oxford Utd

THIRD DIVISION
Bury v Northampton Town
Chesterfield v Carlisle Utd
Colchester Utd v Lincoln City
Darlington v Rochdale
Exeter City v Barnet
Gillingham v Doncaster Rovers
Hartlepool Utd v Hereford Utd
Mansfield Town v Fulham
Preston North End v Torquay Utd
Scunthorpe Utd v Scarborough
Walsall v Wigan Athletic

SAT. 29th APRIL

FA CARLING PREMIERSHIP
Arsenal v Tottenham Hotspur
Chelsea v QPR
Coventry City v Manchester Utd
Crystal Palace v Nottingham Forest
Everton v Wimbledon
Leeds Utd v Aston Villa
Leicester City v Ipswich Town
Manchester City v Newcastle Utd
Norwich City v Liverpool
Southampton v Sheffield Wed
West Ham Utd v Blackburn Rovers

ENDSLEIGH LEAGUE FIRST DIVISION
Barnsley v Sheffield Utd
Bristol City v Reading
Burnley v Sunderland
Charlton Athletic v Port Vale
Derby County v Southend Utd
Grimsby Town v Wolverhampton
Wdrs
Middlesbrough v Luton Town
Notts County v Watford
Oldham Athletic v Bolton Wdrs
Stoke City v Millwall
Swindon Town v Portsmouth
WBA v Tranmere Rovers

SECOND DIVISION
Birmingham City v Brighton
Bradford City v Blackpool
Brentford v AFC Bournemouth
Cambridge Utd v Huddersfield Town
Cardiff City v Bristol Rovers
Chester City v Leyton Orient
Hull City v Wrexham
Oxford Utd v Swansea City
Shrewsbury Town v Crewe Alexandra
Stockport County v Peterborough Utd
Wycombe Wdrs v Plymouth Argyle
York City v Rotherham Utd

THIRD DIVISION
Barnet v Northampton Town
Colchester Utd v Carlisle Utd
Darlington v Chesterfield
Doncaster Rovers v Scarborough
Exeter City v Fulham
Gillingham v Hereford Utd
Lincoln City v Bury
Mansfield Town v Torquay Utd
Preston North End v Hartlepool Utd
Rochdale v Wigan Athletic
Walsall v Scunthorpe Utd

SAT. 6th MAY

FA CARLING PREMIERSHIP
Arsenal v Wimbledon
Aston Villa v Liverpool
Blackburn Rovers v Newcastle Utd
Crystal Palace v West Ham Utd
Everton v Southampton
Ipswich Town v Coventry City
Leeds Utd v Norwich City
Leicester City v Chelsea
Manchester Utd v Sheffield Wed
Nottingham Forest v Manchester City
QPR v Tottenham Hotspur

ENDSLEIGH LEAGUE FIRST DIVISION
Bolton Wdrs v Burnley
Luton Town v Stoke City
Millwall v Bristol City
Port Vale v Notts County
Portsmouth v Oldham Athletic
Reading v Charlton Athletic
Sheffield Utd v Grimsby Town
Southend Utd v Barnsley
Sunderland v WBA
Tranmere Rovers v Middlesbrough
Watford v Derby County
Wolverhampton Wdrs v Swindon
Town

SECOND DIVISION
AFC Bournemouth v Shrewsbury
Town
Blackpool v Hull City
Brighton v Bradford City
Bristol Rovers v Brentford
Crewe Alexandra v Cardiff City
Huddersfield Town v Birmingham City
Leyton Orient v Wycombe Wdrs
Peterborough Utd v York City
Plymouth Argyle v Oxford Utd
Rotherham Utd v Stockport County
Swansea City v Chester City
Wrexham v Cambridge Utd

THIRD DIVISION
Bury v Darlington
Carlisle Utd v Lincoln City
Chesterfield v Colchester Utd
Fulham v Rochdale
Hartlepool Utd v Mansfield Town
Hereford Utd v Barnet
Northampton Town v Exeter City
Scarborough v Walsall
Scunthorpe Utd v Preston North End
Torquay Utd v Gillingham
Wigan Athletic v Doncaster Rovers

SAT. 13th MAY

FA CARLING PREMIERSHIP
Chelsea v Arsenal
Coventry City v Everton
Liverpool v Blackburn Rovers
Manchester City v QPR
Newcastle Utd v Crystal Palace
Norwich City v Aston Villa
Sheffield Wed v Ipswich Town
Southampton v Leicester City
Tottenham Hotspur v Leeds Utd
West Ham Utd v Manchester Utd
Wimbledon v Nottingham Forest

Key to abbreviations

QPR	Queens Park Rangers
WBA	West Bromwich Albion
Brighton	Brighton & Hove Albion
Wdrs	Wanderers
Sheffield Wed	Sheffield Wednesday